REASSEMBLING THE SOCIAL

The Clarendon Lectures in Management Studies are jointly organised by Oxford University Press and the Saïd Business School. Every year a leading international academic is invited to give a series of lectures on a topic related to management education and research, broadly defined. The lectures form the basis of a book subsequently published by Oxford University Press.

Reassembling the Social

An Introduction to Actor-Network-Theory

Bruno Latour

OXFORD
UNIVERSITY PRESS

OXFORD
UNIVERSITY PRESS

Great Clarendon Street, Oxford OX2 6DP

Oxford University Press is a department of the University of Oxford.
It furthers the University's objective of excellence in research, scholarship,
and education by publishing worldwide in

Oxford New York

Auckland Cape Town Dar es Salaam Hong Kong Karachi
Kuala Lumpur Madrid Melbourne Mexico City Nairobi
New Delhi Shanghai Taipei Toronto

With offices in

Argentina Austria Brazil Chile Czech Republic France Greece
Guatemala Hungary Italy Japan Poland Portugal Singapore
South Korea Switzerland Thailand Turkey Ukraine Vietnam

Oxford is a registered trade mark of Oxford University Press
in the UK and in certain other countries

Published in the United States
by Oxford University Press Inc., New York

British Library Cataloguing in Publication Data
Data available

Library of Congress Cataloguing in Publication Data
Data available

Typeset by SPI Publisher Services, Pondicherry, India
Printed and bound in Great Britain by Clays Ltd, St Ives plc
on acid-free paper by
Ashford Colour Press Ltd, Gosport, Hampshire

ISBN 978-0-19-925604-4 (Hbk.)   978-0-19-925605-1 (Pbk.)

To the doctoral students I had the good fortune of accompanying through some of their travails

Figure 1

CONTENTS

Conclusion: From Society to Collective—Can the
Social Be Reassembled?

ACKNOWLEDGEMENTS

This book has passed through many avatars. It began almost thirty years ago when I had the chance of being taught primate sociology by Shirley Strum and her baboons in Kenya. Although that project with Shirley has remained in limbo, it has been the staple of my teaching of sociology to young engineers at the School of Mines in Paris. When, in 1996, I was offered to give the Leclerc lectures in Louvain-la-Neuve, I decided it was about time to synthesize what I had learned from Michel Callon, John Law, Madeleine Akrich, Andy Barry, Annemarie Mol, Antoine Hennion, and many others in what had become known as 'Actor-Network-Theory'. Time and again, I have found that readers were puzzled not so much by our views on scientific practice and various other topics, but rather by the unusual meaning we gave to the words 'social' and 'social explanations'. And yet, this alternative social theory has never been the object of a systematic introduction. Instead of complaining that this small school of thought had become a monster that had escaped its Frankensteinian makers, I decided it might be fairer to present interested readers with its intellectual architecture.

It was only in 1999, when Barbara Czarniawska asked me to give a crash course in social theory 'compatible with the needs of organization studies', that I began to write down a complete draft. Although the present text has not made use of the transcript Barbara had so kindly arranged for, I owe much to her and to her Göteborg students for the organization of the material that, in addition, had been rehearsed at the London School of Economics in the Department of Information Systems in the winters of 1999, 2000 and 2001. When my old friend Steve Woolgar, through the auspices of the Saïd Business School, asked me to give the Clarendon Lectures in the fall of 2002, I wrote another draft which has since been discussed in varying degrees of detail by Andrew Barry, Howie Becker, Geof Bowker, François Cooren, Didier Debaise, Gerard de Vries, Emilie Gomart, Fabian Muniesa, Noortje Marres, Shirley Strum, Albena Yaneva, Benedikte Zitouni, and Edgar Whitley that has resulted in this new version. Finally, it was submitted to a second round of critiques by Michael Flower, Jean-Toussaint Leca, Michael Lynch, Paolo Quattrone, Isabelle Stengers and Eduardo Vargas. I wish I could say that all remaining defects are theirs and not mine.

My greatest debt goes, however, to the doctoral students who have participated over the years in my 'thesis-writing workshops'. In a discipline in which I have never been trained but to which I have never despaired of contributing, they have been my best and most patient teachers.

I hope that such a protracted and idiosyncratic genesis goes some way toward explaining the opinionated nature of this piece of work. Now that this alternative social theory has been presented in an orderly fashion, readers can decide to put it to use, to distort it beyond recognition, or, most likely, to drop it altogether—but this time knowingly! As for me, I have finally discovered in writing this book the conditions under which I could be proud of being called a sociologist.

Introduction: How to Resume the Task of Tracing Associations*

The argument of this book can be stated very simply: when social scientists add the adjective 'social' to some phenomenon, they designate a stabilized state of affairs, a bundle of ties that, later, may be mobilized to account for some other phenomenon. There is nothing wrong with this use of the word as long as it designates what is *already* assembled together, without making any superfluous assumption about the *nature* of what is assembled. Problems arise, however, when 'social' begins to mean a type of material, as if the adjective was roughly comparable to other terms like 'wooden', 'steely', 'biological', 'economical', 'mental', 'organizational', or 'linguistic'. At that point, the meaning of the word breaks down since it now designates two entirely different things: first, a movement during a process of assembling; and second, a specific type of ingredient that is supposed to differ from other materials.

What I want to do in the present work is to show why the social cannot be construed as a kind of material or domain and to dispute the project of providing a 'social explanation' of some other state of affairs. Although this earlier project has been productive and probably necessary in the past, it has largely stopped being so thanks in part to the success of the social sciences. At the present stage of their development, it's no longer possible to inspect the precise ingredients that are entering into the composition of the social domain. What I want to do is to redefine the notion of social by going back to its original meaning and making it able to trace connections again. Then it will be possible to resume the traditional goal of the social sciences but

* A shortened reference format is used in the notes; the complete bibliography is at the end. This somewhat austere book can be read in parallel with the much lighter Bruno Latour and Emilie Hermant (1998), *Paris ville invisible*, which tries to cover much of the same ground through a succession of photographic essays. It's available online in English (*Paris the Invisible City*) at http://bruno.latour.name.

with tools better adjusted to the task. After having done extensive work on the 'assemblages' of nature, I believe it's necessary to scrutinize more thoroughly the exact content of what is 'assembled' under the umbrella of a society. This seems to me the only way to be faithful to the old duties of sociology, this 'science of the living together'.[1]

Such a project entails, however, a redefinition of what is commonly understood by that discipline. Translated from both the Latin and Greek, 'socio-logy' means the 'science of the social'. The expression would be excellent except for two drawbacks, namely the word 'social' and the word 'science'. The virtues that we are prepared nowadays to grant the scientific and technical enterprises bear little relation with what the founders of the social sciences had in mind when they invented their disciplines. When modernizing was in full swing, science was a rather powerful urge to be prolonged indefinitely without any misgivings to slow its progress down. They had no idea that its extension could render it almost coextensive with the rest of social intercourse. What they meant by 'society' has undergone a transformation no less radical, which is thanks in large part to the very expansion of the products of science and technology. It is no longer clear whether there exists relations that are specific enough to be called 'social' and that could be grouped together in making up a special domain that could function as 'a society'. The social seems to be diluted everywhere and yet nowhere in particular. So, neither science nor society has remained stable enough to deliver the promises of a strong 'socio-logy'.

In spite of this double metamorphosis, few social scientists have drawn the extreme conclusion that the object as well as the methodology of the social sciences should be modified accordingly. After having been so often disappointed, they still hope to reach one day the promised land of a true science of a real social world. No scholars are more aware of this painful hesitation than those who, like me, have spent many years practicing this oxymoron: 'sociology of science'. Because of the many paradoxes triggered by this lively but more than slightly perverse subfield and the numerous changes in the meaning of 'science', I think time has come to modify what is meant by 'social'. I therefore wish to devise an alternative definition for

---

[1] This expression is explained in Laurent Thévenot (2004), 'A science of life together in the world'. This logical order—the assemblies of society after those of nature—is the exact opposite of how I came to think about it. The twin books—Bruno Latour (1999), *Pandora's Hope: Essays on the reality of science studies* and Bruno Latour (2004), *Politics of Nature: How to Bring the Sciences into Democracy*—were written long after my colleagues and I had developed an alternative social theory to deal with the new puzzles uncovered after carrying out our fieldwork in science and technology.

'sociology' while still retaining this useful label and remaining faithful, I hope, to its traditional calling.

What is a society? What does the word 'social' mean? Why are some activities said to have a 'social dimension'? How can one demonstrate the presence of 'social factors' at work? When is a study of society, or other social aggregates, a good study? How can the path of a society be altered? To answer these questions, two widely different approaches have been taken. Only one of them has become common sense—the other is the object of the present work.

The first solution has been to posit the existence of a specific sort of phenomenon variously called 'society', 'social order', 'social practice', 'social dimension', or 'social structure'. For the last century during which social theories have been elaborated, it has been important to distinguish this domain of reality from other domains such as economics, geography, biology, psychology, law, science, and politics. A given trait was said to be 'social' or to 'pertain to society' when it could be defined as possessing specific properties, some negative—it must not be 'purely' biological, linguistic, economical, natural—and some positive—it must achieve, reinforce, express, maintain, reproduce, or subvert the social order. Once this domain had been defined, no matter how vaguely, it could then be used to shed some light on specifically social phenomena—the social could explain the social—and to provide a certain type of explanation for what the other domains could not account for—an appeal to 'social factors' could explain the 'social aspects' of non-social phenomena.

For instance, although it is recognized that law has it own strength, some aspects of it would be better understood if a 'social dimension' were added to it; although economic forces unfold under their own logic, there also exists social elements which could explain the somewhat erratic behavior of calculative agents; although psychology develops according to its own inner drives, some of its more puzzling aspects can be said to pertain to 'social influence'; although science possesses its own impetus, some features of its quest are necessarily 'bound' by the 'social limitations' of scientists who are 'embedded in the social context of their time'; although art is largely 'autonomous', it is also 'influenced' by social and political 'considerations' which could account for some aspects of its most famous masterpieces; and although the science of management obeys its own rules, it might be advisable to also consider 'social, cultural, and political aspects' that could explain why some sound organizational principles are never applied in practice.

Many other examples can easily be found since this version of social theory has become the default position of our mental software that takes into consideration the following: there exists a social 'context' in which non-social activities take place; it is a specific domain of reality; it can be used as a specific type of causality to account for the residual aspects that other domains (psychology, law, economics, etc.) cannot completely deal with; it is studied by specialized scholars called socio-logists or socio-(x)—'x' being the placeholder for the various discip-lines; since ordinary agents are always 'inside' a social world that encompasses them, they can at best be 'informants' about this world and, at worst, be blinded to its existence, whose full effect is only visible to the social scientist's more disciplined eyes; no matter how difficult it is to carry on those studies, it is possible for them to roughly imitate the successes of the natural sciences by being as objective as other scientists thanks to the use of quantitative tools; if this is impos-sible, then alternative methods should be devised that take into ac-count the 'human', 'intentional', or 'hermeneutic' aspects of those domains without abandoning the ethos of science; and when social scientists are asked to give expert advice on social engineering or to accompany social change, some sort of political relevance might ensue from these studies, but only after sufficient knowledge has been accumulated.

This default position has become common sense not only for social scientists, but also for ordinary actors via newspapers, college educa-tion, party politics, bar conversations, love stories, fashion magazines, etc.[2] The social sciences have disseminated their definition of society as effectively as utility companies deliver electricity and telephone services. Offering comments about the inevitable 'social dimension' of what we and others are doing 'in society' has become as familiar to us as using a mobile phone, ordering a beer, or invoking the Oedipus complex—at least in the developed world.

The other approach does not take for granted the basic tenet of the first. It claims that there is nothing specific to social order; that there is no social dimension of any sort, no 'social context', no distinct do-main of reality to which the label 'social' or 'society' could be attrib-uted; that no 'social force' is available to 'explain' the residual features other domains cannot account for; that members know very well what they are doing even if they don't articulate it to the satisfaction of the observers; that actors are never embedded in a social context and so are always much more than 'mere informants'; that there is thus no meaning in adding some 'social factors' to other scientific specialties; that political relevance obtained through a 'science of society' is not necessarily desirable; and that 'society', far from being the context 'in which' everything is framed, should rather be construed as one of the

---

[2] The diffusion of the word 'actor' itself, which I will keep vague until later—see p. 46—, being one of the many markers of this influence.

many connecting elements circulating inside tiny conduits. With some provocation, this second school of thought could use as its slogan what Mrs Thatcher famously exclaimed (but for very different reasons!): 'There is no such a thing as a society.'

If they are so different, how could they both claim to be a science of the social and aspire to use the same label of 'sociology'? On the face of it, they should be simply incommensurable, since the second position takes as the major puzzle to be solved what the first takes as its solution, namely the existence of specific social ties revealing the hidden presence of some specific social forces. In the alternative view, 'social' is not some glue that could fix everything including what the other glues cannot fix; it is *what* is glued together by many *other* types of connectors. Whereas sociologists (or socio-economists, socio-linguists, social psychologists, etc.) take social aggregates as the given that could shed some light on residual aspects of economics, linguistics, psychology, management, and so on, these other scholars, on the contrary, consider social aggregates as what should be explained by the specific *associations* provided by economics, linguistics, psychology, law, management, etc.[3]

The resemblance between the two approaches appears much greater, however, provided one bears in mind the etymology of the word 'social'. Even though most social scientists would prefer to call 'social' a homogeneous thing, it's perfectly acceptable to designate by the same word a trail of *associations* between heterogeneous elements. Since in both cases the word retains the same origin—from the Latin root *socius*—it is possible to remain faithful to the original intuitions of the social sciences by redefining sociology not as the 'science of the social', but as the *tracing of associations*. In this meaning of the adjective, social does not designate a thing among other things, like a black sheep among other white sheep, but *a type of connection* between things that are not themselves social.

At first, this definition seems absurd since it risks diluting sociology to mean any type of aggregate from chemical bonds to legal ties, from atomic forces to corporate bodies, from physiological to political assemblies. But this is precisely the point that this alternative branch of social theory wishes to make as all those heterogeneous elements *might be* assembled anew in some given state of affairs. Far from being a mind-boggling hypothesis, this is on the contrary the most common experience we have in encountering the puzzling face of the

---

[3] I will use the expression 'society or other social aggregates' to cover the range of solutions given to what I call below the 'first source of uncertainty' and that deals with the nature of social groups. I am not aiming especially here at the 'holist' definitions since, as we shall see, the 'individualist' or the 'biological' definitions are just as valid. See p. 27.

social. A new vaccine is being marketed, a new job description is offered, a new political movement is being created, a new planetary system is discovered, a new law is voted, a new catastrophe occurs. In each instance, we have to reshuffle our conceptions of what was associated together because the previous definition has been made somewhat irrelevant. We are no longer sure about what 'we' means; we seem to be bound by 'ties' that don't look like regular social ties.

The ever shrinking meaning of social
There is a clear etymological trend in the successive variations of the 'social' word family (Strum and Latour 1987). It goes from the most general to the most superficial. The etymology of the word 'social' is also instructive. The root is *seq-, sequi* and the first meaning is 'to follow'. The Latin *socius* denotes a companion, an associate. From the different languages, the historical genealogy of the word 'social' is construed first as following someone, then enrolling and allying, and, lastly, having something in common. The next meaning of social is to have a share in a commercial undertaking. 'Social' as in the social contract is Rousseau's invention. 'Social' as in social problems, the social question, is a nineteenth-century innovation. Parallel words like 'sociable' refer to skills enabling individuals to live politely in society. As one can see from the drifting of the word, the meaning of social shrinks as time passes. Starting with a definition which is *coextensive* with all associations, we now have, in common parlance, a usage that is limited to what is left *after* politics, biology, economics, law, psychology, management, technology, etc., have taken their own parts of the associations.

Because of this constant shrinking of meaning (social contract, social question, social workers), we tend to limit the social to humans and modern societies, forgetting that the domain of the social is much more extensive than that. De Candolle was the first person to create scientometrics—the use of statistics to measure the activity of science—and, like his father, a *plant* sociologist (Candolle 1873/ 1987). For him corals, baboons, trees, bees, ants, and whales are also social. This extended meaning of social has been well recognized by socio-biology (Wilson 1975). Unfortunately, this enterprise has only confirmed social scientists' worst fears about extending the meaning of social. It's perfectly possible, however, to retain the extension without believing much in the very restricted definition of agency given to organisms in many socio-biological panoramas.

Thus, the overall project of what we are supposed to do together is thrown into doubt. The sense of belonging has entered a crisis. But to register this feeling of crisis and to follow these new connections, another notion of social has to be devised. It has to be *much wider* than what is usually called by that name, yet *strictly limited* to the tracing of new associations and to the designing of their assemblages. This is the reason why I am going to define the social not as a special domain, a specific realm, or a particular sort of thing, but only as a very peculiar movement of re-association and reassembling.

In such a view, law, for instance, should not be seen as what should be explained by 'social structure' in addition to its inner logic; on the contrary, its inner logic may explain some features of what makes an association last longer and extend wider. Without the ability of legal precedents to draw connections between a case and a general rule, what would we know about putting some matter 'into a larger context'?[4] Science does not have to be replaced by its 'social framework', which is 'shaped by social forces' as well as its own objectivity, because its objects are themselves dislocating any given context through the foreign elements research laboratories are associating together in unpredictable ways. Those quarantined because of the SARS virus painfully learned that they could no longer 'associate' with parents and partners in the same way because of the mutation of this little bug whose existence has been revealed by the vast institution of epidemiology and virology.[5] Religion does not have to be 'accounted for' by social forces because in its very definition—indeed, in its very name—it links together entities which are not part of the social order. Since the days of Antigone, everyone knows what it means to be put into motion by orders from gods that are irreducible to politicians like Creon. Organizations do not have to be placed into a 'wider social frame' since they themselves give a very practical meaning to what it means to be nested into a 'wider' set of affairs. After all, which air traveler would know the gate to go to without looking anxiously and repeatedly at the number printed on her boarding pass and circled in red by an airline attendant? It might be vacuous to reveal behind the superficial chats of politicians the 'dark hidden forces of society' at work, since without those very speeches a large part of what we understand to be part of a group will be lost. Without the contradictory

---

[4] Patricia Ewick and Susan S Silbey (1998), *The Common Place of Law* and Silbey's contribution to Bruno Latour and Peter Weibel (2005), *Making Things Public: Atmospheres of Democracy*.

[5] Although the study of scientific practice has provided the main impetus for this alternative definition of the social, it will be tackled only later when the fourth uncertainty has been defined, see p. 87.

spiels of the warring parties in Iraq, who in the 'occupied' or 'liberated' Baghdad will know how to recognize friend from foe?

And the same is true for all other domains.[6] Whereas, in the first approach, every activity—law, science, technology, religion, organization, politics, management, etc.—could be related to and explained by the same social aggregates *behind* all of them, in the second version of sociology there exists *nothing* behind those activities even though they might be linked in a way that does produce a society—*or doesn't* produce one. Such is the crucial point of departure between the two versions. To be social is no longer a safe and unproblematic property, it is a movement that may fail to trace any new connection and may fail to redesign any *well-formed* assemblage. As we are going to learn throughout this book, after having rendered many useful services in an earlier period, what is called 'social explanation' has become a counter-productive way to *interrupt* the movement of associations instead of resuming it.

According to the second approach, adherents of the first have simply confused what they should explain with the explanation. They begin with society or other social aggregates, whereas one should end with them. They believed the social to be made essentially of social ties, whereas associations are made of ties which are themselves non-social. They imagined that sociology is limited to a specific domain, whereas sociologists should travel wherever new heterogeneous associations are made. They believed the social to be always already there at their disposal, whereas the social is not a type of thing either visible or to be postulated. It is visible only by the *traces* it leaves (under trials) when a *new* association is being produced between elements which themselves are in no way 'social'. They insisted that we were already held by the force of some society when our political future resides in the task of deciding what binds us all together. In brief, the second school claims to *resume* the work of connection and collection that was abruptly interrupted by the first. It is to help the interested enquirers in *reassembling* the social that this book has been written.

In the course of the book we will learn to distinguish the standard sociology of the social from a more radical subfamily which I will call

---

[6] We will see only in Part II, p. 238, how to reformulate this opposition in a more subtle way than an inversion of cause and effect.

[7] For the distinction between critical sociology and sociology of critique, see Luc Boltanski and Laurent Thévenot (forthcoming) *On Justification*; Luc Boltanski and Laurent Thévenot (1999), 'The Sociology of Critical Capacity'; and especially Luc Boltanski (1990), *L'amour et la justice comme compétences*. If I find it necessary to establish some continuity with the sociology of the social, I will have to be more confrontational with critical sociology and its 'illusion of an illusion'.

critical sociology.[7] This last branch will be defined by the following three traits: it doesn't only *limit* itself to the social but *replaces* the object to be studied by another matter made *of* social relations; it claims that this substitution is unbearable for the social actors who *need* to live under the illusion that there is something 'other' than social there; and it considers that the actors' objections to their social explanations offer the best *proof* that those explanations are right.

To clarify, I will call the first approach 'sociology of the social' and the second 'sociology of associations' (I wish I could use 'associology'). I know this is very unfair to the many nuances of the social sciences I have thus lumped together, but this is acceptable for an introduction which has to be very precise on the unfamiliar arguments it chooses to describe as it sketches the well-known terrain. I may be forgiven for this roughness because there exist many excellent introductions for the sociology of the social but none, to my knowledge, for this small subfield of social theory[8] that has been called—by the way, what is it to be called? Alas, the historical name is 'actor-network-theory', a name that is so awkward, so confusing, so meaningless that it deserves to be kept. If the author, for instance, of a travel guide is free to propose new comments on the land he has chosen to present, he is certainly not free to change its most common name since the easiest signpost is the best—after all, the origin of the word 'America' is even more awkward. I was ready to drop this label for more elaborate ones like 'sociology of translation', 'actant-rhyzome ontology', 'sociology of innovation', and so on, until someone pointed out to me that the acronym A.N.T. was perfectly fit for a blind, myopic, workaholic, trail-sniffing, and collective traveler. An ant writing for other ants, this fits my project very well![9] Ideally, the word *sociology* should work best, but it cannot be used before its two components—what is social and what is a science—have been somewhat revamped. As this book unfolds, I will use it more and more often though, reserving the expression 'sociology of the social' to designate the repertoire to which other social scientists, in my view, limit themselves too readily.

---

[8] A recent guide is presented in John Law (2004) *After Method: Mess in Social Science Research.* Andrew Barry (2001), *Political Machines. Governing a Technological Society* and Anne-Marie Mol (2003), *The Body Multiple: Ontology in Medical Practice (Science and Cultural Theory)* may also be taken as a good introduction along with Bruno Latour (1996), *Aramis or the Love of Technology.*

[9] I have to apologize for taking the exact opposite position here as the one taken in Bruno Latour (1999c), 'On Recalling ANT'. Whereas at the time I criticized all the elements of his horrendous expression, including the hyphen, I will now defend all of them, *including* the hyphen!

How to find one's way in the literature under the heading Actor-Network-Theory

Most of the relevant bibliography can be found on the excellent website 'the Actor Network Resource' maintained by John Law.[10] The origin of this approach can be found in the need for a new social theory adjusted to science and technology studies (Callon and Latour 1981). But it started in earnest with three documents (Latour 1988b; Callon 1986; Law 1986b). It was at this point that non-humans—microbes, scallops, rocks, and ships—presented themselves to social theory in a new way. As I will explain on p. 87 when reviewing the fourth uncertainty, it was the first time for me that the objects of science and technology had become, so to speak, social-compatible. The philosophical foundation of this argument was presented in the second part of (Latour 1988a) although in a form that made it difficult to grasp.

Since then it has moved in many directions, being reviewed and criticized by many papers listed on Law's website. Although there is no clear litmus test for ANT membership, some ad hoc and make-shift ones may be devised. Needless to say, this interpretation of ANT represents only my view. This book does not aim at a more collective presentation, only at a more systematic one. Here are some of the tests that I have found most useful.

One of them is the precise role granted to non-humans. They have to be *actors* (see the definition on p. 64) and not simply the hapless bearers of symbolic projection. But this activity should not be the type of agency associated up to now with matters of fact or natural objects. So if an account employs either a symbolic or a naturalist type of causality, there is no reason to include it in the ANT corpus even though it might claim to be. Conversely, any study that gives non-humans a type of agency that is more open than the traditional natural causality—but more efficient than the symbolic one—can be part of our corpus, even though some of the authors would not wish to be associated in any way with this approach. For instance, a biological book (Kupiec and Sonigo 2000) could pertain to ANT because of the new active role given to the gene.

Another test is to check which direction the explanation is going in. Is the list of what is social in the end the same limited repertoire that has been used to explain (away) most of the elements? If the social remains stable and is used to explain a state of affairs, it's not ANT. For instance, no matter how enlightening it has been for all of us, the Social Shaping of Technology (Bijker 1995) would not be part

---

[10]   See http://www.lancs.ac.uk/FSS/sociology/css/antres/antres.htm.

of the corpus since the social is kept stable all along and accounts for the shape of technological change. But McNeill (1976), although he is in no way an ANT author, would qualify for inclusion, since what is to be associated is being modified by the inclusion of rats, viruses, and microbes into the definition of what is to be 'collected' in an empire. In this way, a book like Cronon's (1991) is certainly a masterpiece of ANT because no hidden social force is added to explain the progressive composition of the metropolis itself. The same would be true of the work done in distributed cognition (Hutchins 1995). This is also what has made much of the history of science and technology important for our program, and why sociology of art has been a continuous companion, especially through the influence of Hennion (1993).

A third and more difficult test would be to check whether a study aims at reassembling the social or still insists on dispersion and deconstruction. ANT has been confused with a postmodern emphasis on the critique of the 'Great narratives' and 'Eurocentric' or 'hegemonic' standpoint. This is, however, a very misleading view. Dispersion, destruction, and deconstruction are not the goals to be achieved but what needs to be overcome. It's much more important to check what are the new institutions, procedures, and concepts able to collect and to reconnect the social (Callon et al. 2001; Latour 2004b).

It's true that in most situations resorting to the sociology of the social is not only reasonable but also indispensable, since it offers convenient shorthand to designate all the ingredients already *accepted* in the collective realm. It would be silly as well as pedantic to abstain from using notions like 'IBM', 'France', 'Maori culture', 'upward mobility', 'totalitarianism', 'socialization', 'lower-middle class', 'political context', 'social capital', 'downsizing', 'social construction', 'individual agent', 'unconscious drives', 'peer pressure', etc. But in situations where innovations proliferate, where group boundaries are uncertain, when the range of entities to be taken into account fluctuates, the sociology of the social is no longer able to trace actors' new associations. At this point, the last thing to do would be to limit in advance the shape, size, heterogeneity, and combination of associations. To the convenient shorthand of the social, one has to substitute the painful and costly longhand of its associations. The duties of the social scientist mutate accordingly: it is no longer enough to limit actors to the role of informers offering cases of some well-known types. You have to grant them back the ability to make up their own theories of what the social is made of. Your task is no longer to impose some order, to limit the range of acceptable entities, to teach actors what they are, or to add some reflexivity to their blind practice. Using a slogan from ANT, you have 'to follow the actors themselves', that is try to catch up with their often wild innovations in order to learn from them what the collective existence has become in their hands, which methods they have elaborated to make it fit together, which accounts could best define the new associations that they have been forced to establish. If the sociology of the social works fine with what has been already *assembled*, it does not work so well to collect anew the participants in what is not— *not yet*—a sort of social realm.

A more extreme way of relating the two schools is to borrow a somewhat tricky parallel from the history of physics and to say that the sociology of the social remains 'pre-relativist', while our sociology has to be fully 'relativist'. In most ordinary cases, for instance situations that change slowly, the pre-relativist framework is perfectly fine and any fixed frame of reference can register action without too much deformation. But as soon as things accelerate, innovations proliferate, and entities are multiplied, one then has an absolutist framework generating data that becomes hopelessly messed up. This is when a relativistic solution has to be devised in order to remain able to move between frames of reference and to regain some sort of commensurability between traces coming from frames traveling at very different speeds and acceleration. Since relativity theory is a well-known example of a major shift in our mental apparatus triggered by very basic questions, it can be used as a nice parallel for the ways in which the sociology of associations reverses and generalizes the sociology of the social.

In what follows I am not interested in refutation—proving that the other social theories are wrong—but in proposition. How far can one go by suspending the common sense hypothesis that the existence of a social realm offers a legitimate frame of reference for the social sciences?[11] If physicists at the beginning of the previous century were able to do away with the common sense solution of an absolutely rigid and indefinitely plastic ether, can sociologists discover new traveling possibilities by abandoning the notion of a social substance as a 'superfluous hypothesis'? This position is so marginal, its chance of success so slim, that I see no reason to be fair and thorough with the perfectly reasonable alternatives that could, at any point, smash it into pieces. So, I will be opinionated and often partial in order to demon-

---

[11] If my treatment of the sociology of the social seems harsh and if I am truly obnoxious with critical sociology, this is only provisional. We will learn in due time how to retrieve what was correct in their original intuitions. If the key notion of standards (Part II, p. 221) allows us to pay full justice to the sociology of the social, critical sociology will have to wait, I am afraid, until the Conclusion when the question of political relevance will be tackled.

strate clearly the contrast between the two viewpoints. In exchange for this breach of fairness, I will try to be as coherent as possible in drawing the most extreme conclusions from the position I have chosen to experiment with. My test will be to see how many new questions can be brought to light by sticking firmly, even blindly, to all the obligations that this new departure point is forcing us to obey. The final test will be to check, at the end of this book, if the sociology of associations has been able to take up the relay of the sociology of the social by following different types of new and more active connections, and if it has been able to inherit all that was legitimate in the ambition of a science of the social. As usual, the result of whether this has been successful or not will be up to the reader.

For those who like to trace a discipline to some venerable ancestor, it is worth noting that this distinction between two contrasted ways of understanding the duties of social science is nothing new. It was already in place at the very beginning of the discipline (at least in France) in the early dispute between the elder Gabriel Tarde and Emile Durkheim, the winner.[12] Tarde always complained that Durkheim had abandoned the task of explaining society by confusing cause and effect, replacing the understanding of the social link with a political project aimed at social engineering. Against his younger challenger, he vigorously maintained that the social was not a special domain of reality but a principle of connections; that there was no reason to separate 'the social' from other associations like biological organisms or even atoms; that no break with philosophy, and especially metaphysics, was necessary in order to become a social science; that sociology was in effect a kind of inter-psychology;[13] that the study of innovation, and especially science and technology, was the growth area of social theory; and that economics had to be remade from top to bottom instead of being used as a vague metaphor to describe the calculation of interests. Above all, he considered the social as a circulating fluid that should be followed by new methods and not a specific type of organism. We don't need to accept all of Tarde's idiosyncrasies—and there are many—but in the gallery of portraits of eminent predecessors he is one of the very few, along with Harold Garfinkel, who believed sociology could be a science accounting for how society is held together, instead of using society to explain something else or to help solve one of the political questions of the time. That Tarde was

[12] The only extensive introduction to Tarde in English is Gabriel Tarde and Terry C. Clark (1969), *On Communication and Social Influence*. For a more recent view see Bruno Latour (2002), 'Gabriel Tarde and the End of the Social'. An older translation is available online of Gabriel Tarde (1899/2000), *Social Laws: An Outline of Sociology*.

[13] By opposition to *intra*-psychology on which he was almost completely silent, see Gabriel Tarde (1895/1999), *Monadologie et sociologie*.

utterly defeated by sociologists of the social to the point of being squeezed into a ghostly existence for a century does not prove that he was wrong. On the contrary, it simply makes this book even more necessary. I am convinced that if sociology had inherited more from Tarde (not to mention Comte, Spencer, Durkheim, and Weber), it could have been an even more relevant discipline. It still has the resources to become so as we will see at the end of this book. The two traditions can easily be reconciled, the second being simply the resumption of the task that the first believed was too quickly achieved. The factors gathered in the past under the label of a 'social domain' are simply some of the elements to be assembled in the future in what I will call not a society but a *collective*.

Gabriel Tarde An alternative precursor for an alternative social theory

Gabriel Tarde (1843–1904) was a judge and then a self-taught criminologist and became the predecessor of Bergson at the Collège de France.

A few quotes will give an idea of the strong contrast between the two lines of thought. Here is Tarde's definition of society:

'But this means that every thing is a society and that all things are societies. And it is quite remarkable that science, by a logical sequence of its earlier movements, tends to strangely generalize the notion of society. It speaks of cellular societies, why not of atomic societies? Not to mention societies of stars, solar systems. All of the sciences seem fated to become branches of sociology.' (Tarde 1999: 58)

Most interestingly, Tarde was head of a statistical institute for many years and always believed simultaneously in monographies and quantitative data, but he disagreed with Durkheim on the type of *quantum* sociology had to trace.

Generalizing Leibniz's monads, but without a God, Tarde's projects reverses the link between micro and macro:

'In a multitude of forms, though on a smaller scale, the same error always comes to light, namely, the error of believing that, in order to see a gradual dawn of regularity, order, and logic in social phenomena, we must go outside of the details, which are essentially irregular, and rise high enough to obtain a panoramic view of the general effect; that the source and foundation of every social coordination is some general fact from which it descends gradually to particular facts, though always diminishing in strength; in short, that man acts but a law of evolution guides him. I hold the contrary, in a certain sense.' (Tarde 1899/2000: 75)

This explains the radical opposition with Durkheim, a generation younger than Tarde:

'This conception is, in fact, almost the exact opposite of the unilinear evolutionists' notion and of M. Durkheim's. Instead of explaining everything by the supposed supremacy of a law of evolution, which compels collective phenomena to reproduce and repeat themselves indefinitely in a certain order rather than explaining lesser facts by greater, and the part by the whole—I explain collective resemblances of the whole by the massing together of minute elementary acts—the greater by the lesser and the whole by the part. This way of regarding phenomena is destined to produce a transformation in sociology similar to that brought about in mathematics by the introduction of infinitesimal calculus.' (Tarde 1899/2000: 35)

The reason why Tarde may pass for an early ancestor of ANT is that his best example of a social connection is always history and sociology of science:

'As regards the structure of science, probably the most imposing of human edifices, there is no possible question. It was built in the full light of history, and we can follow its development almost from the very outset down to our own day.... Everything here originates in the individual, not only the materials but the general design of the whole and the detail sketches as well. Everything, including what is now diffused among all cultured minds and taught even in the primary school, began as the secret of some single mind, whence a little flame, faint and flickering, sent forth its rays, at first only within a narrow compass, and even there encountering many obstructions, but, growing brighter as it spread further, it at length became a brilliant illumination. Now, if it seems plainly evident that science was thus constructed, it is no less true that the construction of every dogma, legal code, government, or economic régime was effected in the same manner; and if any doubt be possible with respect to language and ethics, because the obscurity of their origin and the slowness of their transformations remove them from observation through the greater part of their course, is it not highly probable that their evolution followed the same path?' (Tarde 1899/2000: 84–5)

The entities that Tarde is dealing with are not people but innovations, quanta of change that have a life of their own:

'This is why any social production having some marked characteristics, be it an industrial good, a verse, a formula, a political idea which has appeared one day somewhere in the corner of a brain, dreams like Alexander of conquering the world, tries to multiply itself by thousands and millions of copies in every place where there exists human beings and will never stop except if it is kept in check by some rival production as ambitious as itself.' (Tarde 1895/1999: 96)

What is most useful for ANT is that Tarde does not make the social science break away from philosophy or even metaphysics:

'To exist is to differ; difference, in one sense, is the substantial side of things, what they have most in common and what makes them most different. One has to start from this difference and to abstain from trying

> to explain it, especially by starting with identity, as so many persons wrongly
> do. Because identity is a minimum and, hence, a type of difference, and
> a very rare type at that, in the same way as rest is a type of movement
> and the circle a type of ellipse. To begin with some primordial identity
> implies at the origin a prodigiously unlikely singularity, or else the
> obscure mystery of one simple being then dividing for no special reason.'
> (Tarde 1895/1999: 73)

This book on how to use ANT for reassembling social connections is
organized in three parts corresponding to the three duties that the
sociology of the social has conflated for reasons that are no longer
justified:

How to *deploy* the many controversies about associations without
restricting in advance the social to a specific domain?

How to render fully traceable the means allowing actors to *stabilize*
those controversies?

Through which *procedures* is it possible to reassemble the social not
in a society but in a collective?

In the first part, I will show why we should not limit in advance the
sort of beings populating the social world. Social sciences have become
much too timid in deploying the sheer complexity of the associations
they have encountered.[14] I will argue that it's possible to feed, so to
speak, off controversies and learn how to become good relativists—
surely an indispensable preparation before venturing into new territory. In the second part, I will show how it's possible to render social
connections traceable by following the work done to stabilize the
controversies followed in the first part. Borrowing a metaphor from
cartography, I could say that ANT has tried to render the social world
as *flat* as possible in order to ensure that the establishment of any new
link is clearly visible. Finally, I will conclude by showing why the task
of assembling the collective is worth pursuing, but only after the
shortcut of society and 'social explanation' has been abandoned. If
it's true that the views of society offered by the sociologists of the
social were mainly a way of insuring civil peace when modernism
was under way,[15] what sort of collective life and what sort of knowledge is to be gathered by sociologists of associations once moderniz-

[14] I have left aside in this book the question of quantitative sociology not because I
believe more in qualitative data, but because the very definition of which *quantum* to
tally is at stake in the different definitions of the social vector I am going to follow here.

[15] The first instance of the words 'sociology' and 'social sciences' are found in the
famous pamphlet *Qu'est-ce que le Tiers-Etat?* by Emmanuel Joseph Sieyès (1748–1836) to
designate a fusion of all the 'cameral sciences' in an art of government, see Frédéric
Audren (forthcoming), 'Les juristes et les sociologues'.

ing has been thrown into doubt while the task of finding the ways to cohabit remains more important than ever?

In some ways this book resembles a travel guide through a terrain that is at once completely banal—it's nothing but the social world we are used to—and completely exotic—we will have to learn how to slow down at each step. If earnest scholars do not find it dignifying to compare an introduction of a science to a travel guide, be they kindly reminded that 'where to travel' and 'what is worth seeing there' is nothing but a way of saying in plain English what is usually said under the pompous Greek name of 'method' or, even worse, 'methodology'. The advantage of a travel book approach over a 'discourse on method' is that it cannot be confused with the territory on which it simply overlays. A guide can be put to use as well as forgotten, placed in a backpack, stained with grease and coffee, scribbled all over, its pages torn apart to light a fire under a barbecue. In brief, it offers suggestions rather than imposing itself on the reader. That said, this is not a coffee table book offering glossy views of the landscape to the eyes of the visitor too lazy to travel. It is directed at practitioners as a how-to book, helping them to find their bearings *once* they are bogged down in the territory. For others, I am afraid it will remain totally opaque, since the social ties to be traced will never resemble those they have been trained to follow.

PART I

How to Deploy Controversies About the Social World

Introduction to Part I: Learning to Feed off Controversies

Like all sciences, sociology begins in wonder. The commotion might be registered in many different ways but it's always the paradoxical presence of something at once invisible yet tangible, taken for granted yet surprising, mundane but of baffling subtlety that triggers a passionate attempt to tame the wild beast of the social. 'We live in groups that seem firmly entrenched, and yet how is it that they transform so rapidly?' 'We are made to do things by other agencies over which we have no control and that seem plain and mundane enough.' 'There is something invisible that weighs on all of us that is more solid than steel and yet so incredibly labile.' 'There exist forces that are strangely similar to those studied by natural scientists and yet distinctively different.' 'This puzzling mixture of obdurate resistance and perverse complexity seems wide opened to inquiry, and yet it defies all inquiries.' It would be hard to find a social scientist not shaken by one or more of these bewildering statements. Are not these conundrums the source of our *libido sciendi*? What pushes us to devote so much energy into unraveling them?

There is, however, an increasing distance between what triggers those successive shocks and the solutions that have been devised to explain them. I am going to argue in Part I that although the insights of sociology are correct, the solutions suggested by a shrinking definition of the social has in many ways adulterated what was productive and scientific in them. This is why I want to reexamine each of those successive questions and dissect them so that we can renew our definition of what is an association.

Faithful to relativist principles, instead of dividing the social domain as most textbooks of sociology usually do into a list of actors, methods, and domains *already* taken as members of the social realm, I have organized the first part of this work by types of controversies about *what* this universe is made of. I think it is possible to build upon the

major intuitions of the social sciences by examining five major uncertainties:[16]

- the nature of groups: there exist many contradictory ways for
actors to be given an identity;
- the nature of actions: in each course of action a great variety of
agents seem to barge in and displace the original goals;
- the nature of objects: the type of agencies participating in interaction seems to remain wide open;
- the nature of facts: the links of natural sciences with the rest of
society seems to be the source of continuous disputes;
- and, finally, about the type of studies done under the label of a
science of the social as it is never clear in which precise sense social
sciences can be said to be empirical.

What has made ANT so implausible is that before going anywhere
those five uncertainties have to be piled on top of one another, with
each new one making the former even more puzzling until some
common sense is regained—but only at the end. Most users of ANT
have so far had little patience to wait and I can't blame them.[17]

The reader will discover here a set of complicated instructions to
make displacement more costly and more painful. The reason for this
is that I want to break the habit of linking the notions of 'society',
'social factor', and 'social explanation' with a sudden *acceleration* in
the description. When sociologists of the social pronounce the words
'society', 'power', 'structure', and 'context', they often jump straight
ahead to connect vast arrays of life and history, to mobilize gigantic
forces, to detect dramatic patterns emerging out of confusing interactions, to see everywhere in the cases at hand yet more examples of
well-known types, to reveal behind the scenes some dark powers pulling the strings. Not that they are wrong since its perfectly true that
older social relations have been packaged in such a way as to seem to
provide a ready explanation for many puzzling subjects. But the time
has come to have a much closer look at the type of aggregates thus
assembled and at the ways they are connected to one another.

When you wish to discover the new unexpected actors that have
more recently popped up and which are not yet *bona fide* members of
'society', you have to travel somewhere else and with very different
kinds of gear. As we are going to see, there is as much difference in the

---

[16] I have chosen 'uncertainties'—in a weak allusion to the 'uncertainty principle'—
because it remains impossible to decide whether it resides in the observer or in the
phenomenon observed. As we will see, it's never the case that the analyst knows what
the actors ignore, nor is it the case that the actors know what the observer ignores. This is
the reason why the social needs to be reassembled.

[17] For readers most interested in science studies, it might make more sense to read
Chapter 4 first—p. 87—and then swallow the other sources of uncertainty one by one.
For those more familiar with ANT, it might be easier to start with the interlude, p. 141.

two uses of the word 'social' as there is between learning how to drive on an already existing freeway and exploring for the first time the bumpy territory in which a road has been planned against the wishes of many local communities.[18] There's no question that ANT prefers to travel slowly, on small roads, on foot, and by paying the full cost of any displacement out of its own pocket.

The reason for this change of tempo is that, instead of taking a reasonable position and imposing some order beforehand, ANT claims to be able to find order much better *after* having let the actors deploy the full range of controversies in which they are immersed. It is as if we were saying to the actors: 'We won't try to discipline you, to make you fit into our categories; we will let you deploy your own worlds, and only later will we ask you to explain how you came about settling them.' The task of defining and ordering the social should be left to the actors themselves, not taken up by the analyst. This is why, to regain some sense of order, the best solution is to trace connections *between* the controversies themselves rather than try to decide how to settle any given controversy.[19] The search for order, rigor, and pattern is by no means abandoned. It is simply relocated one step further into abstraction so that actors are allowed to unfold their own differing cosmos, no matter how counter-intuitive they appear.[20]

It is this increased level of abstraction in social theory which makes ANT hard to grasp at first. And yet this shift is comparable to what a cartographer does in trying to record the shape of a foreign coast on

[18] A reader, asking in what sense our theory of the social could be reconciled with 'conventional' sociology, offered as an objection the way AIDS patients mobilized as a group. Looking at traditional 'social movements', it was obvious to her that patients' organizations corresponded to 'conventional' definitions of the social because she had entirely forgotten how deeply innovative it was for patients to make politics out of retroviruses. For us on the other hand, AIDS activism, and more generally patient-based organizations, is just the type of innovation that requires completely new definitions of the social. See Steven Epstein (1996), *Impure Science. Aids, Activism and the Politics of Knowledge*; Michel Callon and Vololona Rabeharisoa (1999), *Le pouvoir des malades*; and Nicolas Dodier (2003), *Leçons politiques de l'épidémie de sida*. These prove how fast people forget the new associations and include them in their 'conventional' definition of what is a society.
[19] A striking example of the richness of this approach has been provided in Boltanski and Thévenot, *On Justification*. In this major work, the authors have shown that it was possible to find a much more solid order once it was accepted that ordinary French persons, when engaged in polemics where they had to justify their positions, could rely not on one but six complete principles of justification (les *Cités* or Orders of Worth: Market, Industrial, Civic, Domestic, Inspired, Opinion) to which the authors later added a possible Green justification. See Claudette Lafaye and Laurent Thevenot (1993), 'Une justification écologique? Conflits dans l'aménagement de la nature'. Although those principles were incommensurable, the sociologists, by moving one step further into abstraction, could nonetheless render them comparable. It's this magnificent example of the power of relativity that I am trying to emulate here.

a piece of paper. She might exert herself to fit the various reports sent by explorers into some existing geometrical format—bays have to be circles, capes triangles, continents squares. But after noticing the hopeless mess created by those records, none of which exactly fall into pre-determined shapes, she will eagerly accept any proposition to displace the quest for geometrical rigor with a totally abstract Cartesian grid. Then she will use this empty grid to patiently record the coastline itself, allowing it to be drawn in as tortuous a way as geological history made it to be. Although it may appear stupid to record every reported point simply by longitude and latitude, it would be even more stupid to insist that only data that fits a preordained geometrical shape be kept. Similarly, ANT claims that it is possible to trace more sturdy relations and discover more revealing patterns by finding a way to register the links between unstable and shifting frames of reference rather than by trying to keep one frame stable. Society is no more 'roughly' made of 'individuals', of 'cultures', of 'nation states' than Africa is 'roughly' a circle, France a hexagon or Cornwall a triangle. There is nothing surprising in this since every scientific discipline is a slow training in devising the right sort of relativism that can be adapted to the data at hand. Why would sociology alone be forbidden to invent its own path and be requested to stick to the obvious? Now that geologists have accepted the notion of cold and rigid continental plates floating freely over the hot, molten seabed that seeps out of deep oceanic rifts, are they not, so to speak, on 'firmer ground'? Similarly, ANT claims that we will find a much more scientific way of building the social world if we abstain from interrupting the flood of controversies. We, too, should find our firm ground: on shifting sands. Contrary to what is so often said, relativism is a way to float on data, not drown in them.

Metaphors borrowed from cartography or from physics break down very fast, however, once the range of uncertainties to be swallowed by sociologists of association begins to be deployed. In some extreme situations, actors seem to have an uncanny ability to disagree with everything sociologists supposedly take for granted in order to begin their work. Abandoning the fixed frame of reference offered by ether, as physicists did, appears in retrospect a rather simple affair when compared with what we will have to let go of if we want to leave the actors free to deploy the full incommensurability of their own world-making activities.[21] Be prepared to cast off agency, structure, psyche,

---

[20] It's only in Part II that we will deal with the other question of stabilizing controversies. For reasons that will become clear only later, sociologists of the social have not been able to keep the two movements distinct.

[21] 'World-making' would be a fine word, see Nelson Goodman (1988), *Ways of World Making*, were it not for the conception of 'making' that goes with it and the definition of

time, and space along with every other philosophical and anthropological category, no matter how deeply rooted in common sense they may appear to be.

Using the example of our cartographer, it is as if she had to deal not only with multiple reports coming from many travelers but also with multiple projection grids, where each point is requesting its own ad hoc coordinates. Faced with this confusion, one may decide to restrain the range of controversies or to unleash all of them. The first pre-relativist solution works fine but risks limiting sociology to routine, cold, and quiet situations. The second relativist solution tackles active, warm, and extreme situations, but then one has to let controversies unfold all the way. Striking some compromise between the two positions would be most absurd since controversies are not simply a nuisance to be kept at bay, but what allows the social to be established and the various social sciences to contribute in its building. Many of the difficulties in developing those disciplines have come from a refusal to be theoretical enough and from a misplaced attempt at clinging to common sense mixed with an ill-timed craving for political relevance. Such is the extreme position I wish to try and sustain for as long as possible. The drawback is that throughout their travels readers have to support themselves on a strange diet: they have to feed off controversies about what the social is made out of.

Traveling with ANT, I am afraid to say, will turn out to be agonizingly slow. Movements will be constantly interrupted, interfered with, disrupted, and dislocated by the five types of uncertainties. In the world ANT is trying to travel through, no displacement seems possible without costly and painful translations. Sociologists of the social seem to glide like angels, transporting power and connections almost immaterially, while the ANT-scholar has to trudge like an ant, carrying the heavy gear in order to generate even the tiniest connection. At the end of this book, we will attempt to summarize what differentiates a good ANT account from a bad one—a crucial quality test—by asking three questions: have all the difficulties of traveling been recognized? Has the complete cost of the travel from one connection to the next been fully paid? Has the traveler not cheated by surreptitiously getting a ride from an already existing 'social order'? In the meantime, my advice is to pack as little as possible, don't forget to pay your ticket, and prepare for delays.

the 'one world'. This expression is thus taken as a provisional placeholder until we can redefine constructivism—see p. 88—and then much later what it means to compose 'one common world'—p. 247.

First Source of Uncertainty: No Group, Only Group Formation

Where should we start? As always, it is best to begin in the middle of things, *in medias res*. Will the reading of a newspaper do? Sure, it offers a starting point as good as any. As soon as you open it, it's like a rain, a flood, an epidemic, an infestation. With every two lines, a trace is being left by some writer that some group is being made or unmade. Here it's the CEO of a big company who deplores the fact that five years after the merger the firm's various branches are still not fully integrated. She wonders how to 'promote a common corporate culture'. A few lines further down finds an anthropologist explaining that there is no 'ethnic' difference between Hutus and Tutsis in Rwanda, but that it's really a 'class difference' that has been 'instrumentalized' by colonialists and then 'naturalized' as a 'cultural' one. In the letters section, a Scot reminds his readers of the 'Glorious Alliance' between France and Mary Queen of Scots, which explains why Scotland should not share the rabid Europhobia of Englishmen. A correspondent from France tries to explain why second generation girls from Algeria that show up at school with an Islamic veil are seen by their teachers as 'fanatics' who 'exclude themselves' from the French Republic. In the Europe section, it is explained that EU functionaries are more and more thinking 'as Europeans' and are no longer 'loyal to their nationalities'. In the Music section, a fierce dispute divides Baroque ensembles according to the frequency of their tuning forks, pelting one another with accusations such as 'modernist', 'unfaithful to the tradition', 'academic'. In the Computer section, the writer mocks the attachment of Macintosh users to their utterly marginal machines and puts forward a 'cultural interpretation' for what he calls a form of 'techno-fanaticism'. Further down an editorialist predicts that Iraq, though its borders are fairly recent, will exist as a nation and will not split up along the older dividing lines of religion and historical 'zones of influence'. Another column mocks the accusation that those against the war in Iraq are 'anti-American'. It never stops.

Relating to one group or another is an on-going process made up of uncertain, fragile, controversial, and ever-shifting ties. Is this not odd? If we simply follow the newspapers' cues, the central intuition of sociology should be that at any given moment actors are *made to fit* in a group—often in more than one. And yet, when you read social theorists, it seems that the main, the crucial, the most urgent question should be which grouping is *preferable* to start a social enquiry. Should we take social aggregates to be made of 'individuals', 'of organizations', 'of 'classes', of 'roles', of 'life trajectories', of 'discursive fields', of 'selfish genes', of 'forms of life', of 'social networks'? They never seem to tire in designating one entity as real, solid, proven, or entrenched while others are criticized as being artificial, imaginary, transitional, illusory, abstract, impersonal, or meaningless. Should we focus on the micro-level of interactions or should we consider the macro-level as more relevant? Is it better to view markets, organizations, or networks as the essential ingredients of our collective life?

While the most common experience we have of the social world is of being simultaneously seized by several possible and contradictory calls for regroupings, it seems that the most important decision to make before becoming a social scientist is to decide first which ingredients are already there in society. While it is fairly obvious that we are *enrolled* in a group by a series of interventions that renders visible those who argue for the relevance of one grouping and the irrelevance of others, everything happens as if social scientists had to claim that there exists 'out there' one type that is real, whereas the other sets are really inauthentic, obsolete, irrelevant, or artificial. While we are well aware that the first feature of the social world is this constant tracing of boundaries by people over some other people, sociologists of the social consider that the main feature of this world is to recognize, independently of who is tracing them and with what sort of tools, the unquestionable existence of boundaries. Even stranger is that while social scientists, economists, historians, psychologists, and political scientists are at work with their newspaper columns, demonstrations, teachings, reports, enquiries, commissions, and statistics to help define and redefine groups, social theories still seem as if the existence of the relevant actors was fully independent of this massive amount of work by the professionals, or worse, as if this inevitable reflexive loop precluded sociology from ever becoming a science. And yet, who would know how to invoke the 'unconscious' without Freud? Who would be able to denounce 'alienation' without Marx? Who would be able to declare themselves 'upper-middle class' without social statistics? Who would learn to 'feel European' without the editorials of the liberal press?

To sum up, whereas for sociologists the first problem seems to settle on one privileged grouping, our most common experience, if we are faithful to it, tells us that there are lots of contradictory group formations, group enrollment—activity to which social scientists are obviously crucial contributors. The choice is thus clear: either we follow social theorists and begin our travel by setting up at the start which kind of group and level of analysis we will focus on, or we follow the actors' own ways and begin our travels by the traces left behind by their activity of forming and dismantling groups.

The first source of uncertainty one should learn from is that there is no relevant group that can be said to make up social aggregates, no established component that can be used as an incontrovertible starting point.[22] Many a sociological enquiry has begun by setting up one—or several—type of groupings, before apologizing profusely for this somewhat arbitrary limitation made necessary, it is often argued, by the 'obligation to limit one's scope' or 'by the right of a scientist to define one's object'. But this is not at all the sort of setting, the sort of obligation, the sort of apologies, sociologists of associations wish to start with. Their duty is not to stabilize—whether at the beginning for clarity, for convenience, or to look reasonable—the list of groupings making up the social. Quite the opposite: their starting point begins precisely with the controversies about which grouping one pertains to, including of course the controversies among social scientists about what the social world is made of.

If someone pointed out to me that words like 'group', 'grouping', and 'actor' are meaningless, I would answer: 'Quite right.' The word 'group' is so empty that it sets neither the size nor the content. It could be applied to a planet as well as to an individual; to Microsoft as well as to my family; to plants as well as to baboons. This is exactly why I have chosen it.

This is a larger point about the vocabulary of ANT with which I should familiarize the reader at this early stage in order to avoid confusing the language of this book with the landscape we are going to visit. I find it best to use the most general, the most banal, even the most vulgar repertoire so that there will be no risk of confusing the

---

[22] Garfinkel's ethnomethods would take the same starting points, beginning with mundane accounts instead of controversies or through the clever idea of 'breaching', which transforms even mundane encounters into controversies. See Harold Garfinkel (1967), *Studies in Ethnomethodology*. In both cases, the point is the same: it's not the sociologist's duty to decide in advance and in the member's stead what the social world is made of—a very common idea for chemists, physicists, and naturalists, but it is still seen as provocative in the social sciences.

actors' own prolific idioms. Sociologists of the social, as a rule, do just the opposite. They are keen to produce precise, well chosen, sophisticated terms for what they say the actors say. But then they might run the risk of confusing the two meta-languages—since actors, too, have their own elaborate and fully reflexive meta-language. If they practice critical sociology, then there is an even greater risk to render actors mute altogether. ANT prefers to use what could be called an *infra-language*, which remains strictly meaningless except for allowing displacement from one frame of reference to the next. In my experience, this is a better way for the vocabulary of the actors to be heard loud and clear—and I am not especially worried if it is the social scientists' jargon that is being downplayed. If I had to provide a checklist for what is a good ANT account—this will be an important indicator of quality—are the concepts of the actors allowed to be *stronger* than that of the analysts, or is it the analyst who is doing all the talking? As far as writing reports is concerned, it means a precise but difficult trial: Is the text that comments on the various quotes and documents more, less, or as interesting as the actors' own expressions and behaviors? If you find this test too easy to meet, then ANT is not for you.

A list of traces left by the formation of groups

From the many disputes among social theorists and among actors themselves about what should be the basic building block of society, there is no reason to draw the conclusion that we should despair of social science. ANT doesn't claim that we will ever know if society is 'really' made of small individual calculative agents or of huge macro-actors; nor does it claim that since anything goes one can pick a favorite candidate at whim. On the contrary, it draws the relativist, that is, the scientific conclusion that those controversies provide the analyst with an essential resource to render the social connections traceable. ANT simply claims that once we are accustomed to these many shifting frames of reference a very good grasp of how the social is generated can be provided, since a relativist connection between frames of reference offers a better source of objective judgment than the absolute (that is, arbitrary) settings suggested by common sense. This is the reason why it is so crucial *not* to begin with a pronouncement of the sort: 'Social aggregates are mainly made of (x).' It makes no difference if (x) stands for 'individual agent', 'organizations', 'races', 'small bands', 'states', 'persons', 'members', 'will power', 'libido', 'biographies', 'fields', etc. ANT simply doesn't take as its job to stabilize the social on behalf of the people it studies; such a duty is to be left entirely to the 'actors themselves'—a much maligned cliché which we will visit in due time.

While at first sight it would seem easier for sociologists to settle on one group instead of mapping the controversies about group formation, it is exactly the opposite and for a good empirical reason. Group formations leave many more traces in their wake than already established connections which, by definition, might remain mute and invisible. If a given ensemble simply lies there, then it is invisible and nothing can be said about it. The ensemble generates no trace and thus produces no information whatsoever; if it is visible, then it is being performed and will then generate new and interesting data. The solution is to substitute the list of groupings composed of social aggregates—an impossible task—with the list of the elements always present in *controversies* about groups—a much simpler one. This second list is more abstract to be sure since it deals with the work necessary to delineate any grouping, but it also generates much more data since every time a new grouping is alluded to the fabrication mechanism necessary to keep it alive will be made visible and thus traceable. While, after one hundred and fifty years, sociologists are still unclear on what the 'right' social aggregates should be,[23] it is a rather simpler matter to agree that in any controversy about group formation—including of course academic disputes—some items will always be present: groups are made to talk; anti-groups are mapped; new resources are fetched so as to make their boundaries more durable; and professionals with their highly specialized paraphernalia are mobilized.

First, to delineate a group, no matter if it has to be created from scratch or simply refreshed, you have to have spokespersons which 'speak for' the group existence—and sometimes are very talkative, as the newspaper example made clear. Whichever example you take, be they feminist dog-owners in California, Kosovars in former Serbia, *'chevaliers du tastevin'* in my native Burgundy, Achuars in the Amazon, accountants, anti-globalists, sociologists of science, egos, Trotskyites, working class, market forces, conspiracies, etc., all need some people defining who they are, what they should be, what they have been. These are constantly at work, justifying the group's existence, invoking rules and precedents and, as we shall see, measuring up one definition against all the others. Groups are not silent things, but rather the provisional product of a constant uproar made by the millions of contradictory voices about what is a group and who pertains to what. Just think of the mass of talks and writings that went

---

[23] One reason for this continuing uncertainty over the departure point—individual, structures, fields, trajectories, etc.—is due to the belief that society is ranked according to sizes ranging from Small to XXL. The origin of this misapprehension and the ways to avoid it will not be tackled until the second part of this book—see p. 175.

into the delineation of this extraordinary set: *homo oeconomicus*.[24] There is no group without some kind of recruiting officer. No flock of sheep without a shepherd—and his dog, his walking stick, his piles of vaccination certificates, his mountain of paperwork to get EU subsidies. If you still believe groupings exist 'by themselves', for instance the 'individual', just try to remember how much labor had to be done before each of you could 'take your life into your own hands'. How many admonitions from parents, teachers, bosses, partners, and colleagues before we learned that we had better be a group of our own (the ego)? And how quickly we forgot that lesson.[25] Although groups seem to be already fully equipped, ANT sees none existing without a rather large retinue of group makers, group talkers, and group holders.

Second, whenever some work has to be done to trace or retrace the boundary of a group, other groupings are designated as being empty, archaic, dangerous, obsolete, and so on. It is always by comparison with other competing ties that any tie is emphasized. So for every group to be defined, a list of *anti-groups* is set up as well. This is quite convenient for observers because it means that actors are always engaged in the business of mapping the 'social context' in which they are placed, thus offering the analyst a full-blooded theory of what sort of sociology they should be treated with.[26] This is why it is so important *not* to define in advance what sort of social aggregates could provide the context for all these maps. Group delineation is not only one of the occupations of social scientists, but also the very constant task of the actors themselves. Actors do the sociology for the sociologists and sociologists learn from the actors what makes up their set of associations.

While this should seem obvious, such a result is actually in opposition to the basic wisdom of critical sociologists. For them, actors do not see the whole picture but remain only 'informants'. This is why they have to be *taught* what is the context 'in which' they are situated and 'of which' they see only a tiny part, while the social scientist, floating above, sees the 'whole thing'. The excuse for occupying such a

---

[24] Gabriel Tarde (1902), *Psychologie économique*. The main work remains Karl Polanyi (1944), *The Great Transformation*, but see also Albert O. Hirshmann, *The Passions and the Interests* and Michel Callon (1998b), *The Laws of the Markets* as well as the fields of anthropology and economics. For recent empirical studies on an ANT perspective, see Fabian Muniesa (2004), Des marchés comme algorithmes: sociologie de la cotation électronique à la Bourse de Paris' and Vincent Lépinay (2003), 'Les formules du marché. Ethno-Economie d'une innovation financière: les produits à capital garanti'.

[25] It's the great achievement of Tarde's inter-psychology to relate the amount of influence with the increase in individualisation, see Gabriel Tarde (1901[1989]), *L'opinion et la foule* and Tarde, *On Communication and Social Influence*.

[26] No one has developed this as thoroughly as Garfinkel. See the famous case of Agnes's uncertain gender affiliation and its critique in Norman K. Denzin (1990), 'Harold and Agnes: A Feminist Narrative Undoing'.

bird's eye view is usually that scientists are doing 'reflexively' what the informants are doing 'unwittingly'. But even this is doubtful. The little awareness that social scientists may gather is exacted out of the reflexive group formation of those they simply, at this point of their enquiry, use like a parasite. In general, what passes for reflexivity in most social sciences is the sheer irrelevancy of questions raised by the analyst about some actors' serious concerns.[27] As a rule, it's much better to set up as the default position that the inquirer is always one reflexive loop *behind* those they study.

Third, when groups are formed or redistributed, their spokesperson looks rather frantically for ways to *de-fine* them. Their boundaries are marked, delineated, and rendered fixed and durable. Every group, no matter how small or how big, requires a *limes* like the mythical one traced by Romulus around nascent Rome. This is very convenient for the analyst as every group formation will be accompanied by the digging out of a wide range of features, mobilized to make the group boundary hold against the contradictory pressures of all the competing anti-groups that threaten to dissolve it. There exist endless ways of rendering the group definition a finite and sure thing, so finite and sure that, in the end, it looks like the object of an unproblematic definition. You may appeal to tradition or to law. You may invent strange hybrids like 'strategic essentialism' or entrench the boundary in 'nature'. You may even turn it into a 'genetic make-up', associate it with 'blood and soil', make it a 'folk tradition', sink it into customs or habits. On the contrary, you may tie it to freedom, emancipation, artifice, fashion, or history. In the end it will have become so unquestionable that it will be taken for granted and thus will no longer produce any trace, spark, or information. The ensemble is now entirely *out of* the social world—in the ANT sense—even though it is now, in the usual sense, a *bona fide* member of the social.

Fourth, among the many spokespersons that make possible the durable definition of groups, one must include social scientists, social sciences, social statistics, and social journalism. This is one of the essential differences between the two schools of thought. For the sociologists of the social, sociology should strive to become a science in the traditional disinterested sense of a gaze directed to a world outside, allowing for a description that is somewhat independent of the groups being materialized by the actors. For the sociologists of associations, any study of any group by any social scientist is part and parcel of what makes the group exist, last, decay, or disappear. In

---

[27] Reflexivity is a tricky term that has an interesting meaning when given to actors and objects and a deleterious one when taken as an epistemological virtue protecting the sociologist from a breach of objectivity. See Antoine Hennion (2004), 'Pragmatics of Taste'.

the developed world, there is no group that does not have at least some social science instrument attached to it. This is not some 'inherent limitation' of the discipline due to the fact that sociologists are also 'social members' and have difficulties in 'extracting themselves' out of the bonds of their own 'social categories'. It is simply because they are on par with those they study, doing exactly the same job and partici- pating in the same tasks of tracing social bonds, albeit with different instruments and for different professional callings. Although in the first school actors and scholars are in two different boats, in the second they remain in the same boat all along and play the same role, namely group formation. If the social is to be assembled, every hand is needed. We will draw only at the end the consequence of this fundamental equality.

No matter how gross and tentative my list appears, it is already possible to learn how to trace with it many social connections, instead of being constantly bogged down in the impossible task of deciding once and for all what is the right unit of analysis sociology should chose to focus on. This is, however, a very partial advantage of ANT. On the one hand, we are freed from one impossible task that would have slowed us down. On the other, we now have to take into account many more contradictory cartographies of the social than we would have wished for—and *that* is going to slow us down even more.

No work, no group

The choice, as we just saw, is not between certainty and confusion, between the arbitrariness of some a priori decision and the morass of endless differences. What we have lost—a fixed list of groups—we have regained because groupings have constantly to be made, or re- made, and during this creation or recreation the group-makers leave behind many traces that can be used as data by the informer. One way to mark this difference is to say that social aggregates are not the object of an *ostensive* definition—like mugs and cats and chairs that can be pointed at by the index finger—but only of a *performative* definition. They are made by the various ways and manners in which they are said to exist. This distinction, however, entails many delicate linguistic and metaphysical difficulties. I don't want to suggest that groups are made by *fiat* or, worse still, out of speech acts by mere conventions.[28] I want

[28] Not in the sense applied to social science in John Searle (1995), *The Construction of Social Reality*, but rather in that proposed in Ian Hacking (1992), 'The Self-Vindication of the Laboratory Sciences' to account for the success of natural science. To save naturalism, Searle defined the social world by bootstrapping, thus making the abyss even bigger

to use it simply to underline the difference between groups endowed with some inertia and groupings that need to be constantly kept up by some group-making effort. Sociologists of the social like to appeal to 'social inertia', as if there existed somewhere a stock of connections whose capital could be eroded only over a long time. For ANT, if you stop making and remaking groups, you stop having groups. No reservoir of forces flowing from 'social forces' will help you. For sociologists of the social, the rule is order while decay, change, or creation are the exceptions. For the sociologists of associations, the rule is performance and what has to be explained, the troubling exceptions, are any type of stability over the long term and on a larger scale. It is as if, in the two schools, background and foreground were reversed.

The consequences of this inversion are enormous. If inertia, durability, range, solidity, commitment, loyalty, adhesion, etc. have to be accounted for, this cannot be done without looking for vehicles, tools, instruments, and materials able to provide such a stability—see the third and fourth uncertainties. Whereas, for the sociologists of the social, the great virtue of appeals to society is that they offer this long lasting stability on a plate and for free, our school views stability as exactly what has to be explained by appealing to costly and demanding *means*. And by definition those instruments should have another quality than that of being 'social', since they have to make the grouping *reach* a bit further and *stand* a bit longer. The problem with any ostensive definition of the social is that no extra effort seems necessary to maintain the groups in existence, while the influence of the analyst seems to count for nothing—or simply as a perturbing factor that should be minimized as much as possible. The great benefit of a performative definition, on the other hand, is just the opposite: it draws attention to the means necessary to ceaselessly upkeep the groups and to the key contributions made by the analysts' own resources. Sociology of associations has to pay the price, in small change, of what sociology of the social seems to stock on its shelves in infinite supply.

In pointing out the practical means necessary to delineate groups and keep them in existence, we encounter a conflict of duties that marks a clear departure point—not the last!—between the freeways of the sociologists of the social and the delicate trails of the regions we wish to map. It all depends on what is designed by 'means'. While the first enquirers exclaim: 'Surely we need to start somewhere, so why not

between matters of fact and social law. One minute of inquiry breaks down the distinction, however, since it would be totally impossible to maintain something like money—his favorite example—without materials and that not one single matter of fact can be defined without categories, formalism, convention, and translation starting with measurements. See p. 109.

begin by defining society as being made of (x)?' The others exclaim
with as much energy: 'Let the actors do the job for us. Don't define for
them what makes up the social!' The reason for this difference in
duties is that, in the eyes of the former group, the choice of a departure
point is not absolutely crucial since the social world already exists. For
them, if you highlight 'classes' instead of 'individuals', 'nations' instead of 'classes', 'life trajectories' instead of 'social roles', or 'social
networks' instead of 'organizations', all the paths will merge in the end
since they are simply somewhat arbitrary ways to delineate the same
big animal—in the same fashion as for the proverbial elephant seized
successively by the leg, the ear, the trunk, or the tusk. However, the
situation is entirely different for ANT because neither society nor the
social exists in the first place. They have to be retraced by subtle
changes in connecting non-social resources. Thus, every choice of a
departure point will lead to the drawing of a completely different
animal, fully incommensurable with the others. For the first school,
society is always there putting its full weight behind whatever vehicle
can carry it; in the second approach, social links have to be traced *by
the circulation* of different vehicles which cannot be substituted by one
another.

For example, if an informant says that she lives 'in a God ordained
world', this statement is not really different from that of another
informant who claims he is 'dominated by market forces', since both
of these terms—'God' and 'market'—are mere 'expressions' of the *same*
social world. But it makes a huge, an insurmountable, an incommensurable difference for the ANT-trained sociologist. An association with
God is *not* substitutable by any other association, it is utterly specific
and cannot be reconciled with another one made up of market forces
which, in turn, designs a pattern completely different from those
drawn by legal ties. Sociologists of the social always have at their
disposal a stable and absolute third term in which to translate all the
vocabularies of the informants, a master vocabulary which acts as a
sort of clearing house for instantaneous exchanges between goods that
all share the same basic homogeneous quality—namely, to be social.
ANT-sociologists, on the other hand, possess no such common currency. The word social cannot replace anything, cannot express anything better, cannot be substituted—in any form or guise—for
anything else. It is not the common measure of all things, like a credit
card widely accepted everywhere. It is only a movement that can be
seized indirectly when there is a slight change in one older association
mutating into a slightly newer or different one. Far from a stable and
sure thing, it is no more than an occasional spark generated by the
shift, the shock, the slight displacement of other non-social phenomena. Does this mean that we have to take seriously the real and

sometimes exquisitely small differences between the many ways in which people 'achieve the social'? I am afraid so.

Mediators vs. intermediaries

It would be possible to attenuate the differences between the two schools by saying that 'naturally' all social scientists agree that groups have to be made and remade anew through some other non-social means, and that there is never a grouping that can sustain its existence without some keeping up. To be sure, everyone will agree that, for instance, popular festivals are necessary to 'refresh social ties'; that propaganda is indispensable to 'heat up' the passions of 'national identities'; that traditions are 'invented'; that it is good for a company to distribute a journal to 'build loyalties'; that without price tags and bar codes it would be very difficult to 'calculate' a price; that for a child to become 'responsible' early spanking cannot do any harm; that without a totem it would be difficult for a tribe to recognize that they are 'members' of the same clan. These sorts of expressions flow effortlessly from our keyboards. But their precise effect depends on how exactly we understand ways of speaking which all allude to the 'making' of groups. For sociologists of the social, such terms designate the many avatars that the *same* social order can take or the variegated tools with which it 'represents' itself or through which it is 'reproduced'.[29] For them, 'social forces' are always already present in the background so that the precise means to achieve their presence matters a great deal—but not that crucially.

For the sociologists of associations, they make all the difference in the world because there exists no society to begin with, no reservoir of ties, no big reassuring pot of glue to keep all those groups together. If you don't have the festival now or print the newspaper today, you simply lose the grouping, which is not a building in need of restoration but a movement in need of continuation. If a dancer stops dancing, the dance is finished. No inertia will carry the show forward. This is why I needed to introduce the distinction between ostensive and performative: the object of an ostensive definition remains there, whatever happens to the index of the onlooker. But the object of a performative definition vanishes when it is no longer performed—or if

---

[29] The word 'reproduction', so often used in expressions like 'social reproduction', takes up two entirely different meanings depending on the relationship between the product and the 'reproducer'. Most of the time, the product is fully predicted by the progenitor. Thus nothing is added by the 're'-production, which is seen only as a chain of necessary but largely passive intermediaries.

it stays, then it means that *other* actors have taken over the relay. And this relay, by definition, cannot be 'the social world', since it is that very world which is in dire need of a fresh relay.

Durkheim having a Tardian moment

As the following quotes from Durkheim's famous passage on the role of totems in group-making show, the difference is extremely subtle between a mediator and an intermediary. Does the totem express the group, facilitate its cohesion, or is it what allows the group to exist as a group?

Here is how Durkheim (1915/1947: 230–31, 233) addresses the issue:

'That an emblem is useful as a rallying center for any sort of a group it is superfluous to point out. By expressing the social unity in a material form, it makes this more obvious to all, and for that very reason the use of emblematic symbols must have spread very quickly once thought of. But more than that, this idea should spontaneously arise out of the conditions of common life; for the emblem is not merely a convenient process for clarifying the sentiment the society has of itself: it also serves to create this sentiment; it is one of its constituent elements.

Moreover, without symbols, social sentiments could have only a precarious existence.... But if the movements by which these sentiments are expressed are connected with something that endures, the sentiments themselves become more durable. These other things are constantly bringing them to mind and arousing them; it is as though the cause which excited them in the first place continued to act. Thus these systems of emblems, which are necessary if society is to become conscious of itself, are no less indispensable for assuring the continuation of this consciousness.

So we must refrain from regarding these symbols as simple artifices, as sorts of labels attached to representations already made, in order to make them more manageable: they are an integral part of them (...)

The unity of the group is visible, therefore, only in the collective emblem reproducing the object designated by this name. A clan is essentially a reunion of individuals who bear the same name and rally around the same sign. Take away the name and the sign which materializes it and the clan is no longer representable.'

To take two of the very few technical terms I will need in this introductory book, it makes a huge difference whether the means to produce the social are taken as *intermediaries* or as *mediators*. At the beginning, the bifurcation seems small, but it will later on lead us into different territories. To be sure, this nuance will be fully visible only at the close of this book—if the reader is patient enough to reach it! Yet we should try to get familiar with it as early as possible as it will be our shibboleth throughout.

An *intermediary*, in my vocabulary, is what transports meaning or force without transformation: defining its inputs is enough to define its outputs. For all practical purposes, an intermediary can be taken not only as a black box, but also as a black box counting for one, even if it is internally made of many parts. *Mediators*, on the other hand, cannot be counted as just one; they might count for one, for nothing, for several, or for infinity. Their input is never a good predictor of their output; their specificity has to be taken into account every time.[30] Mediators transform, translate, distort, and modify the meaning or the elements they are supposed to carry. No matter how *complicated* an intermediary is, it may, for all practical purposes, count for just one— or even for nothing at all because it can be easily forgotten. No matter how apparently simple a mediator may look, it may become *complex*; it may lead in multiple directions which will modify all the contradictory accounts attributed to its role. A properly functioning computer could be taken as a good case of a complicated intermediary while a banal conversation may become a terribly complex chain of mediators where passions, opinions, and attitudes bifurcate at every turn. But if it breaks down, a computer may turn into a horrendously complex mediator while a highly sophisticated panel during an academic conference may become a perfectly predictable and uneventful intermediary in rubber stamping a decision made elsewhere.[31] As we will slowly discover, it is this constant uncertainty over the intimate nature of entities—are they behaving as intermediaries or as mediators?—that is the source of all the other uncertainties we have decided to follow.

Once this definition is in place, we can see that it is not enough for sociologists to recognize that a group is made, 'reproduced', or 'constructed' through many means and expressed through many tools. As a matter of fact, when seeing what most sociologists call 'construction', one is not sure they have ever built anything as simple as a shack, not to mention a 'society' (more on this later, see p. 88). The real difference between the two schools of thought becomes visible when the 'means' or 'tools' used in 'construction' are treated as mediators and not as mere intermediaries. If this looks like splitting hairs, well it is, but this is because the tiny difference in direction taken by the two sociologies is no larger than a hair's width. After all, if physicists

---

[30] That the relations between causes and effects are to be altered requires nothing out of the ordinary. Before the lily has learned to extract the sun energy through photosynthesis, the sun is not the 'cause' of the lily; before Venice learned to rise out of the water, the lagoon was not one of the reasons for its development. Causes and effects are only a retrospective way of interpreting *events*. This is true of 'social' and 'natural' events. On this philosophy of causality, see Isabelle Stengers (2002), *Penser avec Whitehead*.

[31] For a use of this distinction between complexity and complication, see Shirley Strum and Bruno Latour (1987), 'The Meanings of Social: from Baboons to Humans'.

have been able to dispose with the ether, it was thanks to quite a lot of hair-splitting.

If the nuance looks moot, its effects are radical. If, for instance, a social difference is 'expressed in' or 'projected upon' a detail of fashion, but that this detail—let's say a shine of silk instead of nylon—is taken as an intermediary transporting faithfully some social meaning—'silk is for high-brow', 'nylon for low-brow'—then it is in vain that an appeal has been made to the detail of the fabric. It has been mobilized purely for illustrative purposes. Even without the chemical difference between silk and nylon, the social difference between high- and low-brow will have existed anyhow; it has simply been 'represented' or 'reflected' on a piece of cloth that has remained wholly indifferent to its composition. If, on the contrary, the chemical and manufacturing differences are treated as so many mediators, then it may happen that *without* the many indefinite material nuances between the feel, the touch, the color, the sparkling of silk and nylon, *this* social difference might not exist at all.[32] It is this infinitesimal distinction between mediators and intermediaries that will produce, in the end, all the differences we need between the two types of sociologies. To sum up the contrast in a rudimentary way, the sociologists of the social believe in *one* type of social aggregates, *few* mediators, and *many* intermediaries; for ANT, there is *no* preferable type of social aggregates, there exist *endless* number of mediators, and when those are transformed into faithful intermediaries it is not the rule, but a *rare* exception that has to be accounted for by some extra work—usually by the mobilization of even more mediators![33] No two viewpoints of the same object could be more different.

It is puzzling to see such a basic intuition not shared by mainstream sociology, although I claimed earlier that ANT was nothing but the recasting of the central hopes of social science. A possible reason for not recognizing earlier the essential parity between actors and social scientists all engaged in controversies about groups is that sociology has been involved, very early on, in *social engineering*. Since the beginning, there has been a sort of confusion of duties. By deciding that their job was to define what the social world is made of, sociologists in the middle of the 19th century took upon themselves the task of politics.[34] If politics is defined, as we shall see later, as the progressive

---

[32] For the socio-chemical history of nylon, see Susannah Handley (2000), *Nylon: The Story of a Fashion Revolution: A Celebration of Design from Art Silk to Nylon and Thinking Fibres*. See the Coco Chanel biography by Axel Madsen (1991), *Chanel: A Woman of Her Own*.

[33] This stabilization of controversies through the key notions of forms and standards will be tackled in Part II.

[34] On the place of social sciences among the sciences of government, see Paolo Napoli (2003), *Naissance de la police moderne: Pouvoirs, normes, société* and Audren, 'Les juristes et les sociologues'.

composition of collective life, some sociologists, tired of the revolutionary period, found a way to shortcut the slow and painful process of composition and decided to sort out by themselves what were the most relevant units of society. The simplest way was to get rid of the most extravagant and unpredictable ways in which actors themselves defined their own 'social context'. Social theorists began to play legislator, strongly encouraged in this endeavor by the state that was engaged in the ruthless task of modernizing.[35] In addition, this gesture could pass for proof of scientific creativity as scientists since Kant have had to 'construct their own object'. Human actors were reduced to mere informants simply answering the questions of the sociologist *qua* judge, thus supposedly producing a discipline as scientific as chemistry or physics.[36] Without this strong obligation to play the legislating role, sociologists would not have limited the first obvious source of uncertainty, cutting all the links with the explicit and reflexive labor of the actors' own methods. Anthropologists, who had to deal with premoderns and were not requested as much to imitate natural sciences, were more fortunate and allowed their actors to deploy a much richer world. In many ways, ANT is simply an attempt to allow the members of contemporary society to have as much leeway in defining themselves as that offered by ethnographers. If, as I claim, 'we have never been modern', sociology could finally become as good as anthropology.[37]

I believe that with the extremely light equipment defined above, we are now prepared to profit from the first source of uncertainty. Readers can begin mapping the many contradictory ways in which social aggregates are constantly evoked, erased, distributed, and reallocated. For scientific, political, and even moral reasons, it is crucial that enquirers do not in advance, and *in place* of the actors, define what sorts of building blocks the social world is made of. This lesson is

[35] I am using here the argument made most clearly in Zygmunt Bauman (1992), *Intimations of Postmodernity*, who differentiates between 'legislators' and 'interpreters'. Tarde is interesting precisely because he escaped, as did Garfinkel later, from the legislating role.

[36] The epistemology of the social sciences has been obsessed with this theme of the right of the observer to define the type of entities one had to deal with, this theme itself being a strange philosophy of science borrowed, in the French case at least, from Gaston Bachelard's interpretation of physics. See Pierre Bourdieu, Jean-Claude Chamboredon and Jean-Claude Passeron (1991), *Craft of Sociology: Epistemological Preliminaries*, which is almost exclusively built on Bachelard's philosophy of science. It's clear that any change in the conception of science will modify the claims and duties of the *social* science.

[37] Although I have written on this question of modernism—how to define it, how to study it, and how to overcome it in Bruno Latour (1993), *We Have Never Been Modern*—I have left it aside here to concentrate instead on the social theory that an alternative to modernism would require—the other requirement being a parallel change in the conception of nature, as I have shown in Latour, *Politics of Nature*.

negative, to be sure, but it's a powerful way to reverse the political urge that itches so many critical sociologists. It might be time to put Marx's famous quote back on its feet: 'Social scientists have *transformed* the world in various ways; the point, however, is to *interpret* it.' But to interpret, we need to abandon the strange idea that all languages are translatable in the already established idiom of the social. Such a preparatory training is important since, as we will see in the next chapter, social aggregates might not be made of *human* ties.

Second Source of Uncertainty: Action Is Overtaken

In most situations, we use 'social' to mean that which has already been assembled and acts as a whole, without being too picky on the precise nature of what has been gathered, bundled, and packaged together. When we say that 'something is social' or 'has a social dimension', we mobilize one set of features that, so to speak, march in step together, even though it might be composed of radically different types of entities. This unproblematic use of the word is fine as long as we don't confuse the sentence 'Is social what goes together?', with one that says, 'social designates a particular kind of stuff'. With the former we simply mean that we are dealing with a routine state of affairs whose *binding* together is the crucial aspect, while the second designates a sort of substance whose main feature lies in its *differences* with other types of materials. We imply that some assemblages are built out of social stuff *instead* of physical, biological, or economical blocks, much like the houses of the Three Little Pigs were made of straw, wood, and stone. To avoid this confusion between the two meanings of social, we have to open a second source of uncertainty, one dealing this time with the heterogeneous nature of the ingredients making up social ties.

When we act, who else is acting? How many agents are also present? How come I never do what I want? Why are we all held by forces that are not of our own making? Such is the oldest and most legitimate intuition of those sciences, that which has fascinated since the time when crowds, masses, statistical means, invisible hands, and unconscious drives began to replace the passions and reasons, not to mention the angels and demons that had pushed and pulled our humble souls up to then. In the previous chapter, we learned to trace social connections using the unexpected trails left by the controversies about group formation. Social scientists and actors were on par with each other and both raised essentially the same type of question: How do we know what the social world is made of? We now have to learn how to exploit a second source of uncertainty, one that is even more fundamental and which resides at the heart of all the social sciences, namely that which sees action as not transparent. Action is not done under the full control of consciousness; action should rather be felt as a node, a knot, and a conglomerate of many surprising sets of agencies that have to be slowly disentangled. It is this venerable source of uncertainty that we wish to render vivid again in the odd expression of actor-network.

That we are never alone in carrying out a course of action requires but a few examples. For instance, you have become so estranged from your parents by a university degree that you have become ashamed of how dumb they are. Reading critical sociologists, you realize that this is the common experience of a whole generation of 'upwardly mobile' young kids from 'lower class' families lacking 'cultural capital'. And this is when you begin to wonder *who* has estranged you from your very kin, who has molded your voice, your manners, your face so differently from theirs? Perhaps a strange beast that pertains to no one in particular and who is nobody's responsibility. It is a force to be sure, maybe a *habitus*. Second, you think you are in love with your future partner. You read a statistical study of marriage patterns where his age, his height, his revenue, his degrees, the distance between his town and yours fit, within a very small margin, in the mean range of what thousands of other young girls are in love with at almost exactly the same period. So, who is in love then? *Others* for sure, a strange alien agency that does not look like you, which has no eyes, no mouth, no ears but which acts all the same. But how exactly?

Villages appear to dot the landscape haphazardly until an archaeologist excavates the ancient road networks and realizes that all the settlements align perfectly on some ancient causeways, simply separated by the mean day march of the Roman legions. Who has created the settlement there? What force has been exerted? How could Caesar still be acting through the present landscape? Is there some other *alien* agency endowed with the long-lasting subterranean power to make settlers 'freely choose' the very place it has allotted them? Here again you wonder, and you wonder even more when you realize, watching the stock exchange one morning, that ten million of your fellow shareholders have sold the same stocks that day, as if your collective mind had been solidly swayed by the invisible hand of some invisible giant. At the school's open-house party, you wonder why all the parents look eerily familiar: same clothes, same jewels, same ways of articulating words, same ambitions for their kids. What makes all of us do the same thing at the same time? In the long and variegated history of their disciplines, the social scientists, sociologists, historians, geographers, linguists, psychologists, and economists had to multiply— like their colleagues in the natural sciences—agencies to account for the complexity, diversity, and heterogeneity of action. Each had to find a way to tame those many *aliens* who barged in as uninvited guests in everything we seem to be doing.

That these examples have spurred on the development of the social sciences is something we nowadays take for granted. And ANT wishes for nothing else than to inherit this tradition and this intuition. Action is *overtaken* or, as one Swedish friend transcribed this dangerous Hegelian expression, action is *other-taken*! So it is taken up by others and shared with the masses. It is mysteriously carried out and at the same time distributed to others. We are not alone in the world. 'We', like 'I', is a wasp's nest; as the poet Rimbaud wrote: *'Je est un autre'*.[38]

But there is a huge, an insurmountable, an abysmal gap in going from this intuition—action is overtaken—to the usual conclusion that a social force has taken over. While ANT wishes to inherit from the first, it wants to inhibit the second step; it wants to show that between the premise and the consequence there exists a huge gap, a complete *non sequitur*. For the social sciences to regain their initial energy, it's crucial *not* to conflate all the agencies overtaking the action into some kind of agency—'society', 'culture', 'structure', 'fields', 'individuals', or whatever name they are given—that would *itself* be social. Action should remain a surprise, a mediation, an event. It is for this reason that we should begin, here again, not from the 'determination of action by society', the 'calculative abilities of individuals', or the 'power of the unconscious' as we would ordinarily do, but rather from the *under-determination of action*, from the uncertainties and controversies about who and what is acting when 'we' act—and there is of course no way to decide whether this source of uncertainty resides in the analyst or in the actor. If we have to readily accept the central intuition of social sciences—if not there would be no reason to call oneself a 'social' scientist—we should move very slowly so as to remove the poison that is secreted when this intuition is transformed into 'something social' that *carries out* the acting. Contrary to what so many 'social explanations' seem to imply, the two arguments not only don't follow one another, but they are in complete contradiction with

---

[38] 'Between the acting of a dreadful thing
And the first motion, all the interim is
Like a phantasma or a hideous dream
The genius and the mortal instruments
Are then in counsel, and the state of man
Like a little kingdom, suffers then
The nature of an insurrection"
   Brutus in Shakespeare, *Julius Caesar*, II. i. 63–69.

one another. Since that which makes us act is *not* made of social stuff, it can be *associated* together in new ways.[39]

An actor is what is *made to* act by many others

An 'actor' in the hyphenated expression actor-network is not the source of an action but the moving target of a vast array of entities swarming toward it. To retrieve its multiplicity, the simplest solution is to reactivate the metaphors implied in the word *actor* that I have used so far as an unproblematic placeholder.

It is not by accident that this expression, like that of 'person', comes from the stage. Far from indicating a pure and unproblematic source of action, they both lead to puzzles as old as the institution of theater itself—as Jean-Paul Sartre famously showed in his portrait of the *garçon de café* who no longer knows the difference between his 'authentic self' and his 'social role'.[40] To use the word 'actor' means that it's never clear who and what is acting when we act since an actor on stage is never alone in acting. Play-acting puts us immediately into a thick imbroglio where the question of who is carrying out the action has become unfathomable. As soon as the play starts, as Irwin Goffman has so often showed, nothing is certain: Is this for real? Is it fake?[41] Does the audience's reaction count? What about the lighting? What is the backstage crew doing? Is the playwright's message faithfully transported or hopelessly bungled? Is the character carried over? And if so, by what? What are the partners doing? Where is the prompter? If we accept to unfold the metaphor, the very word actor directs our attention to a complete dislocation of the action, warning us that it is not a coherent, controlled, well-rounded, and clean-edged affair. By definition, action is *dislocated*.[42] Action is borrowed, distributed, suggested, influenced, dominated, betrayed, translated. If an actor is said to be an *actor*-network, it is first of all to underline that it represents the major source of uncertainty about the origin of action—the turn of the word 'network' will come in due time. Like Jesus on the cross, it is of the

---

[39]   This is the exact opposite of the limitation proposed very sensibly by Weber: 'Action is social in so far as, by virtue of the subjective meaning attached to it by the acting individual (or individuals), it takes account of the behavior of others and is thereby oriented in its course.' Max Weber (1947), *The Theory of Social and Economic Organization*, p. 88.

[40]   The famous episode is in Jean-Paul Sartre (1993), *Being and Nothingness*.

[41]   Many examples have been made famous in Erving Goffman (1959), *The Presentation of Self in Everyday Life*.

[42]   'Dislocal' as proposed in François Cooren (2001), *The Organizing Property of Communication*.

actor that one should always say: 'Forgive them Father, they know not what they do.'

It's not because there is some hesitation about the source of action that we have to hurry to say where it springs from, taking for instance the 'global forces of society', the 'transparent calculations of the self', the 'inner passions of the heart', the 'intentionality of the person', the 'gnawing scruples of moral consciousness', 'the roles given to us by social expectations', or 'bad faith'. Uncertainty should remain uncertain throughout because we don't want to rush into saying that actors may not know what they are doing, but that we, the social scientists, know that there exists a social force 'making them do' things unwittingly. Inventing a hidden social drive, an unconscious, would be a sure way of reintroducing this ether of the social that we try to dispense with. Not because actors know what they are doing and social scientists don't, but because both have to remain puzzled by the identity of the participants in any course of action if they want to assemble them again.

It's precisely because the social is not yet made that sociologists of associations should keep as their most cherished treasure all the traces that manifest the hesitations actors themselves feel about the 'drives' that make them act. It is the only way to render productive again the central intuition of the social sciences—before it gets sterilized into an argument about the action *of* some social stuff. This is why we should paradoxically take all the uncertainties, hesitations, dislocations, and puzzlements as our foundation. Just as actors are constantly engaged by others in group formation and destruction (the first uncertainty), they engage in providing controversial accounts for their actions as well as for those of others. Here again, as soon as the decision is made to proceed in this direction, traces become innumerable and no study will ever stop for lack of information on those controversies. Every single interview, narrative, and commentary, no matter how trivial it may appear, will provide the analyst with a bewildering array of entities to account for the hows and whys of any course of action. Social scientists will fall asleep long before actors stop deluging them with data.

The mistake we must learn to avoid is listening distractedly to these convoluted productions and to *ignore* the queerest, baroque, and most idiosyncratic terms offered by the actors, following *only* those that have currency in the rear-world of the social. Alas, this mistake is made so often that it passes for good scientific method, producing most of the artifacts of social explanations. When a criminal says, 'It is not my fault, I had bad parents', should we say that 'society made her a criminal' or that 'she is trying to escape her own personal culpability by diluting it in the anonymity of society'—as Mrs Thatcher would have certainly commented. But the criminal said nothing of that sort. She simply said, 'I had bad parents.' Bad parenting, if we take it seriously, is not automatically translatable into something else and certainly not into society—and she did not say 'castrating mother' either. We have to resist the idea that there exists somewhere a dictionary where all the variegated words of the actors can be translated into the few words of the social vocabulary.[43] Will we have the courage *not* to substitute an unknown expression for a well-known one? Here lies the most morally, politically, and scientifically relevant difference between the two sociologies.

Even more difficult is when a pilgrim says, 'I came to this monastery because I was called by the Virgin Mary.' How long should we resist smiling smugly, replacing at once the agency of the Virgin by the 'obvious' delusion of an actor 'finding pretext' in a religious icon to 'hide' one's own decision? Critical sociologists will answer: 'Just as far as to be polite, it's bad manners to sneer in the presence of the informant.' A sociologist of associations meanwhile must learn to say: 'As long as possible in order to seize the chance offered by the pilgrim to fathom the diversity of agencies acting at once in the world.' If it is possible to discover today that 'the Virgin' is able to induce pilgrims to board a train against all the scruples that tie them to home, that is a miracle indeed.[44] When a famous soprano says, 'It is my voice who tells me when to stop and when to begin', how quickly should the sociologist jump to the conclusion that the singer offers here a 'typical case' of 'false consciousness', artists being always too ready to take what is of their own making as the fetish that makes them do things?[45] Is it not abundantly clear that this singer should not be listened to but instead 'freed from her own delusion' by the courageous exposition of her lies. Down with Muses and other undocumented aliens! And yet, the soprano did say that she shared her life with her voice that *made her do* certain things. Are we able to treasure this odd way of speaking or not? It was very precise, very revealing, very telling, and also very moving. Is not being moved, or rather, *put into motion* by the informants exactly what we should mean by an enquiry?

[43] A powerful example of this nuance has been provided by drug addicts when they moved from being 'patients' or 'delinquents' to 'drug-users'. On this see Emilie Gomart (1999), *Surprised by Methadone. Thèse de doctorat,* Emilie Gomart (2002), 'Methadone: Six Effects in Search of a Substance' as well as the argument made in Isabelle Stengers (1991), *Drogues, le défi hollandais.*

[44] I am following here the marvellous lesson in methods provided in Elizabeth Claverie (2003), *Les Guerres de la Vierge: Une anthropologie des apparitions.* See also Patricia de Aquino (1998), 'La mort défaite. Rites funéraires du candomblé'.

[45] Julia Varady in Bruno Monsaingeon's film, *Le chant possédé,* dir. Bruno Monsaingeon (Idéale Audience, 1998).

The painful lesson we must learn is exactly the opposite of what is still being taught all over the world under the name of a 'social explanation', namely we must not substitute a surprising but precise expression that is the well-known repertoire of the social which is supposed to be hidden behind it. We have to resist pretending that actors have only a language while the analyst possesses the *meta*-language in which the first is 'embedded'. As I said earlier, analysts are allowed to possess only some *infra*-language whose role is simply to help them become attentive to the actors' own fully developed meta-language, a reflexive account of what they are saying. In most cases, social explanations are simply a superfluous addition that, instead of revealing the forces behind what is said, dissimulates what has been said, as Garfinkel has never tired of showing.[46] And it is no use claiming that natural scientists also keep adding hidden entities in order to make sense of phenomena. When natural scientists invoke invisible entities, it is to account for the trickiest details of the matter at hand, not to look away from embarrassing information to less recalcitrant ones!

Of course, there exist perfectly respectable reasons for this confusion as I briefly indicated already: the political agenda of many social theorists has taken over their *libido sciendi*. They considered that their real duty was not so much to inventory active agencies in the world as to clean out the many forces that, in their eyes, are cluttering the world and that maintain people in a state of alienation—'Virgins' and 'fetishes' being among the worst offenders. The task of emancipation to which they have devoted themselves requires that they rarefy the number of acceptable entities. So they think they are entitled to change their job description, forgetting that their duty is not to decide how the actors should be made to act, but rather to retrace the many different worlds actors are elaborating for one another. At which point they begin deciding for themselves what is an acceptable list of entities to make up the social world. But it seems obvious that a policy aimed at artificially withdrawing from the world most of the entities to be taken into account cannot claim to lead to emancipation.

What is even more dangerous in the inconsiderate acceptance of hidden variables is to shift from the sociology of the social to critical sociology.[47] This is the only discipline that finds itself scientific when

[46] An ethno-method is the discovery that members possess a complete vocabulary and a complete social theory for understanding their behavior. See p. 57

[47] It comes into existence when the acceptable limits of social theory are exaggerated to the point where the existence of society is taken as stronger than the existence of everything else, including law, religion, economics, science, and technology, thus reversing the order of explanation and transforming all the actors into so many victims of illusions. At this point, critical sociology becomes indistinguishable from conspiracy theory, that is, a hybrid of the two most extreme forms of scepticism and gullibility.

it not only ignores data and *replaces* it with uncontroversial data from already assembled social forces, but also when it takes the indignant reactions of those who are thus 'explained' as what *proves* the unbearable truth of the critics' interpretations. At this point sociology stops being empirical and becomes 'vampirical'. It's the great tragedy of the social sciences that this lesson was not heeded and that critical sociologists still consider as their treasure what they should rather be ashamed of, namely confusing what obfuscates data with what is revealed by it. Would you qualify as 'scientific' a discipline that puts to one side the precise information offered by fieldwork and replaces it by instances of *other* things that are *invisible* and those things people have *not* said and have vocally denied? For once, it's sociologists of associations who are following common sense. For them, controversies about agencies have to be deployed to the full, no matter how difficult it is so as not to simplify in advance the task of assembling the collective.

This does not mean that we should abstain from alluding to hidden variables forever, or that we have to believe that actors live the pristine clarity of some *ego cogito* in full command of their own actions. Quite the contrary, we have just seen that the most powerful insight of social sciences is that other agencies over which we have no control make us do things. In the next chapter, we will have many occasions to see how action is distributed among agents, very few of whom look like humans.[48] The reason why we want to be cautious with any social explanation is for the simple fact that hidden variables have become packaged in such a way that there is no control window to check what is inside. Explaining in 'instant sociology' has become a cinch, much like 'instant psychoanalysis'. Their accounts have become as impossible to probe and repair as a black-boxed electronic appliance. It's because the very success of social explanations has rendered them so cheap that we now have to increase the cost and the quality control on what counts as a hidden force.[49]

An enquiry into practical metaphysics

If we call *metaphysics* the discipline inspired by the philosophical tradition that purports to define the basic structure of the world,

---

[48] At the end of Part II, we will encounter the strange figure of the 'plasma', which takes the bottom out of any bottom line when accounting for action.

[49] It also means that there might be many other ways for an agency to be hidden than simply acting from behind and from the outside. Ethnomethodologists have now made familiar the famous formula 'seen but not noticed' and we will soon meet another one: to be *made* to act.

then *empirical metaphysics* is what the controversies over agencies lead to since they ceaselessly populate the world with new drives and, as ceaselessly, contest the existence of others.[50] The question then becomes how to explore the actors' own metaphysics. Sociologists of the social have answered by abstaining from metaphysics altogether and by cutting all relations with philosophy, that fanciful and non empirical discipline which represents the lowly infancy of the now mature social sciences. They have also strictly limited the set of agencies 'really acting' in the world so as to free actors from their delusion, prepare the ground for social engineering on a grand scale, and smooth the path toward modernization.[51]

It is no wonder that this program ended up going nowhere. As anthropologists have tirelessly shown, actors incessantly engage in the most abstruse metaphysical constructions by redefining all the elements of the world. Only a researcher trained in the conceptual calisthenics offered by the philosophical tradition could be quick, strong, daring, and pliable enough to painstakingly register what they have to say. Agency is about the most difficult problem there is in philosophy. How could enquirers listen to a housewife, a clerk, a pilgrim, a criminal, a soprano, and a CEO and still succeed in following what they express if they had no Hegel, no Aristotle, no Nietzsche, no Dewey, no Whitehead to help them? Have those writers not done quite a lot of useful work to open up what an agency could be? It does not mean that philosophers will know better, go deeper, be more profound than social scientists, nor does it mean that they will provide sociology with its 'foundation' or indulge in 'meta-theory'. It means that cutting the social sciences from the reservoirs of philosophical innovations is a recipe to make sure that no one will ever notice the metaphysical innovations proposed by ordinary actors— which often go beyond those of professional philosophers. And the situation will be even worse if social scientists not only abstain from metaphysics, but take as their duty to cling to the most limited list of agencies, ceaselessly translating the indefinite production of actors into their

---

[50] Most social scientists would adamantly resist the idea that they have to indulge in metaphysics to define the social. But such an attitude means nothing more than sticking to one metaphysics, usually a very poor one that in no way can pay justice to the multiplicity of fundamental questions raised by ordinary actors. No one has gone further in criticizing this move than Tarde, especially in Tarde *Monadologie et sociologie*.

[51] A telling example of this confusion is provided by Randall Collins's 'social history' of philosophers in Randall Collins (1998), *The sociology of philosophies: a global theory of intellectual change*. At no point does he realize that the philosophers whose ideas he is 'explaining' have dozens more arguments about what is a society, what is an influence, what is a group. To stick to the same impoverished meta-language for all the philosophers throughout history does not prove that one provides a social explanation of those philosophies.

short one. Actors have many philosophies but sociologists think they should stick to only a few. Actors fill the world with agencies while sociologists of the social tell them which building blocks their world is 'really' made of. That they often do this for high-minded reasons, to be 'politically relevant', to be 'critical' for the good of the actors they wish to 'free from the shackle of archaic powers', does not reassure me. Even if it were excellent politics, which it is not as we shall see, it would still be bad science.

There is, of course, a more respectable and practical reason to limit in advance the list of agencies that make actors do things. Apart from the social theorists' infatuation with emancipation politics, it is the sheer difficulty of following their proliferation. And it is true that to ask enquirers to indulge in empirical metaphysics, to send them trotting behind the actors themselves, is no easy task. However, if agencies are innumerable, *controversies* about agency have a nice way of ordering themselves. The solution is the same as with the former source of uncertainty: although there exists an indefinite list of groups, we could devise a small list of handles allowing the sociologist to move from one group formation to the next. In the same way, I think it is possible to propose a limited set of grips to follow the ways in which actors credit or discredit an agency in the accounts they provide about what makes them act.

It might still appear paradoxical, although less so as this book proceeds, but feeding off controversies offers a much safer way than the implausible task of setting up a priori, and in the actors' stead, what groups and which agencies will, from now on, be allowed to fill the social world. Once again, displacement from one frame of reference to the next allows for more freedom of movement than any absolute or arbitrary viewpoint. And to take up again the metaphor of a travel guide, freedom of movement becomes crucial—even if it is to force the traveler to proceed even more slowly!

A list to map out controversies over agency

Although we never know for sure who and what is making us act, we can define a list of features which are always present in contradictory arguments about what has happened: agencies are part of an account; they are given a figure of some sort; they are opposed to other competing agencies; and, finally, they are accompanied by some explicit theory of action.

First, agencies are always presented in an account as *doing* something, that is, making some difference to a state of affairs, transforming some

As into Bs through trials with Cs.[52] Without accounts, without trials, without differences, without transformation in some state of affairs, there is no meaningful argument to be made about a given agency, no detectable frame of reference. An invisible agency that makes no difference, produces no transformation, leaves no trace, and enters no account is *not* an agency. Period. Either it does something or it does not. If you mention an agency, you have to provide the account of its action, and to do so you need to make more or less explicit which trials have produced which observable traces—which does not mean, of course, that you have to speak about it, speech being only one of the many behaviors able to generate an account and far from the most frequent.[53] This seems obvious enough and yet worth pointing out to those intoxicated with too many invisible and unaccountable social forces. In ANT, it is not permitted to say: 'No one mentions it. I have no proof but I know there is some hidden actor at work here behind the scene.' This is conspiracy theory, not social theory. The presence of the social has to be demonstrated each time anew; it can never be simply postulated. If it has no vehicle to travel, it won't move an inch, it will leave no trace, it won't be recorded in any sort of document. Even to detect Polonius behind the arras that became his shroud, the Prince of Denmark needed to hear the squeak of a rat.

Second, if agency is one thing, its *figuration* is another. What is doing the action is always provided in the account with some flesh and features that make them have some form or shape, no matter how vague. 'Figuration' is one of those technical terms I need to introduce to break the knee-jerk reactions of 'social explanation' because it is essential to grasp that there exist many more figures than anthropomorphic ones. This is one of the many cases where sociology has to accept to become more abstract. To endow an agency with anonymity gives it exactly as much a figure as when it is endowed with a name, a nose, a voice, or a face. It's just making it *ideo-* instead of *anthropo-* morphic. Statistical aggregates obtained from a questionnaire and given a label—like A and B types in the search for the causes of heart disease—are as concrete as 'my red-faced sanguine neighbor who died last Saturday from a stroke while planting his turnips because he ate too much fat'. To say 'culture forbids having kids out of wedlock' requires, in terms of figuration, exactly as much work as saying 'my future mother-in-law wants me to marry her daughter'. To be sure the

---

[52] Accountability is a crucial aspect of ethnomethodology as well; it will become a textual account in Chapter 5.

[53] The notion of trial of strength is developed at length in Bruno Latour (1988), *Irreductions*. Trial—*épreuves*—has also become the key notion of the moral sociology developed by Luc Boltanski. See Boltanski and Thévenot, *On Justification*.

first figuration (anonymous) is different from the second one (my mother-in-law), but they both give a figure, a form, a cloth, a flesh to an agency forbidding me or forcing me to do things. As far as the question of figuration is concerned, there is no reason to say that the first is a 'statistical abstraction' while the other would be a 'concrete actor'. Individual agencies, too, need abstract figurations. When people complain about 'hypostasizing' society, they should not forget that my mother-in-law is also a hypostasis—and so are of course individuals and calculative agents as much as the infamous Invisible Hand. This is exactly what the words 'actor' and 'person' mean: no one knows how many people are simultaneously at work in any given individual; conversely, no one knows how much individuality there can be in a cloud of statistical data points. Figuration endows them with a shape but not necessarily in the manner of a smooth portrait by a *figurative* painter. To do their job, sociologists need as much variety in 'drawing' actors as there are debates about figuration in modern and contemporary art.

To break away from the influence of what could be called 'figurative sociology', ANT uses the technical word *actant* that comes from the study of literature. Here are four ways to figure out the same actant: 'Imperialism strives for unilateralism'; 'The United States wishes to withdraw from the UN'; 'Bush Junior wishes to withdraw from the UN'; 'Many officers from the Army and two dozen neo-con leaders want to withdraw from the UN.' That the first is a structural trait, the second a corporate body, the third an individual, the fourth a loose aggregate of individuals makes a big difference of course to the account, but they all provide different figurations of the same actions. None of the four is more or less 'realist', 'concrete', 'abstract', or 'artificial' than the others. They simply lead to the entrenchment of different groups and thus helps to solve the first uncertainty about group formation. The great difficulty in ANT is not to be intimidated by the type of figuration: *ideo-*, or *techno-*, or *bio*-morphisms are 'morphism' just as much as the incarnation of some actant into a single individual.

Because they deal with fiction, literary theorists have been much freer in their enquiries about figuration than any social scientist, especially when they have used semiotics or the various narrative sciences. This is because, for instance in a fable, the same actant can be made to act through the agency of a magic wand, a dwarf, a thought in the fairy's mind, or a knight killing two dozen dragons.[54] Novels,

[54] It would be fairly accurate to describe ANT as being half Garfinkel and half Greimas: it has simply combined two of the most interesting intellectual movements on both sides of the Atlantic and has found ways to tap the inner reflexivity of both actor's

plays, and films from classical tragedy to comics provide a vast playground to rehearse accounts of what makes us act.[55] For this reason, once the difference between actant and agency is understood, various sentences such as 'moved by your own interest', 'taken over by social imitation', 'victims of social structure', 'carried over by routine', 'called by God', 'overcome by destiny', 'made by your own will', 'held up my norms', and 'explained by capitalism' become fully *comparable*. They are simply different ways to make actors *do* things, the diversity of which is fully deployed without having to sort in advance the 'true' agencies from the 'false' ones and without having to assume that they are all translatable in the repetitive idiom of the social.

This is why ANT has borrowed from narrative theories, not all of their arguments and jargon to be sure, but their freedom of movement. It is for the same reason we refuse to be cut off from philosophy. It is not that sociology is fiction or because literary theorists would know more than sociologists, but because the diversity of the worlds of fiction invented on paper allow enquirers to gain as much pliability and range as those they have to study in the real world.[56] It is only through some continuous familiarity with literature that ANT sociologists might become less wooden, less rigid, less stiff in their definition of what sort of agencies populate the world. Their language may begin to gain as much inventiveness as that of the actors they try to follow— also because actors, too, read a lot of novels and watch a lot of TV! It is only by constantly comparing complex repertoires of action that sociologists may become able to register data—a task that seems always very hard for the sociologists of the social who have to filter out everything which does not look in advance like a uniformed 'social actor'. *Recording* not filtering out, *describing* not disciplining, these are the Laws and the Prophets.

accounts and of texts. The classic work in semiotics is best summarized in Algirdas Julien Greimas and Joseph Courtès (1982), *Semiotics and Language: an Analytical Dictionary*. For a recent presentation see Jacques Fontanille (1998), *Sémiotique du discours*.

[55] For some magnificent examples of the metaphysical freedom of semioticians, see Louis Marin (1989), *Opacité de la peinture: Essais sur la représentation*; Louis Marin (1992), *Des pouvoirs de l'image: Gloses*; and Louis Marin (2001) ,*On Representation*. Although an enemy of semioticians, Thomas Pavel (2003), *La pensée du roman* shows the incomparable freedom of movement of literary theorists.

[56] See Thomas Pavel (1986), *Fictional Worlds*.

Richard Powers on what is a firm

In his novel *Gain*, Richard Powers (1998: 349–350) portrays the CEO of a big company as he is trying to prepare a pep talk to his staff:

'To make a profit. To make a consistent profit. To make a profit in the long run. To make a living. To make things. To make things in the most economical way. To make the greatest number of things. To make things that last the longest. To make things for the longest possible time. To make things that people need. To make things that people desire. To make people desire things. To give meaningful employment. To give reliable employment. To give people something to do. To do something. To provide the greatest food for the greatest number. To promote the general welfare. To provide for the common defense. To increase the value of the common stock. To pay a regular dividend. To maximize the net worth of the firm. To advance the lot of all the stakeholders. To grow. To progress. To expand. To increase knowhow. To increase revenues and to decrease costs. To get the job done more cheaply. To compete efficiently. To buy low and sell high. To improve the hand that humankind has been dealt. To produce the next round of technological innovations. To rationalize nature. To improve the landscape. To shatter space and arrest time. To see what the human race can do. To amass the country's retirement pension. To amass the capital required to do anything we want to do. To discover what we want to do. To vacate the premises before the sun dies out. To make life a little easier. To make people a little wealthier. To make people a little happier. To build a better tomorrow. To kick something back into the kitty. To facilitate the flow of capital. To preserve the corporation. To do business. To stay in business. To figure out the purpose of business.'

Third, actors also engage in criticizing other agencies accused of being fake, archaic, absurd, irrational, artificial, or illusory. In the same way group performance maps out for the benefit of the enquirer the anti-groups making up their social world, accounts of agency will constantly add new entities while *withdrawing* others as illegitimate. Thus, each actor will map out for the benefit of the analyst the empirical metaphysics to which they are both confronted. Now let us examine the following statements: 'I refuse to be taken over by the general opinion which is pure propaganda anyway'; 'You are thinking like your whole generation'; 'Social structure is an empty term, there exists only individual action'; 'God is not talking to you, imams are talking in His place'; 'Market forces are much wiser than bureaucrats'; 'Your unconscious has betrayed itself through this clever slip of the tongue'; 'I prefer wild salmon to mankind.'[57] It's as if each of these sentences

---

[57] Quoted in Christelle Gramaglia (2005), 'La mise en cause environnementale comme principe d'association. Casuistique des affaires de pollution des eaux'.

was making some additions and subtractions to the list of agencies endowed with a legitimate role in the world.

The only thing that can stop the enquiry is the decision by analysts to choose among these moves the ones that they deem more reasonable. This does not mean that social scientists are powerless, that they are always on the leash of their informants. However, if they want to propose an alternative metaphysics, they have to first engage in the world-making activities of those they study. It will not be enough to say that they—the analysts—know in advance who the actors really are and what makes them really act. Neither will it do to disguise this sort of voluntarily blindness as a claim for reflexivity. Too often, social scientists—and especially critical sociologists—behave as if they were 'critical', 'reflexive', and 'distanced' enquirers meeting a 'naïve', 'uncritical', and 'un-reflexive' actor. But what they too often mean is that they translate the many expressions of their informants into their own vocabulary of social forces. The analyst simply repeats what the social world is already made of; actors simply ignore the fact that they have been mentioned in the analyst's account.[58]

Fourth, actors are also able to propose their own *theories of action* to explain how agencies' effects are carried over.[59] Being full-blown reflexive and skillful metaphysicians, actors—as ANT's new default position proposes—also have their own meta-theory about how agency acts and more often than not it leaves the traditional metaphysician totally bewildered. They will not only enter into a controversy over which agency is taking over but also on the ways in which it is making its influence felt. And here again, the major distinction will be to decide whether the agency—once provided with existence, figuration, and opponents—is treated as an intermediary or as a mediator. In both cases, the outcome of the actor's account will be deeply different.[60]

It is crucial for what follows to understand that this difference cuts across all agencies, *no matter what their figuration is*. A so-called 'anonymous and cold field of forces' can be made to enter the account as a mediator, while a close, individual, 'warm', 'lived in' intentional

---

[58] And as we will learn when dealing with the fifth uncertainty, since the actor's presence or opinion has made no difference in the analyst's account, they are not real *actors* and have literally not been 'taken into account'. Thus, society, in the ANT sense, has not been reassembled and there is no chance whatsoever for such a sociology of the social to have any political relevance.

[59] So far social scientists have taken it as their duty to choose which one of those theories of action is right and thus intervening directly into the controversies instead of deploying them. This is the originality of Thévenot's enterprise: to map out the various regimes of action simultaneously at work among ordinary members. See Laurent Thévenot (2002), 'Which road to follow? The moral complexity of an "equipped" humanity'.

[60] As in the first uncertainty, social theorists, philosophers, psychologists, and social psychologists will here *add* to the controversies their own versions. A good example is provided by the disputes about the existence of a calculative individual.

person may be played out as a mere intermediary. The choice of a figuration, in other words, is a bad predictor of which theory of action will be invoked. What counts is not the type of figures but the range of mediators one is able to deploy. This is what has so confused the debates among the various schools of social sciences: they have insisted too much on *which* agency to choose and not enough on *how* each of them was supposed to act. It may happen that if one declares, 'the state of productive forces determines the state of social representations', then this becomes *more active*, that is, it generates more mediators than the apparently local, concrete, 'lived' and 'existential' sentence: 'Individual human action is always intentional.' Intentionality, if used to carry meaning as an intermediary, will do *less* than the more abstract and global 'state of productive forces', provided that this agency is treated as a mediator.[61] So, figuration and theory of action are two different items in the list and should not be conflated with one another. If they are, the enquirer will be tempted to privilege some figurations as being 'more concrete' and others as 'more abstract', thus falling back into the legislative and policing role of the sociologists of the social and abandoning the firm ground of relativism.[62]

How to make someone do something

If we decide to accept this second source of uncertainty, then sociology becomes the discipline that respects the dislocation inherent in *making someone do something*. In most theories of action, there is no such dislocation because the second term is predicted by the first: 'Give me the cause and I will have the effect.' But this is not the case when the two terms are taken as mediators. For intermediaries, there is no mystery since inputs predict outputs fairly well: nothing will be present in the effect that has not been in the cause. But there is always a problem with this apparently scientific way of speaking. If it were really the case that input predicts output, then it would be better to disregard the effects and be attentive to the causes where everything interesting has already happened—at least potentially. For mediators, the situation is different: causes do not allow effects to be deduced as

[61] For instance, the typically postmodern slogan 'I insist on specificity, locality, peculiarity' may be as complacent as it is empty, while a 'Great Narrative' may trigger more acting voices in the end. Once again, the difference is not in the figures that are chosen, but in the relative proportion of mediators allowed to exist.

[62] To detect those differences we need a benchmark of textual quality that allows us to measure, so to speak, the relative density of mediators over intermediaries, something like taking the temperature of the textual account. As we will see in reviewing the fifth source of uncertainty, this will become a shibboleth for objectivity.

they are simply offering occasions, circumstances, and precedents. As a result, lots of surprising *aliens* may pop up in between.[63]

Such a distinction affects all agencies, whether it is the one whose figuration seems 'abstract'—like 'state of productive forces'—or 'concrete'—like 'my friend Julie'. As long as they are treated as causes simply transported through intermediaries, nothing will be added by the vehicles chosen to carry their effect forward. Causes, in such a strange and very archaic theology, are supposed to create things *ex nihilo*. But if vehicles are treated as mediators triggering other mediators, then a lot of new and unpredictable situations will ensue (they make things do *other* things than what was expected). Again it might look like hair-splitting, but the differences in the type of cartography are immense. The first solution draws maps of the world which are composed of a few agencies, followed by trails of consequences which are never much more than effects, expressions, or reflections of something else. The second solution, the one preferred by ANT, pictures a world made of *concatenations of mediators* where each point can be said to fully act.[64] Thus, the key question for a social science is to decide whether it tries to deduce from a few causes as many of the effects that were there 'in potentia', or whether it tries to replace as many causes as possible by a series of actors—such is the technical meaning that the word 'network' will later take.

This point is horrendously difficult but for now it can be simplified through the use of a vignette. Sociologists are often accused of treating actors like so many puppets manipulated by social forces. But it appears that puppeteers, much like sopranos, possess pretty different ideas about *what* it is that makes their puppets *do* things. Although marionettes offer, it seems, the most extreme case of direct causality— just follow the strings—puppeteers will rarely behave as having total control over their puppets. They will say queer things like 'their marionettes suggest them to do things they will have never thought

---

[63] That this is true also of experiments, we have learned from science studies starting with Harry Collins (1985), *Changing Order. Replication and Induction In Scientific Practice* and his most recent book, Harry Collins (2004), *Gravity's Shadow: The Search for Gravitational Waves*, but also from ethnomethodology, see Michael Lynch (1985), *Art and Artifact in Laboratory Science: A Study of Shop Work and Shop Talk in a Research Laboratory* and Garfinkel in Harold Garfinkel, Michael Lynch and Eric Livingston (1981), 'The Work of a Discovering Science Construed with Materials from the Optically Discovered Pulsar'. Actually, it was the early realization of the real complexity of the causal connections in the most formatted settings of natural sciences that rendered totally moot the description of action in social sciences. This transformation of the duties of social sciences because of the study of natural ones has been detected in Isabelle Stengers (2000), *The Invention of Modern Science*.

[64] In Deleuze's parlance, the first has 'realized potentials', the second 'actualized virtualities'. For a presentation of this opposition of concepts, see François Zourabichvili (2003), *Le vocabulaire de Deleuze*.

possible by themselves'.[65] When a force manipulates another, it does not mean that it is a cause generating effects; it can also be an occasion for other things to start acting. The *hand* still hidden in the Latin etymology of the word 'manipulate' is a sure sign of full control *as well as a lack of it*. So who is pulling the strings? Well, the puppets do in addition to their puppeteers. It does not mean that puppets are controlling their handlers—this would be simply reversing the order of causality—and of course no dialectic will do the trick either. It simply means that the interesting question at this point is not to decide who is acting and how but shift from a certainty about action to an *uncertainty* about action—but to decide what is acting and how. As soon as we open again the full range of uncertainties about agencies, we recover the powerful intuition that lies at the origin of the social sciences. So, when sociologists are accused of treating actors as puppets, it should be taken as a compliment, provided they multiply strings and accept surprises about acting, handling, and manipulating. 'Treating people like puppets' is a curse only when this proliferation of mediators is transformed into one agency—the social—whose effect is simply transported without deformation through a chain of intermediaries. Then, the original intuition has been lost for good.

This is especially important to keep in mind since sociology has been embarrassed—we will have many occasions to witness this in Part II—by the prejudice that there exists a privileged locus in the social domain where action is 'concrete': *'parole'* more than *'langue'*, 'event' more than 'structure', 'micro' more than 'macro', 'individual' more than 'masses', 'interaction' more than 'society', or, on the contrary, 'classes' more than 'individual', 'meaning' more than 'force', 'practice' more than 'theory', 'corporate bodies' more than 'persons', and so on. But if action is dislocal, it does not pertain to any specific site; it is distributed, variegated, multiple, dislocated and remains a puzzle for the analysts as well as for the actors.[66]

This point will help to not confuse ANT with one of the many polemical movements that have appealed to the 'concreteness' of the human individual with its meaningful, interacting, and intentional action against the cold, anonymous, and abstract effects of the 'determination by social structures', or that has ignored the meaningful lived world of individual humans for a 'cold anonymous technical

---

[65] See Victoria Nelson (2002), *The Secret Life of Puppets*.

[66] The point has been excellently made by the disciplines of 'situated' or 'distributed' cognition and whose results have been so important for ANT. See Edwin Hutchins (1995), *Cognition in the Wild*; Jean Lave *(1988)*, *Cognition in Practice: Mind, Mathematics and Culture in Everyday Life*; and Lucy Suchman (1987), *Plans and Situated Actions*. The relation between ANT and those studies will be even stronger when the third uncertainty is considered. They will part company only when the fourth and fifth sources are considered.

manipulation' by matter. Most often inspired by phenomenology, these reform movements have inherited all its defects: they are unable to imagine a metaphysics in which there would be other real agencies than those with intentional humans, or worse, they oppose human action with the mere 'material effect' of natural objects which, as they say, have 'no agency' but only 'behavior'.[67] But an 'interpretative' sociology is just as much a sociology of the social than any of the 'objectivist' or 'positivist' versions it wishes to replace. It believes that certain types of agencies—persons, intention, feeling, work, face-to-face interaction—will *automatically* bring life, richness, and 'humanity'.

This belief in the 'lived world' is a nice case of 'misplaced concreteness' to use Whitehead's term: an account full of individuals might be more abstract than another consisting only of collective actors. A billiard ball hitting another one on the green felt of a billiard table might have exactly as much agency as a 'person' directing her 'gaze' to the 'rich human world' of another 'meaningful face' in the smoke-filled room of the pub where the tables have been set up. This is not what phenomenologists and sociologists of the social might say, but then listen to what the players themselves are saying about their own 'behaviors' and the unpredictable 'action' of their billiard balls. They seem to produce quite a lot of the very imbroglios which are strictly forbidden by the theory that states that a radical difference should be maintained between 'action' and 'behavior'.[68] Here again, social scientists have too often confused their role of analyst with some sort of political call for discipline and emancipation.

It is in these kinds of spots that we have to take a decision if we want to trace social connections in new and interesting ways: we must either part company with the analysts who have only one fully worked out metaphysics or 'follow the actors themselves' who are getting by with more than one. Concreteness does not come from choosing some figuration over some other ones in the place of the actors, but from the increase, in the accounts, of *the relative share of mediators over intermediaries*. This will be the tell tale sign that indicates to us what is a good ANT study. For all these reasons, if there is one thing not to set up at the onset, it is the choice of a privileged locus where action is said to

[67] In spite of many efforts, especially in Don Ihde and Evan Selinger (2003), *Chasing Technoscience. Matrix for Materiality*, to reconcile ANT and phenomenology, the gaps between the two lines of interest remain too wide because of the excessive stress given by phenomenologists to the human sources of agency. It will grow even bigger when the three other uncertainties are piled up. This does not mean that we should deprive ourselves of the rich descriptive vocabulary of phenomenology, simply that we have to extend it to 'non-intentional' entities.

[68] This in spite of the spirited defence of the distinction in Harry Collins and Martin Kusch (1998), *The Shape of Actions. What Human and Machines can Do.*

be more abundant. 'Concrete' and 'abstract' do not designate a specific type of character—the usual suspects of critical sociology. The only important differences to keep for now are the following: Which agencies are invoked? Which figurations are they endowed with? Through which mode of action are they engaged? Are we talking about causes and their intermediaries or about a concatenation of mediators? ANT is simply the social theory that has made the decision to follow the natives, no matter which metaphysical imbroglios they lead us into—and they quickly do as we shall see now!

Third Source of Uncertainty: Objects too Have Agency

I f sociology has been marked from the start by the discovery that action was overtaken by other agencies, it has been spurred even more forcefully by the ethical, political, and empirical discovery that there exist hierarchies, asymmetries, and inequalities; that the social world is just as differentiated a landscape as a rugged and mountainous terrain; that no amount of enthusiasm, free will, or ingenuity can make those asymmetries go away; that they all seem to weigh as heavily as the pyramids, which hampers individual action and explains why society should be considered as a specific *sui generis* entity; that any thinker who denies those inequalities and differences is either gullible or somewhat reactionary; and, finally, that ignoring social asymmetry is as ridiculous as claiming that Newtonian gravitation does not exist.

How could we be faithful to this intuition and still maintain, as I just did with the first two sources of uncertainty, that groups are 'constantly' being performed and that agencies are 'ceaselessly' debated? Has the choice of those two departure points not been inspired by a naive attitude that has smoothed the highly unequal social domain into a level playing field where everyone, it seems, has the same chance to generate one's own metaphysics? Is ANT not one of the symptoms of this market spirit that claims, against all evidence, that everyone has the same chance—and too bad for the losers?[69] 'What have you done', people could ask in exasperation, 'with power and domination?' But it is just because we wish to *explain* those asymmetries that we don't want to simply *repeat* them—and even less to *transport* them further unmodified. Once again, we don't want to confuse the cause and the effect, the *explanandum* with the *explanans*. This is

[69] In Luc Boltanski and Eve Chiapelllo (2005), *The New Spirit of Capitalism*, the authors have made quite explicit this critique of ANT as does the scathing attack in Philip Mirowski and Edward Nik-Khah (2004), 'Markets Made Flesh: Callon, Performativity, and a Crisis in Science Studies, augmented With Consideration of the FCC auctions'. We will have to wait until the Conclusion to tackle again the question of political relevance and answer those critiques.

why it's so important to maintain that power, like society, is the final result of a process and not a reservoir, a stock, or a capital that will automatically provide an explanation. Power and domination have to be produced, made up, composed.[70] Asymmetries exist, yes, but where do they come from and what are they made out of?

To provide an explanation, sociologists of associations must make the same radical decision as when they wanted to feed off the second source of uncertainty. It is *because* they wanted to keep the original intuition of social sciences that they had to adamantly *reject* the impossible solution that was proposed, namely that society is unequal and hierarchical; that it weighs disproportionably on some parts; and that it has all the character of inertia. To state that domination breaks down bodies and souls is one thing whereas concluding that these hierarchies, dissymmetry, inertia, powers, and cruelties are made *of* social stuff is a different argument altogether. Not only the second point has no logical continuity with the first, but it is also, as we shall see, in complete contradiction with it. In the same way as the over-taking of action by other agencies does not mean that society is taking over, the flagrant asymmetry of resources does not mean that they are generated by social asymmetries. It just leads to the opposite conclusion: if inequalities have to be generated, this is proof that other types of actors than the social ones are coming into play. As Marx did with Hegel's dialectics, it's time we put social explanation back on its feet.

The type of actors at work should be increased

So far, I have insisted mostly on the difference between 'social' as in 'social ties' and 'social' as in 'associations'—bearing in mind that the second meaning is closer to the original etymology. I have argued that most often in social sciences, 'social' designates a type of link: it's taken as the name of a specific domain, a sort of material like straw, mud, string, wood, or steel. In principle, you could walk into some imaginary supermarket and point at a shelf full of 'social ties', whereas other aisles would be stocked with 'material', 'biological', 'psychological', and 'economical' connections. For ANT, as we now understand, the definition of the term is different: it doesn't designate a domain of reality or some particular item, but rather is the name of a movement, a displacement, a transformation, a translation, an

---

[70] See John Law (1986a), 'On Power And Its Tactics: A View From The Sociology Of Science' and John Law (1992), *A Sociology of Monsters. Essays on Power, Technology and Domination.*

enrollment. It is an association between entities which are in no way recognizable as being social in the ordinary manner, *except* during the brief moment when they are reshuffled together. To pursue the metaphor of the supermarket, we would call 'social' not any specific shelf or aisle, but the multiple modifications made throughout the whole place in the organization of all the goods—their packaging, their pricing, their labeling—because those minute shifts reveal to the observer which new combinations are explored and which paths will be taken (what later will be defined as a 'network').[71] Thus, social, for ANT, is the name of a type of momentary association which is characterized by the way it gathers together into new shapes.[72]

Once this second meaning of social as association is in place, we can understand what was so confusing about the sociologists of the social. They use the adjective to designate two entirely different types of phenomena: one of them is the local, face-to-face, naked, unequipped, and dynamic interactions; and the other is a sort of specific force that is supposed to explain why those same temporary face-to-face interactions could become far-reaching and durable. While it's perfectly reasonable to designate by 'social' the ubiquitous phenomenon of face-to-face relations, it cannot provide any ground for defining a 'social' force that is nothing more than a tautology, a sleight of hand, a magical invocation, since it begs the question of how and through which means this increase in durability has been practically achieved. To jump from the recognition of interactions to the existence of a social force is, once again, an inference that does not follow from the premise.

This distinction is especially crucial since what could be called the basic social skills are actually difficult to isolate in human societies. As we will see in Part II when criticizing the notion of 'local interactions', it's mostly in non-human societies (ants, monkeys, and apes) that it's possible to generate a social world understood as an entanglement of interactions. In humans, the basic social skills, although still present, offer an ever-present but nonetheless restricted repertoire. Most of the far-reaching and long-lasting associations are made by something else that could not be detected as long as the notion of social force was not submitted to scrutiny. With ANT, one needs to place the first definition within a very limited sphere and do away with the second, apart from using it as a kind of shorthand to describe what has been already

---

[71] On this notion of adjustment, see Franck Cochoy (2002), *Une sociologie du packaging ou l'âne de Buridan face au marché*.

[72] The term 'fluid' was introduced in Annemarie Mol and John Law (1994), 'Regions, Networks, and Fluids: Anaemia and Social Topology'—but see also Zygmunt Bauman (2000), *Liquid Modernity*. The word 'fluid' allows analysts to insist better than if they used the word network on the circulation and on the nature of what is being transported.

assembled together.[73] In summary, no tie can be said to be durable and made of social stuff.

The main advantage of dissolving the notion of social force and replacing it either by short-lived interactions or by new associations is that it's now possible to distinguish in the composite notion of society what pertains to its durability and what pertains to its substance.[74] Yes, there may exist durable ties, but this does not count as proof that they are made of social material—quite the opposite. It's now possible to bring into the foreground the practical means to keep ties in place, the ingenuity constantly invested in enrolling other sources of ties, and the cost to be paid for the extension of any interaction.

If we consider the basic social skills, it's easy to understand that the connections they are able to weave are always too weak to sustain the sort of weight that social theorists would like to grant to their definition of social. Left to its own devices, a power relationship that mobilizes nothing but social skills would be limited to very short-lived, transient interactions. But where has this situation ever been observed? Even baboon troops, although they are closest to the ideal world invented by many social theorists, cannot provide such an extreme case. As Hobbes and Rousseau have remarked long ago, no giant is strong enough not to be easily overcome in his sleep by a dwarf; no coalition is solid enough not to be run over by an even larger coalition. When power is exerted for good, it is because it is not made of social ties; when it has to rely only on social ties, it is not exerted for long. So, when social scientists appeal to 'social ties' they should always mean something that has great trouble spreading in time and space, that has no inertia and is to be ceaselessly renegotiated. It's precisely because it's so difficult to maintain asymmetries, to durably entrench power relations, to enforce inequalities, that so much work is being constantly devoted in shifting the weak and fast-decaying ties to *other types* of links. If the social world was made of local interactions, it will retain a sort of provisional, unstable, and chaotic aspect and never this strongly differentiated landscape that the appeals to power and domination purport to explain.

As soon as the distinction between the basic social skills and the non-social means mobilized to expand them a bit longer is not carefully kept, analysts run the risk of believing that it's the invocation of

---

[73] For an early presentation of this argument, see Strum and Latour, 'The Meanings of Social'.

[74] In the complex notion of nature, I have been able to distinguish its outside reality from its unity: the two did not go together in spite of so much philosophy (see Latour, *Politics of Nature*). The same is true of society: durability does not point to its materiality, only to its movement.

social forces that will provide an explanation. Sociologists will claim that when they appeal to the durability of social ties they bring in something that really possesses the necessary durability, solidity, and inertia. It is 'society', or 'social norm', or 'social laws', or 'structures', or 'social customs', or 'culture', or 'rules', etc., they argue, which have enough steel in them to account for the way it exerts its grip over all of us and accounts for the unequal landscape in which we are toiling. It is, indeed, a convenient solution but does not explain where their 'steely' quality is coming from that reinforces the weak connections of social skills. And sociologists, in a careless move, might take a wrong turn and say that durability, solidity, and inertia are provided by the durability, solidity, and inertia of society itself. They might go even further and take this tautology not for the starkest of contradictions, but from what should be admired most in the miraculous force of a society that is, as they say, *sui generis*, by which they mean that it is generated out of itself.[75]

Even if this way of talking is innocuous enough when taken as some shorthand to describe what is already bundled together, the consequences of such an argument are disastrous. The temptation is too strong to act as if there now existed some formidable force that could provide all the short-lived asymmetries with the durability and expansion that social skills could not manage to produce by their own impetus. At which point the causes and effects would be inverted and the practical means for making the social hold would vanish from view. What had begun as a mere confusion of adjectives has become a wholly different project: to this base world has been added a world which is just as intractable as the heaven of ancient Christian theology—except it does not offer any hope of redemption.

Are sociologists of the social so foolish that they are unable to detect such a tautology in their reasoning? Are they really stuck in the mythical belief of another world behind the real world? Do they really believe in this strange bootstrapping of a society born out of itself?[76] Of course not, since they never really use it in practice and so are never confronted by the contradiction inherent in the notion of a 'self-production' of society. The reason why they never draw the logical conclusion that their argument is contradictory is that they use it somewhat more loosely. When they invoke the durability of some social aggregates they always, wittingly or unwittingly, lend to the

---

[75] Cornelius Castoriadis (1998), *The Imaginary Institution of Society* extends the fallacy even further, considering this tautology itself as the imaginary foundation of society. But once this foundation is accepted, there is no longer any way to detect the composition of the social.

[76] Bootstrapping is taken as one characteristic of the social itself. See Barry Barnes (1983), 'Social Life as Bootstrapped Induction'.

weak social ties the heavy load coming from the masses of other non-social things. It is always things—and I now mean this last word literally—which, in practice, lend their 'steely' quality to the hapless 'society'. So, in effect, what sociologists mean by the 'power of society' is not society itself—that would be magical indeed—but some sort of summary for all the entities already mobilized to render asymmetries longer lasting.[77] This use of a shorthand is not tautological, but it is dangerously misleading since there is no empirical way to decide how all that stuff has been mobilized any longer—and worst of all, there is no way to know if such a load is still active. The idea of a society has become in the hands of later-day 'social explainers' like a big container ship which no inspector is permitted to board and which allows social scientists to smuggle goods across national borders without having to submit to public inspection. Is the cargo empty or full, healthy or rotten, innocuous or deadly, newly made or long disused? It has become anyone's guess, much like the presence of weapons of mass destruction in Saddam Hussein's Iraq.

ANT's solution is not to engage in polemics against sociologists of the social, but simply to multiply the occasions to quickly detect the contradiction in which they might have fallen into. This is the only way to gently force sociologists again to trace the non-social means mobilized whenever they invoke the power of social explanations.[78] What ANT does is that it keeps asking the following question: Since every sociologist loads things into social ties to give them enough weight to account for their durability and extension, why not do this explicitly instead of doing it on the sly? Its slogan, 'Follow the actors', becomes, 'Follow the actors in their weaving through things they have added to social skills so as to render more durable the constantly shifting interactions.'

It's at this point that the real contrast between sociology of associations and sociology of *the social* will be most clearly visible. So far, I might have exaggerated the differences between the two viewpoints. After all, many schools of social science might accept the two first uncertainties as their departure point (especially anthropology, which is another name for empirical metaphysics), and of course ethnomethodology. Even adding controversies does not radically alter the type of phenomena they might want to study, only the difficulties of

[77] In Part II, we will discover that this tautology is the hidden presence of the Body Politic: the paradoxical relation of the citizen with the Republic has fully contaminated the entirely different relation of actor and system—see p. 161.

[78] Important in organization studies is the fact that whenever the big animal is implied tautologically, look for accounts, documents, and the circulation of forms. See Barbara Czarniawska (1997), *A Narrative Approach To Organization Studies*; Cooren, James R. Taylor (1993), *Rethinking the Theory of Organizational Communication: How to Read an Organization*.

listing them. But now the gap is going to be considerably enlarged, because we are not going to limit in advance to one small repertoire only that which is needed for actors to generate social asymmetries. Instead, we are going to accept as full-blown actors entities that were explicitly *excluded* from collective existence by more than one hundred years of social explanation. The reasons are twofold: first, because the basic social skills provide only one tiny subset of the associations making up societies; second, because the supplement of force which seems to reside in the invocation of a social tie is, at best, a convenient shorthand and, at worst, nothing more than a tautology.

Shirley Strum's baboons

To understand the link between the basic social skills and the notion of society, a detour through the study of apes and monkeys is required. In recalling the first meeting on baboon studies that she organized in 1978 in a castle near New York City, Shirley Strum (1987: 157–58) wrote:

'Still, I knew my work painted a picture of baboon societies that others would find difficult to accept. My shocking discovery was that males had no dominance hierarchy; that baboons possessed social strategies; that finesse triumphed over force; that social skill and social reciprocity took precedence over aggression. This was the beginning of sexual politics, where males and females exchanged favors in return for other favors. It appeared that baboons had to work hard to create their social world, but the way in which they created it made them seem "nicer" than people. They needed one another in order to survive at the most basic level—the protection and advantage that group living offered the individual—and also at the most sophisticated level, one marked by social strategies of competition and defense. They also seemed "nice" because, unlike humans, no member of Pumphouse [the name of the troop] possessed the ability to control essential resources: each baboon got its own food, water and place in the shade, and took care of its own basic survival needs. Aggression could be used for coercion, but aggression was a roped tiger. Grooming, being close, social goodwill and cooperation were the only assets available for barter or to use as leverage over another baboon. And these were all aspects of "niceness", affiliation not aggression. Baboons were "nice" to one another because such behavior was as critical to their survival as air to breathe and food to eat. What I had discovered was a revolutionary new picture of baboon society. Revolutionary, in fact, for *any* animal society as yet described. The implications were breathtaking. I was arguing that aggression was not as pervasive or important an influence in evolution as had been thought, and that social strategies and social reciprocity were extremely important. If baboons possessed these, certainly, the precursors of our early human ancestors must have had them as well.'

If sociologists had the privilege to watch more carefully baboons repairing their constantly decaying 'social structure', they would have witnessed what incredible cost has been paid when the job is to maintain, for instance, social dominance with no *thing* at all, just social skills. They would have documented empirically the price to pay for the tautology of social ties made out of social ties.[79] It's the power exerted through entities that don't sleep and associations that don't break down that allow power to last longer and expand further— and, to achieve such a feat, many more materials than social compacts have to be devised. This does not mean that the sociology of the social is useless, only that it might be excellent for studying baboons but not for studying humans.

Making objects participants in the course of action

The contrast between the two schools cannot be made more dramatic. As soon as you start to have doubts about the ability of social ties to durably expand, a plausible role for objects might be on offer.[80] As soon as you believe social aggregates can hold their own being propped up by 'social forces', then objects vanish from view and the magical and tautological force of society is enough to hold *every thing* with, literally, *no thing*. It's hard to imagine a more striking fore-ground/background reversal, a more radical paradigm shift. This is of course the reason why ANT first attracted attention.[81]

Social action is not only taken over by aliens, it is also shifted or delegated to different types of actors which are able to transport the action further through other modes of action, other types of forces altogether.[82] At first, bringing objects back into the normal course of

---

[79] See Hans Kummer (1995), *In Quest of the Sacred Baboon* for the key notion of 'social tools' about Hamadryas baboons.

[80] The word object will be used as a placeholder until the next chapter where it will be defined as a 'matter of concern'. There is no way to speed things up since ANT is defined in this book by laying out the five sources of uncertainty in succession.

[81] It cannot be understood apart from the two other uncertainties about groups and about action. Without them, ANT is immediately reduced to a rather silly argument about the causal agency of technical objects, that is, a clear return to technical determinism.

[82] For the word delegation to hold, the ANT theory of action, that is, how someone makes another do things, has to be kept in mind. If such a dislocation is missed, delegation becomes another causal relation and a resurrection of a *Homo faber* fully in command of what he—it's almost always a 'he'—does with tools.

action should appear innocuous enough. After all, there is hardly any doubt that kettles 'boil' water, knifes 'cut' meat, baskets 'hold' provisions, hammers 'hit' nails on the head, rails 'keep' kids from falling, locks 'close' rooms against uninvited visitors, soap 'takes' the dirt away, schedules 'list' class sessions, prize tags 'help' people calculating, and so on. Are those verbs not designating actions? How could the introduction of those humble, mundane, and ubiquitous activities bring any news to any social scientist?

And yet they do. The main reason why objects had no chance to play any role before was not only due to the definition of the social used by sociologists, but also to the very definition of actors and agencies most often chosen. If action is limited a priori to what 'intentional', 'meaningful' humans do, it is hard to see how a hammer, a basket, a door closer, a cat, a rug, a mug, a list, or a tag could act. They might exist in the domain of 'material' 'causal' relations, but not in the 'reflexive' 'symbolic' domain of social relations. By contrast, if we stick to our decision to start from the controversies about actors and agencies, then *any thing* that does modify a state of affairs by making a difference is an actor—or, if it has no figuration yet, an actant. Thus, the questions to ask about any agent are simply the following: Does it make a difference in the course of some other agent's action or not? Is there some trial that allows someone to detect this difference?

The rather common sense answer should be a resounding 'yes'. If you can, with a straight face, maintain that hitting a nail with and without a hammer, boiling water with and without a kettle, fetching provisions with or without a basket, walking in the street with or without clothes, zapping a TV with or without a remote, slowing down a car with or without a speed-bump, keeping track of your inventory with or without a list, running a company with or without bookkeeping, are exactly the same activities, that the introduction of these mundane implements change 'nothing important' to the realization of the tasks, then you are ready to transmigrate to the Far Land of the Social and disappear from this lowly one. For all the other members of society, it does make a difference under trials and so these implements, according to our definition, are actors, or more precisely, *participants* in the course of action waiting to be given a figuration.

This, of course, does not mean that these participants 'determine' the action, that baskets 'cause' the fetching of provisions or that hammers 'impose' the hitting of the nail. Such a reversal in the direction of influence would be simply a way to transform objects into the causes whose effects would be transported through human action now limited to a trail of mere intermediaries. Rather, it means that there might exist many metaphysical shades between full causality and sheer inexistence. In addition to 'determining' and serving as a 'back-drop for human action', things might authorize, allow, afford, encourage, permit, suggest, influence, block, render possible, forbid, and so on.[83] ANT is not the empty claim that objects do things 'instead' of human actors: it simply says that no science of the social can even begin if the question of who and what participates in the action is not first of all thoroughly explored, even though it might mean letting elements in which, for lack of a better term, we would call *non-humans*. This expression, like all the others chosen by ANT is meaningless in itself. It does not designate a domain of reality. It does not designate little goblins with red hats acting at atomic levels, only that the analyst should be prepared to look in order to account for the durability and extension of any interaction.[84] The project of ANT is simply to extend the list and modify the shapes and figures of those assembled as participants and to design a way to make them act as a durable whole.

For sociologists of associations, what is new is not the multiplicity of objects any course of action mobilizes along its trail—no one ever denied they were there by the thousands; what is new is that objects are suddenly highlighted not only as being full-blown actors, but also as what explains the contrasted landscape we started with, the over-arching powers of society, the huge asymmetries, the crushing exercise of power. This is the surprise from which sociologists of associations wish to start instead of considering, as do most of their colleagues, that the question is obviously closed and that objects do nothing, at least nothing comparable or even *connectable* to human social action, and that if they can sometimes 'express' power relations, 'symbolize' social hierarchies, 'reinforce' social inequalities, 'transport' social power, 'objectify' inequality, and 'reify' gender relations, they cannot be at the origin of social activity.

---

[83] This is why the notion of affordance, introduced in James G. Gibson (1986), *The Ecological Approach to Visual Perception*, has been found so useful. The multiplicity of modes of action when dealing with technology—hard and soft—is marvellously followed by Suchman, *Plans and Situated Actions*, C. Goodwin and M. Goodwin (1996), 'Formulating planes: Seeing as a situated activity', and Bernard Conein, Nicolas Dodier and Laurent Thévenot (1993), *Les objets dans l'action. De la maison au laboratoire*.

[84] There is a bit of anthropocentric bias in using the expression *non*-humans. I have explained in detail elsewhere how the couple human/non-human should be substituted for the insurmountable dichotomy between subject and object (see Latour, *Politics of Nature*). No extra meaning should be looked for in this notion: it does not specify any ontological domain, but simply replaces another conceptual difference. For a complete panorama of humans/non-humans relations, see Philippe Descola (2005), *La nature des cultures*.

A good example of an asymmetric definition of actors is offered by Durkheim (1966: 113) when he states:

'The first origins of all social processes of any importance should be sought in the internal constitution of the social group. [italics in text]

It is possible to be even more precise. The elements which make up this milieu are of two kinds: things and persons. Besides material objects incorporated into the society, there must also be included the products of previous social activity: law, established customs, literary and artistic works, etc. But it is clear that the impulsion which determines social transformations can come from neither the material nor the immaterial, for neither possesses a motivating power [*puissance motrice*]. There is, assuredly, occasion to take them into consideration in the explanations one attempts. They bear with a certain weight on social evolution, whose speed and even direction vary according to the nature of these elements; but they contain nothing of what is required to put it in motion. They are the matter upon which the social forces of society act, but by themselves they release no social energy [*aucune force vive*]. As an active factor, then, the human milieu itself remains.'

This, for me, has always been a great surprise: How is it that, in spite of this massive and ubiquitous phenomenon, sociology remains 'without object'? It is even more startling when you realize that this discipline emerged a full century after the Industrial Revolution and has been evolving in parallel with the largest and most intensive technical developments since the Neolithic. Not only that, but how to explain that so many social scientists pride themselves in considering 'social meaning' *instead* of 'mere' material relations, 'symbolic dimension' *instead* of 'brute causality'? Much like sex during the Victorian period, objects are nowhere to be said and everywhere to be felt. They exist, naturally, but they are never given a thought, a social thought. Like humble servants, they live on the margins of the social doing most of the work but never allowed to be represented as such. There seems to be no way, no conduit, no entry point for them to be knitted together with the same wool as the rest of the social ties. The more radical thinkers want to attract attention to humans in the margins and at the periphery, the less they speak of objects. As if a damning curse had been cast unto things, they remain asleep like the servants of some enchanted castle. Yet, as soon as they are freed from the spell, they start shuddering, stretching, and muttering. They begin to swarm in all directions, shaking the other human actors, waking them out of their dogmatic sleep. Would it be too childish to say that ANT played the role of the Charming Prince's kiss tenderly touching Sleeping

Beauty's lips? At any rate, it is because it was an object-oriented sociology for object-oriented humans that this school of thought was
noticed in the first place—and that it makes sense to write an introduction to it.

Objects help trace social connections only intermittently

It is true that, at first sight, the difficulty of registering the role of
objects comes from the apparent *incommensurability* of their modes
of action with traditionally conceived social ties. But sociologists of
the social have misunderstood the nature of such incommensurability.
They have concluded that because they are incommensurable they
should be kept separate from proper social ties, without realizing that
they should have concluded precisely the opposite: it's because they
are incommensurable that they have been fetched in the first place! If
they were as weak as the social skills they have to reinforce, if they were
made of the same material quality, where would the gain be? Baboons
we were, baboons we would have remained![85]

It's true that the force exerted by a brick unto another brick, the spin
of a wheel onto an axis, the balance of a lever onto a mass, the gearing
down of a force through a pulley, the effect of fire on phosphorus, all of
those modes of action seem to pertain to categories so obviously
different from the one exerted by a 'stop' sign on a cyclist or that of a
crowd over an individual mind that it seems perfectly reasonable to
put material and social entities on two different shelves. Reasonable
but absurd, once you realize that any *human* course of action might
weave together in a matter of minutes, for instance, a shouted order to
lay a brick, the chemical connection of cement with water, the force of
a pulley unto a rope with a movement of the hand, the strike of a
match to light a cigarette offered by a co-worker, etc. Here, the apparently reasonable division between material and social becomes just
what is obfuscating any enquiry on how a *collective* action is possible.
Provided of course that by collective we don't mean an action carried
over by homogeneous social forces, but, on the contrary, an action
that collects different types of forces woven together because they are

---

[85] This is the power of the now outdated but still beautiful synthesis offered in André
Leroi-Gourhan (1993), *Gesture and Speech*. For a more recent review of the state of the art,
see Pierre Lemonnier (1993), *Technological Choices. Transformation in Material Cultures
since the Neolithic* and Bruno Latour and Pierre Lemonnier (1994), *De la préhistoire aux
missiles balistiques - l'intelligence sociale des techniques*.

different.[86] This is why, from now on, the word 'collective' will take the place of 'society'. Society will be kept only for the assembly of already gathered entities that sociologists of the social believe have been made in social stuff. Collective, on the other hand, will designate the project of assembling new entities not yet gathered together and which, for this reason, clearly appear as being not made of social stuff.

Any course of action will thread a trajectory through completely foreign modes of existence that have been brought together by such heterogeneity. Social inertia and physical gravity might seem unconnected, but they need no longer be when a team of workers is building a wall of bricks: they part company again only *after* the wall is completed. But while the wall is being built, there is no doubt that they are connected. How? The enquiry will determine this. ANT claims that we should simply not believe the question of the connections among heterogeneous actors to be closed, that what is usually meant by 'social' has probably to do with the reassembling of new types of actors. ANT states that if we wish to be a bit more realistic about social ties than 'reasonable' sociologists, then we have to accept that the continuity of any course of action will rarely consist of human-to-human connections (for which the basic social skills would be enough anyway) or of object-object connections, but will probably zigzag from one to the other.

To get the right feel for ANT, it's important to notice that this has nothing to do with a 'reconciliation' of the famous object/subject dichotomy. To distinguish a priori 'material' and 'social' ties before linking them together again makes about as much sense as to account for the dynamic of a battle by imagining a group of soldiers and officers stark naked with a huge heap of paraphernalia—tanks, rifles, paperwork, uniforms—and then claim that 'of course there exist some (dialectical) relation between the two'.[87] One should retort adamantly 'No!' There exists no relation whatsoever between 'the material' and 'the social world', because it is this very division which is a complete

---

[86] This is what was at stake in the dispute about the exact role of non-humans and known as the 'Bath controversy'. See Harry Collins and Steven Yearley (1992), 'Epistemological Chicken' and Michel Callon and Bruno Latour (1992), 'Don't throw the Baby out with the Bath School! A reply to Collins and Yearley'—a tiny landmark for our little field.

[87] See Diane Vaughan (1996), *The Challenger Launch Decision: Risky Technology, Culture and Deviance at NASA*. 'But I believed that with sufficient immersion in the case materials and by consulting technical experts, I could sufficiently master the technical details necessary to get at the sociological questions. It was, after all, human behavior I wanted to explain, and I was trained to do that' (p. 40). This position is reasonable but is it the best way to follow a course of action like this one: 'At approximately 7:00 a.m., the ice team made its second launch pad inspection. On the basis of their report, the launch time was slipped to permit a third ice inspection' (p. 328). Where is the split here between engineering and sociology?

artifact.[88] To reject such a divide is not to 'relate' the heap of naked soldiers 'with' the heap of material stuff: it is to redistribute the whole assemblage from top to bottom and beginning to end. There is no empirical case where the existence of *two* coherent and homogeneous aggregates, for instance technology 'and' society, could make any sense. ANT is not, I repeat is not, the establishment of some absurd 'symmetry between humans and non-humans'. To be symmetric, for us, simply means *not* to impose a priori some spurious *asymmetry* among human intentional action and a material world of causal relations. There are divisions one should never try to bypass, to go beyond, to try to overcome dialectically. They should rather be ignored and left to their own devices, like a once formidable castle now in ruins.[89]

This interest for the object has nothing to do with a privilege given to 'objective' matter in opposition to 'subjective' language, symbols, values, or feelings. As we will see when absorbing the next source of uncertainty, the 'matter' of most self-proclaimed materialists does not have a great deal to do with the type of force, causality, efficacy, and obstinacy non-human actants possess in the world. 'Matter', we will soon realize, is a highly politicized interpretation of causality. In order to absorb the third source of uncertainty, we should be ready to inquire about the agency of all sorts of objects. But since objects have such poor and constricted roles in most of the social sciences, it's very difficult to extend their original activity to other types of material like documents, writings, charts, files, paper clips, maps, organizational devices, in brief intellectual technologies.[90] As soon as some

---

[88] Psychologists have shown that even a two-month-old baby can clearly differentiate intentional and non-intentional movements. Humans and objects are clearly distinct. See Olivier Houdé (1997), *Rationalité, développement et inhibition: Un nouveau cadre d'analyse* and Dan Sperber, David Premack and Ann James Premack (1996), *Causal Cognition: A Multidisciplinary Debate*. But a difference is not a divide. Toddlers are much more reasonable than humanists: although they recognize the many differences between billiard balls and people, this does not preclude them to follow how their actions are woven into the *same* stories.

[89] This is the reason why I have abandoned most of the geometrical metaphor about the 'principle of symmetry' when I realized that readers concluded from it that nature and society had to be 'maintained together' so as to study 'symmetrically' 'objects' *and* 'subjects', 'non-humans' *and* 'humans'. But what I had in mind was not *and*, but *neither*: a joint *dissolution of both collectors*. The last thing I wanted was to give nature and society a new lease on life through 'symmetry'.

[90] Distributed cognition, situated knowledge, history of intellectual technologies, science studies, administrative sciences, and social accounting have each in its own way multiplied the range of objects engaged in making interactions longer lasting and further reaching. This long trend to materialize non-material technologies goes back to Jack Goody (1977), *The Domestication of the Savage Mind*; see Geoffrey C. Bowker and Susan Leigh Star (1999), *Sorting Things Out: Classification and Its Consequences*; Paolo Quattrone (2004), 'Accounting for God. Accounting and Accountability Practices in the Society of Jesus (Italy, 16th–17th centuries)'; and the now classical work of Michel Foucault (1973), *The Birth of the Clinic. An Archaeology of Medical Perception*.

freedom of movement is granted back to non-humans, the range of agents able to participate in the course of action extends prodigiously and is no longer restricted to the 'middle size dry goods' of analytical philosophers. What makes ANT difficult to grasp is that it fills in precisely the space that is emptied by critical sociologists with the damning words of 'objectification' and 'reification'.

Yet sociologists of the social are not fools. They have good reason to hesitate before following the social fluid wherever it leads them. What is so difficult to comprehend at first is that an ANT study has to tackle both continuity and discontinuity among modes of action. We have to become able to follow the smooth continuity of heterogeneous entities and the complete *discontinuity* between participants that, in the end, will always remain incommensurable. The social fluid does not offer to the analyst a continuous and substantial existence, but rather puts up only a provisional appearance much like a shower of physical particles in the brief instant it's forced into existence. You begin with assemblages that look vaguely familiar and you end up with completely foreign ones. It is true that this oscillation makes the tracing of social connections especially tricky once you begin to add non-humans to the list of *bona fide* social ties.

A shepherd and his dog remind you nicely of social relations, but when you see her flock behind a barbed wire fence, you wonder where is the shepherd and her dog—although sheep are kept in the field by the piercing effect of wire barbs more obstinately than by the barking of the dog. There is no doubt that you have become a couch potato in front of your TV set thanks largely to the remote control that allows you to surf from channel to channel[91]—and yet there is no *resemblance* between the causes of your immobility and the portion of your action that has been carried out by an infrared signal, even though there is no question that your behavior has been *permitted* by the TV command.

Between a car driver that slows down near a school because she has seen the '30 MPH' yellow sign and a car driver that slows down because he wants to protect the suspension of his car threatened by the bump of a 'speed trap', is the difference big or small? Big, since the obedience of the first has gone through morality, symbols, sign posts, yellow paint, while the other has passed through the same list to which has been added a carefully designed concrete slab. But it is small since they both have obeyed something: the first driver to a rarely manifested altruism—if she had not slowed down, her heart would have been broken by the moral law; the second driver to a largely distributed

---

[91] Try it for yourself: throw it away and see how long you will spend moving back and forth from the couch to the set.

selfishness—if he had not slowed down his suspension would have been broken by the concrete slab. Should we say that only the first connection is social, moral and symbolic, and that the second is objective and material? No. But, if we say that both are social, how are we going to justify the difference between moral conduct and suspension springs? They might not be social all the way through, but they certainly are *collected* or *associated* together by the very work of road designers. One cannot call oneself a social scientist and pursue only some links—the moral, legal, and symbolic ones—and stop as soon as there is some physical relation interspersed in between the others. That would render any enquiry impossible.[92]

How long can a social connection be followed without objects taking the relay? A minute? An hour? A microsecond? And for how long will this relay be visible? A minute? An hour? A microsecond? One thing is certain: if we interrupt our fieldwork at each relay by focusing only on the list of already gathered connections, the social world would become immediately opaque, shrouded into those strange autumn fogs that leave visible only tiny and unpredictable smears of the landscape. And yet, on the other hand, if sociologists have also to become engineers, artisans, craftsmen, designers, architects, managers, promoters etc., they will never end up following their actors through those many intermittent existences. So, we have to take non-humans into account only as long as they are rendered commensurable with social ties and also to accept, an instant later, their fundamental incommensurability.[93] To travel around using an ANT definition of 'social' requires quite a lot of nerve. No wonder then that sociologists of the social balked at that difficulty! That they had good reasons to abstain from following those oscillations does not mean, however, that they were right. It only means that sociology requires an extended range of tools.

---

[92] Since ANT is often accused of being indifferent to morality, it's worth recalling that there are good deontological reasons in having at least as much freedom of movement as the actors we study. This principle is as old as the notion of translation. See Michel Callon (1981) 'Struggles and Negotiations to Decide What is Problematic and What is Not: The Sociology of Translation'.

[93] This is clearly at odds with the explicitly asymmetric program offered in Weber 'To be devoid of meaning is not identical with being lifeless or non-human; every artifact, such as for example a machine, can be understood only in terms of the meaning which its production and use have had or will have for human action; a meaning which may derive from a relation to exceedingly various purposes. Without reference to this meaning such an object remains wholly unintelligible.' Max Weber (1947), the Theory of Social and Economic Organization (p. 93) Then follows a definition of means and ends completely at odds with the notion of mediators.

A list of situations where an object's activity is made easily visible

In exploring the new associations making up the social, ANT scholars have to accept two contradictory demands: on the one hand, we don't want the sociologist to limit oneself to social ties; on the other, we don't ask the enquirer to become a specialized technologist. One solution is to stick to the new definition of social as a fluid visible *only* when new associations are being made. Such is the rightful 'domain' of ANT, even though it is not a specific stretch of land nor an enclosed turf but only a brief flash which may occur everywhere like a sudden change of phase.

Fortunately for the analysts, those situations are not as rare as one might think. To be accounted for, objects have to enter into accounts. If no trace is produced, they offer no information to the observer and will have no visible effect on other agents. They remain silent and are no longer actors: they remain, literally, unaccountable. Although the situation is the same for groups and agencies—no trial, no account, no information—it is clearly more difficult for objects, since carrying their effects while becoming silent is what they are so good at as Samuel Butler noted.[94] Once built, the wall of bricks does not utter a word—even though the group of workmen goes on talking and graffiti may proliferate on its surface. Once they have been filled in, the printed questionnaires remain in the archives forever unconnected with human intentions until they are made alive again by some historian. Objects, by the very nature of their connections with humans, quickly shift from being mediators to being intermediaries, counting for one or nothing, no matter how internally complicated they might be. This is why specific tricks have to be invented to *make them talk*, that is, to offer descriptions of themselves, to produce *scripts* of what they are making others—humans or non-humans—do.[95]

Again, this situation is not different for groups and agencies we reviewed earlier since humans, too, have to be made to talk; and this is why very elaborate and, often, artificial situations have to be devised to reveal their actions and performances (more on this in the fifth uncertainty). But still, there is a difference: once humans become mediators again, it is hard to stop them. An indefinite stream of data springs forth, whereas objects, no matter how important, efficient,

---

[94] Samuel Butler (1872), *Erewhon*.
[95] Madeleine Akrich (1992), 'The De-Scription of Technical Objects'; Madeleine Akrich (1993), 'A Gazogene in Costa Rica: An Experiment in Techno-Sociology'; and Madeleine Akrich and Bruno Latour (1992), 'A Summary of a Convenient Vocabulary for the Semiotics of Human and Non-Human assemblies'.

central, or necessary they may be, tend to recede into the background very fast, interrupting the stream of data—and the greater their importance, the faster they disappear. It does not mean they stop acting, but that their mode of action is no longer *visibly connected* to the usual social ties since they rely on types of forces chosen precisely for their differences with the normal social ones. Speech acts always look comparable, compatible, contiguous, and continuous with other speech acts; writing with writing; interaction with interaction; but objects appear associable with one another and with social ties only *momentarily.*[96] This is quite normal since it is through their very heterogeneous agencies that social ties have been provided with completely different shape and figures—normal but tricky.

Fortunately, it is possible to multiply the occasions where this momentary visibility is enhanced enough to generate good accounts. Much of ANT scholars' fieldwork has been devoted to trigger these occasions so I can go quickly.

The first solution is to study *innovations* in the artisan's workshop, the engineer's design department, the scientist's laboratory, the marketer's trial panels, the user's home, and the many socio-technical controversies. In these sites objects live a clearly multiple and complex life through meetings, plans, sketches, regulations, and trials. Here, they appear fully mixed with other more traditional social agencies. It is only once in place that they disappear from view. This is why the study of innovations and controversies has been one of the first privileged places where objects can be maintained longer as visible, distributed, accounted mediators before becoming invisible, asocial intermediaries.

Second, even the most routine, traditional, and silent implements stop being taken for granted when they are approached by users rendered ignorant and clumsy by *distance*—distance in time as in archaeology, distance in space as in ethnology, distance in skills as in learning. Although those associations might not trace an innovation per se, the same situation of novelty is produced, for the analyst at least, by the irruption into the normal course of action of strange, exotic, archaic, or mysterious implements. In those encounters, objects become mediators, at least for a while, before soon disappearing again through know-how, habituation, or disuse. Anyone who has tried to make sense of a user's manual will know how time-consum-

---

[96] Both impressions are only superficially true. A human's course of action is never homogeneous and there is never a technology that is so well organized that it runs automatically. And yet, the practical difference remains for someone who is carrying out the inquiry.

ing—and how painful—it is to read what is ironically called an 'assembly drawing'.[97]

The third type of occasion is that offered by accidents, breakdowns, and strikes: all of a sudden, completely silent intermediaries become full-blown mediators; even objects, which a minute before appeared fully automatic, autonomous, and devoid of human agents, are now made of crowds of frantically moving humans with heavy equipment. Those who watched the *Columbia* shuttle instantly transformed from the most complicated human instrument ever assembled to a rain of debris falling over Texas will realize how quickly objects flip-flop their mode of existence. Fortunately for ANT, the recent proliferation of 'risky' objects has multiplied the occasions to hear, see, and feel what objects may be doing when they break other actors down.[98] Official enquiries are happening everywhere to map out for us the fabulous extension of what social ties have become in the hands of technical setups. Here again, it will never be the lack of material that will stop the studies.[99]

Fourth, when objects have receded into the background for good, it is always possible—but more difficult—to bring them back to light by using archives, documents, memoirs, museum collections, etc., to artificially produce, through historians' accounts, the state of crisis in which machines, devices, and implements were born.[100] Behind each bulb Edison can be made visible, and behind any microchip is the huge, anonymous Intel. By now, the history of technology should have forever subverted the ways in which social and cultural histories are narrated.[101] Even the humblest and most ancient stone tools from the Olduvai Gorge in Tanzania have been turned by paleontologists into the very mediators that triggered the evolution of 'modern man'.

---

[97] See Donald A. Norman (1988), *The Psychology of Everyday Things,* Donald Norman (1993), *Things that Make Us Smart*; Madeleine Akrich and Dominique Bouiller (1991), 'Le mode d'emploi: genèse et usage'; and Chapter 6 in Garfinkel (2002), *Ethnomethodology's Program: Working Out Durkheim's Aphorism.*

[98] The multiplication of those 'risky' objects is at the heart of Ulrich Beck (1992), *Risk Society. Towards a New Modernity.* Although he uses an entirely different social theory, Beck's attention to the new forms of objectivity (what he calls 'reflexive modernisation') has his innovative sociology in very close conversation with ANT, especially through its political, or rather, 'cosmopolitical' interests.

[99] Thanks to the proliferation of accidents and the extension of democratic interests, those sources of data multiply. See Michel Callon, Pierre Lascoumes and Yannick Barthe (2001), *Agir dans un monde incertain. Essai sur la démocratie technique*; Richard Rogers (2005), *Information Politic on the Web*; and Vaughan, *The Challenger Launch Decision.*

[100] The encounter with Thomas P. Hughes (1983), *Networks of Power. Electrification in Western Society, 1880–1930* was important because Hughes abstained from giving an explanation in terms of social shaping of technology and had coined the expression 'seamless web'. See Thomas P. Hughes (1986), 'The Seamless Web: Technology, Science, Etcetera, Etcetera'.

[101] There is no difference, on that score, between history of technology and ANT, except when the social theory is made explicit—but often this sociological packaging has so little relation to the cases at hand that it makes no real difference.

Finally, when everything else has failed, the resource of fiction can bring—through the use of counterfactual history, thought experiments, and 'scientifiction'—the solid objects of today into the fluid states where their connections with humans may make sense. Here again, sociologists have a lot to learn from artists.[102]

Whatever solution is chosen, the fieldwork undertaken by ANT scholars has demonstrated that if objects are not studied it is not due to a lack of data, but rather a lack of will. Once the conceptual difficulty of the flip-flop between commensurability and incommensurability has been lifted, all of the remaining problems are matters of empirical research: they are not a matter of principle any more. The impassable boundary marked by some Herculean Columns to stop the social sciences reaching beyond the narrow confines of social ties has been left behind. It's thus possible now for social scientists to catch up with what paleontologists call 'anatomically modern humans', who have already been settled for tens of thousands of years beyond the limits dictated to them by *social* science.

Who has been forgetting power relations?

We can now at last put our finger on what upset ANT so much in the pretensions of the sociology of the social to explain asymmetries in order to be faithful to the central intuition of their science: they could not deliver. The word 'social' meant either local face-to-face interactions that were too transient to account for asymmetries or a magical appeal to tautological forces whose exact price in object-load they were never ready to fully pay.

Social explanations run the risk of hiding that which they should reveal since they remain too often 'without object'.[103] In their study, sociologists consider, for the most part, an object-less social world, even though in their daily routine they, like all of us, might be constantly puzzled by the constant companionship, the continuous intimacy, the inveterate contiguity, the passionate affairs, the convoluted attachments of primates with objects for the past one

---

[102] It ranges from Francis Ponge's (1972), *The Voice of Things* to the thought experiments allowed by science fiction or Richard Powers's decisive work as a novelist of science studies in, for instance, Richard Powers (1995), *Galatea 2.2*.

[103] Even though objects proliferate in the works of Simmel, Elias, and Marx, the presence of objects is not enough to load the social. It's their way of entry that makes the difference. Hence the necessity to add the fourth uncertainty (see next chapter) to the one on agency and later the redefinition of politics (see Conclusion). For a very useful collection of cases on the effect of technology studies on materialism, see Donald MacKenzie and Judy Wajcman (1999), *The Social Shaping of Technology*.

million years. When we define the quality control of ANT accounts, we have to be very scrupulous in checking whether power and domination are explained by the multiplicity of objects given a central role and transported by vehicles which should be empirically visible—and we will not be content to have power and domination *themselves* be the mysterious container that holds inside of it that which makes the many participants in the action move.

To follow the social links even when they weave their way through non-social objects might be difficult for a reason that has nothing to do with theory. For the social scientists, there were some serious motives behind the need to ceaselessly patrol the border separating the 'symbolic' from the 'natural' domain, namely a good—that is, a bad—polemical argument. To carve out a little niche for themselves, they had abandoned, early in the 19th century, things and objects to the scientists and engineers. The only way to plead for a little autonomy was to forsake the vast territories they had given up and stick forcefully to the shrinking plot allotted to them: 'meaning', 'symbol', 'intention', 'language'. When a bicycle hits a rock, it is not social. But when a cyclist crosses a 'stop' sign, it becomes social. When a new telephone switchboard is installed, this is not social. But when the colors of telephone sets are discussed, this becomes social because there is, as designers say, 'a human dimension' in the choice of such a fixture. When a hammer hits a nail, it is not social. But when the image of a hammer is crossed with that of a sickle, then it graduates to the social realm because it enters the 'symbolic order'. Every object was thus divided in two, scientists and engineers taking the largest part—efficacy, causality, material connections—and leaving the crumbs to the specialists of 'the social' or 'the human' dimension. Thus, any allusion by ANT scholars to the 'power of objects' over social relations was a painful reminder, for sociologists of the social, of the clout of the other 'more scientific' departments on their independence—not to mention grant money—and on the territories they were no longer allowed to walk through freely.

But polemics among disciplines does not produce good concepts, only barricades made of any available debris. When any state of affairs is split into one material component to which is added as an appendix a social one, one thing is sure: this is an artificial division imposed by the disciplinary disputes, not by any empirical requirement. It simply means that most of the data has vanished, that the collective course of action has not been followed through. To be 'both material and social' is not a way for objects to exist: it is simply a way for them to be artificially cut off and to have their specific agency rendered utterly mysterious.

It is fair to say that social scientists were not alone in sticking polemically to one metaphysic among the many at hand. Their 'dear colleagues' in the other hard science departments were also trying to claim that all material objects have only 'one way' to act and that was to 'causally determine' other material objects to move. As we shall see in the next chapter, they were granting the social no other role than that of an intermediary faithfully 'transporting' the causal weight of matter. When the social realm is given such an infamous role, great is the temptation to overreact and to turn matter into a mere intermediary faithfully 'transporting' or 'reflecting' society's agency. As usual with those polemics among disciplines, stupidity breeds stupidity. To avoid the threat of 'technical determinism', it is tempting to defend adamantly 'social determinism', which in turn becomes so extreme (the steam engine becoming, for instance, the 'mere reflection' of 'English capitalism') that even the most open-minded engineer becomes a fierce technical determinist bumping the table with virile exclamations about the 'weight of material constraints'. These gestures have no other effect but to trigger even a moderate sociologist to insist even more vehemently on the importance of some 'discursive dimension'.[104]

What renders these disputes moot is that the choice between these positions is unrealistic. It would be incredible if the millions of participants in our courses of action would enter the social ties through three modes of existence and *only three*: as a 'material infrastructure' that would 'determine' social relations like in the Marxian types of materialism; as a 'mirror' simply 'reflecting' social distinctions like in the critical sociologies of Pierre Bourdieu; or as a backdrop for the stage on which human social actors play the main roles like in Erving Goffman's interactionist accounts. None of those entries of objects in the collective are wrong, naturally, but they are only primitive ways of packaging the bundle of ties that make up the collective. None of them are sufficient to describe the many entanglements of humans and non-humans.

Talking of 'material culture' would not help very much since objects, in this case, would be simply connected *to one another* so as to form an homogeneous layer, a configuration which is even less likely than one which imagines humans linked to one another by nothing else than

[104] See examples of this tug-of-war and on the ways to pacify it in Philippe Descola and Gisli Palsson (1996), *Nature and Society. Anthropological Perspectives*. See also Tim Ingold (2000), *Perception of the Environment: Essays in Livelihood, Dwelling and Skill* and the early discussions around Bijker's volumes in Wiebe Bijker and John Law (1992), *Shaping Technology-Building Society: Studies in Sociotechnical Change*; Wiebe E. Bijker, Thomas P. Hughes and Trevor Pinch (1987), *The Social Construction of Technological Systems. New Directions in the Sociology and History of Technology*; and Wiebe Bijker (1995), *Of Bicycles, Bakelites, and Bulbs. Towards a Theory of Sociotechnical Change*.

social ties. Objects are never assembled together to form some other realm anyhow, and even if it were the case they would be neither strong nor weak—simply 'reflecting' social values or being there as mere decorum. Their action is no doubt much more varied, their influence more ubiquitous, their effect much more ambiguous, their presence much more distributed than these narrow repertoires. The best proof of this multiplicity is provided by a close look at what objects really do in the texts of the writers alluded to above: they deploy many *other* ways for objects to act than the ones granted to them by their author's own philosophy of matter. Even as textual entities, objects overflow their makers, intermediaries become mediators.[105] But in order to learn this lesson, the research field should be made wide open to begin with and it cannot be opened if the difference between human action and material causality is maintained as adamantly as Descartes's distinguished mind from matter (*res extensa* from the *res cogitans*) as a proof of scientific, moral and theological virtue—and even *he* kept open the tiny conduit of the pineal gland that sociologists of the social have cut off as well.

There exists, however, an even more important reason for rejecting adamantly the role given to objects in the sociology of the social: it voids the appeals to power relations and social inequalities of any real significance. By putting aside the practical means, that is the mediators, through which inertia, durability, asymmetry, extension, domination is produced and by conflating all those different means with the powerless power of social inertia, sociologists, when they are not careful in their use of social explanations, are the ones who hide the real causes of social inequalities. If there is one point where confusing cause and effect makes a huge difference, it is at this juncture when an *explanation* should be provided for the vertiginous effect of domination. Of course, appealing to 'social domination' might be useful as shorthand, but then it is much too tempting to *use* power instead of *explaining* it and that is exactly the problem with most 'social-explainers': in their search for *powerful explanations*, is it not *their* lust for power that shines through? If, as the saying goes, absolute power corrupts absolutely, then gratuitous use of the concept of power by so many critical theorists has corrupted them absolutely—or at least rendered their discipline redundant and their politics impotent. Like the 'dormitive virtue of opium' ridiculed by Molière, 'power' not only puts analysts to sleep, which does not matter so much, it also try to anesthetize the actors as well—and that is a political crime. This

---

[105] A crucial case is fetishism in *The Capital* where the textual fetish does much more in the text of Marx than what Marx himself reduces the fetish to do. See William Pietz (1985), 'The Problem of the Fetish, I' and William Pietz (1993), 'Fetishism and Materialism: the Limits of Theory in Marx'.

rationalist, modernist, positivist science nurtures in its bosom the most archaic and magical ghost: a self-generated, self-explicative society. To the *studied* and *modifiable* skein of means to achieve powers, sociology, and especially critical sociology, has too often substituted an invisible, unmovable, and homogeneous world of power for itself.[106] In sociology, powerful explanations should be counterchecked and counterbalanced.

Thus, the accusation of forgetting 'power relations' and 'social inequalities' should be placed squarely at the door of the sociologists of the social. If sociologists of associations wish to inherit this ancient, venerable, and fully justified intuition of the social science—power is unequally distributed—they also have to explain how domination has become so efficacious and through which unlikely means. Quite reasonably, it is for them the only way to make it modifiable. But to do so, a fourth uncertainty has to be accepted, a fourth can of worms opened—and this one is a Pandora's box.

---

[106] That this lesson is easy to forget is shown dramatically by the transatlantic destiny of Michel Foucault. No one was more precise in his analytical decomposition of the tiny ingredients from which power is made and no one was more critical of social explanations. And yet, as soon as Foucault was translated, he was immediately turned into the one who had 'revealed' power relations *behind* every innocuous activity: madness, natural history, sex, administration, etc. This proves again with what energy the notion of social explanation should be fought: even the genius of Foucault could not prevent such a total inversion.

Fourth Source of Uncertainty: Matters of Fact vs. Matters of Concern

G roups are made, agencies are explored, and objects play a role. Such are the three first sources of uncertainty we rely on if we want to follow the social fluid through its ever-changing and provisional shapes. So far, our core hypothesis may still remain acceptable to those who define social in the traditional sense of the word. To be sure, it requires more work: an extension of the list of actors and agencies; a deepening of the conflicts about practical metaphysics; an abandonment of the artificial divide between social and technical 'dimensions'; a pursuit through areas scarcely visited until now; a new practice of finding controversies more rewarding and, in the end, more stable than absolute departure points; and, finally, an invitation to develop a puzzling new custom to generously share metalanguage, social theory, and reflexivity with the actors themselves who are no longer considered as mere 'informants'. Still, the travels that are made possible by such a new departure point, although rougher and bumpier, have not requested any basic changes in the *scientific* outlook itself. After all, sociology may remain a science even though this means paying a higher price than expected, visiting sites that had not been anticipated, accepting more relativity, and deploying more contradictory philosophies than seemed necessary at first glance. On the whole, abandoning the ether of society to feed off of controversies doesn't seem to be that much of a sacrifice. No matter how startling at first, new habits of thought might be quick to form.

Unfortunately, the difficulties we have to tackle do not stop at these three. A fourth source of uncertainty has to be accepted, and this one will lead us to the trickiest points of the sociology of associations as well as to its birthplace. Sociology of science, or what is known as 'science studies', is a convenient although banal translation into

English of the Greek word 'epistemology'.[107] After having doubted the 'socio' in the word socio-logy, we now have to doubt its 'logy'. Once this double revision is completed, we might finally be able to use the word positively again and without too many qualms. At this juncture problems become so numerous that all our travels would come to a stop if we were not careful enough to prepare the visitors to get through this tangle. Once again, in order to gain some freedom of movement we have to learn how to go even slower.

Constructivism vs. social constructivism

ANT is the story of an experiment so carelessly started that it took a quarter of century to rectify it and catch up with what its exact meaning was. It all started quite badly with the unfortunate use of the expression 'social construction of scientific facts'. We now understand why the word 'social' could entail so much misunderstanding; it confused two entirely different meanings: a kind of stuff and a movement for assembling non-social entities. But why has the introduction of the word 'construction' triggered even more confusion? In accounting for this difficulty, I first hope to make clear why I give so much prominence to the tiny subfield of science studies. It has renewed the meaning of all the words making up this innocent little expression: what is a fact, what is a science, what is a construction, and what is social. Not so bad for an experiment so recklessly conducted!

In plain English, to say something is constructed means that it's not a mystery that has popped out of nowhere, or that it has a more humble but also more visible and more interesting origin. Usually, the great advantage of visiting construction sites is that they offer an ideal vantage point to witness the connections between humans and non-humans. Once visitors have their feet deep in the mud, they are easily struck by the spectacle of all the participants working hard at the time of their most radical metamorphosis.[108] This is not only true of science but of all the other construction sites, the most obvious being those that are at the source of the metaphor, namely houses and

---

[107] A striking proof of the impact of science studies on social theory is provided by the parallel effect it had on Haraway. See Donna J. Haraway (1991), *Simians, Cyborgs, and Women: The Reinvention of Nature*. Pickering's critique of the earlier explanations provided by the Edinburgh school (Andy Pickering (1995), *The Mangle of Practice. Time, Agency and Science*) as well as Karin Knorr-Cetina's definition of agencies in science (Karin Knorr-Cetina (1999), *Epistemic Cultures: How the Sciences Make Knowledge*). They all had to take a similar turn.

[108] This is of course Marx's decisive insight and remains the crucial advantage of any historicization.

buildings fabricated by architects, masons, city planners, real estate agents, and homeowners.[109] The same is true of artistic practice.[110] The 'making of' any enterprise—films, skyscrapers, facts, political meetings, initiation rituals, haute couture, cooking—offers a view that is sufficiently different from the official one. Not only does it lead you backstage and introduce you to the skills and knacks of practitioners, it also provides a rare glimpse of what it is for a thing to emerge out of inexistence by adding to any existing entity its time dimension. Even more important, when you are guided to any construction site you are experiencing the troubling and exhilarating feeling that things *could be different,* or at least that *they could still fail*—a feeling never so deep when faced with the final product, no matter how beautiful or impressive it may be.

So, using the word 'construction' seemed at first ideal to describe a more realistic version of what it is for anything to *stand.* And indeed, in all domains, to say that something is constructed has always been associated with an appreciation of its robustness, quality, style, durability, worth, etc. So much so that no one would bother to say that a skyscraper, a nuclear plant, a sculpture, or an automobile is 'constructed'. This is too obvious to be pointed out. The great questions are rather: How well designed is it? How solidly constructed is it? How durable or reliable is it? How costly is the material? Everywhere, in technology, engineering, architecture, and art, construction is so much a *synonym* for the real that the question shifts immediately to the next and really interesting one: Is it *well* or *badly* constructed?

At first, it seemed obvious to us—the early science students—that if there existed building sites where the usual notion of constructivism should be readily applied, it had to be the laboratories, the research institutes, and their huge array of costly scientific instruments. Even more so than in art, architecture, and engineering, science offered the most extreme cases of complete *artificiality* and complete *objectivity* moving in parallel. There could be no question that laboratories, particle accelerators, telescopes, national statistics, satellites arrays, giant computers, and specimen collections were artificial places the history of which could be documented in the same way as for buildings, computer chips, and locomotives. And yet there was not the slightest doubt that the products of those artificial and costly sites were the most ascertained, objective, and certified results ever

[109] See two totally different but equally remarkable examples in Tracy Kidder (1985), *House* (1985) and Rem Koolhas and Bruce Mau (1995), *Small, Medium, Large, Extra-Large*. No one should use the word 'construction' without reading first the 'constructors'.
[110] See Albena Yaneva (2001), *L'affluence des objets. Pragmatique comparée de l'art contemporain et de l'artisanat'* and Albena Yaneva (2003), 'When a Bus Meet a Museum. To Follow Artists, Curators and Workers in Art Installation'.

obtained by collective human ingenuity. This is why it was with great enthusiasm that we began using the expression 'construction of facts' to describe the striking phenomenon of artificiality and reality marching in step. Moreover, to say that science, too, was constructed gave the same thrill as with all the other 'makings of': we went back stage; we learned about the skills of practitioners; we saw innovations come into being; we felt how risky it was; and we witnessed the puzzling merger of human activities and non-human entities. By watching the fabulous film that our colleagues the historians of science were shooting for us, we could attend, frame after frame, to the most incredible spectacle: truth being slowly achieved in breathtaking episodes without being sure of the result. As far as suspense was concerned, history of science outdid any plot Hollywood could imagine. Science for us became better than simply objective, it became *interesting*, just as interesting as it was for its practitioners engaged in its risky production.[111]

Unfortunately, the excitation went quickly sour when we realized that for other colleagues in the social as well as natural sciences the word construction meant something entirely different from what common sense had thought until then. To say that something was 'constructed' in their minds meant that something was not true. They seemed to operate with the strange idea that you had to submit to this rather unlikely choice: *either* something was real and not constructed, *or* it was constructed and artificial, contrived and invented, made up and false. Not only could this idea not be reconciled with the sturdy meaning one had in mind when talking about a 'well constructed' house, a 'well designed' software, or a 'well sculpted' statue, but it flew in the face of everything we were witnessing in laboratories: to be contrived and to be objective went together. If you began breaking the seamless narratives of fact making into two branches, it made the emergence of any science simply incomprehensible. Facts were facts—meaning exact—*because* they were fabricated—meaning that they emerged out of artificial situations. Every scientist we studied was proud of this connection between the quality of its construction and the quality of its data. This strong connection was actually one's main claim to fame. While the epistemologists might have forgotten this, etymology was there to remind everybody.[112] We were prepared to answer the more interesting question: Is a given fact of science *well* or

---

[111] Before the 'anti-whiggish' reactions in the history of science, it was impossible to share the *libido sciendi* of practitioners: faced with the final product, the public had no other way to get interested in science but the pedagogical injunction: 'It's true, so you should know about it.'

[112] The French epistemologist Gaston Bachelard has often insisted on this double etymology. For an English presentation see Mary Tiles and Robert B. Pippin (1984), *Bachelard: Science and Objectivity.*

badly constructed? But certainly not to sway under this most absurd alternative: 'Choose! Either a fact is real or it's fabricated!'

And yet, it became painfully clear that if we wanted to go on using the word construction we would have to fight on two fronts: against the epistemologists who went on claiming that facts were 'of course' not constructed—which had about as much sense as saying that babies are not born out of their mother's wombs—and against our 'dear colleagues' who seemed to imply that if facts were constructed then they were as weak as fetishes—or at least what they *believed* fetishists 'believed' in. At which point, it could have been safer to abandon the word 'construction' entirely—especially since the word 'social' had the same built-in defect of maddening our readers as surely as a torero's cape in front of a bull. On the other hand, it remained an excellent term for all the reasons just mentioned. Especially useful was the clear fashion in which 'construction' focused on the scene in which humans and non-humans were fused together. Since the whole idea of the new social theory we were inventing was to renew in both directions what was a social actor and what was a fact, it remained crucial not to lose sight of those most extraordinary building sites where this double metamorphosis was occurring. This is why I thought it more appropriate to do with constructivism what we had done for relativism: thrown at us like insults, both terms had a much too honorable tradition not to be reclaimed as a glorious banner. After all, those who criticized us for being relativists never noticed that the opposite would be *absolutism*.[113] And those who criticized us for being constructivists would have probably not wished to see that the opposite position, if words have any meaning, was *fundamentalism*.[114]

On the one hand, it seemed easy enough to reclaim a sturdy meaning for this much maligned term construction: we simply had to use the new definition of social that was reviewed in the earlier chapters of this book. In the same way as a Socialist or an Islamic Republic is the opposite of a Republic, adding the adjective 'social' to 'constructivism' completely perverts its meaning. In other words, 'constructivism' should not be confused with 'social constructivism'. When we say that a fact is constructed, we simply mean that we account for the solid objective reality by mobilizing various entities whose assemblage could fail; 'social constructivism' means, on the other hand, that we *replace* what this reality is made of with some *other stuff*, the social in which it is 'really' built. An account about the heterogeneous genesis of a building is substituted by another one dealing with the homogeneous

---

[113] David Bloor (1991), *Knowledge and Social Imagery*.

[114] Bruno Latour (2003a), 'The Promises of Constructivism'. I am following here in this chapter the clarifying work of Ian Hacking (1999), *The Social Construction of What?*

social matter in which it is built. To bring constructivism back to its feet, it's enough to see that once social means again association, the whole idea of a building made of social stuff vanishes. For any construction to take place, non-human entities have to play the major role and this is just what we wanted to say from the beginning with this rather innocuous word.

But obviously this rescue operation was not enough since the rest of the social sciences seemed to share a completely different notion of the same term. How could that be? Our mistake was that since we had never shared the idea that construction could mean a reduction to only one type of material, we produced antibodies against the accusation that we had reduced facts to 'mere construction' only very slowly. Since it was obvious to us that 'social construction' meant a renewed attention to the number of heterogeneous realities entering into the fabrication of some state of affairs, it took years for us to react in a balanced way to the absurd theories with which we appeared to be associated.[115] Even though constructivism was for us a synonym for an *increase* in realism, we were feted by our colleagues in social critique as having shown at last that '*even* science is bunk'! It took me a long time to realize the danger of an expression that, in the hands of our 'best friends', apparently meant some type of revenge against the solidity of scientific facts and an exposé of their claim to truth. They seemed to imply that we were doing for science what they were so proud of having done for religion, art, law, culture, and everything the rest of us believe in, namely reducing it to dust by showing it was made up. For someone who had never been trained in critical sociology, it was hard to imagine that people could use the causal explanation in their own discipline as proof that the phenomena they were accounting for didn't really exist, not to mention that they were associating the artificiality of the construction with a *deficit* in reality. Unwittingly, constructivism had become a synonym of its opposite number: deconstruction.

No wonder that our excitement in showing the 'social construction of scientific fact' was met with such fury by the actors themselves! For physicists, it is far from the same thing to settle complex controversies about black holes or to be presented instead with 'power struggles among physicists'. For a religious soul, it is far from the same thing to address God in prayer and to be said to pray only to 'the personalization

---

[115] Since, in the French tradition, constructivist and rationalist are synonymous, it was especially difficult for the French. The association of the word 'construction' with any suspicion about the reality of science crossed our 'Duhemian' (see Pierre Duhem (1904), *La Théorie Physique. Son objet sa structure*), 'Bachelardian', or 'Canguilhemian' mind only very slowly. See Georges Canguilhem (1968 [1988]), *Ideology and Rationality in the History of the Life Sciences*.

of Society'. For a lawyer, it is not the same thing to obey the Constitution or to yield to powerful lobbies hidden behind the law. For a haute couture seamstress, it is not the same to cut through thick and shiny velvet or to be said to make 'social distinction' visible. For a follower of a cult, it's not the same thing to be tied to the existence of a divinity and to be told that one adores a fetish made out of wood. The substitution of the social with other stuff seems to every actor a catastrophic loss to be adamantly resisted—and rightly so! If, however, the word social is not used to replace one kind of stuff by another, but is used instead to deploy the associations that have rendered some state of affairs solid and durable, then another social theory might become audible at last.

How could there be, we wondered, such a divide in the basic duties of social science? This is why it slowly dawned on us that there was something deeply flawed not only in the standard philosophy of science, but also in the standard social theories used to account for *other domains* than science. This is what made ANT scholars at first look either too critical—they were accused of attacking 'even' matters of facts and of not 'believing' in 'Nature' or in 'outside reality'—or much too naive—they believed in the agencies of 'real things' that were 'out there'.[116] In effect, what ANT was trying to modify was simply the use of the whole critical repertoire by abandoning *simultaneously* the use of Nature and the use of Society, which had been invented to reveal 'behind' social phenomena what was 'really taking place'. This, however, meant a complete reinterpretation of the experiment that we had conducted, at first unwittingly, when trying to account sociologically for the production of science. After all, there is a lot to be said in favor of red flags in the hands of clever toreros as they might, in the end, allow one to tame the wild beast.

The fortunate wreck of sociology of science

Let me first dispose of a mistake frequently made about our original subfield by people who are not conversant with it—and that means, I am afraid, most of the world. The field of science studies is often presented as the *extension* of the same normal sociology of the social to a new object: scientific activities. After having studied religion, class struggles, politics, law, popular cultures, drug addiction, urbanism,

---

[116] The first critique has been offered during the 'Science Wars' episode, the second can be seen in Collins and Yearley 'Epistemological Chicken'; Simon Schaffer (1991a), 'The Eighteenth Brumaire of Bruno Latour'; and Steve Woolgar (1991), 'The Turn to Technology in Social Studies of Science'.

corporate culture, etc., social scientists, so the story goes, had no reason to stop at what is the hallmark of contemporary societies: science and technology. According to this view, laboratories and research institutes were no more than the next items in a list of topics to be tackled by using the normal ingredients of social methodology that had been used elsewhere 'with so much success'. This was the almost unanimous opinion—including that of our colleagues with whom, years ago, we started our enquiries and who are called 'sociologists of scientific knowledge' (SSK) or more vaguely 'science and technology students' (S&TS).[117]

Had I to write an introduction to science studies, I would be glad to march behind such a flag.[118] But since I am trying to define ANT, I have to show how it emerged out of sociology of science by drawing extreme conclusions not only for science but also for social theory. ANT is not the branch of social science that has *succeeded* in extending its methods to scientific activity and then to the rest of society, but the branch (or rather the twig) made of those who have been thoroughly shaken when trying to give a social explanation of the hard facts of science. ANT scholars are mainly defined as those who have drawn, from the thirty odd years of sociology of science, a completely different conclusion than those of their best and closest colleagues. Whereas the later have decided that social theory works *even on science*, we have concluded that, overall and in the details, social theory has failed on science *so radically* that it's safe to postulate that it had *always failed* elsewhere as well. Social explanations cannot be 'extended' to science, thus they cannot expand anywhere else. If sociology claims to become somewhat of a science—and we do share this claim—it has to come to grasps with such an obstacle without flinching.

To check that this argument is not an empty paradox, I have to explain why we had to abandon our friends' positions—without of course abandoning either close collaboration or friendship! In effect, four conclusions had been drawn from the development of sociology of science—I can ignore the fifth position, but I wonder whether it really even exists. It supposedly concluded that science is a 'social fiction like all the other social fictions' because it is obviously no longer interested in elaborating a social science and does not grasp the first thing about fiction anyhow.[119]

---

[117] Although I have never used those labels, precisely because they maintain in existence the different domains that they have to dissolve, I have no problem in saying that ANT pertains to the fields of science, technology and society.

[118] There exist several ones. See Mario Biagioli (1999), *The Science Studies Reader*; Massimiano Bucchi (2004), *Science in Society: An Introduction to the Social Studies of Science*; and Dominique Vinck (1995), *La sociologie des sciences*.

[119] I have seen the accusation often but have never read anyone who had actually stated the argument. Disproving a non-existing position has nonetheless become

The first position is quite predictable: science studies *had to fail* completely because no social explanation of objective science can be offered; facts and theories are too hard, too technical, too real, too eternal, and too remote from human and social interest. Trying to explain science sociologically is a contradiction since, by definition, the scientific is only what has escaped from the narrow constraints of society—by which they probably mean ideology, political passions, subjective mood, and endless, empty debates. Scientific objectivity has to remain forever the rock on which all the ambitions of sociology will wreck, the stone that will always humiliate its pride. Such is the majority reaction of philosophers, epistemologists and, strangely enough, most social scientists: there can be a sociology of knowledge, of pseudo-sciences, of belief, of the superficial aspects of science— 'scientists are humans, too' says the cliché—but not of the cognitive, objective, atemporal aspects of the incontrovertible results of science.[120] *Exeunt* sociologists.

The second, less extreme conclusion can be stated in this way: in order to be respected and to succeed, sociology should stick to just those points deemed superficial by the former position. Indeed, sociology of science should limit itself to career patterns, institutions, ethics, public understanding, reward systems, legal disputes and it should propose only with great prudence to establish 'some relations' between some 'cognitive' factors and some 'social' dimensions, but without pressing the point too hard. Such is the position of a sociology of *scientists* (as opposed to a sociology of *science*) put forward, for instance, by Robert K. Merton and later Pierre Bourdieu.[121]

The third conclusion is the one drawn by most of our colleagues in science studies: in their eyes, sociologists of the former persuasion are much too timid. As to those who have predicted with glee the failure of all scientific explanations of science, they have embraced a form of pure obscurantism. They were never able to offer a reason why science itself could not be scientifically studied.[122] For scholars in SSK and

---

somewhat of a cottage industry (see the book with the apt title by Noretta Koergte (1998), *A House Built on Sand: Exposing Postmodernist Myths about Science*). As usual the confusion between relativism (anything goes) and relativity is made at a price. As Deleuze said, 'Relativism is not the relativity of truth but the truth of relation.' Gille Deleuze (1993), *The Fold: Leibnitz and the Baroque*.

[120] This default position can be found in the cleverest version in Philip Kitcher (2003), *Science, Truth, and Democracy* as well as in the superficial Paul R. Gross, Norman Levitt and Martin W. Lewis (1997), *The Flight from Science and Reason*.

[121] R.K. Merton (1973), *The Sociology of Science. Theoretical and Empirical Investigations*. The rather crepuscular book written by Bourdieu to 'explain' the difference between his sociology of scientists and science studies bears witness to this distinction. See Pierre Bourdieu (2001), *Science de la science et réflexivité*.

[122] Bloor *Knowledge and Social Imagery*; Harry M. Collins and Trevor Pinch (1982), *Frames of Meaning: the Social Construction of Extraordinary Science*.

more generally STS, cognitive and technical aspects of science, on the whole, are thoroughly studiable by sociologists. It requires invention, adaptation and precaution, but the usual tools of the trade are adequate enough—even though tricky questions of reflexivity and realism might make some people dizzy and queasy.[123] Such has become, and with good reason, the common sense of sociologists of science.

But from the very same experiment we have drawn a completely different fourth conclusion—or rather the 'we' I use in this book is defined as those who have drawn the following consequences:[124]

a) a thorough sociology of science is perfectly possible—against the philosophers of science and in agreement with the whole of science studies;

b) such a sociology cannot be limited to the superficial and social context of science—against those who wish to limit the ambitions of their discipline to the study of scientists and who voluntarily shun away from the technical and cognitive content;

c) scientific practice is too hard to be cracked by ordinary social theory and a new one has to be devised which can be used to throw a new light on 'softer' topics as well—against our colleagues in the field of science studies who chose not to see the threat to their original discipline raised by their own work.[125]

I am not claiming that this conclusion to the thrilling adventure of science studies is the only necessary and inevitable one. I am simply saying that to be called 'ANT scholars' it is necessary to transform the failure of providing a convincing social explanation of scientific hard facts into a proof. It is not that sociology of science was doomed to fail, but that social theory instead had to be redone.[126] Since there exist

[123]   See Steve Woolgar (1988), *Science The Very Idea*. Woolgar has done a remarkable job at trying to make his colleagues even dizzier, although he has always remained safely and wisely inside the strict limits given by the anthropocentric repertoire of discourse about objects of science and technology. He made sure that the gap between words and worlds became even wider, without noticing that science studies in addition to a lesson in irony could also be a lesson in realism.

[124]   I would not attempt to define the real size of this incredibly small 'we', not being sure that it extends much beyond the 62 boulevard St Michel in Paris, and even that might be limited to the ground floor! I can only pretend to be a 'representative sample' of a non-existing group.

[125]   The departure point is easy to locate in the two disputes with our SSK friends. See Collins and Yearley 'Epistemological Chicken'. See our response in Callon and Latour, 'Don't throw the Baby out with the Bath School! A reply to Collins and Yearley'; see also David Bloor (1999), 'Anti-Latour' and my response in Bruno Latour (1999b), 'For Bloor and Beyond - a Response to David Bloor's "Anti-Latour"'.

[126]   This shibboleth could nicely dispense with reading much of what passes for ANT as this social theory has been put on its head and used as an all-purpose, all-terrain 'methodology', which can be 'applied' to any field without itself undergoing any change (see the Interlude p. 141). Conversely, masses of work in the history of science and technology could count as ANT.

experimenta crucis (decisive experiments) neither in physics nor in sociology, I cannot demonstrate that this is the only way to go, but I can claim that by using this failure as a springboard—no social explanation of science is possible—a new path opens up for social theory: the social has never explained anything; the social has to be explained instead. It's the very notion of a social explanation that has to be dealt with. Our colleagues prefer to say: 'Social explanation of science has failed because it is contradictory.' Or they might say: 'It has succeeded fairly well, let's go on with business as usual.' But ANT proposes: 'It's a great opportunity now that it has failed so thoroughly since it may finally bring social theory to its senses.' In the same way as church fathers celebrated Adam's sin as a *felix culpa* (a fortunate fall from grace) because it had triggered Christ's redemption, I could say that the failure of a social explanation on science has been the great chance for social theory.

If our decision to draw those conclusions from this experiment cannot be proven, it is nonetheless far from being frivolous, as if we had made it just for the fun of it, simply *'pour épater le bourgeois'*. There is an excellent reason, retrospectively at least, why the special case of science should have wrecked social theory so completely: it was the first time that social scientists were really studying *up*.

Until laboratories, machineries, and markets were carefully scrutinized, Objectivity, Efficacy and Profitability—the three Graces of modernism—were simply taken for granted. Social scientists had fallen into the dangerous habit of studying only those activities that *differed* from those default positions: irrationality should be accounted for; rationality was never in need of any additional justification; the straight path of reason did not require any social explanation, only its crooked deviations.[127] Thus, no real test had ever been proposed to see whether a social explanation of anything actually held up or not, since rationality itself was never questioned. Even when they were tycoons, artistic geniuses, movie stars, boxing champions, or statesmen, sociologists' informants were always branded by the stigma of being less rational, less objective, less reflexive, less scientific, or less academic than those doing the study. Thus, in spite of what they often claimed, sociologists had always studied *down*, since the power of science remained on their side and was not itself scrutinized. Religion, popular culture, mythical cosmologies, markets, corporations—even works of art—were never as strong as the science of the social, which was *replacing* all those softer things by the harder stuff of some hidden

---

[127] This remains the durable contribution of David Bloor's principle of symmetry because it was the only way to break away from the stifling influence of sociology of knowledge that was limited to irrationalism.

social aggregates as well as their powers, structure, and inertia. The wheels of the *explanans* had always been forged in more solid steel than those of the *explanandum*. No wonder they easily grinded out proofs and effortlessly cranked out data.

For example, religious people never screamed in anger when they were 'socially explained'. Who would have listened to them anyway? If anything, their sobs would have been further proof that they could not stand witnessing their fanciful and archaic illusions explained by the cold glare of hard social facts. And the same would have happened if politicians, the poor, workers, farmers, and artists had whined at being 'put into a social context'. Who would have listened to the three-century long string of objections raised by tropical worshippers accused of fetishism? They might have grumbled and shrugged, but never did they bite *back* at the sociologists' proofs. So who would have checked the efficacy of social explanation? Certainly not critical sociologists, especially because their 'explanations' always fell on concerns they did not much care for. So not only did the social explanation never run into a counter case, but its acid also had no difficulty in dissolving issues for which social scientists could not care less about since, in their almost prophetic drive for emancipation, they tried to help people out of them! What event could have awaked them out of their dogmatic slumber? How about the gentle hum of laboratory air conditioning!

This is the Archimedean point social theory was looking for.... Science represented a completely different challenge and this is exactly the reason why we tackled it first—even though, for reasons of logic, I place it fourth in this book. Not only did social scientists care wholeheartedly about science, but it was also their only treasure left after the cruel disenchantment of modernism had struck down all the older ideals. Beyond objectivity, universality, and scientificity, there was nothing worth clinging to. Their only hope was to become full-fledged scientists. And yet, for the first time, social scientists had to study something that was *higher*, *harder*, and *stronger* than them. For the first time, the *explanandum* resisted and grinded the teeth of the *explanans'* cogs to mere stumps. Not only that, but the screams of those being studied could be heard loud and clear—and they were not coming from Bali, the ghettos, TV studios, corporate board rooms, or the US Senate, but from departments next door, from colleagues in the very same hiring and grant committees.

Now, at last, it was time to carry out in the social sciences the experiment which had never been carried out before: What proof do we have that a social explanation holds when we study *up*? When the reactions of those studied cannot be ignored? When the 'cultural capital' of those studied is infinitely higher than those doing the study? When the objects to be replaced by 'social force' are obviously much stronger, varied, longer lasting than this very social force that is supposed to explain them? When the truths to be explained are equally valued by those who study and by those who are studied as the only treasure on earth worth fighting for? After two centuries of easily explaining away the behavior and beliefs of farmers, the poor, fetishists, fanatics, priests, lawyers, and businessmen whose anger was rarely registered and by providing explanations that could never be compared one to one with what was explained, we were going to finally see whether or not the social could *explain* anything *else*. Chemists, rocket scientists, and physicists are used to seeing their laboratories explode, but it had been quite a while before the sociologist's office could run an experiment risky enough even to have a chance to fail! And, this time, it did explode. After a week in Roger Guillemin's laboratory thirty years ago, I remember how inescapable I found the conclusion: the social cannot be substituted for the tiniest polypeptide, the smallest rock, the most innocuous electron, the tamest baboon. Objects of science may explain the social, not the other way around. No experience was more striking than what I saw with my own eyes: the social explanation had vanished into thin air.

Naturally, many branches of social science made the same effort, especially feminist studies, queer studies, some cultural studies and most of anthropology. But is it really unfair to say that those bodies of work risked remaining peripheral, marginal, and exotic as long as they were *contrasted* with scientific objectivity, which was supposed to escape from that sort of treatment? The service provided by science studies and similar branches of social science was to remove the standard that made them by comparison marginal or simply 'special'. After science studies, every social science can study 'up'.[128]

No social explanation is necessary

The difficulty was to make sense of this experience—and this took a very long time. That scientists were sometimes angry at us was not in itself that significant. Studying up does not mean being submitted to the agenda of those we study: what some disgruntled scientists concluded from our research remains their business, not ours. As far as I can tell from the confusing episodes of what has been called the

---

[128] Such is the source of my chauvinist attachment for my beloved little subfield. From now on science, too, is 'special' instead of being that which makes all the other activities 'special'.

'Science Wars', they might have concluded that the white purity of science should never be sullied by the dark and greasy fingers of mere sociologists.[129] If they have not learned anything from their encounters with us, this is too bad for them and there is not much we can do. But even if they drew the wrong conclusion, their furor at what sociologists were so clearly missing in trying to explain their work was for me a crucial sign. No matter how misguided their reactions, it showed that whenever a social explanation was provided there was something very tricky going on. Instead of establishing some connection between two entities, it often happens that one entity is *substituted* by another one. At which point the necessary search for causality has become a wholly different enterprise dangerously close to prestidigitation.

How can this sleight of hand be done? It happens when a complex, unique, specific, varied, multiple, and original expression is replaced by a simple, banal, homogeneous, multipurpose term under the pretext that the latter may explain the former. For instance, when you try to relate the revolution in medicine introduced by Louis Pasteur to a small set of terms summarizing the French Second Empire; or when you try to account for Van Gogh's *Chambre à Arles* with a small number of all-purpose expressions having to do with artists' markets. What begins as a classical and fully respectable search for an explanation ends up by replacing the *explanandum* with the *explanans*. While other sciences keep *adding* causes to phenomena, sociology might be the only one whose 'causes' risk having the strange effect of making the phenomena they are supposed to explain vanish altogether.

Such is the interpretation I chose to give to the 'Science Wars': scientists made us realize that there was not the slightest chance that the type of social forces we use as a cause could have objective facts as their effects.[130] Not only because we lacked respect for them—in which case we could have ignored or even taken pride in debunking their pretensions[131]—but because we could not detect any *continuity* between the causalities we were putting forward and the objects to which they were attached. Thanks to the scientists knee-jerk reactions,

---

[129] See Baudoin Jurdant (1998), *Impostures intellectuelles. Les malentendus de l'affaire Sokal* and Yves Jeanneret (1998), *L'affaire Sokal ou la querelle des impostures*.

[130] I am using 'Science Wars' to designate the entire reaction of scientists to the studies made of them even though it took about twenty years between the beginning of real hard core science studies and the bitter episodes triggered by the publications of 'science warriors'.

[131] This is what has rendered making a critique so dangerous. The urge for debunking has become the best way to protect the analyst from even hearing the scream of those they misinterpret, while draping themselves in the role of courageous iconoclasts who alone 'see through' the mysteries to which ordinary people are naively attached. On this anthropology of iconoclasm, see Bruno Latour and Peter Weibel (2002), *Iconoclash: Beyond the Image Wars in Science, Religion and Art*.

which could not be ignored because they dealt with harder facts than ours and occupied an academic position dangerously close to us, we slowly came to realize—provided we wished to—that such a slick substitution might have been occurring *unnoticed* in *all* the other subfields of social sciences as well, even when we were studying down and not up. In which case, it was not only science but the *whole of social theory* that had always provided harder objects than the social forces used to explain it—fetishes, beliefs, religions, cultures, art, law, markets. Even when no actor screamed back, no alarm ringed, the social scientists' legislation seemed to run smoothly and to everyone's satisfaction, celebrating still a new success for its 'scientific method'.

ANT does not assert that all the other domains of social science are fine and that only science and technology require a special strategy because they are so much harder, so much more important, and so much more respectable. It claims that since social accounts have failed on science so pitifully, it must have failed everywhere, science being special only in the sense that its practitioners did not let sociologists pass through their turf and destroy their objects with 'social explanations' without voicing their dissent loud and clear. Elsewhere the 'informants' had always resisted but in a way that was not so noticeable because of their lower status or, when it was noticed, their furor was simply added to the data of the critical theorist as further proof that 'naive actors' cling to their pet illusions even in the face of the most blatant refutations. Scientists do not offer a special case of *recalcitrance*: we have simply rediscovered, thanks to science studies, that it should have remained the case *everywhere*, be it in the social or natural sciences.[132] As we will see later on, our job as social scientists is to generate recalcitrant hard facts and passionate objectors that *resist* social explanations. In effect, sociologists have always studied *up*.[133] Could this lead to a science of the social after so many attempts to engage sociology 'on the sure path of science' as Kant had said? This remains to be seen. What is clear at this point is that science as an activity is *part of the problem* as well as part of the solution, and that no social science is now possible without a strong-minded sociology of

[132] I would have never navigated this move without Isabelle Stengers (1997), *Power and Invention* and Stengers, *The Invention of Modern Science*. See an essay interpreting her argument in Bruno Latour (2004a), 'How to Talk about the Body? The Normative Dimension of Science Studies'.

[133] Such was Harold Garfinkel's crucial insight from the very beginning. And it is the right attitude of almost anyone else in the social sciences because in practice it's very rare that good observers can stick to their social theory. This is what makes Pierre Bourdieu (1972), *Outline of a Theory of Practice* such an insightful book. This attitude of full respect is at the heart of the Chicago School of sociology and in all the work of Howie Becker. See Howard Becker (1982), *Art Worlds*.

science at its core to remove the snake of social explanation it has nurtured up to now. So far, what passes as 'epistemology of social sciences' has simply accumulated the defects built in the traditional conceptions of epistemology and sociology.

To use this point positively, and not simply as some example of how reflexive sociologists are sawing the branch on which they are uncomfortably seated, a little more work has to be done. The discovery—I see no reason to abstain from this rather grandiose word—that giving an explanation should not be confused with substituting a phenomenon with (and not for) a social one has to be fully absorbed if we wish to continue our travels.

The difficulty resides with the word 'substitution'. I know full well that even the most positivist sociologists of the social will naturally object that they never 'really meant' that when giving a social explanation of, let's say, religious fervor, they 'literally meant' *replacing* statues, incense, tears, prayers, and pilgrimages by 'some stuff' like 'social cohesion' that would be hidden 'beneath' the clouds of smoke. They are not, they argue, that stupid. What they 'really mean' is that there must exist 'behind' the varieties of religious experience another deeper, stronger force that is 'due to society' and which explains why religious fervor holds 'in spite of the fact' that entities mobilized in prayers (gods, divinities) have no 'real existence'. Similarly, since objects of art have no intrinsic properties, the passions they trigger must come from some other source that can account for the durable interest people invest in masterpieces.

So, sociologists don't 'really mean' that a social force could be made visible 'instead of' gods and divinities or 'in addition' to works of art, only that this force is what gives them a durable existence *in the absence* of what actors say must be the solid and substantial flesh of their divinities and masterpieces. It should thus be noted that, contrary to what usually happens in natural sciences, the task of explaining starts only after a profound *suspicion* has been introduced about the very existence of the objects to be accounted for. Critical theorists would add that such a revelation of the social entity would be unbearable, since it would actually destroy the necessary illusion that makes society maintain its 'veil of false consciousness'. So, in their account, social forces play the complicated role of being simultaneously what has to be postulated to explain everything and what, for many reasons, has to remain invisible. Those contradictory requirements are very reminiscent of the 19th century ether that had to be at once infinitely rigid and infinitely elastic. No wonder: like the ether of physicists, the social of sociologists is an artifact caused by the same lack of relativity in the description.

This is a difficult spot.[134] When I begin to ask naive questions about what is really meant by social explanation, I am told not to take the existence of social forces 'literally', since no reasonable sociologists ever claimed that they could really *substitute* society for the object it explains. They would rather say that they try to give familiar causes to unfamiliar phenomena or, like the natural sciences they are so fond of, unfamiliar causes to familiar phenomena. Fine, but the difficulty comes from the double meaning of social we have already detected: behind the innocuous epistemological claim that social explanations have to be ferreted out, lies the ontological claim that those causes have to mobilize forces made *of* social stuff. For reasons that will become clearer in the second part of this book, to explain is not a mysterious cognitive feat, but a very practical world-building enterprise that consists in connecting entities with other entities, that is, in tracing a network. So, ANT cannot share the philosophy of causality used in social sciences. Every time some A is said to be related to some B, it's the social itself that is being generated. If my questioning of social explanations looks unfair, blind, and obsessively literal, it's because I don't want to confuse the assembling of the collective with the mere review of the entities already assembled or with a bundle of homogeneous social ties. It's thus essential to detect as early as possible any sleight of hand in the ways the collective is being composed. Is it unfair to say that in the hands of later day 'social explainers' allusions to the social risk becoming empty repetitions? That alluding to the rear-world of society has become even more superfluous than the promise of an afterlife?

If they don't literally replace some phenomenon by some social force, what do social explainers mean when they say that there is some force 'behind the illusory appearances' that constitutes the 'real stuff' out of which gods, arts, law, markets, psychology, and beliefs are 'really' made? What is an entity that plays the main part *without doing anything*? What sort of absence/presence is this? To me, this looks even more mysterious than the dogma of the Holy Trinity, and I am not reassured when it is *this* mystery that is supposed to explain the whole of religion, law, art, politics, economics, empires, or just plain everything—including the Holy Trinity! And I don't find it fair at this time to hedge by claiming that sociology is not philosophy anyway; that theories are moot; that good social scientists have no time to split hairs; and that they are too busy with empirical questions or that the tasks of emancipation are too pressing. If sociology

---

[134] I thank Gerard de Vries for his help in those treacherous straits. If I drown, it's not his fault.

suddenly falls back onto an anti-intellectualist stance whenever things get delicate, why does it call itself a science?

It is exactly at such a juncture that we have to choose to be literal, naive, and myopic. Refusing to understand only half is sometimes a virtue. After all, physicists got rid of the ether only when one of them was moronic enough to ask how the small handle of a clock could be 'superimposed' on the big one: everyone else knew, he chose not to.[135] With all due respect, I propose to do the same with this great mystery of the social. Everyone seems to know what it means to 'relate' religion and society, law and society, art and society, market and society, to have something at once 'behind', 'reinforced', 'invisible', and 'denied'. But I don't!

With my voluntarily narrowed mind I'd say that if social element A is said to 'cause' the existence of B, C, and D, then not only should it be able to generate back B, C, and D, but it should also account for the *differences* between B, C, and D, except if it can be shown that B, C, and D are the *same* thing, in which case their differences can be declared unimportant. If you peruse the social history literature and look at the *number of things* that are supposed to be *caused* by 'the force of society', the rise of the modern state, the ascent of the petty bourgeoisie, the reproduction of social domination, the power of industrial lobbies, the invisible hand of the market, individual interactions, then the relation might just be one where a single cause has a million effects.[136] But a cause is a cause is a cause. Is the causing element able to account *for the differences* between millions of effects—in which case can I generate B, C, and D as consequences when I hold A as a cause? Or are these differences between millions of events really immaterial—in which case sticking simply to cause A implies that I hold everything as important, minus marginal perturbations? In both cases, the A cause is indeed, for all practical purposes, *substitutable* with the millions of B, C, Ds, etc. But with the 'ascent of the petty bourgeoisie', do I really grasp what happened in England, France, and Germany from the 15th to the 20th century? With the 'automatic feedback of the invisible hand', do I really grasp the millions of market interactions throughout the whole world? When holding the law of falling bodies, do I grasp everything pertinent there is to say about the planet's interactions as

[135] See Albert Einstein (1920), *Relativity, the Special and the General Theory.* For a staging of this rematerialization, see Peter Galison (2003), *Einstein's Clocks, Poincarés's Maps.*

[136] This is just what social explainers find so convincing in their causality and what makes them so proud of their scientific achievements. It's so powerful that it can explain so much! But they should look more carefully at the ways in which natural scientists establish connections between phenomena and their causalities. It usually means that the unknown can generate not only the known, but also probe deep into the future unknown. See the telling example in Bernadette Bensaude-Vincent (1986), 'Mendeleev's periodic system of chemical elements'.

well as in the pendulum movement of my mother's old clock? Does 'society' or the 'market' contain *in potentia* what it is supposed to cause or not? 'Of course not' would respond the unanimous choir of social theorists, 'we never claimed such a stupid philosophy of causes'. But then what exact role do they really give to 'social forces'?

I am inventing of course an experiment that has never occurred because social observers never meant to test their causalities that harshly. They would easily grant that social gravitation is not like Newtonian gravitation. Forced to retreat, I guess they would say that they tried to imagine a more modest, fuzzy, and uncertain type of causality: 'some relations' and 'correlations' between different 'factors'. But this is just the place not to be fuzzy: What is precisely the relation imagined between a social factor and some other phenomenon? This is where we have to use again the crucial distinction I introduced earlier between intermediary and mediator. Is the element B, whose emergence is triggered by a factor, treated as a *mediator*, or is it construed as an *intermediary* for some force simply transported intact through the agency of the 'factor'? We have to be very practical again and as myopic as possible: we are not talking here about grandiose epistemological questions but about vehicles, movements, displacements, and transportation systems.[137] We have to be as pigheaded as possible. If some 'social factor' is *transported* through intermediaries, then everything important is *in the factor*, not in the intermediaries. For all practical purposes, it can be substituted by them without any loss of the nuances. If society explains religion, then society is enough. If society explains law, then society is enough. If society explains science, then...

At this point, everything falls apart. Why? Because in this case, *and only in this one*, from the start it has been obvious to the enquirers as well as to the informants that 'factors' are unable to transport any action through any event reduced to the status of intermediary. Yes, Einstein had a turbulent youth and called his theory 'revolutionary' and 'relativist', but that does not lead you all the way *through* his use of Maxwell's equations, only *in their vicinity*;[138] yes, Pasteur was somewhat reactionary and adored the Empress Eugenie but that does not carry you very far through his bacteriology, even though 'it might not be unrelated' to his rejection, for instance, of spontaneous generation.[139]

---

[137] This obstinacy will pay itself back at the very end of this book when we will render possible the encounters with the beings that make action possible, encounters that have been so far delayed by the ill-timed assemblage of the collective in the form of a society—see p. 232.

[138] A classical example of such an explanation is offered in Lewis S. Feuer (1974), *Einstein and the Generations of Science*.

[139] See the typical case presented in John Farley and Gerald L. Geison (1974), 'Science, Politics and Spontaneous generation in 19th-century France: the Pasteur-Pouchet Debate' and Gerald G. Geison (1995), *The Private Science of Louis Pasteur*.

When they have to transport social explanations to the sanctuary of science, factors have an unfortunate tendency to run out of gas! Naturally, this had always been true for the transportation of all the other entities to the various sanctuaries of law, religion, technology, markets, and subjectivities. But before science studies, it was never noticed how quickly they came to a full stop. The experiment that never took place in social theory about what is really meant by a social explanation of anything has been going on in our little field every day when papers are written about the history and sociology of the natural sciences. This is what has made science studies such a perfect crucible for the whole of sociology: finally, thanks to the attempts at socially explaining hard scientific facts, we are going to know what they all had meant before by 'social'. Here is the place for the decisive big jump: *Hic Rhodus, hic salta.*

Translation vs. transportation

We have now reached the very birthplace of what has been called 'actor-network-theory' or, more accurately, 'sociology of translation'—unfortunately the label never held in English. As I said, ANT is simply the realization that something unusual had happened in the history and sociology of scientific hard facts, something so unusual that social theory could no more go through it than a camel through the eye of a needle.

The Rubicon was crossed, for me at least, when successive connections were accepted of three former non-social objects (microbes, scallops, and reefs) that insisted on occupying the strange position of being *associated* with the former social entities we were trying to describe.[140] Either they were rejected out of social theory because they did not look social enough, or they were welcomed into it. But then the very concept of social had to be deeply altered. This second solution was the defining moment of what was later called ANT.

For instance, fishermen, oceanographers, satellites, and scallops might have some *relations* with one another, relations of such a sort that they *make* others do unexpected things—this is the definition of a mediator, as we have now seen several times. Is there one element in this concatenation that can be designated as 'social'? No. Neither the functioning of satellites nor the life habits of scallops would be

---

[140] See Bruno Latour (1984), *Les microbes, guerre et paix, suivi de Irréductions*; John Law (1986b), 'On the Methods of Long-Distance Control Vessels Navigation and the Portuguese Route to India'; and of course the now mythical paper on scallops Michel Callon (1986), 'Some elements of a sociology of translation domestication of the scallops and the fishermen of St Brieux Bay' that I here summarize in this section.

clarified in any way by *adding something social* to the description. The social of sociologists thus appears exactly as it always was, namely a superfluity, a purely redundant rear-world adding nothing to the real world except artificial conundrums—just like the ether before relativity theory helped physicists to re-describe dynamics. Stage one: the social has vanished.

On the other hand, is there anything in the chain deployed that could be said to be *non social*, in the sense of pertaining to a world apart from associations, for instance a 'material objective' one, a 'subjective symbolic' one, or a realm of 'pure thoughts'? No. Scallops *make* the fisherman *do* things just as nets placed in the ocean lure the scallops into attaching themselves to the nets and just as data collectors bring together fishermen and scallops in oceanography. From the first three uncertainties, we have learned that studying their relations might be empirically difficult but is no longer a priori forbidden by the 'obvious objections' that 'things don't talk', 'fish nets have no passion', and 'only humans have intentions'. Social is *nowhere* in particular as a thing among other things but may circulate *everywhere* as a movement connecting non-social things. Stage two: social is back as association.

We don't know yet how all those actors are connected, but we can state as the new default position before the study starts that all the actors we are going to deploy might be *associated* in such a way that they *make others do things*. This is done not by transporting a force that would remain the *same* throughout as some sort of faithful intermediary, but by generating *transformations* manifested by the many unexpected *events* triggered in the other mediators that *follow* them along the line. This is what I dubbed the 'principle of irreduction' and such is the philosophical meaning of ANT: a concatenation of mediators does not trace the same connections and does not require the same type of explanations as a retinue of intermediaries transporting a cause.

When science studies writers set out to account for Einstein's relativity, Pasteur's bacteriology, Kelvin's thermodynamics, and so on, they have to draw connections between entities that are completely different from what before was considered to be a string of social explanations. Those writers state that a factor is an *actor* in a *concatenation* of actors instead of a *cause* followed by a *string* of intermediaries. As soon as they do that, to their great surprise, the practical details of the case at hand seem to provide some explanation of the context that was supposed to explain it. Suddenly, it's Pasteur's own bacteria that appears to explain, through the new tracer of infectious diseases, a large part of what it meant, during the Second Empire in France, to be 'socially connected': contagious and uncontaminated people didn't establish the same solidarity as, say, the rich and the poor. The direction of causality between what is to be explained and what provides an explanation is not simply reversed, but thoroughly subverted: the contagion redraws the social maps. The British Empire is not only 'behind' Lord Kelvin's telegraph experiments, it is also given a reach, a faster reaction time, a durability it will never have without the tiny cables laid out on the ocean. Kelvin's science creates, in part, the Empire, which is no longer in the background manipulating him unwittingly but made to exist by telegraph wires that are turned into full-blown mediators.[141] It is this reversal in causality that ANT tried to register first for science and technology and then for every other topic.[142] This is where it got the strange idea that the social was to be explained instead of providing the explanation. We all began to wonder: if we were good enough at describing so many mediators, we would realize that there is no need anymore for a society that lies 'behind'.[143]

As I have said in the introduction, to use the word social for such a process is legitimated by the oldest etymology of the word *socius*: 'someone following someone else', a 'follower', an 'associate'. To designate this thing which is neither one actor among many nor a force behind all the actors transported through some of them but a connection that transports, so to speak, transformations, we use the word *translation*—the tricky word 'network' being defined in the next chapter as what is *traced* by those translations in the scholars' accounts.[144] So, the word 'translation' now takes on a somewhat specialized meaning: a relation that does not transport causality but induces two mediators into coexisting. If some causality appears to be transported in a predictable and routine way, then it's the proof that other mediators have been put in place to render such a displacement smooth and predictable (see Part II). I can now state the aim of this sociology of associations more precisely: there is no society, no social realm, and no social ties, *but there exist translations between mediators that may generate traceable associations.* Through this book, we will hopefully learn to widen the gap between an account that makes use of the social as traditionally construed and this other one that purports to deploy

[141] See Crosbie Smith and Norton Wise (1989), *Energy and Empire: A Biographical Study of Lord Kelvin* and Brian Cantwell Smith (2003), 'The Devil in the Digital Details. Digital Abstraction and Concrete Reality'.
[142] Once again, everyone else in history, anthropology, art history, and business history had been doing the same all along. See the stunning example in Carlo Ginzburg (1980), *The Cheese and the Worms: The Cosmos of a 16th-Century Miller* for the way to respect the metaphysics of a miller. See Alfred D. Chandler (1977), *The Visible Hand: The Managerial Revolution in American Business* for an account of the growth of companies that does not presuppose scale.
[143] Had we known Gabriel Tarde earlier, we would have saved a lot of effort or at least would not have had to indulge in the rather silly posture that we had invented a brand new social theory.
[144] Callon refers explicitly to Michel Serres (1974), *La Traduction (Hermès III)*.

strings of mediators. To learn ANT is nothing more than to become sensitive to the differences in the literary, scientific, moral, political, and empirical dimensions of the two types of accounts.

There is more to experience than meets the eye

What may appear really shocking in such a definition of association is not only the strange new meaning it gives to 'social' but also the unusual place offered to so-called 'natural' objects. And yet both ends of these chains, the social and the natural, have to be dissolved simultaneously. This symmetry is rarely understood by those who define ANT as a sociology 'extended to non-humans'—as if non-humans themselves had not undergone a transformation as great as those of the social actors. And yet, if both are not put aside at the same time, it is in vain that we will do our fieldwork: whatever new connections we will have traced, some agencies will take up the label 'social' and others the label 'natural', and the incommensurability between the two will render invisible the drawing of what we mean by social connections. How they are *associated* will be lost for good: scallops will sink back into the deep ocean of natural, material, objective, and unintentional matters of fact, while fishermen will assemble in the shabby hut at the entrance of which is written, as in the bad old days of Apartheid, 'for intentional humans only'. Meantime, sociologists will come back from the field empty-handed, all their data spoiled by a division that contradicts the very practice they tried to account for: fish and fishermen do not face one another like 'natural' and 'social', 'object' and 'subject', 'material' and 'symbolic'—and oceanographers even less. Social theory does not have to be confused with Kantism.

To make this possible, we have to free the matters of fact from their reduction by 'Nature' exactly as much as we should liberate objects and things from their 'explanation' by society. Without this double move, our argument is nothing more than a return to classical materialism that closely resembles a 'sociology of engineers' complete with its 'technical determinism'. The problem is that if it's already difficult to show that the social is an artifact produced by the application of an ill-adapted notion of causality, it is even trickier to show that 'Nature', conceived as the gathering of all non-social matters of fact, should be dispensed with as well. And the utterly puzzled reactions to ANT over the years is proof enough that this is quite tricky and that the chances of success are indeed slim.

Durkheim against pragmatism
No one offers a more striking proof of the close link between the definition of society and the theory of science than Durkheim when he set himself the task of criticizing pragmatism, then a novel philosophy. This is how he opened his first 1914 class:

'We are currently witnessing an attack on reason which is truly militant and determined. Consequently the problem is of threefold importance.
1) In the first place, it is of general importance. Pragmatism is in a better position than any other doctrine to make us see the need for a reform of traditional rationalism, for it shows us what is lacking in it.
2) Next, it is of national importance. Our whole French culture is basically and essentially a rationalist one. The 18th century is a prolongation of Cartesianism. A total negation of rationalism would thus constitute a danger, for it would overthrow our whole national culture. If we had to accept the form of irrationalism represented by pragmatism, the whole French mind would have to be radically changed.
3) Lastly, it is of philosophical importance. Not only our culture, but the entire philosophical tradition, right from the very beginnings of philosophical speculation is inspired by rationalism. If pragmatism were valid, we should have to embark upon a complete reversal of this whole tradition.' (Durkheim 1955)

So this is where the fourth source of uncertainty can help us. If we accept to learn also from the controversies about non-humans, we soon realize that matters of fact do not describe what sort of agencies are populating the world any better than the words 'social', 'symbolic', and 'discursive' describe what is a human actor and the *aliens* overtaking it. This is no wonder since 'Society' and 'Nature' do not describe domains of reality, but are two *collectors* that were invented together, largely for polemical reasons, in the 17th century.[145] Empiricism, conceived as a clear-cut distinction between sensory impressions on the one hand and mental judgment on the other, cannot certainly claim

---

[145] On this long history I can only refer the reader to Steven Shapin and Simon Schaffer (1985), *Leviathan and the Air-Pump: Hobbes, Boyle and the Experimental Life*. The link between sociology and modernization is so strong that it's impossible to disentangle one from the other. See Ulrick Beck, Anthony Giddens and Scott Lash (1994), *Reflexive Modernization: Politics, Tradition and Aesthetics in the Modern Social Order*; Zygmunt Bauman (1997), *Postmodernity and its Discontents*; and Bruno Karsenti (1997), *L'Homme total: Sociologie, anthropologie et philosophie chez Marcel Mauss*.

to be a complete description of what 'we should be attentive to in experience'.[146]

To pursue our project we don't have to tackle these difficult philosophical questions. We just need to be open-minded about the shape in which former objects of nature might present themselves in the new associations we are following. To our great surprise, once the artificial boundary between social and natural was removed, non-human entities were able to appear under an unexpected guise. For instance, rocks might be useful to knock an idealist back to his senses, but rocks *in geology* seemed to be much more varied, much more uncertain, much more open, and deploy many more types of agencies than the narrow role given to them in empiricist accounts.[147] Steel desks offer a great opportunity for angry realists to thump the table in the name of 'material constraints' so as to bring sociologists back to reality, but laminated steel *in metallurgy* offers so many conundrums on the ways material resistance may occur that there is almost no relation between what positivist philosophers and material scientists call 'matter'.[148] The inflexible drive of genetic make-up may be great for socio-biologists to ridicule the socialist dream of nurturing a better humanity, but genes *in biogenetics* take so many contradictory roles, obey so many opposite signals, are 'made up' of so many influences that if there is one thing that cannot be done with them it is to silence an adversary.[149] Computers might offer an advertisement for the best example of hype, but chips *in computer science* require vast institutions in order to live up to their reputation as 'formal machines'.[150] Everywhere, the empirical multiplicity of former 'natural' agencies overflows the narrow boundary of matters of fact. There exists no direct relation between being real and being indisputable.

Empiricism no longer appears as the solid bedrock on which to build everything else, but as a very poor rendering of experience. This poverty, however, is not overcome by moving *away* from material experience, for instance to the 'rich human subjectivity', but *closer* to the

---

[146] This is Whitehead's expression. See William James (1890), *The Principles of Psychology*, John Dewey (1930 reprinted in 1948 complete works 1982), *Reconstruction in Philosophy*, and Stengers *Penser avec Whitehead*. That empiricism has never been simply about matters of fact is marvellously shown in Lorraine Daston (1988), 'The Factual Sensibility: an Essay Review on Artifact and Experiment' and Jessica Riskin (2002), *Science in the Age of Sensibility: The Sentimental Empiricists of The French Enlightenment.*

[147] See the chapter on rocks in Hacking, *The Social Construction of What?*

[148] See Pablo Jensen (2001), *Entrer en matière: Les atomes expliquent-ils le monde?*

[149] See Evelyn Fox-Keller (2000), *The Century of the Gene*; Sophie Houdart (2000), 'Et le scientifique tint le monde: Ethnologie d'un laboratoire japonais de génétique du comportement'; and Richard Lewontin (2000), *The Triple Helix: Gene, Organism and Environment.*

[150] Brian Cantwell Smith (1997), *On the Origins of Objects.*

much variegated lives materials have to offer.[151] It's not true that one should fight reductionism by adding some human, symbolic, subjective, or social 'aspect' to the description since reductionism, to begin with, does not render justice to objective facts. What could be called the first empiricism managed, for political reasons, to obscure the many tours and detours of objectivity and to reduce non-humans to shadows. Far from 'owning objectivity', positivists are more like absentee landowners who don't seem to know what to do with their properties. It just happens that we, in science studies, might know.

The great chance of ANT is that objectivity's many folds become visible as soon as one moves a bit *closer* to where agencies are made to express themselves, namely scientific laboratories—or where laboratories are brought into more intimate contact with daily life, which is quite often nowadays. Positivists were not very inspired when they chose 'facts' as their elementary building blocks to build their cathedral of certainty. They acted as if it was the most primitive, solid, incontrovertible, undisputable material, as if all the rest could be reduced to it. But there was more than one straw in the solid matter they chose as their foundation.[152] The etymology itself should have made them shudder: How could a fact be that solid if it is also fabricated? As the shortest inquiry in the most primitive laboratory shows, and as Ludwik Fleck proved long ago, facts are about the least primitive, the most complex, the most elaborated, and the most collective makeup there is![153]

Fleck on Wasserman's reaction to detect syphilis
In his pioneering book, the founder of sociology of science elaborates a much finer description of the 'genesis' of scientific fact that is usually recognized by those who read it through a Kantian or a Kuhnian lens:[154]

'To give an accurate historical account of a scientific discipline is impossible. It is as if we wanted to record in writing the natural course of an excited conversation among several persons all speaking simultaneously among themselves and each clamoring to make himself heard, yet which nevertheless permitted a consensus to crystallize.' (Fleck 1981: 15)

---

[151] The unlikely case of sugar beets has helped François Mélard to provide one of the best applications of what happens to society when things are brought in. See François Mélard (2001) 'L'autorité des instruments dans la production du lien social: le cas de l'analyse polarimétrique dans l'industrie sucrière belge'.

[152] Durkheim had not much chance either when he proposed to treat 'social facts as things', since what is social, what is a fact, and what is a thing are probably the three most controversial, uncertain, and shaky concepts of philosophy!

[153] See Ludwig Fleck (1981) *Genesis and Development of a Scientific Fact* and Ludwik Fleck, Robert S. Cohen and Thomas Schnelle (1986) *Cognition and Fact: Materials on Ludwik Fleck*.

[154] The metaphor of lens or presupposition is actually the one used by Kuhn in his foreword to Fleck's book.

But his definition of social is clearly positive and non negative, that is, the more social there is, the more realism there is:

'Every epistemological theory is trivial that does not take this sociological dependence of all cognition into account in a fundamental and detailed manner. But those who consider social dependence a necessary evil and unfortunate human inadequacy which ought to be overcome fail to realize that without social conditioning no cognition is even possible. Indeed, the very word "cognition" acquires meaning only in connection with a thought collective.' (Fleck 1981: 43)

This is what makes him at odds with sociologists like Durkheim:

'All these thinkers trained in sociology and classics, however, no matter how productive their ideas, commit a characteristic error. They exhibit an excessive respect, bordering on pious reverence for scientific facts'. (Fleck 1981: 47)

But the ambiguous notion of 'thought collective' is in no way akin to traditionally conceived social influence:

'If we define "thought collective" as a *community of persons mutually exchanging ideas or maintaining cultural interaction, we will find by implication that it also provides the special "carrier" for the historical development of any field of thought, as well as for the given stock of knowledge and level of culture. This we have designated thought style.* The thought collective thus supplies the missing component'. (Fleck 1981: 39)

Thought collective is not what conditions or limits the fact production, but what allows it to emerge:

'This is how a fact arises. At first there is a signal of resistance in the chaotic initial thinking, then a definite thought constraint, and finally a form to be directly perceived. A fact always occurs in the context of the history of thought and is always the result of a definite thought style'. (Fleck 1981: 95)

This realist attitude toward the social allows Fleck to shift from the notion of collective practice to that of the event:

'We can summarize as follows our theory of the recognition of the relation between the Wassermann reaction and syphilis. The discovery—or the invention—of the Wasserman reaction occurred during a unique historical process, which can be neither reproduced by experiment nor confirmed by logic. The reaction was worked out, in spite of many errors, through socio-psychological motives and a kind of collective experience. *From this point of view the relation between the Wassermann reaction and syphilis-an undoubted fact-becomes an event in the history of thought'*. (Fleck 1981: 97)

The notion of event becomes the way to overcome the symmetric limits of sociologists and epistemologists:

'Truth is not "relative" and certainly not "subjective" in the popular sense of the word. It is always, or almost always, completely determined within a thought style. One can never say that the same thought is true for

> A and false for B. If A and B belong to the same thought collective, the thought will be either true or false for both. But if they belong to different thought collectives, it will just *not* be the *same* thought! It must either be unclear to, or be understood differently by, one of them. Truth is not a convention but rather (1) in historical perspective, an event in the history of thought, (2) in its contemporary context, stylized thought constraint'. (Fleck 1981: 100)

ANT is not interested only in freeing human actors from the prison of the social but in offering natural objects an occasion to escape the narrow cell given to matters of fact by the first empiricism.[155] This is what I have always found so refreshing in science studies: until its development, the conversation between philosophers, sociologists, and political scientists about the right divide between 'Nature' and 'Society' had always been illustrated by boring, routine, millenary old matters of fact such as stones, rugs, mugs, and hammers that were basically things Neanderthals could have been using already. Those objects are perfectly respectable but, as we saw in the preceding chapter, they no longer leave a trace, and thus there is no way they could appear again as mediators.[156]

The discussion begins to shift for good when one introduces not matters of fact, but what I now call *matters of concern*. While highly uncertain and loudly disputed, these real, objective, atypical and, above all, *interesting* agencies are taken not exactly as object but rather as *gatherings*.[157] You cannot do with Monte Carlo calculations what you do with mugs; you cannot do with genetically modified organisms what you do with mats; you cannot do with quaternions what you do with black swans.[158] This is exactly what the fourth uncertainty wishes to thrive from: the mapping of scientific controversies about matters of concern should allow us to renew from top to bottom the very scene of empiricism—and hence the divide between 'natural' and 'social'. A natural world made up of matters of fact does not look quite the same as a world consisting of matters of concern and thus cannot be

---

[155] Latour, *Politics of Nature*, Chapter 2.

[156] Except of course in the expert hands of archaeologists and ethnographers. See Pierre Lemonnier, *Technological Choices*.

[157] Martin Heidegger (1977), *The Question Concerning Technology and Other Essays*. On the rereading of this argument, see Graham Harman (2002), *Tool-Being: Heidegger and the Metaphysics of Objects*.

[158] See Peter Galison (1997), *Image and Logic: A Material Culture of Microphysics* and Pickering *The Mangle of Practice*.

used so easily as a foil for the 'symbolic-human-intentional' social order. This is why what could be referred to as the *second* empiricism doesn't look at all like the first: its science, its politics, its esthetics, its morality are all different from the past. It is still real and objective, but it is livelier, more talkative, active, pluralistic, and more mediated than the other.

There is, however, nothing radical or revolutionary in going from the first to the second empiricism. The shift from one world to the other did not require great ingenuity, courage, and originality from ANT scholars. Scientists and engineers in their laboratories were every day making the production of facts *more* visible, *more* risky, *more* costly, *more* debatable, *more* interesting, and *more* publicly relevant as even a cursory look at any technical magazine easily showed. Matters of fact may remain silent, they may allow themselves to be simply kicked and thumped at, but we are not going to run out of data about matters of concern as their *traces* are now found everywhere. If there is something disheartening for sociologists of associations, it is not the deep silence of a mute 'Nature' that would render their enquiries impossible and force them to stick to the 'symbolic' human realm, but the sheer flood of information on the many modes in which matters of concern exist in the contemporary world. How could we be up to the task and do justice to such a rising mass of evidence?

A list to help deploy matters of concern

The solution, once again, is to learn how to feed off uncertainties, instead of deciding in advance what the furniture of the world should look like. The inquiry can go on as long as we learn how to take the poison out of the concept of nature in the same way we did for the twin concept of society. In 'society' we learned to distinguish the associations—which we kept—from a substance made of social stuff—which we rejected. Similarly, in 'nature' we are going to keep the deployment of reality and reject its premature unification into matters of fact. If it was a mistake to jump from the idea of association to the conclusion that they are phenomena made of social *stuff*, it's a symmetric error to conclude from an interest in non-humans that they will look like matters of facts—which are nothing more than a dumbed-down version of matters of concern as any reading in science studies will show.

For instance, spermatozoids used to be obstinate little machos swimming forcefully toward the powerless ovule; they are now attracted, enrolled, and seduced by an egg the agency of which is becoming so subtle now that it can select the good sperm from the bad—or at least this is what is now *disputed* in developmental physiology.[159] Genes were supposed to transport information coding for the proteins, but they are also considered as competing with one another for food, thus ruining the information transfer metaphor—or at least this is what is now *disputed* among some geneticists.[160] Chimpanzees were supposed to be nice sociable partners offering the image of a good savage paradise but now look fiercely competitive, prone to assassination and to devious Machiavellian plots—or at least this is what is *disputed* in primatology.[161] Topsoil was supposed to be a compact set of inert matter arranged in layers of different colors that soil scientists learned how to map; it now swarms with such a great number of micro organisms that only microzoologists can explain this miniaturized jungle—or at least this is what is *disputed* among some pedologists.[162] Computers were supposed to be stupid digital machines but now appear to be achieving digitality through a bewildering set of material analog signals bearing no relation with formal calculations—or at least this is what is *disputed* among some theorists of computing.[163]

Such a multiplicity does not mean that scientists don't know what they are doing and that everything is just fiction, but rather that science studies has been able to pry apart exactly what the ready-made notion of 'natural objective matters of fact' had conflated too fast, namely reality, unity, and indisputability.[164] When you look for the first, you do not get automatically the two others. And this has nothing to do with the 'interpretive flexibility' allowed by 'multiple points of views' taken on the 'same' thing. *It is the thing itself that has been allowed to be deployed as multiple* and thus allowed to be grasped through different viewpoints, before being possibly unified in some later stage depending on the abilities of the collective to unify them.[165] There are simply more agencies in the *pluriverse*, to use William James's expression, than philosophers and scientists thought possible.

The important ethical, scientific, and political point here is that when we shift from the world of matters of fact to the *worlds* of matters of concern, we can no longer be satisfied either by the *indifference* to

---

[159] See the chapter in Shirley Strum and Linda Fedigan (2000), *Primate Encounters* by Tang-Martinez, Z. 'Paradigms and Primates: Bateman's Principles, Passive Females, and Prospectives from Other Taxa. pp. 260–274.

[160] See Jean-Jacques Kupiec and Pierre Sonigo (2000), *Ni Dieu ni gène*.

[161] See Frans De Waal (1982), *Chimpanzee Politics: Power and Sex Among Apes*.

[162] See Alain Ruellan and Mireille Dosso (1993), *Regards sur le sol*.

[163] See Adam Lowe and Simon Schaffer (1999), *N01se*.

[164] This is the decisive lesson I draw from Marc Berg and Anne-Marie Mol (1998), *Differences in Medicine: Unraveling Practices, Techniques and Bodies* and Mol, *The Body Multiple*.

[165] This is also the dividing line between postmodernism, which believes that its task is to add multiplicity to a world overly unified by 'master Narratives', and ANT which feels that multiplicity is a property of things, not of humans interpreting things.

reality that goes with multiple 'symbolic' representations of the 'same' nature or with the *premature unification* provided by 'nature'. By including the many results of the sciences into the zoos of agencies at work together in the world, we have crossed another Rubicon, the one leading from *metaphysics* to *ontology*.[166] If traditional social theory was against delving into the first, it is even more hesitant to sink into the second, which reminds it too much of its own philosophical infancy. And yet, if we wish to travel, we have to learn how to swim these turbulent waters.

To go from metaphysics to ontology is to raise again the question of what the *real* world is *really* like. As long as we remain in metaphysics, there is always the danger that deployment of the actors' worlds will remain *too easy* because they could be taken as so many *representations* of what the world, in the singular, is like. In which case we would not have moved an inch and would be back at square one of social explanation—namely back to Kant's idealism.

The danger cannot be exaggerated when we consider that the open-mindedness shown, for instance, by anthropologists about the 'other's' cosmologies is often due to their certainty that those representations have no serious relation to the solid world of matters of fact. In the scholar's tolerance for wild beliefs, a great deal of condescension might seep through. There may be thousands of ways of imagining how kinships bring children into existence, but there is only, it is argued, *one* developmental physiology to explain how babies really grow in the womb. There may be thousands of ways to design a bridge and to decorate its surface, but only one way for gravity to exert its forces. The first *multiplicity* is the domain of social scientists; the second *unity* is the purview of natural scientists. Cultural relativism is made possible only by the solid absolutism of the natural sciences. Such is the default position of the endless debates going on, for instance, between physical and human geography, physical and cultural anthropology, biological psychiatry and psychoanalysis, material and social archaeology, and so on. There is unity and objectivity on one side, multiplicity and symbolic reality on the other.

This is just the solution that ANT wishes to render untenable. With such a divide between one reality and many interpretations, the continuity and commensurability of what we call the associations would immediately disappear, since the multiple will run its troubled historical course while the unified reality will remain intact, untouched, and remote from any human history. But it's not the case that shifting

---

[166] I made no pretence to follow standard definitions, given the long and variable history of those words. In what follows, 'ontology' is the same thing as 'metaphysics', to which the question of truth and unification have been added.

from social to natural objects means shifting from a bewildering multiplicity to a welcoming unity. We have to shift, yes, but from an impoverished repertoire of intermediaries to a highly complex and highly controversial set of mediators. Controversies over ontologies turn out to be just as interesting and controversial as metaphysics, except that *the question of truth* (of what the world is really like) *cannot be ignored* with a blasé pose or *simplified* a priori by thumping on desks and kicking at stones.[167] Even once reality has fully set in, the question of its unity is still pending. The common world has still to be collected and composed. As we shall see at the end of this book, this is where the social sciences may regain the political relevance that they seem to have lost by abandoning the ether of the social and the automated use of the critical repertoire that it allowed. There is no rear-world behind to be used as a judge of this one, but in this lowly world there lie in wait many more worlds that may aspire to become one—or not, depending on the assembly work we will be able to achieve.

Fortunately, we don't have to solve those arduous questions all at once in order to do our work as sociologists. We don't even have to deploy the complete set of agencies manifested by matters of concern. We simply have to make sure that their diversity is not prematurely closed by one *hegemonic* version of one kind of matter of fact claiming to be what is present in experience—and that goes, of course, for 'power' and 'Society' as well as for 'matter' and 'Nature'. Once again, the key training for practicing ANT is negative at first.

A to-do list will help us maintain the empirical grasp needed as the considerable difficulties of this theory might force us to lose our way.

First, the great advantage of following scientific facts is that as the name indicates they are fabricated, they exist in many different shapes and at very different stages of completion. While all these differences were shamelessly hidden when they were used as the 'elementary building blocks' of 'the world' in the singular, they provide massive amounts of information as soon as they are brought back into their 'factories', namely their laboratories and research institutes. Science studies now offers many devices to follow facts in the making and to multiply the sites where they have not yet become cold, routine matters of fact.

Second, those sites are no longer limited to laboratories. This is the great virtue of contemporary science and technology. It has extended itself so much, in so many settings, in ever closer intimacy with daily life and ordinary concerns, that it is hard to follow a course of action

---

[167] I maintain the plural for ontologies to remind the reader that this unity is not the result of what the world is like at first encounter, but what the world might become provided it's collected and assembled.

anywhere in industrial societies without bumping into one of their outcomes. The more science and technology extend, the more they render social ties physically *traceable*. A material infrastructure provides everyday more proof of a precise follow up of associations, as any look at the World Wide Web turned World Wide Lab shows.

Third, experiments and the controversies they generate provide a sort of continuous site to check what metaphysics and ontology could mean practically for scientists at work. The very organization of science—through grant application, large scale experiments, congresses, publications, controversies, consensus conferences—offers to the analyst a continuous source of information on how to raise the question of ontology. It is in the scientific institutions that we may find the *easiest* access to understand what it means to increase the range of agencies, to explore alternative theories of actions, without abandoning the quest for reality. Scientific practice is the drosophila of social theory since it offers an exaggerated and scaled up version of what can later be studied in much more inaccessible domains. Once you learn how to respect shifting ontologies, you can tackle more difficult entities for which the question of reality has been simply squeezed out of existence by the weight of social explanations.[168] Compared to other domains, science is easier because the debates about the detours of objectivity are much more traceable.

Fourth, without any help from sociologists of science, the very difference between matters of fact and matters of concern has been made publicly visible by the growing intensity of controversies over 'natural things'. The difference between reality and unity becomes palpable when courts have to decide on expert knowledge, when heads of state have to make decisions about natural phenomena, when consensus conferences are brought together to stabilize some geopolitical controversy, when scientists are criticizing their peers in the press for not having followed adequate protocols, when public discussions are going on about the fate of the Gulf Stream, etc. While before you had to go back and forth between reality and fiction as if it was the only road worth taking, it is now possible to distinguish the procedures allowing for realities—now in the plural—and those leading to stability and unity.[169] To maximize the fabulous power of their etymology, objects have now become *things* again: the disputed topic of a virtual assembly.[170]

---

[168] A useful case of this is offered by a study of religion that takes the Catholic God as an instance of actor-network. See Albert Piette (1999), *La religion de près: L'activité religieuse en train de se faire*.

[169] See Callon, Lascoumes and Barthe, *Agir dans un monde incertain*.

[170] See Latour and Weibel, *Making Things Public*.

As should now be clear, what has limited inquiries so far is not the lack of traces nor the inherent technical difficulties of the task, but the conceptual obstacles rendering them a priori impossible. Even though these obstacles look formidable since they deal with the two main defects of social science—the concept of 'social' and the concept of 'science' —they might be no more than paper tigers once the fourth source of uncertainty has been added to the three others. What is sure is that the empirical domain that is opened is so vast, so rewarding, so varied that it is already hard to remember that it had been forbidden for so long to social scientists. If the third source of uncertainty allowed sociologists to catch up with 'anatomically modern humans', whose existence has been shared with artifacts for hundreds of thousands of years, it might be time, using the fourth, to catch up with a world made of matters of concern.

When we list the qualities of an ANT account, we will make sure that when agencies are introduced they are never presented simply as matters of fact but always as matters of concern, with their mode of fabrication and their stabilizing mechanisms clearly visible. In addition, we will be especially attentive to counteract the deconstruction mood by making sure that multiplicity is not associated with 'interpretive flexibility' or with a weakening of the empirical grasp. Finally, we will be attentive to the procedures through which the multiplicity of reality—metaphysics—can be distinguished from its progressive unification—ontology.

Alas, if it takes just a few hours to get rid of the obstacles of the sociology of the social (the time needed to read the previous chapters), then the harder part is before us. Just when conceptual obstacles have been removed, the real hurdles become visible: how to *write an account* that could live up to the prospects of the sociology of associations. That is the new difficulty—and hopefully the last one—we now have to tackle before starting our travels.

Fifth Source of Uncertainty: Writing Down Risky Accounts

This introduction to ANT begins to look like another instance of Zeno's paradox, as if every segment was split up by a host of mediators each claiming to be taken into account. 'We will never get there! How can we absorb so many controversies?' Having reached this point, the temptation is great to quit in despair and to fall back on more reasonable social theories that would prove their stolid common sense by ignoring most of the sources of uncertainty I have reviewed. We could swallow one, maybe two, but not four in a row. Unfortunately, I have not found a way to speed things up: *this* type of science for *that* type of social should be as slow as the multiplicity of objections and objects it has to register in its path; it should be as costly as it is necessary to establish connections among the many mediators it finds swarming at every step; and it should be as reflexive, articulated, and idiosyncratic as the actors cooperating in its elaboration. It has to be able to register differences, to absorb multiplicity, to be remade for each new case at hand. This is why the four sources of uncertainty have to be tackled courageously all at once, each adding its set of differences to the others. If one is missing, the whole project falls apart.

But I confess the difficulty: Is it not counterproductive in the end to abandon the convenient shorthand of social explanations, to split hairs indefinitely about what is or is not a group, to trick intermediaries into behaving as mediators, to register the queerest idiosyncrasies of the humblest actors, to set up long lists of objects participating in action, and to drop the background made of solid matters of fact for the foreground of shifty matters of concern? How ridiculous is it to claim that inquirers should 'follow the actors themselves', when the actors to be followed swarm in all directions like a bee's nest disturbed by a wayward child? Which actor should be chosen? Which one should be followed and for how long? And if each actor is made of another bee's nest swarming in all directions and it goes on indefinitely, then when the hell are we supposed to stop? If there is something especially stupid, it is a method that prides itself in being so meticulous, so radical, so all encompassing, and so object-oriented as to be totally impractical. This is not a sociology any more but a *slow*ciology! Zen masters can puzzle over the many conundrums of their austere discipline, but not the writer of a sociology treatise. Either she proposes a project that is affordable and manageable or we sue her for disinformation.

We write texts, we don't look through some window pane

Fortunately, there is a solution out of these many difficulties and, like all the solutions I have given so far, it is a very practical one: only by sticking obstinately to our decision to feed off uncertainties can we eventually get back on our feet. If we want to have a chance to mop up all the controversies already mentioned, we have to add a fifth and last source of uncertainty, namely one *about the study itself*. The idea is simply to bring into the foreground the very making of reports. As the reader should have understood by now, the solution to relativism is always more relativity. All things being equal, we should do for our study what Einstein did when he decided to tackle—instead of the sublime questions of ether—the apparently moronic and mundane questions of how anyone equipped with a rod and a clock could catch any signal from someone else equipped with a rod and a clock. What is requested from us is not the impossible task of jumping, in one *salto mortale*, from our mental representation to the four former sources of uncertainty, but to ask the simple question: What do we do when we trace social connections? Are we not, in effect, writing down accounts?

What is an account?[171] It is typically a *text*, a small ream of paper a few millimeters thick that is darkened by a laser beam. It may contain 10,000 words and be read by very few people, often only a dozen or a few hundred if we are really fortunate. A 50,000 word thesis might be read by half a dozen people (if you are lucky, even your PhD advisor

---

[171] This is where ANT crosses the resources of ethnomethodology—including the key notion of 'accountability'—with those of semiotics. Strangely enough, for all his attention to practice Garfinkel never points out the practice of writing—which might go some way toward explaining his style! After years of teaching in England and America, I have been forced to recognize that semiotics does not survive sea travels. Attention to text *qua* text remains a continental obsession.

would have read parts of it!) and when I say 'read', it does not mean 'understood', 'put to use', 'acknowledged', but rather 'perused', 'glanced at', 'alluded to', 'quoted', 'shelved somewhere in a pile'. At best, we add an account to all those which are simultaneously launched in the domain we have been studying. Of course, this study is never complete. We start in the middle of things, *in medias res*, pressed by our colleagues, pushed by fellowships, starved for money, strangled by deadlines. And most of the things we have been studying, we have ignored or misunderstood. Action had already started; it will continue when we will no longer be around. What we are doing in the field—conducting interviews, passing out question-naires, taking notes and pictures, shooting films, leafing through the documentation, clumsily loafing around—is unclear to the people with whom we have shared no more than a fleeting moment. What the clients (research centers, state agencies, company boards, NGOs) who have sent us there expect from us remains cloaked in mystery, so circuitous was the road that led to the choice of this investigator, this topic, this method, this site. Even when we are in the midst of things, with our eyes and ears on the lookout, we miss most of what has happened. We are told the day after that crucial events have taken place, just next door, just a minute before, just when we had left exhausted with our tape recorder mute because of some battery failure. Even if we work diligently, things don't get better because, after a few months, we are sunk in a flood of data, reports, transcripts, tables, statistics, and articles. How does one make sense of this mess as it piles up on our desks and fills countless disks with data? Sadly, it often *remains* to be written and is usually delayed. It rots there as advisors, sponsors, and clients are shouting at you and lovers, spouses, and kids are angry at you while you rummage about in this dark sludge of data to bring light to the world. And when you begin to write in earnest, finally pleased with yourself, you have to sacrifice vast amounts of data that cannot fit in the small number of pages allotted to you. How frustrating this whole business of studying is.

And yet, is this not the way of all flesh? No matter how grandiose the perspective, no matter how scientific the outlook, no matter how tough the requirements, no matter how astute the advisor, the result of the inquiry—in 99% of the cases—will be a report prepared under immense duress on a topic requested by some colleagues for reasons that will remain for the most part unexplained.[172] And that is excellent because *there is no better way.* Methodological treatises might

---

[172] I use report as a generic term. It might be an article, a file, a website, a poster, a PowerPoint presentation, a performance, an oral exam, a documentary film, an artistic installation.

dream of another world: a book on ANT, written by ants for other ants, has no other aim than to help dig tiny galleries in this dusty and earthly one.

Bringing the writing of reports into the foreground might irritate those who claim to know what the social is made of. They would much prefer to be like 'hard' scientists and try to understand the existence of a given phenomenon, refusing to consider the written account and relying instead on direct contact with the thing at hand via the transparent medium of a clear and unambiguous technical idiom. But we, who have been trained in science studies, don't need to ignore the thickness of any given text, its pitfalls, its dangers, its awful way to make you say things you don't want to say, its opacity, its resistance, its mutability, its tropism. We know too well that, even in 'hard' sciences, authors clumsily try to write texts about difficult matters of concern. There is no plausible reason why our texts would be more transparent and unmediated than the reports coming out of their laboratories.[173] Since we are all aware that fabrication and artificiality are not the opposite of truth and objectivity, we have no hesitation in highlighting the text itself as a mediator. But for this very same reason, we don't have to abandon the traditional goal of reaching objectivity simply because we consider with great care the heavy textual machinery. Our texts, like those of our fellow scientists, run the parallel course of being artificial *and* accurate: all the more accurate *because* they are artificial. But our texts, like those of our fellow scientists, run the risk of being *simply* artificial, that is full of artifacts. The difference is not between those who know for certain and those who write texts, between 'scientific' and 'literary' minds, between '*esprit de géométrie*' and '*esprit de finesse*', but between those who write *bad* texts and those who write *good* ones.[174] One must put forth the following questions: What is a good laboratory and what is a good textual account? The latter question, far from being belated and irrelevant, becomes central to the definition of what is for us a science of the social. To put it in the most provocative way: good sociology has to be well written; if not, the social doesn't appear through it.

The question is not whether to place objective texts in opposition to subjective ones. There are texts that pretend to be objective because they claim to imitate what they believe to be the secret of the natural

[173] See Françoise Bastide (2001), *Una notte con Saturno: Scritti semiotici sul discorso scientifico* for a collection of essays. For work in English, see Françoise Bastide (1990), 'The Iconography of Scientific Texts: Principle of Analysis'; F. Bastide, M. Callon and J.P. Courtial (1989), 'The Use Of Review Articles In The Analysis Of A Research Area', Françoise Bastide and Greg Myers (1992), 'A Night With Saturne'.

[174] In an otherwise fascinating book on the writing of history, Carlo Ginzburg (1999), *History, Rhetoric, and Proof* is still trying to reconcile the two opposites of rhetoric and reference without realizing this other crucial difference.

sciences; and there are those that try to be objective because they track objects which are given a chance to *object* to what is said about them. It's because ANT claims to renew what it means to be a science and what it means to be social, that it has also to renew what it is an *objective* account. The word does not refer to the traditional sense of matters of fact—with their cold, disinterested claims to 'objectifica-tion'—but to the warm, interested, controversial building sites of matters of concern. Objectivity can thus be obtained either by an objectivist style—even though no object is there to be seen—or by the presence of many *objectors*—even though there is no pretence for parodying the objectivist genre.

It's thus a fair question to ask why the literature of social science is often so badly written. There are two reasons for this: first, scholars strive to imitate the sloppy writings of hard scientists; second, because *contrary to the latter*, they do not convoke in their reports actors recal-citrant enough to interfere with the bad writing.

No matter how illiterate they pretend to be, natural scientists will be forced to take into account at least some of the many quirks of their recalcitrant objects. On the other hand, it seems that only sociologists of the social—especially critical sociologists—can manage to effi-ciently muffle their informants' precise vocabulary into their own all-purpose meta-language. Even though natural scientists take great pains to be as boring as possible, matters of concern inundate scientific writings in such a way as to make physics, biology, and natural history papers the most fascinating of operas—as literary students of science have shown so forcefully.[175] But social scientists too often succeed, at great cost, in being boring for good! This might be the only real difference between the 'hard' and the 'soft' sciences: you can never stifle the voice of non-humans but you can do it to humans. People have to be treated much more delicately than objects because their many objections are harder to register. Whereas subjects easily behave like matters of fact, material objects never do.[176] This is why the question of what is a good account is so much more crucial for the social than for the natural sciences. To introduce the words 'textual account' into a discourse on method might be like dynamite, but not because it blows apart the claims of scientists to objectivity. Rather, it destroys forever sociologists' entitlement to sloppy writing under the pretext that they have to write 'like' scientists. Because science stu-dents had many occasions to probe the slow emergence of objectivity

---

[175] A scholarly association, 'Science and Literature', is now devoted in part to this task. See their journal *Configurations*.

[176] This is all the less surprising since matters of fact are a political invention, a sort of ideal citizenship invented in the 17th century to convoke the assembly of nature. Humans may comply with this political role but why would non-humans?

in scientific writings, they were delivered from the burden of trying to wear the false attires of the objectivist prose.[177] Because they were not living under the shadow of a borrowed objectivity, they could explore other ways to make the object resist in their textual accounts.

Foregoing the word 'textual' in textual accounts remains dangerous however because, for people unaware of science studies and of semiotics, texts are often construed as 'stories' or, even worse, as 'just stories'. Against such a blasé attitude, I will be using the expression 'textual account' to mean a text for which the question of its accuracy and truthfulness has *not* been put aside.[178] And yet the temptation to confuse the two is all the greater because there are scholars—if this honorable word can be applied to them—who claim that the social sciences generate 'only' narratives, and they sometimes add: 'just like fiction'.[179] Like footballers scoring a goal against their own team, sophisticated humanists have begun to use the words 'narratives' and 'discourses' as a way to say that there are no truthful scriptures. As if the absence of an absolute Text meant that all the texts were relative. Of course, all those who are ready to denigrate the social sciences have applauded in agreement since that is just what they have been saying all along: 'Sociologists are mere storytellers. It's about time some of them confess it at last.' If it is one thing to say that social sciences produce written accounts—every science on earth does the same and this is why they all end with the –logy or –graphy suffixes—it's quite another to conclude from this trite that we can only write *fiction* stories.

First, such an appreciation betrays a remarkable ignorance of the hard work of fiction writers. Those in anthropology, sociology, cultural studies—who pride themselves on 'writing fictional narratives'—should be inspired in being at least as disciplined, as enslaved by reality, as obsessed by textual quality, as good writers can be. They don't realize that if social science was 'fiction anyway', it would have

---

[177] This will be probably taken as another instance of my science studies chauvinism, but a characteristic of our subfield is that it is remarkably free of jargon.

[178] I am perfectly happy with the resonance of the word not only with Garfinkel's accountability but also with 'accounting books', since the weak but essential link of accounting with economics has been one of the most productive, and unlikely, domains of science studies. See Alain Desrosières (2002), *The Politics of Large Numbers: A History of Statistical Reasoning* and Michael Power (1995), *Accounting and Science: Natural Inquiry and Commercial Reason*. For an even more surprising case, see Quattrone 'Accounting for God'.

[179] Those reviewed in Lindsay Waters (2004), *Enemies of Promise: Publishing, Perishing, and the Eclipse of Scholarship* have often taken their cues from France, without realizing that the French steeped in Bachelard and Canguilhem never for a moment believed that they were extending their arguments to science. In France, you can be at once naively rationalist and a great admirer of deconstruction. Once transported across the Atlantic, this innocent passion became a dangerous binary weapon.

to submit to an ordeal that would be even more discriminating than what they imagine to be those of experimental science. You can object by asking 'What is a good writer?' But I will answer: 'What is a good scientist?' There is no general answer to these two questions.

But more importantly, an account which accepts to be 'just a story' is an account that has lost its main source of uncertainty: it does not fret any longer at being accurate, faithful, interesting, or objective. It has forsaken the project of translating the four sources of uncertainty that we have reviewed so far. And yet, no social scientist can call oneself a *scientist* and abandon the *risk* of writing *a true and complete* report about the topic at hand. It's not because you become attentive to the writing that you have to shed the quest for truth. Conversely, it's not because a text is bland and boring, that it is accurate. Too often, social scientists believe that an 'objective style', by which they usually mean a few grammatical tricks like the passive form, the royal 'we', and lots of footnotes, will miraculously disguise the absence of objects. The thick sauce of 'objective style' cannot hide for long the lack of meat. But if you have the meat, you may add an extra condiment or dispense with it.

Textual accounts are the social scientist's laboratory and if laboratory practice is any guide, it's *because* of the artificial nature of the place that objectivity might be achieved on conditions that artifacts be detected by a continuous and obsessive attention. So, to treat a report of social science as a textual account is not a weakening of its claims to reality, but an extension of the number of precautions that have to be taken onboard and of the skills requested from the enquirers. As it should be clear by now, rendering the production of objectivity *more* difficult is the name of the game. There is no reason why sociologists of association should abandon that constraint when they abandon the sociology of the social and when they add to the discussion a fifth source of uncertainty, this one generated by the writing of their own studies. In fact, it is quite the opposite. If the social is something that circulates in a certain way, and not a world beyond to be accessed by the disinterested gaze of some ultra-lucid scientist, then it may be *passed along* by many devices adapted to the task—*including* texts, reports, accounts, and tracers. It may or *it may not*. Textual accounts can fail like experiments often do.[180]

By contrast, it seems that too often sociologists of the social are simply trying to 'fix a world on paper' as if this activity was never in risk of failing. If that is the case, there is no way they can succeed, since

---

[180] The same epistemologists who have fallen in love with Popper's falsifiability principle would be well advised to prolong his insight all the way to the text itself and to render explicit the conditions under which their writing can fail as well.

the world they wish to capture remains invisible because the mediating constraints of writing are either ignored or denied. No matter what pains they have taken to be accurate during the course of their inquiries, their textual account has been missed. Sociologists of association try an experiment altogether different: Can the materiality of a report on paper, a story, or rather a fiction—there is no need to abstain from a word that is so close to the fabrication of facts—*extend* the exploration of the social connections a little bit *further*? The careers of mediators should be pursued all the way to the final report because a chain is only as weak as its weakest link. If the social is a trace, then it can be *re*traced; if it's an assembly then it can be *re*assembled. While there exists no material continuity between the society of the sociologist and any textual account—hence the wringing of hands about method, truth, and political relevance—there might exist a plausible *continuity* between what the social, in our sense of the word, does and what a text may achieve—a *good* text, that is.

Defining at last what a network is

But what is a good text? We are not concerned here by good style because no matter how well we learn to write, we will always remain, alas, mere social scientists and we will never be able to do more than emulate from far away the skills of writers, poets, playwrights, and novelists. For this reason, we need a less sophisticated shibboleth. Surprisingly, it's the search for just such a touchstone that will help us define at last the most confusing of the words used in our alternative social theory. I would define a good account as one that *traces a network*.

I mean by this word a string of actions where each participant is treated as a full-blown mediator. To put it very simply: A good ANT account is a narrative or a description or a proposition where all the actors *do something* and don't just sit there. Instead of simply transporting effects without transforming them, each of the points in the text may become a bifurcation, an event, or the origin of a new translation. As soon as actors are treated not as intermediaries but as mediators, they render the movement of the social visible to the reader. Thus, through many textual inventions, the social may become again a circulating entity that is no longer composed of the stale assemblage of what passed earlier as being part of society.[181] A text,

---

[181] This is referred to as 'objects of value'. See usage in Greimas's study of Maupassant, Algirdas Julien Greimas (1988), *Maupassant: The Semiotics of Text. Practical Exercises.*

in our definition of social science, is thus a test on how many actors the writer is able to treat as mediators and how far he or she is able to achieve the social.

Thus, the network does not designate a thing out there that would have roughly the shape of interconnected points, much like a telephone, a freeway, or a sewage 'network'. It is nothing more than *an indicator of the quality of a text* about the topics at hand.[182] It qualifies its objectivity, that is, the ability of each actor to *make* other actors *do* unexpected things. A good text elicits networks of actors when it allows the writer to trace a set of relations defined as so many translations.

A terminological precision about network

The word network is so ambiguous that we should have abandoned it long ago. And yet the tradition in which we use it remains distinct in spite of its possible confusion with two other lines. One is of course the technical networks—electricity, trains, sewages, internet, and so on. The second one is used, in sociology of organization, to introduce a difference between organizations, markets, and states (Boyer 2004). In this case, network represents one informal way of associating together human agents (Granovetter 1985).

When (Castells 2000) uses the term, the two meanings merge since network becomes a privileged mode of organization thanks to the very extension of information technology. It's also in this sense that Boltanski and Chiapello (2005) take it to define a new trend in the capitalist mode of production.

But the other tradition, to which we have always referred, is that of Diderot especially in his *Le rêve de d'Alembert* (1769), which includes twenty-seven instances of the word *réseaux*. This is where you can find a very special brand of active and distributed materialism of which Deleuze, through Bergson, is the most recent representative.[183] Here is one example:

'This one should satisfy you for today. There was a woman who had just given birth to a child; as a result, she suffered a most alarming attack of the vapors—compulsive tears and laughter, a sense of suffocation, convulsions, swelling of the breasts, melancholy silence, piercing shrieks—all the most serious symptoms—and this went on for several years. Now this woman was passionately in love, and eventually she began to think she saw signs indicating that her lover had grown wary of her illness and complaints

---

[182] In that sense it is the equivalent of the ethnomethodologists' notion of 'unique adequacy', provided the notion of account has been enriched by that of *textual* account.

[183] On Diderot's network philosophy of nature, see Wilda Anderson (1990), *Diderot's Dream*.

and was beginning to break off their affair. That was when she decided that she must either get well or make an end of herself. In this way there began a sort of civil war inside her own consciousness. Sometimes this war would turn to the advantage of the master; sometimes the subjects would get the upper hand. Whenever the two sides were equal, so that the force exerted by the fibers exactly counterbalanced that of the center of the bundle [*S'il arrivait que l'action des filets du réseau fût égale à la réaction de leur origine*], she would fall to the ground as though dead. Then, when carried to her bed, she would lie for hours on end, entirely motionless and almost lifeless. On other occasions the effect would be only one of general lassitude or exhaustion or loss of consciousness from which it often seemed she would never recover. For six months she kept up the struggle. Whenever the rebellion began in her fibers she was able to feel it coming on. She would stand up, run about, busy herself with the most vigorous forms of physical exercise, climb up and down stairs, saw wood or shovel dirt. She would make the center of her network, the organ of will power, as rigid as possible by saying to herself: You must conquer or die.' (Diderot 1964)

It's clear from this quote that *réseau* has nothing to do with the social as normally construed, nor is it limited to human ties. But it's certainly close to Tarde's definition of 'society' and 'imitative rays' (Karsenti 2002).

So how can we define by contrast a bad textual account? In a bad text only a handful of actors will be designated as the causes of all the others, which will have no other function than to serve as a backdrop or relay for the flows of causal efficacy. They may go through the gestures to keep busy as characters, but they will be without a part in the plot, meaning they will not act. Nothing is translated from one to the other since action is simply carried through them. Remember that if an actor makes no difference, it's not an actor. The report has not been produced in an ad hoc fashion to be *uniquely adequate* to the description of specific actors and for the eyes of specific readers.[184] It is standard, anonymous, across the board; nothing happens in it. There are just repeat clichés of what has been assembled before as the social past. It has watered down translations into mere displacements without transformation. It simply transports causalities through mere intermediaries.

This is where the literary contrast between ANT and sociology of the social—and even more so with critical sociology—is the greatest. What is often called a powerful and convincing account, because it is made

---

[184] To say that it's an actor-network is to say that it's specific and that the principles of its expansion are rendered visible and the price for its deployment fully paid.

of a few global causes generating a mass of effects, ANT will take as a weak and powerless account that simply repeats and tries to transport an already composed social force without reopening what it is made of and without finding the extra vehicles necessary to extend it further. Masses of social agents might have been invoked in the text, but since the principle of their assembly remains unknown and the cost of their expansion has not been paid, it's as if nothing was happening. No matter what their figuration is, they don't do very much. Since the reassembling of new aggregates has not been rendered traceable through the text, *it's as if the social world had not been made to exist.* Although the common definition of the social seems to be everywhere in full view, *our* definition of what is social has failed to appear. Conversely, when our definition of the social is retraced, the common definition of the social has to vanish first. It's hard to see a more extreme contrast: it is either a society or a network.

So, network is an expression to check how much energy, movement, and specificity our own reports are able to capture. Network is a concept, not a thing out there. It is a tool to help describe something, not what is being described. It has the same relationship with the topic at hand as a perspective grid to a traditional single point perspective painting: drawn first, the lines might allow one to project a three-dimensional object onto a flat piece of linen; but they are not *what* is to be painted, only what has allowed the painter to give the impression of depth before they are erased. In the same way, a network is not what is represented in the text, but what readies the text to take the relay of actors as mediators. The consequence is that you can provide an actor-network account of topics which have in no way the shape of a network—a symphony, a piece of legislation, a rock from the moon, an engraving. Conversely, you may well write about technical networks—television, e-mails, satellites, salesforce—without at any point providing an actor-network account.

But is it not somewhat disingenuous to retain the tricky word network to describe such a benchmark of literary quality? I agree that it does not resemble other words I have used up to now like group, actor, actant, group, fluid, and non-human, which are chosen voluntarily because of their benighted meaninglessness. This one, on the contrary, has too many meanings! The confusion took place—it is our fault entirely—because some of the earlier objects described by ANT were networks in the technical sense—metrology, subways, telephones— and also because when this term was introduced twenty-five years ago, the Internet had not struck—nor had al-Qaida for that matter. So, network was a novelty that could help in eliciting a contrast with

'Society', 'institution', 'culture', 'fields', etc. which were often conceived as surfaces, floods of causal transfers, and real matters of
fact. But nowadays, networks have become the rule and surfaces the
exception. It has lost its sharp edge.[185] If I believed in jargon and if
worknet or *action net* had any chance to hold, I would offer it as a
substitute so as to make the contrast between technical networks and
worknets, the latter remaining a way for social scientists to make sense
of the former.[186] *Work*-nets could allow one to see the labor that goes
on in laying down *net*-works: the first as an active mediator, the second
as a stabilized set of intermediaries.

Whatever the word, we need something to designate flows of translations. Why not use the word network, since it is now there and
solidly attached by a little hyphen to the word actor that I redefined
earlier? There exists no good word anyway, only sensible usage; in
addition, the original material metaphor still retains the three important features I wish to induce with this expression:

a) a point-to-point connection is being established which is physically
traceable and thus can be recorded empirically;
b) such a connection leaves *empty* most of what is *not* connected, as
any fisherman knows when throwing his net in the sea;[187]
c) this connection is not made for free, it requires effort as any fisherman knows when repairing it on the deck.

To make it fit our purposes, we have to add a fourth feature that,
I agree, breaks down the original metaphor somewhat: a network
is not made of nylon thread, words or any durable substance but
is the trace left behind by some moving agent. You can hang your
fish nets to dry, but you can't hang an actor-network: it has to be
traced anew by the passage of another vehicle, another circulating
entity.

The weakness of the notion derives partly from the dissemination of
rather simple-minded visual representations. At first, the graph representation of networks, seen as star-like embranchments out of which
lines leave to connect other points that have nothing but new
connections, provided a rough but faithful equivalent to those

---

[185] As Boltanski and Chiapello's, *The New Spirit of Capitalism* has shown, it can even be
used to characterize what is worst in the recent metamorphosis of capitalist modes of
production.
[186] Action net, as proposed in Barbara Czarniawska (2004), 'On Time, Space, and
Action Nets'.
[187] This point will become even more essential when, at the end of Part II, we will deal
with the notion of 'plasma'. Emptiness is the key in following the rare conduits in which
the social circulates.

associations.[188] It had the advantage of defining specificity not by any substantial content, but by a list of associations: the more connected, the more individualized a point was. But those visual graphs have the drawback of not capturing movements and of being visually poor. Yet even those limits have their advantage since the very poverty of graphical representation allows the inquirer not to confuse his or her infra-language with the rich objects that are being depicted: the map is not the territory. At least there is no risk of believing that the world itself is made of points and lines, while social scientists too often seem to believe that the world is made of social groups, societies, cultures, rules, or whatever graphic displays they have devised to make sense of their data.

In order to trace an actor-network, what we have to do is to add to the many traces left by the social fluid another medium, the textual accounts, through which the traces are rendered again present, provided something happens in it. In an actor-network account the relative proportion of mediators to intermediaries is increased. I will call such a description a *risky* account, meaning that it can easily fail—it does fail most of the time—since it *can put aside neither the complete artificiality of the enterprise nor its claim to accuracy and truthfulness.* As to its relevance for the actors themselves and the political impact it might have, this is even less automatic—as we shall see in the Conclusion. The whole question is to see whether the *event* of the social can be extended all the way to the *event* of the reading through the medium of the text. This is the price to pay for objectivity, or rather '*objectfullness*' to be achieved.

Back to basics: a list of notebooks

The best way to proceed at this point and to feed off this fifth source of uncertainty is simply to keep track of all our moves, even those that deal with the very production of the account. This is neither for the sake of epistemic reflexivity nor for some narcissist indulgence into one's own work, but because from now on *everything is data*: everything from the first telephone call to a prospective interviewee, the first appointment with the advisor, the first corrections made by a

---

[188] This was shown in the early Leximappe tools in Michel Callon, John Law and Arie Rip (1986), *Mapping the Dynamics of Science and Technology.* However, there are now many more graphic devices that have been developed. See Alberto Cambrosio, Peter Keating and Andrei Mogoutov (2004), 'Mapping Collaborative Work and Innovation in Biomedicine'. Viewed as representation it is naive, but viewed as theory it's a formidable help to abstraction. See their early use in Geneviève Teil (1991), 'Candide®, un outil de sociologie assistée par ordinateur pour l'analyse quantitative de gros corpus de textes'.

client on a grant proposal, the first launching of a search engine, the first list of boxes to tick in a questionnaire. In keeping with the logic of our interest in textual reports and accounting, it might be useful to list the different notebooks one should keep—manual or digital, it no longer matters much.[189]

The first notebook should be reserved as a *log* of the enquiry itself. This is the only way to document the transformation one undergoes by doing the travel. Appointments, reactions to the study by others, surprises to the strangeness of the field, and so on, should be documented as regularly as possible. Without it, the artificial experiment of going into the field, of encountering a new state of affairs, will be quickly lost. Even years after, it should remain possible to know how the study was conceived, which person was met, what source was accessed, and so on, at a precise date and time.

A second notebook should be kept for gathering information in such a way that it is possible simultaneously to keep all the items in a chronological order *and* to dispatch them into categories which will evolve later into more and more refined files and subfiles. There exists lots of software nowadays that maintain this contradictory specification, but older hands like me have benefited enormously from the tedious rewriting of data onto cards. Whatever the solution, the movement through one frame of reference to the next is greatly facilitated if the data set can be kept at once unspoiled while still being reshuffled in as many arrangements as possible. This is the only way to become as pliable and articulate as the subject matter to be tackled.

A third notebook should be always at hand for *ad libitum* writing trials. The unique adequacy one should strive for in deploying complex imbroglios cannot be obtained without continuous sketches and drafts. It is impossible to imagine that one would gather the data for a period of time and only then begin to write it down. Writing a report is too risky to fall into this divide between enquiring and reporting. What comes spontaneously out of the keyboard are generalities, clichés, transportable definitions, substitutable accounts, ideal-types, powerful explanations, abstractions, in brief, the stuff out of which more social genres write themselves effortlessly. To counteract this trend, many efforts have to be made to break the automatic writing up; it's not easier to write textual accounts as it is in a laboratory to discover the right experimental design. But ideas, paragraphs, metaphors, and tropes might come haphazardly during the course of the study. If they are not allowed to find a place and an outlet, they will either be lost or, worse yet, will spoil the hard work of data collecting

---

[189] I am using notebooks rather metaphorically since they now include digital files as well as films, interviews, and websites.

by mixing the meta-language of the actors with that of the analysts. So it is always good practice to reserve a separate space for the many ideas that may spring to mind even if they will only be used years later.

A fourth type of notebook should be carefully kept to register the effects of the written account on the actors whose world has been either deployed or unified. This second experiment, added to the fieldwork itself, is essential to check how an account plays its role of assembling the social. The study might be finished, but the experiment goes on: the new account adds its performative action to all the others, and that too produces data. It does not mean that those who have been studied have the right to censor what has been written about them, nor does it mean that the analyst has the incredible right of ignoring what his 'informants' say about the invisible forces that make them act. Rather, it means that a new negotiation begins to decide what are the ingredients out of which the one common world might be made—or not.[190] Since the relevance of a risky account might occur much later, the trails left in its wake also have to be documented.

It might be disappointing for the reader to realize that the grand questions of group formation, agency, metaphysics, and ontology that I have reviewed so far have to be tackled with no more grandiose resources than tiny notebooks to be kept during the fully artificial procedure of fieldwork and enquiries. But I warned the reader in advance: there is nothing more rewarding to be had and there is no faster way. After all, Archimedes was in need of nothing more than a fixed point to raise the world. Einstein equipped his observers with only a rod and a stopwatch: Why would we require heavier equipment to creep through the dark tiny conduits traced by blind ants? If you don't want to take notes and to write them down well, don't try to get into sociology: it's the only way there is to become slightly more objective. If those textual accounts are said to be not 'scientific enough', I will retort that although they might not look scientific in the clichéd definition of the adjective, they might be according to the only definition that interests me here: they try to grasp some recalcitrant objects through some artificial device with utmost accuracy, even though this enterprise may very well come up empty. If only a fraction of the energy devoted in social sciences to the commentary of our eminent predecessors was converted into fieldwork! As Garfinkel has taught us: it's practice all the way down.

---

[190] Witness the length of time it took from the long experiment of science studies of the first publications to the Science Wars. And yet, as I have shown in the previous chapter, without a careful documentation the experiment of science studies would have been wasted.

Deployment not critique

To add in a messy way to a messy account of a messy world does not seem like a very grandiose activity. But we are not after grandeur: the goal is to produce a science of the social uniquely suited to the specificity of the social in the same way that all other sciences had to invent devious and artificial ways to be true to the specific phenomena on which they wished to get a handle on. If the social circulates and is visible only when it shines through the concatenations of mediators, then this is what has to be replicated, cultivated, elicited, and expressed by our textual accounts. The task is to *deploy* actors *as* networks of mediations—hence the hyphen in the composite word 'actor-network'. Deployment is not the same as 'mere description', nor is it the same as 'unveiling', 'behind' the actors' backs, the 'social forces at work'. If anything, it looks more like a PCR amplification of some small DNA sample.[191]

And what is so wrong with 'mere descriptions'?[192] A good text is never an unmediated portrait of what it describes—nor for that matter is a portrait.[193] It is always part of an artificial experiment to replicate and emphasize the traces generated by trials in which actors become mediators or mediators are turned into faithful intermediaries. There is nothing less natural than to go into fieldwork and remain a fly on the wall, pass out questionnaires, draw maps, dig up archives, record interviews, play the role of a participant-observer, compile statistics, and 'Google' one's way around the Internet. De-scribing, inscribing, narrating, and writing final reports are as unnatural, complex, and painstaking as dissecting fruit flies or sending a telescope into space. If you find Faraday's experiments oddly artificial, what about Pitt-Rivers's ethnographic expeditions? If you believe Lord Kelvin's laboratory contrived, what about Marx compiling footnotes in the British Library, Freud asking people to free-associate on his Viennese couch, or Howard Becker learning how to play jazz in order to take notes on jazz playing? The simple act of recording anything on paper is already an immense transformation that requires as much skill and just as much artifice as painting a landscape or setting up some elaborate biochemical reaction. No scholar should find humiliating the task of

---

[191] See Law, *After Method*, p. 112. See also the beautiful term 'enactement' used by Mol and 'choreography' in Charis Cussins (1996), 'Ontological Choreography: Agency through Objectification in Infertility Clinics'.

[192] The useful notion of 'thick description' provides a welcome attention to details but not necessarily to style. 'Thickness' should also designate: 'Have I assembled enough?' It should give the word 'assembling' a political meaning, something we will come across in the Conclusion.

[193] See Joseph Leo Koerner (1997), *The Moment of Self-Portraiture in German Renaissance Art.*

sticking to description. This is, on the contrary, the highest and rarest achievement.

However, we worry that by sticking to description there may be something missing, since we have not 'added to it' something else that is often call an 'explanation'. And yet the opposition between description and explanation is another of these false dichotomies that should be put to rest—especially when it is 'social explanations' that are to be wheeled out of their retirement home. Either the networks that make possible a state of affairs are fully deployed—and then adding an explanation will be superfluous—or we 'add an explanation' stating that some other actor or factor should be taken into account, so that it is the *description* that should be *extended* one step further. If a description remains in need of an explanation, it means that it is a bad description. There is an exception, however, if it refers to a fairly stable state of affairs where some actors do indeed play the role of fully determined—and thus of fully 'explained' intermediaries—but in this case we are back to simpler pre-relativist cases. This new diffidence for an explanation 'added' to a description is all the more important because it is usually when a 'frame' is called in that the sociology of the social insinuates its redundant cause. As soon as a site is placed 'into a framework', everything becomes rational much too fast and explanations begin to flow much too freely. The danger is all the greater because this is the moment most often chosen by critical sociology, always lurking in the background, to take over social explanations and replace the objects to be accounted for with irrelevant, all-purpose 'social forces' actors that are too dumb to see or can't stand to be revealed. Much like 'safe sex', sticking to description protects against the transmission of explanations.

Here again, it is the attempt at imitating a false view of the natural sciences that bogs down the social ones: it is always felt that description is too particular, too idiosyncratic, too localized. But, contrary to the scholastic proverb, there is science only of the particular.[194] If connections are established between sites, it should be done through *more* descriptions, not by suddenly taking a free ride through all-terrain entities like Society, Capitalism, Empire, Norms, Individualism, Fields, and so on. A good text should trigger in a good reader this reaction: 'Please, more details, I want more details.' God is in the details, and so is everything else—including the Devil. It's the very character of the social to be specific. The name of the game is not reduction, but irreduction. As Gabriel Tarde never tired of saying: 'To exist is to differ.'

---

[194] Monographs in social science is one of the contributions of Tarde. See Tarde, *Social Laws*, p. 92. In Tarde's general view of societies, human societies are typical because of the small number of agents they mobilize, contrary to biology or physics that deal with millions or billions of elements. So being particular is what encountering the social is all about.

To deploy simply means that through the report concluding the enquiry the number of actors might be increased; the range of agencies making the actors act might be expanded; the number of objects active in stabilizing groups and agencies might be multiplied; and the controversies about matters of concern might be mapped. Only those who have never tried to write about mediators instead of intermediaries will say that this is an easy task, something akin to 'mere description'. For us, on the contrary, it requires exactly as much invention as a laboratory experiment for every new case at hand—and success is just as rare. If we succeed, which is not automatic and is not obtained simply by putting 'PhD' at the bottom of one's signature, a good account will *perform* the social in the precise sense that some of the participants in the action—through the controversial agency of the author—will be *assembled* in such a way that they can be *collected* together. It does not sound like much, and yet it is far from being totally negligible.

The problem is that social scientists too often alternate between *hubris*—each of them dream to be the Newton of social science as well as the Lenin of social change—or desperation—they despise themselves for merely piling on more reports, stories, and statistics that no one will read. But the choice between complete mastery and total irrelevance is a very superficial one. To despair of one's own written text doesn't make any more sense than for the head of a chemistry laboratory to want to be relevant to the NIH. Relevance, like everything else, is an achievement. A report is interesting or not depending on the amount of work done to interest, that is, to place it between other things.[195] This is exactly what the five uncertainties added together might help to reveal: What is the social made up of? What is acting when we are acting? What sort of grouping do we pertain to? What do we want? What sort of world are we ready to share? All those questions are raised not only by scholars, but also by those they study. It is not that we, social scientists, know the answer that would reside behind the actors, nor is it the case that they, the famous 'actors themselves', know the answer. The fact is that *no one* has the answers—this is why they have to be collectively staged, stabilized, and revised. This is why the social sciences are so indispensable to the reassembling of the social. Without them we don't know what we have in common, we don't know through which connections we are associated together, and we would have no way to detect how we can live in the same common world.

---

[195] Science studies have followed many of the relevance-making strategies in hard sciences and documented many failures. See Michel Callon (1989), *La science et ses réseaux: Genèse et circulation des faits scientifiques* and John Law (2002), *Aircraft Stories: Decentering the Object in Technoscience*. On the notion of interest, see also Stengers, *Power and Invention*.

In order to generate those answers, every new artifice might be welcome, *including that of a social scientist's tiny interpretation.* Failure is not more certain than success. It's certainly worth a try. This is precisely because all the five sources of uncertainty are nested into one another, that a report written by some humble colleague who does not even wear a white coat may make a difference. It may offer a provisional staging of the connections it has managed to deploy. It offers an artificial site (the textual account) that might be able to solve for some particular audience the question of which common world they pertain to. Assembled around the 'laboratory' of the text, authors as well as readers may begin to render visible the two mechanisms that account for the plurality of associations to be taken into account and for the stabilization or unification of the world they wish to live in.[196] On the one hand, it is just a text made up of reams of paper sullied by an inkjet or burnt by a laser beam. On the other, it is a precious little institution to represent, or more exactly to re-represent—that is, to present *again*—the social to all its participants, to *perform* it, to give it a form. It is not much, but to ask for more is often settling for less. Many 'powerful explanations' might turn out to be less convincing than weaker ones.

In the last page of his book on sociology of science, Pierre Bourdieu defines the possibility for the sociologist to reach the famous God's eye view of nowhere after having purged himself of all perspectives through an extreme application of critical reflexivity:

'While [the sociologist] must also beware, lest he forget that like any other scientist he is to attempt to help build science's aperspectival perspective, as a social agent he is also placed within the object which he takes as his object, and on these grounds he has a perspective which does not coincide with others, nor with the overview and over-arching perspective of the quasi-divine observer, which he can reach if the field's demands are satisfied. Thus he knows that the particularity of the social sciences calls upon him to work (as I have tried to do for the case of the gift and of labor in the pascalian meditations) to construct a scientific truth capable of integrating the observer's vision and the truth of the agent's practical vision, into a perspective not known as such which is put to the test in the illusion of the absolute.' (Bourdieu 2001)[197]

This is probably the most honest version ever given of the dream of critical sociology as this was written a few months before Bourdieu's untimely disappearance.

---

[196] Those two functions are part of the definition of politics. See Conclusion.
[197] Kindly translated by Simon Schaffer.

To anguish over the potential efficacy of sociological texts is to show lack of modesty or lack of ambition. If anything, the success of social sciences in spreading through the social world is even more astounding than the expansion of the natural sciences and technological devices. Can we overestimate the changes achieved in the way every one of us is now 'having a gender' that has been brought about by the tiny texts of feminist scholars? What would we know about the 'Other' without anthropologists' accounts? Who could size up one's past without archaeologists and historians? Who would be able to navigate without the geographers? Who would have an unconscious without the psychologists? Who would know whether or not a profit is made without the accountants? To be sure, texts look like miserable pathways to move between the many contradictory frames of reference, and yet their efficacy is unmatched by the more grandiose and powerful social explanations that are proposed to humiliate them. It is not because the sociologist cannot occupy the place of the all-encompassing and all-seeing God of social science that he or she has to be imprisoned blind in a cellar. We, the little ants, should not settle for heaven or hell, as there are plenty of things on this earth to munch our way through.

On the Difficulty of Being an ANT: An Interlude in the Form of a Dialog

An office at the London School of Economics on a dark Tuesday afternoon in February before moving upstairs to the *Beaver* for a pint. A quiet but insistent knock is heard. A student peers into the office.[198]

Student: Am I bothering you?

Professor: Not at all. These are my office hours. Come in, have a seat.

S: Thank you.

P: So... I take it that you are a bit lost?

S: Well, yes. I am finding it difficult, I have to say, to apply Actor Network Theory to my case study on organizations.

P: No wonder! It isn't applicable to anything.

S: But we were taught... I mean... it seems like hot stuff around here. Are you saying it's useless?

P: It might be useful, but only if it does not 'apply' to something.

S: Sorry, but are you playing some sort of Zen trick here? I have to warn you that I'm just a straight Organization Studies doctoral student, so don't expect... I'm not too much into French stuff either, just read a bit of *Thousand Plateaus* but couldn't make much sense of it...

P: Sorry, I wasn't trying to say anything cute. Just that ANT is first of all a *negative* argument. It does not say anything positive on any state of affairs.

S: So what can it do for me?

P: The best it can do for you is to say something like, 'When your informants mix up organization, hardware, psychology, and politics in one sentence, don't break it down first into neat little pots; try to follow the link they make among those elements that would have

[198] A version of this dialog has appeared in *The Social Study of Information and Communication Technology*, edited by C. Avgerou, C. Ciborra, and F.F. Land, Oxford University Press, 2004, pp. 62–76.

looked completely incommensurable if you had followed normal procedures.' That's all. ANT can't tell you positively what the link is.

S: So why is it called a 'theory' if it says nothing about the things we study?

P: It's a theory, and a strong one I think, but about *how* to study things, or rather how *not* to study them—or rather, how to let the actors have some room to express themselves.

S: Do you mean that other social theories don't allow that?

P: In a way, yes, and because of their very strengths: they are good at saying *substantive* things about what the social world is made of. In most cases that's fine; the ingredients are known; their repertoire should be kept short. But that doesn't work when things are changing fast. Nor is it good for organization studies, information studies, marketing, science and technology studies or management studies, where boundaries are so terribly fuzzy. *New* topics, that's what you need ANT for.

S: But my agents, I mean the people I am studying at the company, they form a lot of networks. They are connected to a lot of other things, they are all over the place . . .

P: But see, that's the problem! You don't need Actor-Network to say that. Any available social theory would do. It's a waste of time for you to pick such an outlandish argument simply to show that your informants are 'forming a network'.

S: But they are! They form a network. Look, I have been tracing their connections: computer chips, standards, schooling, money, rewards, countries, cultures, corporate boardrooms, everything. Haven't I described a network in your sense?

P: Not necessarily. I agree this is terribly confusing, and it's largely our fault—the word we invented is a pretty horrible one. But you should not confuse the network that is drawn by the description and the network that is used to make the description.

S: Come again?

P: Surely you'd agree that drawing *with* a pencil is not the same thing as drawing the *shape* of a pencil. It's the same with this ambiguous word: network. With Actor-Network you may describe something that doesn't at all look like a network—an individual state of mind, a piece of machinery, a fictional character; conversely, you may describe a network—subways, sewages, telephones—which is not all drawn in an 'Actor-Networky' way. You are simply confusing the object with the method. ANT is a method, and mostly a negative one at that; it says nothing about the *shape* of what is being described with it.

S: This is confusing! But my company executives, are they not forming a nice, revealing, powerful network?

P: Maybe, I mean, surely they are—but so what?

S: Then I can study them with Actor-Network-Theory!

P: Again, maybe yes, but maybe not. It depends entirely on what *you yourself* allow your actors (or rather, your actants) to do. Being connected, being interconnected, or being heterogeneous is not enough. It all depends on the sort of action that is flowing from one to the other, hence the words 'net' and 'work'. Really, we should say 'worknet' instead of 'network'. It's the work, and the movement, and the flow, and the changes that should be stressed. But now we are stuck with 'network' and everyone thinks we mean the World Wide Web or something like that.

S: Do you mean to say that once I have shown that my actors are related in the shape of a network, I have not yet done an ANT study?

P: That's exactly what I mean: ANT is more like the name of a pencil or a brush than the name of a specific shape to be drawn or painted.

S: But when I said ANT was a tool and asked you if it could be applied, you objected!

P: Because it's not a tool, or rather, because tools are never 'mere' tools ready to be applied: they always modify the goals you had in mind. That's what 'actor' means. Actor Network (I agree the name is silly) allows you to produce some *effects* that you would not have obtained by some other social theory. That's all that I can vouch for. It's a very common experience. Just try to draw with a lead pencil or with charcoal, you will feel the difference; and cooking tarts with a gas oven is not the same as with an electric one.

S: But that's not what my supervisor wants. He wants a frame in which to put my data.

P: If you want to store more data, buy a bigger hard disk.

S: He always says: 'Student, you need a framework.'

P: Maybe your supervisor is in the business of selling pictures! It's true that frames are nice for showing: gilded, white, carved, baroque, aluminum, etc. But have you ever met a painter who began his masterpiece by first choosing the frame? That would be a bit odd, wouldn't it?

S: You're playing with words. By 'frame' I mean a theory, an argument, a general point, a concept—something for making sense of the data. You always need one.

P: No you don't! Tell me, if some X is a mere 'case of' Y, what is more important to study: X that is the special case or Y which is the rule?

S: Probably Y...but X too, just to see if it's really an application of...well, both I guess.

P: I would bet on Y myself, since X will not teach you anything new. If something is simply an 'instance of' some other state of affairs, go study this state of affairs instead. A case study that needs a frame in addition, well, it is a case study that was badly chosen to begin with!

S: But you always need to put things into a context, don't you?

P: I have never understood what context meant, no. A frame makes a picture look nicer, it may direct the gaze better, increase the value, allows to date it, but it doesn't add anything to the picture. The frame, or the context, is precisely the sum of factors that make no difference to the data, what is common knowledge about it. If I were you, I would abstain from frameworks altogether. Just describe the state of affairs at hand.

S: 'Just describe'. Sorry to ask, but is this not terribly naive? Is this not exactly the sort of empiricism, or realism, that we have been warned against? I thought your argument was, um, more sophisticated than that.

P: Because you think description is easy? You must be confusing it, I guess, with strings of clichés. For every hundred books of commentaries and arguments, there is only one of description. To describe, to be attentive to the concrete state of affairs, to find the uniquely adequate account of a given situation, I myself have always found this incredibly demanding.

S: I have to say that I'm lost here. We have been taught that there are two types of sociology, the interpretative and the objectivist. Surely you don't want to say you are of the objectivist type?

P: You bet I am! Yes, by all means.

S: You? But we have been told you were something of a relativist! You have been quoted as saying that even the natural sciences are not objective. Surely you are for interpretative sociology, for viewpoints, multiplicity of standpoints and all that.

P: I have no real sympathy for interpretative sociologies. No. On the contrary, I firmly believe that sciences are objective—what else could they be? They're all about objects, no? What I have said is simply that objects might look a bit more complicated, folded, multiple, complex, and entangled than what the 'objectivist', as you say, would like them to be.

S: But that's exactly what 'interpretative' sociologies argue, no?

P: Oh no, not at all. They would say that *human* desires, *human* meanings, *human* intentions, etc., introduce some 'interpretive flexibility' into a world of inflexible objects, of 'pure causal relations', of 'strictly material connections'. That's not at all what I am saying. I would say that this computer here on my desk, this screen, this keyboard are objects made of multiple layers, exactly as much as you sitting here are: your body, your language, your worries. It's the object itself that adds multiplicity, or rather the thing, the 'gathering'. When you speak of hermeneutics, no matter which precaution you take, you always expect the second shoe to drop: someone inevitably will add:

'But of course there *also* exists "natural", "objective" things that are "not" interpreted'.

S: That's just what I was going to say! There are not only objective realities, but also subjective ones! This is why we need both types of social theories...

P: See? That's the inevitable trap: 'Not only... but also'. Either you extend the argument to everything, but then it becomes useless— 'interpretation' becomes another synonym for 'objectivity'—or else you limit it to one aspect of reality, the human, and then you are stuck—since objectivity is always on the other side of the fence. And it makes no difference if the other side is considered richer or poorer; it's out of reach anyway.

S: But you wouldn't deny that you also possess a standpoint, that ANT is situated as well, that you also add another layer of interpretation, a perspective?

P: No, why would I 'deny' it? But so what? The great thing about a standpoint is that you can stand on it and modify it! Why would I be 'stuck with' it? From where they are on earth, astronomers have a limited perspective. Take for instance Greenwich, the Observatory down the river from here. Have you been there? It's a beautiful place. And yet, they have been pretty good at shifting this perspective, through instruments, telescopes, satellites. They can now draw a map of the distribution of galaxies in the whole universe. Pretty good, no? Show me one standpoint and I will show you two dozen ways to shift out of it. Listen: all this opposition between 'standpoint' and 'view from nowhere', you can safely forget. And also this difference between 'interpretative' and 'objectivist'. Leave hermeneutics aside and go back to the object—or rather, to the thing.

S: But I am always limited to my situated viewpoint, to my perspective, to my own subjectivity?

P: Of course you are! But what makes you think that 'having a viewpoint' means 'being limited' or especially 'subjective'? When you travel abroad and you follow the sign 'Belvedere 1.5 km', 'Panorama', 'Bella vista', when you finally reach the breath-taking site, in what way is this proof of your 'subjective limits'? It's the thing itself, the valley, the peaks, the roads, that offer you this grasp, this handle, this take. The best proof is that, two meters lower, you see nothing because of the trees and two meters higher, you see nothing because of a parking lot. And yet you have the same limited 'subjectivity' and you transport with you exactly the very same 'standpoint'! If you can have many points of views on a statue, it's because the statue itself is in three-dimensions and allows you, yes, *allows* you to move around it. If something supports many viewpoints, it's just that it's highly complex, intricately folded, nicely organized, and beautiful, yes, *objectively* beautiful.

S: But certainly nothing is objectively beautiful—beauty has to be subjective . . . taste and color, relative . . . I am lost again. Why would we spend so much time in this school fighting objectivism then? What you say can't be right.

P: Because the things people call 'objective' are most of the time the clichés of matters of facts. We don't have a very good description of anything: of what a computer, a piece of software, a formal system, a theorem, a company, a market is. We know next to nothing of what this thing you're studying, an *organization*, is. How would we be able to distinguish it from human emotions? So, there are two ways to criticize objectivity: one is by going *away* from the object to the subjective human viewpoint. But the other direction is the one I am talking about: back to the object. Positivists don't *own* objectivity. A computer described by Alan Turing is quite a bit richer and more interesting than the ones described by *Wired* magazine, no? As we saw in class yesterday, a soap factory described by Richard Powers in *Gain* is much livelier than what you read in Harvard case studies. The name of the game is to get back to empiricism.

S: Still, I am limited to my own view.

P: Of course you are, but again, so what? Don't believe all that crap about being 'limited' to one's perspective. All of the sciences have been inventing ways to *move* from one standpoint to the next, from one frame of reference to the next, for God's sake: that's called relativity.

S: Ah! So you confess you are a relativist!

P: But of course, what else could I be? If I want to be a scientist and reach objectivity, I have to be able to travel from one frame of reference to the next, from one standpoint to the next. Without those displacements, I would be limited to my own narrow point of view for good.

S: So you associate objectivity with relativism?

P: 'Relativity', yes, of course. All the sciences do the same. Our sciences do it as well.

S: But what is *our* way to change our standpoints?

P: I told you, we are in the business of descriptions. Everyone else is trading on clichés. Enquiries, survey, fieldwork, archives, polls, whatever—we go, we listen, we learn, we practice, we become competent, we change our views. Very simple really: it's called inquiries. Good inquiries always produce a lot of new descriptions.

S: But I have lots of descriptions already! I'm drowning in them. That's just my problem. That's why I'm lost and that's why I thought it would be useful to come to you. Can't ANT help me with this mass of data? I need a framework!

P: 'My Kingdom for a frame!' Very moving; I think I understand your desperation. But no, ANT is pretty useless for that. Its main tenet is that actors themselves make everything, including their own frames, their own theories, their own contexts, their own metaphysics, even their own ontologies. So the direction to follow would be more descriptions I am afraid.

S: But descriptions are too long. I have to *explain* instead.

P: See? This is where I disagree with most of the training in the social sciences.

S: You would disagree with the need for social sciences to provide an explanation for the data they accumulate? And you call yourself a social *scientist* and an objectivist!

P: I'd say that if your description needs an explanation, it's not a good description, that's all. Only bad descriptions need an explanation. It's quite simple really. What is meant by a 'social explanation' most of the time? Adding another actor to provide those already described with the energy necessary to act. But if you have to add one, then the network was not complete. And if the actors already assembled do not have enough energy to act, then they are not 'actors' but mere intermediaries, dopes, puppets. They do nothing, so they should not be in the description anyhow. I have never seen a good description in need of an explanation. But I have read countless bad descriptions to which nothing was added by a massive addition of 'explanations'. And ANT did not help.

S: This is very distressing. I should have known—the other students warned me not to touch ANT stuff even with a long pole. Now you are telling me that I shouldn't even try to explain anything!

P: I did not say that. I simply said that either your explanation is relevant and, in practice, this means you are adding a new agent to the description—the network is simply longer than you thought—or it's not an actor that makes any difference and you are merely adding something irrelevant which helps neither the description nor the explanation. In that case, throw it away.

S: But all my colleagues use them. They talk about 'IBM corporate culture', 'British isolationism', 'market pressure', 'self-interest'. Why should I deprive myself of those contextual explanations?

P: You can keep them as shorthand or to quickly fill in the parts of your picture that make no difference to you, but don't believe they explain anything. At best they apply equally to all your actors, which means they are probably superfluous since they are unable to introduce a difference among them. At worst, they drown all the new interesting actors in a diluvium of older ones. Deploy the content with all its connections and you will have the context in addition.

As Rem Koolhaas said, 'context stinks'. It's simply a way of stopping the description when you are tired or too lazy to go on.

S: But that's exactly my problem: to stop. I have to complete this doctorate. I have just eight more months. You always say 'more descriptions' but this is like Freud and his cures: indefinite analysis. When do you stop? My actors are all over the place! Where should I go? What is a complete description?

P: Now that's a good question because it's a practical one. As I always say: a good thesis is a thesis that is done. But there is another way to stop than just by 'adding an explanation' or 'putting it into a frame'.

S: Tell me it then.

P: You stop when you have written your 50,000 words or whatever is the format here, I always forget.

S: Oh! That's really great. So my thesis is finished when it's completed. So helpful, really, many thanks. I feel so relieved now.

P: Glad you like it! No seriously, don't you agree that any method depends on the size and type of texts you promised to deliver?

S: But that's a *textual* limit, it has nothing to do with method.

P: See? That's again why I dislike the way doctoral students are trained. Writing texts has *everything* to do with method. You write a text of so many words, in so many months, based on so many interviews, so many hours of observation, so many documents. That's all. You do nothing more.

S: But I do more than that. I learn, I study, I explain, I criticize, I . . .

P: But all those grandiose goals, you achieve them through a text, don't you?

S: Of course, but it's a tool, a medium, a way of expressing myself.

P: There is no tool, no medium, only mediators. A text is thick. That's an ANT tenet, if any.

S: Sorry, Professor, I told you, I have never been into French stuff; I can write in C and even C ++, but I don't do Derrida, semiotics, any of it. I don't believe the world is made of words and all of that . . .

P: Don't try to be sarcastic. It doesn't suit the engineer in you. And anyway I don't believe that either. You ask me how to stop and I am just telling you that the best you will be able to do, as a PhD student, is to *add* a text—which will have been read by your advisors, maybe a few of your informants, and three or four fellow doctoral students—to a given state of affairs. Nothing fancy in that: just plain realism. One solution for how to stop is to 'add a framework', an 'explanation'; the other is to put the last word in the last chapter of your damn thesis.

S: I have been trained in the sciences! I am a systems engineer—I am not coming to Organization Studies to abandon that. I am willing to add flow charts, institutions, people, mythologies, and psychology to what I already know. I am even prepared to be 'symmetric' as you teach us about those various factors. But don't tell me that science is about telling nice stories. This is the difficulty with you. One moment you are completely objectivist, perhaps even a naive realist—'just describe'—and the other you are completely relativist—'tell some nice stories and run'. Is this not so terribly French?

P: And that would make you so terribly what? Don't be silly. Who talked about 'nice stories'? Not me. I said you were *writing* a PhD thesis. Can you deny that? And then I said that this so-many-words-long PhD thesis—which will be the only lasting result of your stay among us—is thick.

S: Meaning?

P: Meaning that it's not just a transparent windowpane, transporting without deformation some information about your study. 'There is no in-formation, only trans-formation.' I assume that you agree with this ANT slogan? Well, then this is surely also true of your PhD thesis, no?

S: Maybe, but in what sense does it help me to be more scientific, that's what I want to know. I don't want to abandon the ethos of science.

P: Because this text, depending on the way it's written, will *or will not* capture the actor-network you wish to study. The text, in our discipline, is not a story, not a nice story. Rather, it's the functional equivalent of a laboratory. It's a place for trials, experiments, and simulations. Depending on what happens in it, there is or there is not an actor and there is or there is not a network being traced. And that depends entirely on the precise ways in which it is written—and every single new topic requires a new way to be handled by a text. Most texts are just plain dead. Nothing happens in them.

S: But no one mentions 'text' in our program. We talk about 'studying the organization, not 'writing' about it.

P: That's what I am telling you: you are being badly trained! Not teaching social science doctoral students to *write* their PhDs is like not teaching chemists to do laboratory experiments. That's why I am teaching nothing but writing nowadays. I keep repeating the same mantra: 'describe, write, describe, write.'

S: The problem is that's not what my supervisor wants! He wants my case studies to 'lead to some useful generalization'. He does not want 'mere description'. So even if I do what you want, I will have one nice description of one state of affairs, and then what? I still have to put it into a frame, find a typology, compare, explain, generalize. That's why I'm starting to panic.

P: You should panic only if your actors were not doing that constantly as well, actively, reflexively, obsessively. They, too, compare; they, too, produce typologies; they, too, design standards; they, too, spread their machines as well as their organizations, their ideologies, their states of mind. Why would you be the one doing the intelligent stuff while they would act like a bunch of morons? What they do to expand, to relate, to compare, to organize is what you have to describe as well. It's not another layer that you would have to add to the 'mere description'. Don't try to shift from description to explanation: simply *go on with* the description. What your own ideas are about your company is of no interest whatsoever compared to how this bit of the company itself has managed to spread.

S: But if my people don't act, if they don't actively compare, standardize, organize, generalize, what do I do? I will be stuck! I won't be able to add any other explanations.

P: You are really extraordinary! If your actors don't act, they will leave no trace whatsoever. So you will have no information at all. So you will have nothing to say.

S: You mean when there is no trace I should remain silent?

P: Incredible! Would you raise this question in any of the natural sciences? It would sound totally silly. It takes a social scientist to claim that they can go on explaining even in the absence of any information! Are you really prepared to make up data?

S: No, of course not, but still I want...

P: Good, at least you are more reasonable than some of our colleagues. No trace left, thus no information, thus no description, then no talk. *Don't fill it in.* It's like a map of a country in the 16th century: no one went there or no one came back, so for God's sake, leave it blank! *Terra incognita.*

S: But what about invisible entities acting in some hidden ways?

P: If they act, they leave some trace. And then you will have some information, then you can talk about them. If not, just shut up.

S: But what if they are repressed, denied, silenced?

P: Nothing on earth allows you to say they are there without bringing in the *proof* of their presence. That proof might be indirect, far-fetched, complicated, but you need it. Invisible things are invisible. Period. If they make other things move, and you can document those moves, then they are visible.

S: Proof? What is a proof anyway? Isn't that terribly positivistic?

P: I hope so, yes. What's so great about saying that things are acting whose existence you can't prove? I am afraid you are confusing social theory with conspiracy theory—although these days most of critical social science comes down to that.

S: But if I add nothing, I simply repeat what actors say.

P: What would be the use of adding invisible entities that act without leaving any trace and make no difference to any state of affairs?

S: But I have to make the actors learn something they didn't know; if not, why would I study them?

P: You social scientists! You always baffle me. If you were studying ants, instead of ANT, would you expect ants to *learn* something from your study? Of course not. They are the teachers, you learn from them. You explain what they do to you for your own benefit, or for that of other entomologists, not for them, who don't care one bit. What makes you think that a study is always supposed to teach things to the people being studied?

S: But that's the whole idea of the social sciences! That's why I'm here at the school: to criticize the ideology of management, to debunk the many myths of information technology, to gain a critical edge over all the technical hype, the ideology of the market. If not, believe me, I would still be in Silicon Valley, and I would be making a lot more money—well, maybe not now, since the bubble burst... But anyway, I have to provide some reflexive understanding to the people...

P: ... Who of course were not reflexive before you came to honor them with your study!

S: In a way, yes. I mean, no. They did things but did not know why... What's wrong with that?

P: What's wrong is that it's so terribly cheap. Most of what social scientists call 'reflexivity' is just a way of asking totally irrelevant questions to people who ask other questions for which the analyst does not have the slightest answer! Reflexivity is not a birthright you transport with you just because you are at the LSE! You and your informants have different concerns—when they intersect it's a miracle. And miracles, in case you don't know, are rare.

S: But if I have nothing to add to what actors say, I won't be able to be critical.

P: See, one moment you want to explain and play the scientist, while the next moment you want to debunk and criticize and play the militant...

S: I was going to say: one moment you are a naive realist—back to the object—and the next you say that you just write a text that adds nothing but simply trails behind your proverbial 'actors themselves'. This is totally apolitical. No critical edge that I can see.

P: Tell me, Master Debunker, how are you going to gain a 'critical edge' over your actors? I am eager to hear this.

S: Only if I have a framework. That's what I was looking for in coming here, but obviously ANT is unable to give me one.

P: And I am glad it doesn't. I assume this framework of yours is hidden to the eyes of your informants and revealed by your study?

S: Yes, of course. That should be the added value of my work, not the description since everyone already knows that. But the explanation, the context, that's something they have no time to see, the typology. You see, they are too busy to think. That's what I can deliver. By the way, I have not told you yet, at the company, they are ready to give me access to their files.

P: Excellent, at least they are interested in what you do. It's a good beginning. But you are not claiming that in your six months of field-work, you can by yourself, just by writing a few hundred pages, pro-duce more knowledge than those 340 engineers and staff that you have been studying?

S: Not 'more' knowledge but different. Yes, I hope I can. Shouldn't I strive exactly for that? Is this not why I am in this business?

P: I am not sure what business you are in, but how *different* is the knowledge you produce from theirs, that's the big question.

S: It's the same kind of knowledge as all the sciences, the same way of explaining things: by going from the case at hand to the cause. And once I know the cause, I can generate the effect as a consequence. What's wrong with that? It's like asking what will happen to a pendu-lum that has been moved far from the equilibrium. If I know Galileo's law, I don't even need to look at any concrete pendulum anymore; I know exactly what will happen—provided I forget the perturbations, naturally.

P: Naturally! So what you are hoping for is that your explanatory framework will be to your case study what Galileo's law is to the fall of the pendulum—minus the perturbations.

S: Yes, I guess so, though less precisely scientific. Why? What's wrong with that?

P: Nothing. It would be great, but is it feasible? It means that, whatever a given concrete pendulum does, it will add no new infor-mation to the law of falling bodies. The law holds *in potentia* every-thing there is to know about the pendulum's state of affairs. The concrete case is simply, to speak like a philosopher, the 'realization of a potential' that was already there.

S: Isn't that an ideal explanation?

P: That's just the problem. It's an ideal squared: the ideal of an ideal explanation. I doubt somewhat that your company's subsidiary be-haves that way. And I am pretty confident that you can't produce the law of its behavior that will allow you to deduce everything as the realization *in concreto* of what was already there potentially.

S: Minus the perturbations...

P: Yes, yes, yes, this goes without saying. Your modesty is admirable.

S: Are you making fun of me here? Striving for that sort of framework seems feasible to me.

P: But even it were, would it be desirable? See, what you are really telling me is that the actors in your description make *no difference whatsoever.* They have simply realized a potential—apart from minor deviations—which means they are not actors at all: they simply carry the force that comes through them. So, my dear Student, you have been wasting your time describing people, objects, sites that are nothing, in effect, but passive intermediaries since they do nothing on their own. Your fieldwork has been simply wasted. You should have gone directly to the cause.

S: But that's what a science is for! Just that: finding the hidden structure that explains the behavior of those agents you thought were doing something but in fact are simply placeholders for something else.

P: So you are a structuralist! You've finally come out of the closet. Placeholders, isn't that what you call actors? And you want to do Actor Network Theory at the same time! That's stretching the limits of eclecticism pretty far!

S: Why can't I do both? Certainly if ANT has any scientific content, it has to be structuralist.

P: Have you realized that there is the word 'actor' in actor-network? Can you tell me what sort of action a placeholder does in a structuralist explanation?

S: That's easy, it fulfills a function. This is what is so great about structuralism, if I have understood it correctly. Any other agent in the same position would be forced to do the same.

P: So a placeholder, by definition, is entirely *substitutable* by any other?

S: Yes, that's what I am saying.

P: But that's also what is so implausible and what makes it radically incompatible with ANT. In my vocabulary, an actor that makes no difference is not an actor at all. An actor, if words have any meaning, is exactly what is *not* substitutable. It's a unique event, totally irreducible to any other, except, that is, if you render one commensurable with another one by some process of standardization—but even that requires a *third* actor, a third event.

S: So you are telling me that ANT is not a science!

P: Not a structuralist science, that's for sure.

S: That's the same thing, any science...

P: No! Organization Studies, Science and Technology Studies, Business Studies, Information Studies, Sociology, Geography, Anthropology, whatever the field, they cannot rely, by definition, on any structuralist explanation since information is transformation.

S: 'Systems of transformations', that's exactly what structuralism is about!

P: No way, my friend, since in structuralism nothing is really transformed, it's simply *combined*. You don't seem to fathom the abyss that exists between it and ANT. A structure is just a network on which you have only very sketchy information. It's useful when you are pressed for time, but don't tell me it's more scientific. If I want to have actors in my account, they have to *do* things, not to be placeholders; if they do something, they have to make a difference. If they make no difference, drop them, start the description anew. You want a science in which there is no object.

S: You and your stories. Eventful stories, that's what you want! I am talking about explanation, knowledge, critical edge, not writing scripts for soap operas on Channel 4!

P: I was getting to that. You want your bundle of a few hundred pages to make a difference, no? Well then, you have to be able to prove that your description of what people do, when it comes back to them, *does* make a difference to the way they were doing things. Is this what you call having a 'critical edge'?

S: I guess so, yes.

P: But you would agree that it wouldn't do to provide them with an irrelevant appeal to causes that make no difference to what they do because they are too general?

S: Of course not. I was talking about *real* causalities.

P: But those won't do either because if they existed, which I doubt very much they do, they would have no other effect than transforming your informants into the placeholders of other actors, which you call function, structure, grammar, etc. In effect, they wouldn't be actors anymore but dopes, puppets—and even that would be quite unfair to puppets. Anyway, you are making actors out to be nothing: at best they could add some minor perturbations like the concrete pendulum that only adds slight wobbles.

S: Huh?

P: Now you have to tell me what is so politically great about transforming those you have studied into hapless, 'actless' placeholders for hidden functions that you, and you only, can see and detect?

S: Hmm, you have a way of turning things upside down. Now I am not so sure. If actors become aware of what is imposed on them, if they become more conscious, more reflexive, then is their consciousness not raised somewhat? They can now take their fate into their own hands. They become more enlightened, no? If so, I would say that now, and in part thanks to me, they are more active now, more complete actors.

P: *Bravo, bravissimo!* So an actor for you is some fully determined agent, plus a placeholder for a function, plus a bit of perturbation, plus some consciousness provided by enlightened social scientists? Horrible, simply horrible. And you want to apply ANT to these people! After you have reduced them from actors to placeholders, you want to add insult to injury and generously bring to those poor blokes the reflexivity they had before and that you have taken away by treating them in a structuralist way! Magnificent! They were actors *before* you came in with your 'explanation'. Don't tell me that it's your study that might make them so. Great job, Student! Bourdieu could not have done better.

S: You might not like Bourdieu very much, but at least he was a real scientist, and even better, he was politically relevant. As far as I can tell, your ANT is neither.

P: Thanks. I have been studying the links between science and politics for about thirty years, so I am hard to intimidate with talks of which science is 'politically relevant'.

S: I have learned not to be intimidated by arguments of authority, so your thirty years of study makes no difference to me.

P: *Touché.* But your question was: 'What can I do with ANT?' I answered it: no structuralist explanation. The two are completely incompatible. Either you have actors who realize potentialities and thus are not actors at all, or you describe actors who are rendering virtualities actual (this is Deleuze's parlance by the way) and which require very specific texts. Your connection with those you study requires very specific protocols to work—I guess this is what you would call 'critical edge' and 'political relevance'.

S: So where do we differ? You, too, want to have a critical edge.

P: Yes, maybe, but I am sure of one thing: it's not automatic and most of the time it will fail. Two hundred pages of interviews, observations, etc. will not make any difference whatsoever. To be relevant requires another set of extraordinary circumstances. It's a rare event. It requires an incredibly imaginative protocol. It requires something as miraculous as Galileo with his pendulum or Pasteur with his rabies virus.

S: So what should I do? Pray for a miracle? Sacrifice a chicken?

P: But why do you want your tiny little text to be automatically more relevant to those who might be concerned by it (or not) than say a huge laboratory of natural sciences? Look at how much it takes for Intel® chips to become relevant for mobile phones! And you want everyone to have a label 'LSE® inside' at no cost at all? To become relevant you need extra work.

S: Just what I need, the prospect of even more work!

P: But that's the whole point: if an argument is automatic, across the board, all-purpose, then it can't possibly be scientific. It's simply irrelevant. If a study is really scientific, then it could have failed.

S: Great reassurance, nice of you to remind me that I can fail my thesis!

P: You are confusing science with mastery. 'Being able to lose the phenomenon is essential to scientific practice.'[199] Tell me, can you imagine one single topic to which Bourdieu's critical sociology, which you are so fond of, could possibly *not* apply?

S: But I can't imagine one single topic to which ANT would apply!

P: Beautiful, you are so right, that's exactly what I think.

S: That was not meant as a compliment.

P: But I take it as a true one! An application of anything is as rare as a good text of social science.

S: May I politely remark that, for all your exceedingly subtle philosophy of science, you have yet to tell me how to write one.

P: You were so eager to add frames, context, structure to your 'mere descriptions', how would you have listened to me?

S: But what's the difference between a good and a bad ANT text?

P: Now, that's a good question! Answer: the same as between a good and a bad laboratory. No more, no less.

S: Well, okay, um, thanks. It was nice of you to talk to me. But I think after all, instead of ANT, I was thinking of using Luhmann's system theory as an underlying framework—that seems to hold a lot of promise, 'autopoiesis' and all that. Or maybe I will use a bit of both.

P: Hmmm . . . .

S: Don't you like Luhmann?

P: I would leave aside all 'underlying frameworks' if I were you.

S: But your sort of 'science', from what I see, means breaking all the rules of social science training.

P: I prefer to break them and follow my actors. As you said, I am, in the end, a naive realist, a positivist.

S: You know what would be real nice? Since no one around here seems to understand what ANT is, you should write an introduction to it. That would ensure our teachers know what it is and then, if I may say without being rude, they might not try to push us too hard into it, if you see what I mean . . .

P: So it's really that bad?

S: See, I'm just a PhD student, but you're a professor. You have published a lot. You can afford to do things that I can't. I have to listen to my supervisor. I simply can't follow your advice too far.

P: Why come to me then? Why try to use ANT?

S: For the last half hour, I have to confess, I've been wondering the same thing . . .

---

[199] See Garfinkel, *Ethnomethodology's Program,* p. 264.

PART II

How to Render Associations Traceable Again

Introduction to Part II: Why is it so Difficult to Trace the Social?

It should be the simplest thing in the world. We are all bound by social interactions; we all live in a society; and we are all cultural animals. Why do these ties remain so elusive? In the preceding pages, one reason has been offered up as an explanation. The adjective 'social' designates two entirely different phenomena: it's at once a *substance*, a kind of stuff, and also a *movement* between non-social elements. In both cases, the social vanishes. When it is taken as a solid, it loses its ability to associate; when it's taken as a fluid, the social again disappears because it flashes only briefly, just at the fleeting moment when new associations are sticking the collective together. Although it seemed at first sight that the subject matter of social sciences was easy to locate thanks to the massive and ubiquitous evidence of the social order, it now appears that it's just the opposite: there is nothing more difficult to grasp than social ties. It's traceable only when it's being modified. Physiologists have shown that for a perception to take place, continuous movements and adjustments are necessary: no movement, no feeling. This is true for the senses of sight and hearing as well as for taste, smell, and touch.[200] If you clasp someone's hand and keep the grasp perfectly still, very soon you no longer feel anything but a vague, embarrassing dullness—even if it's the hand of your beloved. With the absence of movements has come a blurring of the senses. The same is true of the 'sense of the social': no new association, no way to feel the grasp.

This is why to renew the feeling for social connections I had to oppose two different types of methods. One that I called 'sociology of the social' tries to keep together as firmly as possible and as long as possible elements which it claims are made of some homogeneous

[200] See the beautiful experiment with rapid-eye movement and its application in portraits in R.C. Miall and John Tchalenko (2001), 'A Painter's Eye Movements: A Study of Eye and Hand Movement during Portrait Drawing'.

stuff; the other—which I referred to as 'sociology of associations'—tries to fathom controversies about the range of heterogeneous elements that may be associated together. In one case, we know roughly what the social world is made of—it's made 'of' or 'in' the social; in the other, we should always begin by *not* knowing what it's made of. Thus, much like the *pharmakon* of the Greeks, the search for the social becomes either a remedy or a powerful poison depending on the dose and on the timing. Freshly grounded into small and timely doses, it allows the observer to detect the new associations that have to be constantly reshuffled in order to gather once more a collective that is threatened by irrelevance. But if you let the elements that have been bundled together pass their 'sell by dates', they will begin to rot. If you persist in ingesting them, they will lead to complete paralysis. You begin to take what has been connected together for a special type of fabric: the social explains the social. You have entered a world that is no longer traceable, a world that is in danger of being quickly invaded by the fairies, dragons, heroes, and witches of critical sociology.

But how is it possible to have two completely opposite meanings for the same adjective? It can be explained, I think, because the social sciences have pursued simultaneously three different tasks: documenting the various ways in which the social is built by its members' ingeniousness; settling the controversies about the social by limiting the range of entities at work in the world; and trying to solve the 'social question' by offering some prosthesis for political action. There is nothing wrong with these goals since sociology, the 'science of living together', should indeed be able to fulfill the three following duties: it should be able to deploy the full range of controversies about which associations are possible; it should be able to show through which means those controversies are settled and how such settlements are kept up; and it can help define the right procedures for the composition of the collective by rendering itself interesting to those who have been the object of study. But what is impossible is to try to fulfill those duties simultaneously without paying attention to their succession.

If you confuse the second with the first, for instance, you start thinking that your main task is to restrict—in advance and in the actor's place—the range of uncertainties in which you are afraid the actors will get lost. This means that you take it upon yourself to narrow down the number of possible social aggregates, to limit the number of agencies that make actors do things, to exclude as many non-human objects as possible, to cling to a strict division of labor between natural and social sciences, and, finally, to maintain a firm belief in sociology as an autonomous scientific discipline. After such a treatment, it is no longer possible to trace the five sources of uncertainty that we have reviewed. Things get even worse when you confuse the third duty—that of political relevance—with the other two. For perfectly respectable reasons that are related to the necessity of modernization, to the project of emancipation, and to the sheer difficulties of empirical inquiries, you begin to substitute the actor's composition of the collective with your own definition of what holds them together. You begin to ask what is a society and in which direction is it headed. Although I am sure that such an intellectual strategy might have been productive in the time of Comte, Spencer, Durkheim, or Parsons, it has now become disastrous. When a social explanation is proposed, there is no longer a way to decide whether it is due to some genuine empirical grasp, to the application of a standard, to an attempt at social engineering, or to mere laziness. With the confusion of the three successive duties of social science, the social has become thoroughly untraceable even though social explanations keep proliferating effortlessly.

To be faithful to the project of a *science of a social*—now that the words social and science have both been refurbished—we have to overcome the mix-up without abandoning any of the three original duties. After having shown in Part I how we could deploy the actors' own world-making abilities, and before tackling in the Conclusion the tricky question of political interest, I now have to show that it's possible to follow the settlement of controversies without confusing such an inquiry with the other two. Yes, controversies are closed and uncertainties are settled, but this is also the labor of the actors themselves so this too products empirical traces and so it can be thoroughly documented. As soon as we let the actors clean up, so to speak, their own mess, some order can be retrieved which is quite different from the inquirers' own attempts at limiting controversies in advance.

Unfortunately, if it's so difficult to deploy the five sources of uncertainty, then it's going to be even trickier to follow the means through which they are stabilized. In this new research I will seem to be even more at loggerheads with 'traditional sociology'. I will argue that what has rendered the social untraceable is the very existence of society or, more generally, of a social realm. This time the problem doesn't come from the ambiguity of the word social, but from a confusion, entertained early on in the history of sociology, between assembling the body politic and assembling the collective. Even though both operations have a lot in common, the two should be kept apart if they are to succeed at all.

To put it broadly, society, this 19th century invention, is an odd transitional figure mixing up the Leviathan of the 18th century and the collective of the 21st.[201] By asking society to do two jobs at once,

---

[201] On the invention of the very notion of society, see Bruno Karsenti (2003), 'Autorité, pouvoir et société: La science sociale selon Bonald' and Michel Foucault (2003), *"Society Must Be Defended": Lectures at the College de France, 1975–1976*.

that is, to make the collective traceable and to play the role of a substitute for politics, it has never been able to do either of them properly. The supposed existence of a society has precluded the emergence of a well-assembled collective as well as thwarted all efforts at defining the odd sort of corporate body that political activities should remain able to form.

Even though it will become clear only at the end of this book, the reason of this double bind can be stated simply: the body politic was supposed, by construction, to be *virtual, total,* and *always already there*. There is nothing wrong with this since it had to solve the impossible problem of political *representation*, fusing the many into one and making the one obeyed by the many. Only political action is able to trace, by a continuous circular movement, this virtual and total assembly that is always in danger of disappearing altogether.[202] This is what Walter Lippmann had designated by the apt word *phantom*, the Phantom Public.[203] From the myth of the social contract onward, the body politic has always been, as John Dewey put it in his answer to Lippmann, a *problem*, a ghost always in risk of complete dissolution. Never was it supposed to become a substance, a being, a sui generis realm that would have existed beneath, behind, and beyond political action. What has struck all readers in Hobbes's sketch of his Leviathan is how fragile 'this mortal god' was and how quickly it could dissolve. For all to see, this giant had feet of clay.[204]

But as soon as you displace the mode of existence of the public into that of a society, so as to save you the immense, contradictory, and arduous task of composing it through political means, its *problematic fragility* vanishes.[205] The body politic transmogrified into a society is supposed to hold up under its own force *even in the absence of* any

[202] On the necessary 'spin' of political enunciation, see Bruno Latour (2003b), 'What if We Were Talking Politics a Little?' (2003).

[203] Walter Lippmann (1927 [1993]), *The Phantom Public*. I am following here the work of Noortje Marres on Dewey and Lippman's political philosophies. See Noortje Marres (2005), 'No Issue, No Politics'. The fragility of political personae is one of the great lessons drawn from Ernst Kantorowicz (1997), *The King's Two Bodies*. This is the reason why the state is always the product of a continuing trial. See Dominique Linhardt (2004), 'La force de l'Etat en démocratie: La République fédérale d'Allemagne à l'épreuve de la guérilla urbaine 1967–1982'.

[204] Although he takes it negatively instead of positively, Bourdieu summarizes perfectly this frailty when defining political representation: 'So delegation – this originary act of constitution in both the philosophical and political senses of the word – is an act of magic which enables what was merely a collection of several persons, a series of juxtaposed individuals, to exist in the form of a fictitious person, a *corporatio*, a body, a mystical body incarnated in a social body, which itself transcends the biological bodies which compose it ("corpus corporatum in corpore corporato").' Pierre Bourdieu (1991), 'Delegation and Political Fetishism', p. 208.

[205] Remember that I have chosen to follow Bauman's decisive insight about the invention of sociology as a substitute to politics. See Bauman, *Intimations of Postmodernity*.

political activity.[206] Although it remains invisible, the giant body politic is now said to have had its feet solidly fastened to a sturdy pedestal. All the difficulties of grasping the social start from such an impossible feat of metallurgical fiction: the moving shape of the Phantom Public now cast in bronze.

Whereas the body politic was ceaselessly traced by politics, society is there whether we like it or not. And instead of seeing this as a contradiction or technical impossibility, social scientists will take this ghostly presence as the best proof of its mysterious existence. Only now does the Phantom become a ghoul, the Leviathan turned into a behemoth. But it does not require much effort to see that a virtual and always present entity is exactly the opposite of what is needed for the collective to be assembled: if it's already there, the practical means to *compose* it are no longer traceable; if it's total, the practical means to *totalize* it are no longer visible; if it's virtual, the practical means to *realize*, *visualize*, and *collect* it have disappeared from view. As long as we detect behind the collective the shadow of society and behind society the shadow of the Leviathan, no science of the social can proceed forward.[207] To put it even more bluntly: *either there is society or there is sociology*. You can't have both at once as Gabriel Tarde warned his readers when he saw the discipline taking such a wrong turn.

Naturally, all social theorists know this perfectly well and this is why each in his or her own way has made efforts to extirpate their inquiries out of the shadows of a society.[208] They all have stated that society is a virtual reality, a *cosa mentale*, a hypostasis, a fiction. But by maintaining it where it was, if only to criticize it, they have never been able to do more than carve a little niche for themselves inside the virtual, total body that they claimed did not really exist. So, through a strange twist of fate, society became at once what was *always criticized* as a fiction and what was *always there* nonetheless as the impassable horizon of all discussions concerning the social world.[209] Whatever the solution, it remained stranded like a whale, yes a leviathan, beached on a seashore

---

[206] See John Dewey (1927 1954), *The Public and Its Problems* and his critique of Hegelianism in politics.

[207] 'The democratic ideal has never defined the function of the public. It has treated the public as an immature shadowy executive of all things. The confusion is deep-seated in a mystical notion of society.' In Lippmann, *The Phantom Public*, p. 137.

[208] For a recent inquiry into the state of the art, see Nicholas Gane (2004), *The Future of Social Theory*.

[209] Thanks to the illusory power of dialectics, it's sometimes this very contradictory nature that is taken as the very circular definition of society itself. This is clear in Castoriadis *The Imaginary Institution of Society* but also in the notion of self-transcendence developed in Jean Pierre Dupuy (1992), *Introduction aux sciences sociales. Logique des phénomènes collectifs* and in the argument by Luhmann regarding the notion of autopoiesis of Humberto R. Maturana and Francisco J. Varela (1980), *Autopoiesis and Cognition: The Realization of the Living*. Although they might all be tracing circles, the body politic, society, and organisms do not carry the same entities and are not transported by the same vehicles.

where Lilliputian social scientists tried to dig it a suitable abode. Of late, the smell of this decaying monster has become unbearable. There is no way to succeed in renewing social theory as long as the beach has not been cleared and the ill-fated notion of society entirely dissolved. To do so we have to extract out of it both the body politic that it has usurped as well as the collective that it keeps hiding.[210]

That society stands in the way of sociology and of politics is not so surprising for those of us in science studies who saw earlier how nature, too, stood in the way. Both monsters are born in the same season and for the same reason: nature assembles non-humans apart from the humans; society collects humans apart from the non-humans. As I have shown elsewhere at length, both are twin freaks generated to stifle the very possibility of a rightful composition of the collective.[211] But if it's relatively easy to show the political composition of nature, so obvious is the difference between matters of concern and matters of fact, society, through some strange perversity, remains more obdurate, more obvious, more taken for granted. The abyss between the social as association and the social as substance seems more difficult to recognize. So much so that even my own efforts at reducing the power of nature have been taken as a reinforcement of that of society! The latter seems to be able to reign where the former has been forced to give up some of its sovereignty. Hence the unfortunate success of the notion of 'social construction' I scrutinized earlier. And yet, there is no escape. After nature, it is society that has to go. If not, we will never be able to collect the collective.

How can we move on and render the social fully traceable again? By following the same strategy as in Part I. We should deploy the full range of controversies instead of attempting to decide by ourselves what is the best starting point to follow it. Once again, we should be more abstract and more relativist than at first anticipated. This time I will take as our point of departure the very difficulty social scientists seem to have had in locating their inquiries at the right locus. By choosing such a roundabout way, we are going to discover that the two collectors they have chosen are simply not there because one specific problem—how to solve the political relations of the Many and the One—has been confused with another: how to compose the collective. This discovery will allow us to escape once and for all the large shadow still cast by the fast disappearing society and, hopefully, to render the social fluid traceable at last.

---

[210] I will account later with the notion of 'panorama' for the reasons why this way of summarizing the social has nonetheless such a powerful grip on imagination, see p. 183.

[211] Even though I don't treat the question of nature as thoroughly here, it's important to remember that my argument makes no sense if the balance between nature and society is not kept firmly in place.

How to Keep the Social Flat

Users of social science seem to consider that it's rather straightforward to assemble, invoke, convoke, mobilize, and explain the social. Practitioners of social science know how painful, costly, arduous, and utterly puzzling it is. The 'easy' social is the one already bundled together, while the 'difficult' social is the new one that has yet to appear in stitching together elements that don't pertain to the usual repertoire. Depending on which tracer we decide to follow we will embark on very different sorts of travels. Sociologists of the social have traced, with *their* definition of a social, a vast domain that bears no relation whatsoever with the maps we are going to need for *our* definition of the social. I am not only saying that existing maps are incomplete, but that they designate territories with such different shapes that they don't even overlap! It is not even clear if they pertain to the same Earth. The job now before us is no longer to go to different places in the same country—less crowded sites, less trodden paths—but to generate an altogether different landscape so we can travel through it. Needless to say, this is not going to speed up our trips: 'slowciology' it was in Part I, 'slowciology' it will remain.

Since what is now at stake is the very topography of the social, there is no way to decide how to draw our itineraries without understanding the principle of projection sociologists of the social have used for theirs. It's only by seeing how they have been led astray that we will grasp why they drew those implausible maps. When you begin to ask this question you realize how arduous their travails have been. They have been forced to constantly migrate between two types of sites—the local interaction and the global context—each so uncomfortable that they had to flee from them as fast as possible. Adam and Eve had been chased out of only one paradise, but sociologists of the social, less fortunate than their forebears, have been forced to leave two resting places in succession, each situated at the polar opposite of the other, and have been shuttling between both. We have to grasp the dynamic of this infernal trip if we wish to escape their fate.

Every social scientist knows quite well that local interactions are not a good place to rest. When, for one reason or another, you happen to

come on the stage, you become quickly aware that most of the ingredients composing the scene have not been brought there by you and
that many have been improvised on the spot by the other participants.
An infant learning to speak finds her language already there in her
mother's competent use. A plaintiff summoned to face the judge
discovers the edifice of law firmly in place and the Old Bailey building
as ancient as London. A worker, who labors all day on the floor of a
sweatshop, discovers quite quickly that his fate has been settled by
invisible agents who are hidden behind the office walls at the other
end of the shop. A pedestrian with a strained ankle learns in the
doctor's office about her skeleton and physiology that predate the
time of her accident. A local 'informant', prodded by the questions
of a visiting ethnographer, realizes that most of his habits of thought
are coming from places and agencies over which he has no control.
And so on. Interactions do not resemble a picnic where all the food is
gathered on the spot by the participants, but rather a reception given
by some unknown sponsors who have staged everything down to the
last detail—even the place to sit might be already pre-inscribed by
some attentive keeper.

So, it is perfectly true to say that any given interaction seems to
overflow with elements which are already in the situation coming from
some other *time*, some other *place*, and generated by some other
agency. This powerful intuition is as old as the social sciences. As
I have said earlier, action is always dislocated, articulated, delegated,
translated. Thus, if any observer is faithful to the direction suggested
by this overflow, she will be led *away* from any given interaction to
some *other places*, *other times*, and *other agencies* that appear to have
molded them into shape. It is as if a strong wind forbade anyone to
stick to the local site and blew bystanders away; as if a strong current
was always forcing us to abandon the local scene.

The problem is where to go from there. It's at this point that the
confusion between body politic and society is threatening to lead us
astray. Although there is indeed, in every interaction, a dotted line
that leads to some virtual, total, and always preexisting entity, this is
just the track that should not be followed, at least for now: virtual and
shadowy it is, virtual and shadowy it should remain. Where political
action has to proceed forward, sociologists should fear to tread. Yes,
interactions are made to exist by other actors but, no, those sites do
not form a context around them.

As we have already witnessed on many occasions, there is often a
wide gap between the correct intuitions of social sciences and the odd
solutions they provide. This is once again the case: they have tended to
confuse the projection of the Phantom Public with the pre-eminence
of society. It's true that both have only a virtual existence but not in

the same way. The first is a constant appeal to resume the impossible feat of politics, while the second is nothing but a way to dissimulate the task of composition by doing as if it was already completed: society is there, above our heads. So, when inquirers begin to look away from local sites because obviously the key of the interactions is not to be found there—which is true enough—they believe they have to turn their attention toward the 'framework' inside of which interactions are supposed to be nested—and here things go terribly wrong. Starting with the right impulse—let's get away from local interactions!—they end up, to borrow from Samuel Butler's famous title, in Erewhon.

Such a direction has been so solidly entrenched by one hundred and fifty years of social science that it now appears as some mass migration along large freeways built at great expenses and guided by huge bright signposts on which is written: 'Context, 15 km, Next Stop'. So automatic has become the custom to reach those sites when you are dissatisfied with local interactions that it is very hard to recognize that it goes nowhere at all. After a short smooth ride, those freeways suddenly vanish into thin air. At Context, there is no place to park. From the infant speech act is it really possible to go to the 'structure' of language? From the plaintiff case is there any way to go to a 'system' of law? From the floor of the sweatshop is there any canal that goes to a 'capitalist mode of production' or to an 'empire'? From the strained ankle of the patient is there a pathway to lead to the 'nature' of the body? From the ethnographer's notebook is it likely that one will reach the 'culture' of this specific people? As soon as those questions are raised, the answer is an embarrassed 'no, yes, maybe'.

To be sure, the structure of language is spoken by nobody in particular and yet it is out of this that all speech acts are generated, although the ways in which *la parole* meets *la langue* have remained totally mysterious ever since the time of Saussure.[212] The system of law doesn't reside anywhere in particular and yet is invoked no less mysteriously in every specific case, even though it is recognized that it has to be made up of some ad hoc totality for each case.[213] Capitalism is certainly the dominant mode of production but no one imagines that there is some *homonculus* CEO in command, despite the fact that many events look like they obey some implacable strategy.[214] The knowledge of the body is what allows specific illnesses to be diagnosed, although

---

[212] For one of the many instances of pragmatics eating up at the structural elements of language, see Alessandro Duranti and Charles Goodwin (1992), *Rethinking Context: Language as an Interactive Phenomenon*.

[213] See Niklas Luhmann (1985), *A Sociological Theory of Law*.

[214] See Philip Mirowski (2001), *Machine Dreams. Economics Becomes a Cyborg Science* and Michel Callon (1998a), 'An Essay on Framing and Overflowing: Economic Externalities Revisited by Sociology'.

it is also clear that it is only from the case at hand that most informa-tion is made relevant.[215] A culture is simultaneously that which makes people act, a complete abstraction created by the ethnographer's gaze, and what is generated on the spot by the constant inventiveness of members' interactions.[216] Even though they seem to be what any inquiry is forced to reach in order to make sense of local interactions, structural features seem to offer resting spots about as comfortable as a bush of poison ivy.

So, the uneasy answer one gets regarding those famed 'contexts' is that there exists something that renders the interaction possible by bringing on the scene most of its necessary ingredients, but that this 'something' is at once *present behind* and *much too abstract* to do anything. Structure is very powerful and yet much too weak and remote to have any efficacy. What is said to be the true source of everything 'real' and 'concrete' that takes place in interactions does not seem to offer any dwelling for long. This is why, as if they had reached the far end of a stretched out rubber band, social scientists are suddenly pulled in the opposite direction from 'deep structural fea-tures' back to the more 'real' and 'concrete' interactions. A second wind, a second current no less violent than the first, is now forcing any visitor *away* from the context and back to the local practical sites. Has the recent history of the social sciences not been in large part a painful oscillation between two opposite poles, one more structural and the other more pragmatic?[217]

Unfortunately, trying to stick to the local scene at the end of the return trip is not much of a solution since the forces that have pushed enquirers away are still in place: it remains obvious that what is 'real' and 'concrete' does not fully reside in those interactions either. Torn between two opposite directions, the enquirer finds herself in an impossible situation. When she sticks to interactions, she is requested to go away and to 'put things in their wider context'. But when she finally reaches that structuring context, she is asked to leave the abstract level for 'real life', 'human size', 'lived-in' sites. But if 'struc-ture' is an abstraction, so is interaction! If one is more real and con-crete, so is the other—the *other* pole, always the other pole. This is enough of a double bind to render any enquirer fully disoriented. Plato claimed that one had to ascend from the confusing and material

---

[215] See Stefan Hirschauer (1991), 'The Manufacture of Bodies in Surgery' and Mol, *The Body Multiple*.

[216] For the dynamic production of culture, see Marshall Sahlins (2000), *Culture in Practice* and Marylin Strathern (1999), *Property, Substance and Effect: Anthropological Essays in Persons and Things*.

[217] The paradigm of this alternation is probably Parsons begetting Garfinkel. To every structuralist an interactionist will be born.

shadows to the real and immaterial ideas. But what if, with exactly as much reason, an anti-Plato was also leading you in the other direction to descend from the abstract ideas to the real and material local world? You would be torn apart by such a tug of war, alternating abruptly between a frame in which interactions have to be situated—in society—and a violent movement to do away with 'overarching frameworks' that goes back to the local and individual setting where things 'really happen' and are 'really lived'. The pull and push of a child's swing is fun, but only for a while and certainly not when shoved so hard that one's stomach begins to feel queasy.

This abrupt alternation has been called the actor/system quandary or the micro/macro debate. The question is to decide whether the actor is 'in' a system or if the system is made up 'of' interacting actors. If only the vertiginous swing could come to a gentle stop. Usually, the strategy is to politely recognize the problem, to declare that it is an artificial question, and then to proceed by carving up some cozy place in what is supposedly an academic debate by imagining some reasonable compromise between the two positions.[218] But if you discover some happy medium between two non-existing positions, what makes you so sure that this third position has not even less claim to existence? Should we try to strike a compromise between actors and system, or should we go somewhere else?

On the face of it, 'actor-network' should be a good candidate for a compromise: the preformatted solution would be to consider *at once* the actor *and* the network in which it is embedded—which would account for the hyphen. Such a lukewarm solution would add itself to the many others which have been proposed in order to reconcile the two obvious necessities of the social sciences: interactions are overflowed by some structures that give shape to them; those structures themselves remain much too abstract as long as they have not instantiated, mobilized, realized, or incarnated into some sort of local and lived interaction. The temptation is all the greater since dialectics, like Ulysses's sirens, might generously offer its profusion of loops to wrap up and tie off such compromises: actors will be said to be simultaneously held by the context and holding it in place, while the context will be at once what makes actors behave and what is being made in turn by the actors' feedback. With circular gestures of the two hands turning faster and faster in opposite directions, it is possible to give an appearance of smooth reason to a connection between two sites whose existence remains as problematic as before. Dialectical thinkers have

---

[218] For some of the many clever attempts, see Bourdieu, *Outline*; Anthony Giddens (1984), *The Constitution of Society*; and Erhard Friedberg (1993), *Le pouvoir et la règle: Dynamiques de l'action organisée.*

the knack to bury artifacts even deeper by claiming that contradictions have been 'overcome'—this being the magic word they use for 'covered up' or 'spirited away'. And again, it's not difficult to see why they remain so convincing even though their hands connect non-existing sites. It is true that the Phantom Public can be drawn only through a looping movement that resembles a dialectic circle.[219] But this indispensable 'lasso' used to draw the paradoxical connection of citizens with their representatives loses all its virtue when it's taken to be the relation of an actor 'inside' a system. While the body politic is artificially made up and vanishes as soon as the loop is interrupted, it seems that society will loom there, whatever we do to it. The actor/system quandary is the unwanted projection onto the plane of social theory of the paradoxical relations citizens entertain with their republic.

This is why the solution explored by ANT, in spite of its somewhat unfortunate label, has nothing to do with offering still another compromise between micro and macro, actor and system—and even less with pushing the swing so forcefully that it circles through some dialectic circles. To follow our argument it's essential, on the contrary, not to try to be clever by striking an even more sophisticated balance between the two clichés of social science. We do not claim that interactions do not really exist because they have to be 'put into' a context, nor that context never really exists because it is always 'instantiated' through individual practice. Instead, we claim that another movement, entirely different from the one usually followed, reveals itself most clearly through the very difficulty of sticking either to a place considered as local or to a place taken as the context for the former one. Our solution is to take seriously the *impossibility* of staying in one of the two sites for a long period. Here again, we have to behave like good ants and to be as moronic, as literalist, as positivist, as relativist as possible. If there is no way to stay in either place, it simply means that those places are not to be reached—either because they don't exist at all or because they exist but cannot be reached with the vehicle offered by sociology.

Just as we decided in Part I to feed off uncertainties instead of cutting through them, it might be possible to profit from this endless alternation between polar opposites to learn something about the real topography of the social. ANT is simply that social theory which has turned 'the Big Problem' of social science from a resource into a topic to solve it. It makes the assumption that the avoidance reflex instantiated twice by sociologists—from the local to the global and from the macro back to the micro—is not the mark of some infamous

---

[219] See Barbara Cassin (1995), *L'effet sophistique*. On the key notion of 'autophuos', see Chapters 7 and 8 of Latour, *Pandora's Hope*.

weakness on their part, but a very important sign that these sites are the shadow image of some entirely different phenomenon. Just as a horse might sense a cliff earlier than his rider, the intuition of the sociologists should be followed, but not the solution they have offered with their mistaken definition of the social. Once again, ANT hopes to be faithful to the tradition while extracting the poison that has debilitated it so much.

Even though the body politic is a shadow, a phantom, a fiction that is produced by the looping move of political action, this doesn't mean that the social world has the same ethereal aspect. Politics, as we will see later, is only one way of composing the collective; it cannot provide the general pattern for a sociology of associations. But since analysts have used society to shortcut politics, they are never in a good position to differentiate the landscapes drawn by those various tracers. Obsessed by the goal of reaching the whole, they have made the task of collecting it much more difficult. Like nature, society is a premature assemblage: it should be put ahead of us and not behind.

Contrary to what Plato said in his *Republic*, there is not one but at least three 'Big Animals': the Body Politic, the Society, the Collective. But to be able to render these different beasts visible, distinguish their movements, track their various ethologies, detect their ecology, one must refuse again to be intelligent. One must remain as myopic as an ant in order to carefully misconstrue what 'social' usually means. One must travel on foot and stick to the decision not to accept any ride from any faster vehicle. Yes, we should follow the suggestion that interactions are overflowed by many ingredients already in place that come from other times, other spaces and other agents; yes, we should accept the idea of moving away to some other sites in order to find the sources of those many ingredients. But as soon as we get out of some interaction, we should ignore the giant signs 'toward Context' or 'to Structure'; we should turn at a right angle, leave the freeways, and choose instead to walk through a tiny path not much wider than a donkey's trail.

Although social scientists are proud of having added volume to flat interactions, it turns out that they have gone too fast. By taking for granted this third dimension—even if it's to criticize its existence—they have withdrawn from inquiry the main phenomenon of social science: the very production of place, size, and scale. Against such a three-dimensional shape, we have to try to keep the social domain completely *flat*. It's really a question of cartography. Because of the underlining necessity of the body politic, social scientists have thought that society provided a third dimension *in which* all the interactions should find a place. This explains why they make such an inordinate consumption of three-dimensional images: spheres, pyramids, monuments, systems, organisms, organizations. To resist this temptation, I am going to offer a 2-D projection. In pursuing the topographic metaphor, it's as if we had to emulate in social theory the marvelous book *Flatland*, which tries to make us 3-D animals live inside a 2-D world only made up of lines. It might seem odd at first but we have to become the Flat-Earthers of social theory.[220] This is the only way to follow how dimensions are generated and maintained. It's as if the maps handed down to us by the tradition had been crumpled into a useless bundle and we have to retrieve them from the wastebasket. Through a series of careful restorations, we have to flatten them out on a table with the back of our hand until they become legible and usable again. Although this ironing out may seem counterintuitive, it is the only way to measure the real distance every social connection has to overcome to generate some sort of tracing. What was hopelessly crinkled must now be fully deployed.

The aim of this second part is to practice a sort of corrective calisthenics. I will proceed in three steps: we will first *relocate* the global so as to break down the automatism that leads from interaction to 'Context'; we will then *redistribute* the local so as to understand why interaction is such an abstraction; and finally, we will *connect* the sites revealed by the two former moves, highlighting the various *vehicles* that make up the definition of the social understood as association.[221] Once this alternative topography has been sketched, it will finally be possible to discuss the political relevance of sociology without confusing the already made society with the delicate and risky loop of the public. Then, and only then, will the collective have enough room to collect itself.

---

[220] Flat Earthers are a subset of fringe science, but I am taking it here as an allusion to Edwin Abbott (1992), *Flatland: a romance of many dimensions*.

[221] To follow Part II, it might be useful to consult online Latour and Hermant, *Paris the Invisible City* because of the many different illustrations.

First Move: Localizing the Global

The first corrective move looks simple enough: we have to lay continuous connections leading from one local interaction to the other places, times, and agencies through which a local site is *made to do* something. This means that we have to follow the path indicated by the process of delegation or translation explained in Part I. As we have also learned in the preceding pages, this deployment might take the shape of a network on the condition that every transport be paid in transformations, that is, if we make sure to pave the whole way from one site to the next not with intermediaries but with full-blown mediators. If we do this, we will render visible the long chains of actors linking sites to one another without missing a single step. It might be empirically hard but we should not expect major theoretical hurdles.

Unfortunately, this would mean counting without the risk of confusing one track with another that has the same departure point—let's get away from local interactions—but not the same end point because that one goes to Context, Structure, and Framework. Depending on which path we follow, the plot ends very differently. Either Little Red Riding Hood will be able to reach grandma's house, or else she will be kidnapped in the forest. How can one plod along safely from one mediator to the next without being swallowed whole by the Wolf of Context? A ploy has to be found to make the two social theories diverge, letting the sociology of the social go its own way while the sociology of associations should be able to keep drawing more and more accurate road maps.

It does not require a deep understanding of topology to realize that the two don't only differ by their end point, but also by the type of deformation they permit: when you put some local site 'inside' a larger framework, you are forced to *jump*. There is now a yawning break between what encloses and what is enclosed, between the more local and the more global. What would happen if we forbade any breaking or tearing and allowed only bending, stretching, and squeezing?

Could we then go *continuously* from the local interaction to the many delegating actors? The departure point and all the points recognized as its origin would now remain *side by side* and a connection, a fold would be made visible.

What is so important for our project is that, in such a flattened topography, if any action has to be transported from one site to the next, you now clearly need a conduit and a vehicle. In the other landscape, the embedded context and the embedded actor were so incommensurable, they were separated by such an unaccountable gap, that there was never any way to detect through which mysterious vehicle action was carried out. But that is not the case if the landscape is kept obsessively flat. The full cost of every connection is now entirely payable. If a site wants to influence another site, it has to levy the means. The tyranny of distance has been underlined again. Actors have become *accountable*. But if something is allowed to be 'inside' something else, then the third dimension of society is added and the whole of Merlin's castle pops up out of the lake. To stop this magic, we have to make sure that no extra dimension will be added. To do so we have to invent a series of *clamps* to hold the landscape firmly flat and to force, so to speak, any candidate with a more 'global' role to sit *beside* the 'local' site it claims to explain, rather than watch it jump on top of it or behind it. In what follows, I am going to draw a rough inventory of some of those clamps.

Textbooks in sociology are organized around various topics—family, institution, nation-states, markets, health, deviance, and so on—which represent the slowly revisable outcome of the many decisions made by social scientists on what the right ingredients of the social world should be. In contrast, all of the idiosyncratic terms I am going to offer designate nothing more than specific tricks to help resist the temptation to jump to the global. Because of the corrective nature of this gymnastic movement, the virtues of those concepts are, first of all, negative. They pertain to our *infra*-language, such as the weak terms of 'group', 'actor', 'agency', 'translation', and 'fluid'. Like the notion of network, they don't designate *what* is being mapped, but *how* it is possible to map anything from such a territory. They are part of the equipment lying on the geographer's desk to allow him to project shapes on a sheet of paper. This is why the terms I am going to review won't say anything substantive about the social realm; they simply allow ANT scholars to render the social fluid collectable again in the same way entomologists learn how to build little bridges so that, without interfering with the ants' travels, they can count them one by one.[222]

---

[222] See Jacques Pasteels and Jean-Louis Deneubourg (1987), *From Individual to Collective Behavior in Social Insects* and Deborah Gordon (1999), *Ants At Work: How An Insect Society Is Organized*.

From Panopticon to Oligopticon

Myopic ANT scholars have a great advantage over sharp-sighted all-encompassing overseers. Not only can they ask gross and silly questions, they can do so obstinately and collectively. The first kind of clamp is the one obtained by this rather naive query: 'Where are the structural effects actually being produced?' I am aware that this geographic question shows a terrible lack of manners, but I am a science student and so, for any piece of scientific knowledge, I am used to supplying its indispensable conditions of production.[223] For example, even linguists need a room, an office, an institution, a department, boxes of archives, a place to stay, a coffee pot, and Xerox machine so as to gather all the elements, which have been extracted from thousands of local interactions and millions of speech acts, and carefully fabricate a linguistic structure.[224] And the same is true of lawyers: the system of law is compiled using folders, libraries, meetings, etc.[225] Even Karl Marx in the British Library needs a desk to assemble the formidable forces of capitalism. No more than language or law, physiology lives a mysterious and ethereal life: it is always produced somewhere, in such and such laboratory at the Royal College of Surgeons, in a freshly revised textbook, in a doctor's cabinet, after a consensus meeting has modified the standard procedure for taking care of sprained ankles. Culture does not act surreptitiously behind the actor's back. This most sublime production is manufactured at specific places and institutions, be it the messy offices on the top floor of Marshal Sahlins's house on the Chicago University campus or the thick Area Files kept at the Pitts River museum in Oxford.[226]

Other sociologists may ignore these production sites as so many transparent intermediaries since, according to their epistemology, they play no other role than to reveal the 'fundamental structures' of human actions, but historians and sociologists of science pay close attention. Ever since we decided to follow how matters of concern are generated by the various disciplines, we have to take into account the practical ways through which the knowledge of others' actions is being daily produced. Is this relativism? I hope so. If no signal travels faster than light, no knowledge travels without scientists, laboratories,

[223] For an up-to-date attempt at spatializing science, see David N. Livingstone (2003), *Putting Science in Its Place: Geographies of Scientific Knowledge*.
[224] See Sylvain Auroux (1999), *La raison, le langage et les normes*.
[225] See Martha Mundy and Alain Pottage (2004), *Law, Anthropology and the Constitution of the Social: Making Persons and Things* and Bruno Latour (2002), *La fabrique du droit - Une ethnographie du Conseil d'Etat*.
[226] For a materialist account of anthropology making, see the classic works of George W. Stocking (ed.) (1983), *Observers Observed: Essays on Ethnographic Fieldwork*; Bourdieu, *Outline*; and Goody *The Domestication of the Savage Mind*.

and fragile reference chains. Our interest for those humble means is not dictated by suspicion about the true efficacy of those structures or by some reflexive urge. It is simply that they offer ideal *tracers* for discovering what sort of relationship may exist for good between the micro and the macro. If the whole of physical space and physical time had to be reshaped because of the realization that no two signals are really sent simultaneously, then how much more social space and time will have to be reshuffled once every structural feature is brought firmly back inside its local conditions of production?

And sure enough, as soon as the local sites that manufacture global structures are underlined, it is the entire topography of the social world that is being modified. Macro no longer describes a *wider* or a *larger* site in which the micro would be embedded like some Russian Matryoshka doll, but another equally local, equally micro place, which is *connected* to many others through some medium transporting specific types of traces. No place can be said to be bigger than any other place, but some can be said to benefit from far safer connections with many *more* places than others. This move has the beneficial effect to keep the landscape flat, since what earlier, in the pre-relativist sociology, was situated 'above' or 'below' remains side by side and firmly on the same plane as the other loci which they were trying to overlook or include. What is now highlighted much more vividly than before are all the connections, the cables, the means of transportation, the vehicles linking places together. This is their strength but also, as we are going to see, their frailty.[227] If you cut some underlying structure from its local application, nothing happens: it remains there in its mysterious empyrean; if you cut a structure-making site from its connections, it simply *stops* being able to structure anything.

Having reached this point, don't try to be intelligent, don't jump, don't switch vehicles: if you do so, you'll miss the embranchment and fail to trace the new landscape. Just follow the trails myopically. Ant you have accepted to be, ANT you will remain! If you stick obstinately enough to the decision of producing a continuous trail instead of a discontinuous one, then another mountain range begins to emerge. It is a landscape which runs through, crosses out, and totally shortcuts the former loci of 'local interaction' and of 'global context'.

It's not that there is no hierarchy, no ups and downs, no rifts, no deep canyons, no high spots. It is simply that if you wish to go from one site to another, then you have to pay the full cost of relation, connection, displacement, and information. No lifts, accelerations, or

---

[227] Even 'vast' master narratives may be produced in these 'local' places. See Michael Lynch and David Bogen (1996), *The Spectacle of History: Speech, Text and Memory at the Iran Contra Hearings*.

shortcuts are allowed. For example, the millions of speech acts that make up a dictionary, a grammar, or a language structure in a linguistics department have been extracted from local speech acts, which have been recorded, transcribed, collated, and classified in various ways using many different mediums.[228] The fact that no structure acts unconsciously 'under' each speech act does not mean that it is made out of thin air by 'local' linguists stuck in their office. It means that the written structure is *related*, connected, associated to all the speech acts *in some ways* the enquiry should discover. Of course, the office of the linguist may have some relationship with what is spoken 'out there', but how would you imagine this relationship to be made without connections and at no cost, without a constant trade going on along the conduits leading to and from the office? These two-way relations are even stronger since grammar has also become, through years of schooling, a common feature of what it is for speakers to interact together. Written grammars have now become part of the equipment of every westernized mother faulting her daughter for defective manners of speech. Viewed in this way, every academic office—the anthropologist's den, the physiologist's lab, the lawyer's library, the social theorist's study, the architect's studio, the consultant's office—begins to take, in the observer's account, a star-like shape with a center surrounded by many radiating lines with all sorts of tiny conduits leading to and fro. The Wolf of Context could gulp down an interaction, but not such a long, flat, folded net in which he would instead find himself fully ensnared.

Provided we follow such a lead without flinching, a new topographical relationship becomes visible between the former micro and the former macro. The macro is neither 'above' nor 'below' the interactions, but *added* to them as *another* of their connections, feeding them and feeding off of them. There is no other known way *to achieve changes in relative scale*. For each of the 'macro places', the same type of questions can be raised. The answer provided by fieldwork will bring attention back to a local site and re-describe them as some disheveled arrays of connections through which vehicles (carrying types of documents, inscriptions, and materials) are traveling via some sort of conduit.

What was true, at the end of Part I, of the sociologists' written account, is true of all the other structure-makers as well: all of them are launching tiny bridges to overcome the gaps created by disparate frames of reference. The precise nature of those moving entities is not important at this point: the enquiry will decide what are the vehicles

---

[228] See Simon Winchester (2003), *The Meaning of Everything: The Story of the Oxford English Dictionary*.

and what are the documents for each case. What counts is the possibility for the enquirer to register that kind of 'networky' shape wherever possible, instead of having to cut off data in two heaps: one local, one global. To tell an actor-network story is to be able to capture those many connections without bungling them from the start by some a priori decision over what is the 'true size' of an interaction or of some social aggregate. As should be clear by now, ANT is first of all an abstract *projection* principle for deploying *any* shape, not some concrete arbitrary decision about *which* shape should be on the map.

Centers of calculation, as I have called them, offer such a star-like shape in a very striking form.[229] Capitalism, for instance, may be an intractable entity endowed with a 'spirit', but a Wall Street trading room does connect to the 'whole world' through the tiny but expeditious conduits of millions of bits of information per second, which, after having been digested by traders, are flashed back to the very same place by the Reuters or Bloomberg trading screens that register all of the transactions and are then wired to the 'rest of the (connected) world' to determine someone's net worth.[230] Once those conduits are taken into account, we now have a choice between two routes: we can still believe that capitalism acts surreptitiously as the 'infrastructure' of all the world's transactions and, if so, we have to jump from the local assessment of a specific company's worth to its 'context', changing vehicles as we go along, shifting gears and flying into stratospheric considerations instead of walking on foot. Or we can continue doing the footwork and study places such as the Wall Street trading room *without* changing vehicles, just to see where this decision will lead us. The landscape drawn in both cases, using these two definitions of tracers, will be completely different.

And so will the leeway left for action: capitalism has no plausible enemy since it is 'everywhere', but a given *trading room* in Wall Street has many competitors in Shanghai, Frankfurt, and London—a computer breakdown, a sneaky movement by a competitor, an unexpected figure, a neglected variable in a pricing formula, a risky accounting procedure—that may shift the balance from an obscene profit to a dramatic loss. Yes, Wall Street is connected to many places and in this sense, but in this sense only, it is 'bigger', more powerful, overarching. However, it is not a wider, larger, less local, less interactive, less an

---

[229] For a definition of the term, see Bruno Latour (1987), *Science In Action: How to Follow Scientists and Engineers through Society*.

[230] See Karin Knorr-Cetina and Urs Bruegger (2002), 'Global Microstructures: The Virtual Societies of Financial Markets'; Muniesa, *Des marchés comme algorithmes*; Donald MacKenzie (forthcoming), *An engine, not a camera: finance theory and the making of markets*; Lépinay 'Les formules du marché'; Mirowski *Machine Dreams*; Andrew Leyshon and Nigel Thrift (1996), *Money/Space: Geographies of Monetary Transformation*; and, although a century old, Tarde *Psychologie économique*.

inter-subjective place than the shopping center in Moulins, France or the noisy and smelly market stands in Bouaké, Ivory Coast. Don't focus on capitalism, but don't stay stuck on the screen of the trading room either: follow the connections, 'follow the actors themselves'. No cold objectification has taken place there, no superior reason is being unfolded. Everywhere, blind termites are busy cranking out data. Just keep sniffing through their galleries, no matter how far this takes you.

The same change of topography occurs every time you replace some mysterious structure by fully visible and empirically traceable sites. An organization is certainly not 'bigger' than those it organizes. Since Bill Gates is not physically larger than all his Microsoft employees, Microsoft itself, as a corporate body, cannot be a vast building in which individual agents reside. Instead, there is a certain type of *movement* going through all of them, a few of which begin and end in Mr Gates's *office*.[231] It's because an organization is even less a society than the body politic that it's made only of movements, which are woven by the constant circulation of documents, stories, accounts, goods, and passions. For an office to be traversed by longer, faster, and more intense connections is not the same thing as being wider.[232] To follow continuous trails is not the same as to jump to structure. To stick to the visible and the graspable is not the same as to gorge oneself with invisible agencies. To remain with one type of vehicle all along is not the same as accepting a ride from faster and fancier modes of transportation. There exists no place that can be said to be 'non-local'. If something is to be 'delocalized', it means that it is being sent from one place to some *other* place, not from one place to *no* place. 'Shouldn't that be common sense?' So mutters the same obsessively blind, trail-following ANT.

An actor-network is traced whenever, in the course of a study, the decision is made to replace actors of whatever size by local *and* connected sites instead of ranking them into micro and macro. The two parts are essential, hence the hyphen. The first part (the actor) reveals the narrow space in which all of the grandiose ingredients of the world begin to be hatched; the second part (the network) may explain through which vehicles, which traces, which trails, which types of information, the world is being brought *inside* those places and then,

---

[231] Strangely enough, this is true of the building itself in spite of the metaphor of structure, since no building is ever visible *in toto* at any point of its construction and use. See Edward Robbins (1994), *Why Architects Draw* and for an ethnography of scaling, Albena Yaneva (2005), 'Scaling Up and Down: Extraction Trials in Architectural Design'.

[232] A stunning example of the fecundity of this approach is offered by the airport project led by Goodwin and Suchman. See Françoise Brun-Cottan et al. (1991), *The workplace project: Designing for diversity and change* and Goodwin and Goodwin *Formulating Planes*.

after having been transformed there, are being pumped back *out* of its narrow walls. This is why the hyphenated 'network' is not there as a surreptitious presence of the Context, but remains what connects the actors together. Instead of being, like Context, another dimension giving volume to a too narrow and flat description, it allows the relations to remain flat and to pay in full the bill for the 'transaction costs'. It's not that there are a macro-sociology and a micro-sociology, but that there are two different ways of envisaging the macro-micro relationship: the first one builds a series of Russian Matryoshka dolls— the small is being enclosed, the big is enclosing; and the second deploys connections—the small is being unconnected, the big one is to be attached.

It is not by accident that ANT started with the study of science. Whenever one looks for a telling example of what it could mean for a social theory to do away with the micro/macro distinction, scientific arrays offer an excellent template. Not only were they much easier to study, they also provided the most extreme examples of how small innovations could, in the end, become a 'macro' feature of the 'whole' world.[233] Sciences have no size, or rather, if there is one thing that does not account well for their power, it is their diminutive size. It's no accident that whenever Gabriel Tarde wanted to find a perfect example of his theory of 'imitative rays', it was to the (then non-existing) sociology of science that he chose to turn. There exists, he insisted, some *indirect but fully traceable* connection between Galileo's cabinet in Florence in the 16th century and what every schoolboy learns when they are asked not to believe their eyes telling them that the sun is setting at dusk.[234] Any laboratory scale is, *potentially*, immensely small or big. It would be foolish, on the observer's part, to decide in advance and for good what its real size is. Scientific disciplines, including the little 'cameral sciences' such as accounting, management, and business organization provide marvelous examples because, like the fruit flies of geneticists, they offer us an exaggerated version of what occurs everywhere in a less clearly, traceable way. As we saw in Part I, the more science and technology develops, the easier it is to physically trace

---

[233] The office at the School of Mines is the birthplace of Schlumberger's early oil detection attempts. On this remarkable story, see Geffrey Bowker (1994), *Science on the Run: Information Management and Industrial Geographics at Schlumberger, 1920–1940*. On the power of network expansion, the classic story remains Hughes, *Networks of Power*. See also the beautiful example of Indian colonialism in Daniel R. Headrick (1988), *The Tentacles of Progress: Technology Transfer in the Age of Imperialism, 1850–1940*.

[234] 'When a young peasant, observing the sunset, is at a loss whether to believe his schoolmaster, who assures him that the fall of night is due to the motion of the earth and not to the motion of the sun, or the testimony of his senses, which tell him the contrary, in such a case there is but a single imitative ray, which, reaching out through his schoolmaster, unites him with Galileo; nevertheless this is sufficient to render his hesitation, his own internal opposition, social in origin.' In Tarde, *Social Laws*, p. 51.

social connections. Satellites, fiber optic networks, calculators, data streams, and laboratories are the new material equipment that underline the ties as if a huge red pen was connecting the dots to let everyone see the lines that were barely visible before.[235] But what is true for laboratories and offices is true for all the other connecting or structuring sites as well.

To designate this first category of landmarks, I propose to use the word *oligopticon* as the generic term, reserving the expression of 'centers of calculation' for the sites where literal and not simply metaphorical *calculations* are made possible by the mathematical or at least arithmetic format of the documents being brought back and forth.[236] As every reader of Michel Foucault knows, the 'panopticon', an ideal prison allowing for a total surveillance of inmates imagined at the beginning of the 19th century by Jeremy Bentham, has remained a utopia, that is, a world of nowhere to feed the double disease of total paranoia and total megalomania.[237] We, however, are not looking for utopia, but for places on earth that are fully assignable. Oligoptica are just those sites since they do exactly the opposite of panoptica: they see much *too little* to feed the megalomania of the inspector or the paranoia of the inspected, but what they see, they *see it well*—hence the use of this Greek word to designate an ingredient at once indispensable and that comes in tiny amounts (as in the 'oligo-elements' of your health store). From oligoptica, sturdy but extremely narrow views of the (connected) whole are made possible—as long as connections hold. Nothing it seems can threaten the absolutist gaze of panoptica, and this is why they are loved so much by those sociologists who dream to occupy the center of Bentham's prison; the tiniest bug can blind oligoptica.

Sometimes, those sites are easy to pinpoint because physical connections do the tracing for us in the same way as with laboratories: it is obvious, for instance, that an army's command and control center is

[235] This is even more true today with quantitative tools. See Peter Keating and Alberto Cambrosio (2003), *Biomedical Platforms: Realigning the Normal and the Pathological in Late-Twentieth-Century Medicine*.

[236] The close study of formalism enables one to distinguish between the two situations. See Claude Rosental (2003), *La Trame de l'évidence*; David Kaiser (2005), *Drawing Theories Apart: The Dispersion of Feynman Diagrams in Postwar Physics*; and, on the other hand, the study of files and bureaucrats in Christian Jacob (1992), *L'empire des cartes. Approche théorique de la cartographie à travers l'histoire*. Suchman uses the expression 'centers of coordination' to insist on the practicalities of the workplace, which she takes to be a hybrid space of forms, calculations, techniques of organizations, and interactions. See Brun-Cottan, *The Workplace Project*.

[237] It's clear that Bentham himself was more than infected by both diseases. See Jérémy Bentham and Michel Foucault (1977), *Le Panopticon précédé de l'oeil du pouvoir: entretien avec Michel Foucault*. It's less clear in the case of Foucault's ironical use of the utopia of the panopticon in Michel Foucault (1975), *Discipline and Punish: The Birth of Prison*.

not 'bigger' and 'wider' than the local front thousands of miles away where soldiers are risking their life, but it is clear nonetheless that such a war room can command and control anything—as the name indicates—*only as long as* it remains connected to the theater of operation through a ceaseless transport of information. So the right topography here is not to include the front line 'into' some overarching power, but to *localize* both and to *connect* through some sort of well-fed cables what in French is called *connectique*.[238] This is what I mean by flattening the landscape. That this is not an easy task, every soldier, commander, and historian of battles knows all too well.[239]

Sometimes the star-shaped oligoptica might be more difficult to detect: a newspaper editor's cubicle resembles a command and control room but only a bit, since what goes out and what comes in is not as formatted and binding as a military order or a dispatch.[240] In still other cases, the connections are barely visible, as when one is asking in which bureau is 'Oedipus' complex', 'governance', 're-engineering' or 'social capital' being produced. And yet, here again, trails could be followed and a map could be drawn of, for instance, the various contradictory social theories that travel through Paris. Even if they appear immaterial, they are physically transported over fieldwork, questionnaires, statistical bureaus, academic polemics, journal articles, bar conversations, and grant applications before making their way back through editorials, textbooks, party officials, strike committees, and war rooms, where they are put to use by some participants as a way to decide, in part, who they are and to which sort of group they pertain. As we learned from the first source of uncertainty, it is hard to pertain to a group nowadays without some help from a social scientist. What does anyone know about 'cultural capital', 'methodological individualism', 'organizational inertia', 'downsizing', 'gender', 'the precautionary principle' without first passing through some research center?[241] In the case of such flimsy tracers, it might be more difficult to draw the map since the tracks might be fainter, the connections

---

[238] Many examples of this fragility can be found in Barry *Political Machines*. For a science studies analysis of bureaucracy at work, see Alberto Cambrosio, Camille Limoges and Denyse Pronovost (1990), 'Representing biotechnology: an ethnography of Quebec Science Policy'.

[239] For a masterly demonstration, see John Keegan (1987), *The Mask of Command*. The recent dispute over weapons of mass destruction offers a stunning example of the limits of all the metaphors of 'gaze' and 'vision', see Hans Blix (2004), *Disarming Iraq*. However, the literary masterpiece remains Tolstoy's *War and Peace*.

[240] For some classical examples, see Walter Lippmann (1922), *Public Opinion*, on journals; Chandler *The Visible Hand* about companies; and Peter Miller (1994), 'The Factory as Laboratory' on accounting.

[241] A good example of this is Boltanski and Chiapello, *The New Spirit of Capitalism* when they use management literature as their guide to understand how companies make use of new social theories—including ANT...

often interrupted. But it remains necessary to try in order to give the impression that we could be put 'in a category' at no cost.[242]

To conclude on this first type of clamp: even though the question seems really odd at first—not to say in bad taste—whenever anyone speaks of a 'system', a 'global feature', a 'structure', a 'society', an 'empire', a 'world economy', an 'organization', the first ANT reflex should be to ask: 'In which building? In which bureau? Through which corridor is it accessible? Which colleagues has it been read to? How has it been compiled?'[243] Inquirers, if they accept to follow this clue, will be surprised at the number of sites and the number of conduits that pop up as soon as those queries are being raised. The social landscape begins to change rather quickly. And as travelers notice right away, it does not produce in them the same feeling as if they were asked to penetrate some intimidating overarching pyramid of power or scan the flattened landscape where many attempts at establishing and securing frail connections circulate. It's this difference in topography that will explain (in the book's concluding chapter) why the two social theories don't aspire to the same sort of political relevance.

Panoramas

And yet, there is no reason to deny that the shadow of a huge social pyramid looms over our heads. It's like a Pavlov reflex, a knee-jerk reaction. Whenever we speak of society, we imagine a massive monument or sphere, something like a huge cenotaph. There is a pecking order from top to bottom. So no matter how many warnings I could flash, every oligopticon used to hold the landscape flat will immediately be engulfed somewhere 'into' a larger social context as snuggly as a pigeon into its pigeon-hole. There is no way to fight this prejudice directly since it has been, for more than two centuries, the default position of our operational systems: society, no matter how it is construed to be, has to be something large in scale. And yet, it is just this default position that makes it impossible to deploy any relativist sociology.

The problem is that social scientists use scale as one of the many variables they need to set up *before* doing the study, whereas scale is

---

[242] See Luc Boltanski (1987), *The Making of a Class: Cadres in French Society* and the early work of Thévenot on socio-economic category making, especially his classic Laurent Thévenot (1984), 'Rules and Implements: Investment in Forms'.

[243] Anke te Heesen (2004), 'Things that talk: News, Paper, Scissors. Clippings in the Sciences and Arts around 1920'.

what actors achieve by *scaling, spacing,* and *contextualizing* each other through the transportation in some specific vehicles of some specific traces.[244] It is of little use to respect the actors' achievements if in the end we deny them one of their most important privileges, namely that they are the ones defining relative scale. It's not the analyst's job to impose an absolute one. As every reader of relativity theory knows, absolute frames of reference generate only horrible deformations, spoiling any hope of superimposing documents in some readable format, while soft and slimy 'mollusks of reference' (Einstein's term) allow physicists to travel from one frame to the next if not smoothly, then at least continuously.[245] Either the sociologist is rigid and the world becomes a mess or the sociologist is pliable enough and the world puts itself in order. Here again the duties of empirical relativism are akin to those of morality.

It is because the prejudice of living inside an overarching framework is seemingly impossible to uproot that I have to devise a second type of artificial clamp. As long as we do not ferret out the places where 'up', 'down', 'total', and 'global' are so convincingly staged, the temptation to jump to the 'context' will not be alleviated and the actors' scale-making activity will never have room to be fully deployed. The social landscape will never be flattened enough for the cost of connecting vehicles to be made fully visible. People will go on believing that the big animal doesn't need any fodder to sustain itself; that society is something that can stand without being produced, assembled, collected, or kept up; that it resides behind us, so to speak, instead of being ahead of us as a task to be fulfilled.

As we saw in the earlier part of the book, it is not the sociologist's job to decide in the actor's stead what groups are making up the world and which agencies are making them act. Her job is to build the artificial experiment—a report, a story, a narrative, an account—where this diversity might be deployed to the full. Even though it seems so odd at first, the same is true of scale: it is not the sociologist's business to decide whether any given interaction is 'micro' while some other one would be 'middle-range' or 'macro'. Too much investment, ingenuity, and energy is expended by participants into modifying the relative scale of all the other participants for sociologists to decide on a fixed standard. As Boltanski and Thévenot have shown, if there is one thing you cannot do in the actor's stead it is to decide where they stand on a scale going from small to big, because at every turn of their many

[244] Those traces are specified in the third move. Once more, patience is requested here.

[245] I have always considered, somewhat infamously, Einstein as a social theorist, that is, as a theorist of associations. See Bruno Latour (1988c), 'A Relativist Account of Einstein's Relativity'.

attempts at justifying their behavior they may suddenly mobilize the whole of humanity, France, capitalism, and reason while, a minute later, they might settle for a local compromise.[246] Faced with such sudden shifts in scale, the only possible solution for the analyst is to take the shifting *itself* as her data and to see through which practical means 'absolute measure' is made to spread.

Scale is the actor's own achievement. Although this is the oldest and, in my view, the most decisive proposition made by ANT,[247] I have never encountered anyone who could accept to even glance at the landscape thus revealed—no more, if I dare the parallel, than Galileo could tempt his 'dear and respected colleagues' to have a look through his makeshift telescope. The reason is that we tend to think of scale— macro, meso, micro—as a well-ordered *zoom*. It is a bit like the marvelous but perversely misleading book *The Powers of Ten,* where each page offers a picture one order of magnitude closer than the preceding one all the way from the Milky Way to the DNA fibers, with a photo somewhere in the middle range that shows two young picnickers on a lawn near Lake Superior.[248] A microsecond of reflection is enough to realize that this montage is misleading—where would a camera be positioned to show the galaxy as a whole? Where is the microscope able to pin down this cell DNA instead of that one? What ruler could order pictures along such a regular trail? Nice assemblage, but perversely wrong. The same is true of the zooming effect in the social realm, except that, in this case, it is taken not as a clever artistic trick, but as a most natural injunction springing from the sturdiest common sense. Is it not obvious that IBM is 'bigger' than its sales force? That France is 'wider' than the School of Mines that is much 'bigger' than me? And if we imagine IBM and France as having the same star-like shape as the command and control war room I mentioned earlier, what would we make of the organizational charts of IBM's corporate structure, of the *map* of France, of the *picture* of the whole Earth? Are they not obviously providing the vastly wider 'framework' into which 'smaller things' have to be 'situated'? Does it not make perfect sense to say that Europe is bigger than France, which is bigger than Paris that is bigger than rue Danton and which is bigger than my flat? Or to say that the 20th century provides the frame 'in which' the Second World War has 'taken place'? That the battle of Waterloo, in Stendhal's *The Charterhouse of Parma*, is a vastly more important event than Fabrizio del Dongo's experience of it? While readers might be ready to listen patiently to the claims of ANT for a new topography, they won't take

---

[246] Boltanski and Thévenot, *On Justification.*
[247] See Michel Callon and Bruno Latour (1981), 'Unscrewing the Big Leviathans. How Do Actors Macrostructure Reality'.
[248] Philip Morrison and Phylis Morrison (1982), *The Powers of Ten.*

it any further if it goes too much against every commonsensical reaction. How could 'putting things into a frame' not be the most reasonable thing to do?

I agree that the point is to follow common sense. I also agree that framing things into some context is what actors constantly do. I am simply arguing that it is this very framing activity, this very activity of contextualizing, that should be brought into the foreground and that it cannot be done as long as the zoom effect is taken for granted. To settle scale in advance would be sticking to one measure and one absolute frame of reference only when it is *measuring* that we are after; when it is *traveling* from one frame to the next that we want to achieve. Once again, sociologists of the social are not abstract enough. They believe that they have to stick to common sense, although what demonstrates, on the contrary, a complete lack of reason is imagining a 'social zoom' without a camera, a set of rails, a wheeled vehicle, and all the complex teamwork which has to be assembled to carry out something as simple as a dolly shot. Any zoom of any sort that attempts to order matters smoothly like the set of Russian dolls is always the result of a script carefully planned by some stage manager. If you doubt it, then go visit Universal Studios. 'Ups' and 'downs', 'local' and 'global' have to be made, they are never given. We all know this pretty well, since we have witnessed many cases where relative size has been instantaneously reversed—by strikes, revolutions, coups, crises, innovations, discoveries. Events are not like tidy racks of clothes in a store. S, M, X, XL labels seem rather confusingly distributed; they wane and wax pretty fast; they shrink or enlarge at lightning speed. But we never seem ready to draw the consequences of our daily observations, so obsessed are we by the gesture of 'placing things into their wider context'.

And yet this gesture should also be carefully documented! Have you ever noticed, at sociological conferences, political meetings, and bar palavers, the hand gestures people make when they invoke the 'Big Picture' into which they offer to replace what you have just said so that it 'fits' into such easy-to-grasp entities as 'Late Capitalism', 'the ascent of civilization', 'the West', 'modernity', 'human history', 'Postcolonialism', or 'globalization'? Their hand gesture is never bigger than if they were stroking a pumpkin! I am at last going to show you the real size of the 'social' in all its grandeur: well, it is not that big. It is only made so by the grand gesture and by the professorial tone in which the 'Big Picture' is alluded to. If there is one thing that is *not* common sense, it would be to take even a reasonably sized pumpkin for the 'whole of society'. Midnight has struck for that sort of social theory and the beautiful carriage has been transformed back into what it should always have remained: a member of the family *Cucurbitaceae*.

I am mean, I know, but sometimes it can be done in a friendly way like when a surgeon quickly removes a painful wart. Size and zoom should not be confused with *connectedness*. Either this pumpkin-size scale is related through many connections to many other sites, in the same way a trading room in Wall Street is to the many arrays making up world economies—and, if so, I want to be convinced that those connections exist, I want to touch the conduits, to check their solidity, to test their realism—or it is *not* related and, in this case, if there is one thing that this threatening gesture of the hands can't do, it is to force me into believing that my small 'local' description has been 'framed' by something 'bigger'. That's right, I don't want to be framed! But I am ready to study very carefully the framing itself, to turn it from such an automatic resource into a fascinating new topic. It is through the staging of the zoom effect that the social of social theorists enters the scene; that it claims to 'embed' local interactions; that it ends up gaining such a powerful grip over the mind of every actor. So powerful is it that when an alternative social theory offers to get rid of such a grip, it is as if God had died again—and indeed there is more than one common feature between the ever dying God of olden days and that position which the God-like sociologist sometimes dreams of occupying.

In effect, the Big Picture is just that: a picture. And then the question can be raised: in which movie theatre, in which exhibit gallery is it *shown*? Through which optics is it *projected*? To which audience is it *addressed*? I propose to call *panoramas* the new clamps by asking obsessively such questions. Contrary to oligoptica, panoramas, as etymology suggests, see *everything*. But they also see *nothing* since they simply *show* an image painted (or projected) on the tiny wall of a room fully *closed* to the outside. The metaphor comes from those early rooms invented in the early 19th century, whose descendants can be found in the Omnimax cinema rooms built near science centers and shopping malls.[249] The Greek word *pan*, which means 'everything', does not signify that those pictures survey 'the whole' but that, on the contrary, they paper over a wall in a blind room on which a *completely* coherent scenery is being projected on a 360° circular screen. Full coherence is their forte—and their main frailty.

Where can we find them now that all of the real panoramas made famous by Walter Benjamin have been destroyed? They are all over the place; they are being painted every time a newspaper editorialist reviews with authority the 'whole situation'; when a book retells the

---

[249] On the history of this 19th century media, see Stephan Oettermann (1997), *The Panorama: History of a Mass Medium*; Bernard Comment (2003), *The Panorama*; and of course Walter Benjamin (2002), *The Arcades Project*.

origins of the world from the Big Bang to President Bush; when a social theory textbook provides a bird's eye view of modernity; when the CEO of some big company gathers his shareholders; when some famous scientist summarizes for the benefit of the public 'the present state of science'; when a militant explains to her cellmates the 'long history of exploitation'; when some powerful architecture—a piazza, a skyscraper, a huge staircase—fills you with awe.[250] Sometimes they are splendid achievements as in the *Palazzo della Ragione* in Padua (yes, the Palace of Reason!), where the large city hall is entirely covered by a fresco depicting a vision of the entire Classical and Christian mythology together with the calendar of all the trades and civic events. Sometimes they are only a rough pell-mell of clichés as in the convoluted plots of conspiracy theorists. Sometimes they are offer entirely new programs as when a new show is offered about the 'end of history', the 'clash of civilizations', or 'risk society'. Sometimes they remake history when they propose a complete rereading of the Zeitgeist as in the *Phenomenology of Spirit* or *The Communist Manifesto*.

What is so powerful in those contraptions is that they nicely solve the question of staging the totality, of ordering the ups and downs, of nesting 'micro', 'meso', and 'macro' into one another. But they don't do it by multiplying two-way connections with other sites—as command and control rooms, centers of calculation and, more generally, oligoptica do.[251] They design a picture which has no gap in it, giving the spectator the powerful impression of being fully immersed in the real world without any artificial mediations or costly flows of information leading from or to the outside. Whereas oligoptica are constantly revealing the fragility of their connections and their lack of control on what is left in between their networks, panoramas gives the impression of complete control over what is being surveyed, even though they are partially blind and that nothing enters or leaves their walls except interested or baffled spectators. To confuse them with oligoptica would be like confusing a war episode monitored from the U.S. Army war room in Tampa, Florida, with the same one related on Fox News when a retired general is commenting on the 'day at the front'. The first account, which is a realist one, knows painfully well that it can become unreal as soon as communications are cut off; the second one might be just as real but it has a smaller chance of telling us whether or not it's fiction. Most of the time, it's this excess of coherence that gives the illusion away.

---

[250] On the link between architecture and power, see Jean-Philippe Heurtin (1999), *L'espace public parlementaire: Essais sur les raisons du législateur.*

[251] Sloterdijk has offered a description of many panoramas under the name of 'globes' in Peter Sloterdijk (1999), *Sphären. Bd.2 Globen.*

Although these panoramas shouldn't be taken too seriously, since such coherent and complete accounts may become the most blind, most local, and most partial viewpoints, they also have to be studied very carefully because they provide the only occasion to see the 'whole story' *as a whole*. Their totalizing views should not be despised as an act of professional megalomania, but they should be *added*, like everything else, to the multiplicity of sites we want to deploy.[252] Far from being the place where everything happens, as in their director's dreams, they are local sites to be added as so many new places dotting the flattened landscape we try to map. But even after such a downsizing, their role may become central since they allow spectators, listeners, and readers to be *equipped with a desire for wholeness and centrality*. It is from those powerful stories that we get our metaphors for what 'binds us together', the passions we are supposed to share, the general outline of society's architecture, the master narratives with which we are disciplined. It is inside their narrow boundaries that we get our commonsensical idea that interactions occur in a 'wider' context; that there is an 'up' and a 'down'; that there is a 'local' nested inside a 'global'; and that there might be a Zeitgeist the spirit of which has yet to be devised.

The status of these panoramas is strangely ambiguous: they are simultaneously what vaccinates against totalization—since they are obviously local and constricted inside blind rooms—and what offers a foretaste for the one world to be lived in. They collect, they frame, they rank, they order, they organize; they are the source of what is meant by a well-ordered zoom. So, no matter how much they trick us, they prepare us for the political task ahead. Through their many clever special effects, they offer a preview of the collective with which they should not be confused. As we now begin to realize, there is always a danger to take the building of those panoramas for the much harder political task of progressively composing the common world. Watching the movies of social theories in those Omnimax rooms is one thing, doing politics is quite another. Durkheim's 'sui generis society', Luhmann's 'autopoietic systems', Bourdieu's 'symbolic economy of fields', or Beck's 'reflexive modernity' are excellent narratives if they prepare us, once the screening has ended, to take up the political tasks of composition; they are misleading if taken as a description of what is the common world. At best, panoramas provide a prophetic preview of

---

[252] John Tresch has shown how many of those collecting devices exist in a given historical situation and how they can produce what he calls cosmograms. See John Tresch (2001), 'Mechanical Romanticism: Engineers of the Artificial Paradise'. This multiplicity disappears as soon as they are put inside a coherent *Zeitgeist* instead of being followed in their contradictory circulations—more on this in the section dealing with collecting statements p. 221.

the collective, at worst they are a very poor substitute for it. It's one of the ambitions of ANT to keep the prophetic urge that has always been associated with the social sciences, but to accompany the master narratives safely back inside the rooms where they are displayed.[253]

So here again, the voluntarily blind ANT scholar should keep asking the same mean and silly questions whenever a well-ordered pecking order between scales has been staged: 'In which room? In which panorama? Through which medium? With which stage manager? How much?' Active, sometimes even beautiful, complex sites will pop up at every corner as soon as this second interrogation is obsessively raised. If you are in doubt, try, as an exercise, to locate the places, the theaters, the stages where 'globalization' is being painted over. You will soon realize that, in spite of so much 'globalonney', globalization circulates along minuscule rails resulting in some glorified form of provincialism.[254]

After 'go slow', the injunctions are now 'don't jump' and 'keep everything flat!' The three pieces of advice reinforce one another, since it is only once the long distance between different points of the territory has been measured up that the full transaction costs to join them will have been reckoned. How could a walker assess in advance the time it will take to reach some mountaintop if the isometric lines had not first been drawn one by one? How could we discover the breadth of the political task ahead of us if *distances* between incommensurable viewpoints had not been fathomed first?

---

[253] The critique of Master Narratives and the appeal to multiplicity, fragmentation, and little narratives becomes moot once panoramas are added to the landscape: multiplicity is not in short supply. To limit oneself to it might also mean that the political task of assembling has been abandoned.

[254] On the localization of the global, see especially the work of Stephan Harrison, Steve Pile and Nigel Thrift (2004), *Patterned Ground: Entanglements of Nature and Culture*.

Second Move: Redistributing the Local

By equipping inquirers' toolboxes with different instruments (oligopticas and panoramas), we have allowed them to localize the global and to accompany it safely back inside the circuits in which it now circulates back and forth. Whenever the urge to go away from local interactions manifested itself, and instead of trying some *salto mortale* toward the invisible rear-world of the social context, I proposed to trudge toward the many local places where the global, the structural, and the total were being assembled and where they expand outward thanks to the laying down of specific cables and conduits. If you keep doing this long enough, the same effects of hierarchy and asymmetry that before were visible will now emerge out of strings of juxtaposed localities. Since they are pinpointed inside the many oligoptica and panoramas, there is nothing wrong any more with using the word 'contexts'. The vehicles that transport their effects have number plates and well-written labels, much like moving vans. From time to time, contexts are gathered, summed up, and staged *inside* specific rooms into coherent panoramas *adding* their many contradictory structuring effects to the sites to be 'contextualized' and 'structured'.

Needless to say, there exists no other place in which to sum up all those sites—at least not yet. So it would be quite foolish to ask 'in which' super-mega-macro-structure they all reside—in the same way as it has become wholly irrelevant to try to detect, after relativity theory, the ether wind 'through which' the Earth passes. There exists no global all-encompassing place where, for instance, the control room of the Strategic Air Command, the Wall Street floor, the water pollution map, the census bureau, the Christian Coalition, and the United Nations would be gathered and summed up. And if someone tries to do so—as I am doing here in this paragraph—it is *another* place, another circuitous route loosely connected to the others with no claim to 'embed' or 'know' them. If a place wishes to dominate all the others for good, that's just fine. But it will have to pay for every item of paraphernalia necessary to reach every one of the other places it purports to sum up, and to establish with it some sort of continuous, costly, two-way relation—if it doesn't foot the bill to the last cent, it becomes a panorama. Even though Leibniz never specified it, for one monad to reflect the dim presence of all the others, some extra work is necessary.

But re-contextualizing context is only part of the job of getting accustomed again to walking on foot inside a flattened landscape. We still have the problem of understanding why we said earlier that interactions were such a dissatisfying starting point because of the number of other ingredients already in place. The reflex of social scientists that led them away from interactions—and which pushed them to look behind, above, or beneath for some other sites of activity—might have been badly directed, but it is still a valid insight. If we understood the first move as a plea to give some privilege to 'local interactions', then we have not gained very much.

Sticking obstinately to the 'localize the global' slogan does not explain what 'local' is, especially if action, as we have witnessed many times earlier, is so clearly 'dislocated'. On the contrary, everything would be lost if, after having revamped the former 'global context', we had to fall back on this other preferred site of social science: the face-to-face encounter between individual, intentional, and purposeful human beings. If the one-way trip from interactions to context led nowhere, as we have just seen, the return trip back to local sites has no reason to be directed at a more accurate target. Far from reaching at last the concrete ground of a 'social hypostasis', we would have simply gone from one artifact to another.[255] If the global has no concrete existence—except when it is brought back to its tiny conduits and onto its many stages—neither has the local. So we now have to ask exactly the same question as earlier, but in reverse: *How is the local itself being generated?* This time it is not the global that is going to be localized, it is the local that has to be *re-dispatched* and *redistributed*.

The reason why it's so important to practice this symmetric operation is that once both corrective movements are done in succession, another entirely different phenomenon will move to the foreground:

---

[255] It's rather astonishing to see even Garfinkel maintain this distinction between formal and informal: 'According to the world wide social science movement and the corpus status of its bibliographies there is no order in the concreteness of things. The research enterprises of the social science movement are defeated by the apparently hopelessly circumstantial overwhelming details of everyday activities—the plenum, the plenty, the plenilunium (sic). To get a remedy, the social sciences have worked out policies and methods of formal analysis. These respecify the concrete details of ordinary activities as details of the analytical devices and of the methods that warrant the use of these devices.' And he adds that ethnomethodology 'consists of evidence to the contrary'. Garfinkel, *Ethnomethodology's Program*, p. 95.

our attention will begin to concentrate on the 'connectors' that will then, and then only, be allowed to freely circulate without ever stopping at a place called 'context' or 'interaction'. When the two moves are carried out together, the social world will begin to transform itself for good; it will take a new and more plausible shape—a shape that allows one to travel without sudden hiccups, a shape that might lend itself to the later work of assembling, collecting, and composing.

Articulators and localizers

To say that every local interaction is 'shaped' by many elements already in place, doesn't tell us anything about the origin of those elements. And yet we have now verified where they *don't* come from: they are not oozing out of a global context, of an overarching framework, of a deep structure. We just went there; there is nothing to be seen except the shadow of the body politic—which is to be reserved for later. Although purely negative, this result clears the way rather nicely. We are now free to search for the existence of another more continuous, more empirically traceable path to reach the places where the ingredients entering into interactions appear to come from. And sure enough, if no label, barcode, certificate of origin, or trademark is able to help us follow the 'actors themselves', there exists what is called in the industry an excellent *traceability* between the sites of production of local interactions, provided we don't forget the lesson of Part I and make good use of all the sources of uncertainty.

The meandering path through which most of the ingredients of action reach any given interaction is traced by the multiplication, enrollment, implication, and folding of non-human actors. If the analyst is not allowed to exert some right of pursuit through multiple types of agencies, then the whole question of local and global becomes intractable. But as soon as non-human agents are brought in, another set of connections appears which are as different to those deployed in the preceding section as veins are to neural pathways.[256] The powerful insight that most of the ingredients of the situation are 'already' in place, that we simply 'occupy' a predetermined position 'inside' some preformatted order, is always due to the transportation of a site into another one at another time, which is produced by someone else through subtle or radical changes in the ways new types of non-social

---

[256] A good example of the crucial importance of not taking the relative size of entities as a given is provided in the case of French water politics in Jean Pierre Le Bourhis (2004), 'La publicisation des eaux. Rationalité et politique dans la gestion de l'eau en France (1964–2003)'.

agencies are mobilized. Others' actions continue to be carried out at some distance, but through the relay of new types of mediators. Paradoxically, it's only once it's allowed to percolate through *non*-social agencies that the social becomes visible.

This process of delegation, dislocation, and translation is never clearer than in the role of material objects—provided we understand 'matter' in the extended sense given earlier (see p. 109). When we talk about an 'overarching framework', 'pillars', 'infrastructure', 'frame', we use loosely the technical terms borrowed from architecture, metallurgy, and cinema. Why not take literally what it means for an interaction to *frame*, to *structure*, or to *localize* another? As long as we use those metaphors in a muted form, we don't see what could connect a place to another via a template. We may continue to believe that leaving a local scene could really mean jumping into the context, or that all of the ingredients of local interactions have to be improvised on the spot through social skills.[257] But as soon as we activate the technical metaphors for good, the connections between sites become visible, even though they are made of many different types of stuff. This heterogeneity, however, no longer represents for us a difficulty since we have learned how to render commensurable various incommensurable materials. We know that objects have the strange capacity of being at once compatible with social skills during certain crucial moments and then totally foreign to any human repertoire of action. This flip-flop renders the inquiry more difficult but not enough to break the newly spun social we use as our Ariadne thread. In effect, what has been designated by the term 'local interaction' is the assemblage of all the *other* local interactions distributed elsewhere in time and space, which have been brought to bear on the scene through the relays of various non-human actors. It is the transported presence of places into other ones that I call *articulators* or *localizers*.[258]

If, to take a trivial enough example, you sit in a chair in a lecture hall surrounded by well-ordered tiers of students listening to you in an amphitheater, I need only half a day's work in the university archives to find out that fifteen years ago and two hundred kilometers away an architect, whose name I have found and whose exploratory scale models I have ferreted out, has drawn the *specifications* of this place down to the centimeter. She had no precise idea that you would be

---

[257] Such is one of the solutions devised by symbolic interactionists to give some maneuvering room to the individual intentional agent without modifying the overall framework of social theory.

[258] The word localizer in computer parlance might be slightly misleading since it is the manifestation of an even larger increase in standards which can then allow the local to be accepted as a mere variation of a more general pattern. We will tackle the question of standardization in the next chapter.

lecturing out loud today, and yet she anticipated, in a gross way, one aspect of such a scene's *script*: you will have to be heard when you speak; you will sit at the podium; you will face a number of students whose maximum number, space requirements, etc. must be taken into consideration. No wonder that, fifteen years later, when you enter this scene, you feel that you have not made it all up and that most of what you need to act is already *in place*. Of course, the space has in fact been tailored for you—the generic you, that is, a large part of you.

Sure enough, no aspect of this structure—and now I can use the term without qualms because there is nothing hidden or discontinuous about it—'determines' what you are going to say, nor even where you will sit. You might decide to stand up, to walk up and down the alleys, or to play the role of the May 1968 rebellious teacher by re-assembling the chairs to form a less 'authoritarian' circle—and nothing can stop the students from falling asleep as soon as you open your mouth. But just because some material element of the place does not 'determine' an action doesn't mean you can conclude that they do nothing. We are now familiar with many more ontological stages than the two foolish extremes of being and nothingness. Fathom for one minute all that allows you to interact with your students without being interfered too much by the noise from the street or the crowds outside in the corridor waiting to be let in for another class. If you doubt the transporting power of all those humble mediators in making this a *local* place, open the doors and the windows and see if you can still teach anything. If you hesitate about this point, try to give your lecture in the middle of some art show with screaming kids and loud speakers spewing out techno music. The result is inescapable: if you are not thoroughly 'framed' by other agencies brought silently on the scene, neither you nor your students can even concentrate for a minute on what is being 'locally' achieved. In other words, what would happen if inter-subjectivity was obtained *for good* by removing, one after the other, all traces of *inter-objectivity*?

In many cases, it is fairly easy to establish some continuous connections that are open to scrutiny between the dreams and drawings of *someone else*, at some *other* time, in some *other* place, and whatever you and your students are now doing locally, face-to-face. This local site has been *made to be a place* by some other locus through the now silent mediation of drawings, specifications, wood, concrete, steel, varnish, and paint; through the work of many workers and artisans who have now deserted the scene because they let objects carry their action in absentia; through the agency of alumni whose generous deeds might be rewarded by some bronze plaque. Locals are *localized*. Places are *placed*.[259] And to remain so, myriads of people, behind the doors, have

---

[259] Koolhas and Mau, *Small, Medium, Large, Extra-Large*.

to keep up the premises so that you can remain, you along with your students, safely 'in it'. Far from offering some primordial autochthony which would be 'so much more concrete' than abstract contexts, face-to-face interactions should be taken, on the contrary, as the terminus point of a great number of agencies swarming toward them.

Although there is no 'underlying hidden structure', this is not to say that there doesn't exist *structuring templates* circulating through channels most easily materialized by techniques—paper techniques and, more generally, intellectual technologies being as important as gears, levers, and chemical bonds. To the inter-subjective relation between you and your students, one should add the inter-objectivity that has dislocated actions so much that someone else, from some other place and some other time, is still acting in it through indirect but fully traceable connections.[260] That does not mean that this faraway site is part of some mysterious context. It simply reveals between these two places—the architect's studio and this classroom today—another circuitry through which masses of entities begin to circulate. Even more than after the first corrective move, one now finds in the foreground the vehicles, the movements, the shifts, and the translation *between* loci rather than the loci themselves. Places do not make for a good starting point, since every one of them are framed and localized by others—including of course the architect's studio that I chose as the provisional origin for my example. We now understand why we had to start, according to Horace's famous expression, in the middle of things, *in medias res*. Circulation is first, the landscape 'in which' templates and agents of all sorts and colors circulate is second. This is probably the oldest intuition of the social sciences, what made us exclaim that the social was an objective, transcendent, ubiquitous, sui generis phenomenon. As usual, the intuition was right but it was difficult to register as long as the circulation of the social was confused with the emergence of a society—itself mixed up with the body politic.

That scale does not depend on absolute size but on the number and qualities of dispatchers and articulators is what I had learned many years ago when I had the chance to follow Shirley Strum and her baboons. When I met her at the first ever 'baboon conference' held in a luxurious castle near New York City, she was a young researcher who had managed to habituate wild monkeys to her close and regular presence. Earlier observers, who watched baboons from afar and from the safe haven of a jeep, had detected a lot of interesting features, but they had situated agonistic encounters 'inside' absent structures—applying to the baboons the stock-in-trade of human sociology.

---

[260] On the condition there exists well-kept archive. Archeologists have to toil much longer to reconstruct the connections.

Animal societies were said to possess, for instance, a rigid dominance pattern 'in which' males had to enter. During this conference, Strum was trying to demonstrate that the dominance 'structure' was not something which male baboons were trying to find, but a *question* all animals raised by testing one another through carefully managed agonistic encounters.[261] In other words, Strum *as well as* young males moving in the troops were raising the same basic questions about what it meant to generate some social structuring effects.[262] And both were slowly discovering, by a series of trials, that it was the females and not the males that were weaving, through daily inter-actions, a pretty solid kind of dominance order that had remained invisible to the (mostly male) observers too far removed to detect those subtle trials. So I was, in effect, following in this beautiful Kenyan landscape a sort of Garfinkel primatologist as she tried to make sense of baboons whom she was gently moving out of their perennial role of 'cultural dopes' so that they could graduate to the new reflexive actions of competent members. In a word, baboons were smart, socially smart.[263]

If there was one social theory mistake not to make, it would be act as if baboons had found a role inside a preexisting structure. But it would be just as wrong to suppose that they were simply interacting with one another. Those furry little beasts were doing just as much social labor as their observers and were living in a world just as complex. And yet, there was a clear difference of *equipment*. The same basic job of testing, achieving, and generating all the ingredients of social life was done, in one case, with 'social tools' only, while the human observer was add-itionally equipped with materials and intellectual technologies. The primates had to decipher the meaning of the interactions with no other tools than the interactions themselves: they had to decide who was friend and enemy, who was displacing whom, who was leading whom, and who was ready to enter in a coalition by using the basic resource of trying and grooming, more grooming and trying. If they kept records, those records had to be 'inscribed' on their own bodies by their own bodies. It was the primatologist who had to rely on written names, statistical charts, notebooks, documentation, blood samples, genetic fingerprints, and visual aids of all sorts. They were achieving

---

[261] Shirley Strum (1982), 'Agonistic Dominance among Baboons an Alternative View' and see Insert p. 69.

[262] This is the dramatic episode narrated in Shirley Strum (1987), *Almost Human: A Journey Into the World of Baboons*.

[263] Since her earlier work, this has become somewhat of a standard for a host of other animals. See Richard Byrne and Andrew Whiten (1988), *Machiavellian Intelligence: Social Expertise and the Evolution of Intellects in Monkeys, Apes and Humans*; Strum and Fedigan *Primate Encounters*; Vinciane Despret (1996), *Naissance d'une théorie éthologique*; and Vinciane Despret (2002), *Quand le loup habitera avec l'agneau*.

the same job of making a social order hold but with vastly different resources. The question then became tantalizing: What's the difference between monkeys and humans if there is no longer a gap dividing nature and culture, instinct and reflection, 'cultural dope' and competent intentional agents? In Strum's description, baboons were getting perilously close to humans, and yet I was not prepared, in spite of the title of her book, to consider myself 'almost' a baboon. Or rather, everything now depended on what is meant by this little 'almost'.

Superficially, we could say that the obvious difference resides in technology. Baboons are not utterly deprived of stabilizing tools. But the point is that even though the males show off their formidable canines and the females parade their irresistible (to the males) swollen bottoms, the baboons still have to maintain their force through *even more* social skills. Chimpanzees have some tools, but baboons only have their 'social tools', namely their bodies which are slowly transformed by years of constant seduction, grooming, and communal life. In a sense, baboon troops could really offer the ideal natural experiment to check what happens when social connections are strictly limited to social skills. In this case, no technology of any sort is available to the participants in order to 'build' the 'superstructure' of their 'society'. Since those architectural terms are completely metaphorical for them as well as for the observer, the baboons have to spend what seems like an inordinate amount of time to repair the shaky 'building' of society, to constantly fix its wobbling hierarchies, to ceaselessly re-establish who is leading whom into foraging forays. They can never rest, nor act on each other at a distance. When they do, it is through the highly *complex* medium of even subtler inter-subjective coalitions. The ways in which baboons have to repair every morning their fast decaying social order remains visible because of the fewer tools at their disposal. Baboons glue the social with ever more complex social interactions while we use interactions that are slightly less social and in a way slightly less complex, even though they may be more *complicated*, that is, made of even more *folds*.[264]

But there might be another way to use this marvelous example of non-human primates as a sort of theoretical baseline. One of the conclusions we could draw is that a face-to-face interaction is not a plausible departure point to trace social connections for both humans and monkeys because in both cases they are being constantly *interfered* with by other agencies. In both cases, action is dislocated, diffracted, re-dispatched and redistributed, not to mention that it has to rely on

---

[264] For the difference between complicated and complex, see Strum and Latour, 'The Meanings of Social: from Baboons to Humans'. For the definition of social tools, see Kummer, *In Quest of the Sacred Baboon*.

successive layers of mediations piled on top of one another. Baboons, too, use some type of 'intellectual technology': their home range, the life history of each interaction, the trajectory of friendships and coalitions, the built-in variations of sizes, sex, anatomical features, etc. It's this constant interference by the action of others that makes life in a baboon group an environment just as selective, just as pressing, and just as taxing as the one made of resources and predators. A baboon that is not socially smart is selected out just as swiftly if it doesn't find food or can't mate. Humans have lived in an environment as taxing, as selective, and as pressing but which is made up of even more mediators, dispatchers, and 'dislocators' that render local interactions even less local.[265] If context was an impossible starting point, so are face-to-face interactions. The difference is no longer between 'simple' baboons and highly 'complex' humans, but rather between complex baboons who have folded themselves into many entities—landscape, predators, groups—and complicated humans who have folded themselves into vastly more entities, some of them having the great advantage of remaining in place, thus simplifying, locally at least, the task of ordering. In humans more so than in monkeys, interference, dispatching, delegation, and articulation are visible and should offer us, in place of local face-to-face interactions, an excellent point of departure.

The implausible locus of face-to-face interactions

Because of the powerful feeling that interactions are 'more concrete', it might be easier for the reader to get rid of the global than the local. As we have seen in reviewing the second source of uncertainty, the same actant may be given different figurations (see p. 57). Although individualized characters might be granted more plausibility because of our habits of reading stories, it requires exactly the same semiotic labor, if I can use this expression, to produce a character as it does a concept or a corporate body. So, while we should remain attuned to small differences in figuration, there is no reason to forget that our own relativistic frame of reference should be indifferent to scale. But it remains true that beliefs in the indisputable existence of individuals is so entrenched, in our western climes at least, that people are only too ready to accept that, even though abstractions like structure, context,

---

[265] This approach of technology as second nature is essential for André Leroi-Gourhan (1993), *Gesture and Speech*; Lewis Mumford (1967), *The Myth of the Machine: Technics and Human Development*; and Tom Hughes (2004), *Human-Built World: How to Think about Technology and Culture*.

or society should be criticized, the *ego* is to be left untouched.[266] Thus, it might be prudent to do more corrective gymnastics to redistribute the local than to localize the global. This is why I have to make up a list of what face-to-face interactions, contrary to so many expectations, cannot possibly deliver. Here again, ANT's lessons will be only negative because clearing the way is what we are after so that the social could be deployed enough to be assembled again.

First, no interaction is what could be called *isotopic*. What is acting at the same moment in any place is coming from many other places, many distant materials, and many faraway actors. If we wanted to project on a standard geographical map the connections established between a lecture hall and all the places that are acting in it at the same time, we would have to draw bushy arrows in order to include, for instance, the forest out of which the desk is coming, the management office in charge of classroom planning, the workshop that printed the schedule that has helped us find the room, the janitor that tends the place, and so on.[267] And this would not be some idle exercise, since each of these faraway sites has, in some indispensable way, anticipated and preformatted this hall by transporting, through many different sorts of media, the mass of templates that have made it a suitable local—and that are still propping it up.

Second, no interaction is *synchronic*. The desk might be made of a tree seeded in the 1950s that was felled two years ago; the cloth of the teacher's dress was woven five years ago, while the firing of neurons in her head might be a millisecond old and the area of the brain devoted to speech has been around for a good hundred thousands years (or maybe less, this is, hotly disputed question among paleontologists). As to the words she uses, some have been introduced into English from foreign languages four hundred years ago, while this rule of grammar might be even older; the metaphor she chooses is just six years old and this rhetoric trope straight out of Cicero; but the computer keyboard she has typed her speech on is fresh from Apple, although the heavy metals making possible the coordination of some of its switches

---

[266] The implausibility of the individual would of course be much easier to detect for instance in India. See Louis Dumont (1982), *Homo Hierarchicus: The Caste System and Its Implications*. This entrenchment of the individual is most extreme in the rational choice mythology since it also includes a stabilized psychology and a stabilized cognition.

[267] I follow here a simple pedagogical example, but see Sequence 3 of Latour and Hermant, *Paris the Invisible City*. This is exactly the type of map that Cronon has been able to draw with his masterful study of Chicago in William Cronon (1991), *Nature's Metropolis. Chicago and the Great West* and that Hutchins has been able to deploy with his study of ship navigation. See also what Law has been able to do with aircraft in Law, *Aircraft Stories*. Cognition is indeed so distributed that the idea of an individual doing a calculation is moot.

will last for as long as the universe. Time is always folded.[268] So the idea of any synchronic interaction where all the ingredients will have the same age and the same pace is meaningless—even for baboons. Action has always been carried on thanks to shifting the burden of connection to longer- or shorter-lasting entities.

Third, interactions are not *synoptic*. Very few of the participants in a given course of action are simultaneously visible at any given point. The lecturer might believe she is center stage, but that does not mean that many others are not acting as well, only that there is no way to sum them up. The wooden desk was not part of the lecture before she pointed it out as an example of design, and yet it does something; it is one of the ingredients that helps put it into shape, allowing inter-action to be framed. So was the slip of paper that advertised the lecture and set the appointed time and space even though she did not high-light it. But if we wanted all the ingredients of this scene to stand up and be counted, we will not be able to do it because there is no way to underline all of them at once, either because there are too many or because they are part of complicated machineries that are necessarily hidden if playing their part as efficient intermediaries. How many distinct entities in this microphone? In this body? In this school's organization? You will never get the same count, no matter how many times you do the counting, because every time different agents will be made visible while others will have become dormant.

Fourth, interactions are not *homogeneous*. We have already under-stood this point earlier, since the relays through which action is carried out do not have the same material quality all along. How many successive shifts in agencies should we have to detect if we wanted to move from the architect's cabinet, fifteen years ago, to the lecture hall? When slides are projected on the screen, how many different successive ingredients are necessary when some writing on a keyboard becomes digitalized, then transformed again in an ana-logical signal before being retransformed in some sort of slower brain wave into the mind of half-asleep students? What is staggering in any given interaction is exactly the opposite of what sociologists with a tropism for 'local sites' find so great in finally reaching face-to-face encounters, namely the crowd of non-human, non-subjective, non-local participants who gather to help carry out the course of action and transport it through channels that do not resemble a social tie, even though all of them are associated together.

Fifth, interactions are not *isobaric*, if I am allowed to borrow a metaphor from the lines of equal pressures that we read in weather

---

[268] See Michel Serres (1995), *Conversations on Science, Culture and Time with Bruno Latour.*

maps when looking for depressions or anticyclones. Some of the participants are pressing very strongly, requesting to be heard and taken
into account, while others are fully routine customs sunk rather mysteriously into bodily habits. Others are black-boxed into some hardware known only by engineers in faraway places in Asia and, very
vaguely, by some techie from the maintenance staff somewhere on
campus. Especially important are the different pressures exerted by
mediators and intermediaries, the later adding, as we know, predict-
ability to the setting, while the former might suddenly make it bifurcate in unexpected ways. At every point during the lecture, something
could break, be it the microphone, the speaker, perhaps even the
teacher. If any of the intermediaries mutates into a mediator, then
the whole set up, no matter how solemn or controlled, may become
unpredictable.

No wonder interactions provided social scientists with the strong
impression that they were overflowing in all directions. They are! That
does not mean that some solid overarching context holds them solidly
in place through the grip of some hidden structural force. It means
that a bewildering array of participants is simultaneously at work in
them and which are dislocating their neat boundaries in all sorts of
ways, redistributing them away and making it impossible to start
anywhere that can be said to be 'local'. Relativity in the social sciences
would be a rather simple affair if we had simply to localize the global; it
becomes relevant only when it is the solid ground of the local that
vanishes. In most situations, actions will already be interfered with by
heterogeneous entities that don't have the same local presence, don't
come from the same time, are not visible at once, and don't press upon
them with the same weight. The word 'interaction' was not badly
chosen; only the number and type of 'actions' and the span of their
'inter' relations has been vastly underestimated. Stretch any given
inter-action and, sure enough, it becomes an actor-network.

The exception, of course, is if we fall back into loose talk and
abandon the arduous task of following all the interferences. In that
case it is perfectly all right to speak of 'structure' and 'face-to-face
interaction'. But this means that we are dealing with more routine
situations and are using a pre-relativist frame of reference. In such an
abbreviated manner of speech, a 'structure' is simply an actor-network
on which there is scant information or whose participants are so quiet
that no new information is required. An 'interaction' is a site so nicely
framed by localizers behaving as intermediaries that it can be viewed,
without too much trouble, as 'taking place locally'.

When you go through this list of features that face-to-face interaction cannot possibly offer, you remain suspicious of the efforts
made to root sociology into inter-subjective interactions, individual

calculations, or personal intentionality.[269] It is clear, on the contrary, that the notion of a local interaction has just as little reality as global structure. Such a result renders, retrospectively, even queerer the attempts done throughout the history of the social sciences to strike some sort of compromise between the so-called global context and the so-called interaction, to negotiate perhaps some subtler 'middle way' between 'actor' and 'system'. These projects make about as much sense now as the Renaissance compilers who tried so earnestly to calibrate the dates of Greek mythology over those of the Bible. The midpoint between two mythologies is still a mythology.

But if we follow the trails left behind by non-human actors, we understand where the right impression of being 'framed' comes from. Every local site is being localized by a flood of localizers, dispatchers, deviators, articulators—whatever word we want to choose. The role of inter-objectivity is to introduce in local interactions some fundamental dislocation. What could be the meaning of *relative* scale without inter-objectivity? How would we know we are small participants in a 'wider' scheme of things if we were not walking, for instance, inside the deep and dark canyons carved inside the massive features of some skyscrapers? *Feeling small* largely depends on how many other people, distributed in time and space, have preformed a place for the anonymous visitor now traveling, for instance, through the streets of New York City. Size is relative indeed—relative to the care with which it *was* designed and the care with which it *is still* enforced. But that does not mean we really are small participants 'inside' some framework. How long do we need to be reminded of this painful lesson? The saddest experimental proof was recently provided when a group of fanatics, equipped with nothing more than paper cutters, undid what many others had so carefully constructed and destroyed buildings in such a way that, although the dark shadow of death remains, the long and oppressing shade that the Twin Towers had projected onto the narrow streets was removed in the space of a few hours. After such an event, should we not be extraordinarily sensitive to the frailty of scale?

Constructing relative scale has a completely different meaning if we take it as a loose metaphor to 'express', 'reproduce', and 'reflect' the always present 'social structure', or if there is no other way to build anything bigger than through the medium of architecture and technology in its literal sense. In the traditional version of social theory, society is strong and nothing can destroy it since it is sui generis; in the

---

[269] This is why, especially for methodological reason, methodological individualism seems a very unfortunate choice of departure in spite of the attempt made in Raymond Boudon (1981), *The logic of social action: an introduction to sociological analysis.*

other, it is so weak that it has to be built, repaired, fixed and, above all, *taken care* of. These two maps of the social drawn with different social tracers lead to two completely different esthetics, ethics, and politics—in addition to generating very different accounts.

Plug-ins

No place dominates enough to be global and no place is self-contained enough to be local. As long as we try to use either local interaction or structure, or some compromise between the two, there is no chance to trace social connections—and the cleverer the compromise, the worse it would be, since we would simply extend the lease of two non-existing sites. On the contrary, I am trying here to be as dumb as possible and multiply clamps to make sure we resist the temptation to cut away in two boxes—global and local—what actors are doing, interrupting at once the deployment of their many fragile and some-times bizarre itineraries. If we stick enough of these clamps firmly in place, we begin to draw another landscape which cuts through the former pathways going from the local to the global and back, and that runs, so to speak, transversally to all of them as if, through some odd cartographic operation, we had slowly morphed the hydrological map of some water catchments into another one. It is as if we had made a west flowing river run along a north-south gradient.

What is so striking in this change of topography is that both the former global and the former local have now taken the same star-shaped aspect—in our projection grid of course, not 'out there'. Context-building sites now look like the intersections of many trails of documents traveling back and forth, but local building sites, too, look like the multiple crossroads toward which templates and formats are circulating. If we take these two 'networky' shapes seriously, then the former landscape flattens itself for good since those two types of star-like shapes cannot be ordered on top of one another inside any three-dimensional structure. They are now side-by-side, every move forcing the analyst to follow the edges without any jump or break, just like the two-dimensional space imagined by Edwin Abbott's *Flatland*. Move-ments and displacements come first, places and shapes second. So in the end, localizing the global and re-dispatching the local are not as difficult as it appeared. After a few minutes of accommodation, the number of traces becomes so great that you would have to be blind not to follow them. Sites no longer differ in shape or size, but in the direction of the movements to and fro as well as in the *nature*, as we shall see, of what is being transported: information, traces, goods, plans, formats, templates, linkages, and so on. It is now the mythical sites of local and global that are hard to locate on a map. Where could those enchanted utopias have resided?

The reason why it's so important to learn how to navigate into this flattened space is that, as soon as we become better at focusing on what circulates, we can detect many other entities whose displacements were barely visible before. Indeed, they were not supposed to circulate at all. It might be possible to pay attention to much subtler phenomena which earlier had to be stocked, because of their apparent subtlety, in the subject's inner sanctuary. Just as a flat, dry, and dusty landscape reveals the trails left by all the animals that have passed through it, we might be able to detect moving entities that leave no trace whatsoever in the bushy undergrowth of the sociology of the social.

Especially important is that which allows actors to *interpret* the setting in which they are located. No matter how many frames are pouring through localizers to format a setting, no matter how many documents are flowing from this setting to oligoptica and back, there is still a huge distance between the *generic* actors preformatted by those movements and the course of action carried out by fully involved *individualized* participants. Everyone has this common experience when they try and make sense of even the most carefully written user's manual. No matter how many *generic* persons an assembly drawing has been designed for, you will surely start grumbling after hours on your newly purchased digital camera and feel that you are not one of these persons. By measuring the distance between instructions addressed to no one in particular and yourself, you have been made painfully aware of what Don Norman has called 'the gap of execution'.[270] It would be foolish to ignore that which gave the impression that face-to-face interactions were so 'concrete' and on such a 'real life' scale, and which gave the feeling that it was individuals who were carrying out the action.

Such a feeling, of course, was immediately lost when sociologists of the social substituted this healthy intuition with the hidden action of some invisible structure—at which point, *nobody* in particular was doing any action any more! It was also lost when interactionists retrieved a purposeful and personalized actor but without dissolving the frame 'in which' members were supposed to deploy their intelligence. *A human agent* is making sense of a world of objects which are by themselves *devoid* of any meaning. At which point we are back to square one, having to choose between meaning without object and

---

[270] See Norman, *The Psychology of Everyday Things* and Garfinkel, *Ethnomethodology's Program*, Chapter 6.

objectivity without meaning. But the powerful insight would be lost just as fast if actors were simply localized by the agency of other sites through the medium of some material or intellectual techniques, without themselves being able to interpret and understand the propositions made by the setting.[271] This is why we have to become sensitive to more elusive tracers than the ones we have reviewed so far.

Let us take the simple-minded example of the lecture hall that we used earlier. No matter how nicely it has been designed, it is still necessary for the teachers and the professors, in order for them to know what to do there, to do quite a lot of work. Without some equipment brought in, human actors would remain, even in the midst of the best-designed frame, unable to interpret what is given; they would remain as unconnected to the meaning of the site as a cat prowling on the Acropolis.

So we have to add something, but what and how? We know already what we don't want to do if we are to pursue our 'flattening' of the landscape all the way: we don't want to jump by resorting to another 'level' or another 'type' of resource. And yet, this would be the safest, the easiest, and the most reasonable strategy. However, as the reader is now painfully aware, reasonableness is not what I am after! I am conducting here a thought experiment that will pay off only if carried out all the way: How far can we maintain a point of view that abstains from ever using the local/global or the actor/system repertoire? Is it possible to resist the temptation? Once again, I am not trying to describe substantively or positively what the landscape is, but simply finding ways to resist the temptation to make a break in its description.

To fill in the 'gap of execution', the solution is usually to shift gears and to abruptly bring in 'subjectivity', 'intentionality', and 'interiority' or at least appeal to some sort of 'mental equipment'. If the social framing from 'outside' is not enough to complete the course of action, then the remainder of the resources has to come from the 'inside' or from the human group locally assembled. At which point, positivism gives way to hermeneutics and sociologists pass the baton to psychologists or to cognitive scientists while structural sociologists shift to interpretative sociology. But if this jump in method is allowed to occur, the continuous trail I have tried to keep from the beginning would suddenly be interrupted; the flat map will be slashed yet again; the scene of an individual subjective actor having 'some leeway' 'inside' a larger system will be reactivated; the two mythical lands of global and local will be drawn anew; Merlin's castle will pop up again.

---

[271] This is the shift introduced by Boltanski and Thévenot in Bourdieu's theory of field: actors are fully able to justify themselves and do not only hide their real motivations. See Luc Boltanski (1999), *Distant Suffering: Morality, Media and Politics*.

So, in keeping with our myopic ANT obsession, we have to keep fumbling in the dark for another clamp.

Surely the question we need to ask then is where are the other vehicles that transport individuality, subjectivity, personhood, and interiority? If we have been able to show that glorified sites like global and local were made out of circulating entities, why not postulate that subjectivities, justifications, unconscious, and personalities would *circulate* as well?[272] And sure enough, as soon as we raise this very odd but inescapable question, new types of clamps offer themselves to facilitate our enquiry. They could be called *subjectifiers, personnalizers,* or *individualisers,* but I prefer the more neutral term of *plug-ins,* borrowing this marvelous metaphor from our new life on the Web. When you reach some site in cyberspace, it often happens that you see nothing on the screen. But then a friendly warning suggests that you 'might not have the right plug-ins' and that you should 'download' a bit of software which, once installed on your system, will allow you to *activate* what you were unable to see before.[273] What is so telling in this metaphor of the plug-in is that competence doesn't come in bulk any longer but literally in bits and bytes. You don't have to imagine a 'wholesale' human having intentionality, making rational calculations, feeling responsible for his sins, or agonizing over his mortal soul. Rather, you realize that to obtain 'complete' human actors, you have to *compose* them out of many successive *layers,* each of which is empirically distinct from the next. Being a fully competent actor now comes in discreet *pellets* or, to borrow from cyberspace, *patches* and *applets,* whose precise origin can be 'Googled' before they are downloaded and saved one by one.[274]

As we have witnessed so many times throughout this book, information technologies allow us to trace the associations in a way that was impossible before. Not because they subvert the old concrete 'humane' society, turning us into formal cyborgs or 'post human' ghosts, but for exactly the opposite reason: they make *visible* what was before only present virtually. In earlier times, competence was a rather mysterious affair that remained hard to trace; for this reason, you had to order it, so to speak, in bulk. As soon as competence can be counted in bauds and bytes along modems and routers, as soon as it can be peeled back layer after layer, it opens itself to fieldwork.

[272] Mol, *The Body Multiple*; Cussins, 'Ontological Choreography'; and Myriam Winance (2001), *Thèse et prothèse. Le processus d'habilitation comme fabrication de la personne: l'association française contre les myopathies, face au handicap* have shown in their own ways what equipment is needed to become a subject and how fragile it is.

[273] I often find that my reader would complain a lot less about my writings if they could download ANT version 6.5 instead of sticking with the beta.

[274] This multiplicity of plug-ins is clearly visible in Thévenot's list of regimes of action. See Thévenot, 'Which road to follow?'

Every pellet leaves a trace behind it that now has an origin, a label, a vehicle, a circuit, sometimes even a price tag.[275] While information technology, standing as one human on a stage, was supposed to be an all-or-nothing affair, it has now clearly become the provisional result of a whole assemblage of plug-ins coming from completely different loci. To be a realistic whole is not an undisputed starting point but the provisional achievement of a composite assemblage.[276]

Just as the division of labor created by the industries and bureaucracies helped Durkheim and Weber to trace their own definitions of social links, information technologies help us realize the work going on in actor-making. It's now much easier to not consider the actor as a subject endowed with some primeval interiority, which turns its gaze toward an objective world made of brute things to which it should resist or out of which it should be able to cook up some symbolic brew. Rather, we should be able to observe empirically how an anonymous and generic body is made to be a person: the more intense the shower of offers of subjectivities, the more interiority you get.[277] Subjects are no more autochthonous than face-to-face interactions. They, too, depend on a flood of entities allowing them to exist. To be an 'actor' is now at last a fully artificial and fully traceable gathering: what was before true only of the Leviathan is now also true for each of its 'components'. Later on, this result will be important for our definition of politics.

Some plug-ins are fairly easy to trace. For instance, there are all of those official and legal papers which designate 'you' as being *someone*. If you doubt the ability of those humble paper techniques to generate *quasi-subjects*, try living in a large European city as an 'undocumented alien' or extricating yourself out of the FBI's grip because of a misspelling of your name. Other vehicles leave such a thin trace as if

---

[275] The massive digitalization of many types of documents may offer Tarde a belated vindication. The poor statistics available at the end of the 19th century could not validate his requirement for a point-to-point 'epidemiology'. It's interesting to think that the possibility of a Tardian quantitative sociology might be opened now. We now have quasi-quantitative tools allowing us to follow in the same fashion rumors, opinions, facts, and fantasies. See Rogers, *Information Politic on the Web*. On the tracing of new *quantum* see Michel Callon (2001), 'Les méthodes d'analyse des grands nombres'.

[276] No one has made this point more emphatically than Donna Haraway (2000), *How like a Leaf: an Interview with Thyrza Goodeve*. But it's probably with queer theory that the notion of multiple layers and artificial construction could be best applied. In spite of some posthuman ideology and masses of critical sociology, it offers a rich building site regarding the number of elements that can be detached and made to circulate. For a different approach see Stefan Hirschauer (1998), 'Performing Sexes and Genders in Medical Practice'.

[277] A splendid allegory of this layered makeup is offered by computer-generated imagery. *Siggraph* meetings in Los Angeles, for example, have entire sessions devoted to it. There is a morning dedicated to the shine of nylon, one afternoon to the refraction of light onto red hair, one evening to the 'realistic rendering' of blows, and so on. As usual 'virtual' reality is a materialization of what is needed for 'natural' reality.

they were really immaterial. But if we maintain our outlook, we can follow them as well: How many circulating *clichés* do we have to absorb before having the competence to utter an opinion about a film, a companion, a situation, a political stance? If you began to probe the origin of each of your idiosyncrasies, would you not be able to deploy, here again, the same star-like shape that would force you to visit many places, people, times, events that you had largely forgotten? This tone of voice, this unusual expression, this gesture of the hand, this gait, this posture, aren't these traceable as well?[278] And then there is the question of your inner feelings. Have they not been given to you? Doesn't reading novels help you to know how to love? How would you know which group you pertain to without ceaselessly downloading some of the cultural clichés that all the others are bombarding you with?[279] Without the avid reading of countless fashion magazines, would you know how to bake a cake? And what about putting on a condom, consoling your lover, brushing your hair, fighting for your rights, or picking out the right clothes? Magazines help here as well. If you take each of the rubrics as the mere 'expression' of some dark social force, then their efficacy disappears. But if you remember that there is nothing beyond and beneath, that there is no rear-world of the social, then is it not fair to say that they make up a part of your own cherished intimacy? We are now familiar with what should no longer appear as a paradox: it's precisely once the overall society disappears that the full range of what circulates 'outside' can be brought to the foreground.

On the condition that we add another flow, another circuitry, through which plug-ins lend actors the supplementary tools—the supplementary souls—that are necessary to render a situation interpretable.[280] A supermarket, for instance, has preformatted you to be a consumer, but only a generic one. To transform yourself into an active and understanding consumer, you also need to be equipped with an ability *to calculate* and *to choose*. In the sociology of the social there were only two sources for such a competence: either you were born with it as a human—as if Darwinian evolution had, from the dawn of time, prepared men and women to be supermarket calculators and optimal maximizers—or you were molded into becoming a clever consumer by the powerful grip of some economic infrastructure. But

---

[278] See Jean Claude Schmitt (1990), *La Raison des gestes dans l'Occident médiéval*; Jan Bremmer and Herman Roodenburg (1992), *A Cultural History of Gesture: From Antiquity to the Present Day*; and Geneviève Calbris (1990), *The Semiotics of French Gesture*.

[279] This is the main reason for the lasting impact of Lev Semenovich Vygotski (1978), *Mind in Society: The Development of Higher Cognitive Processes*.

[280] This is why Bourdieu's notion of habitus, once it is freed from its social theory, remains such an excellent concept. So is the notion of equipment developed in Thévenot, 'Which road to follow?'

with this new topography that we are sketching, another source of competence might be located at your fingertips: there are plug-ins circulating to which you can *subscribe*, and that you can download on the spot to *become* locally and provisionally competent.

If you look at supermarkets in this way, a bewildering array of devices is underlined, each having the capacity to provide you with the possibility of carrying out calculations somewhat more competently. Even when one has to make the mundane decision about which kind of sliced ham to choose, you benefit from dozens of measurement instruments that equip you to become a consumer—from labels, trademarks, barcodes, weight and measurement chains, indexes, prices, consumer journals, conversations with fellow shoppers, advertisements, and so on.[281] The crucial point is that you are sustaining this mental and cognitive competence as long as you *subscribe* to this equipment. You don't carry it with you; it is not your own property. You might have internalized it somewhat, but even for that feat of internalization you need to download another plug-in! If you try to make a rational calculation *away* from such equipment—deciding for example to buy Universal Panoramas in order to become the World Company—you might have nothing more to make your 'macro-decision' with than rough estimates on the back of an envelope; you will no longer *possess* the competence to be rational at all.[282] Here again, it makes much more realistic sense to bypass entirely the two sites: the market forces and the individual agent.

> **Marcel Mauss defines 'habitus' and traces just the same social as Tarde:**
> A kind of revelation came to me in hospital. I was ill in New York. I wondered where previously I had seen girls walking as my nurses walked. I had the time to think about it. At last I realized that it was at the cinema. Returning to France, I noticed how common this gait was, especially in Paris; the girls were French and they, too, were walking in this way. In fact, American walking fashions had begun to arrive over here, thanks to the cinema. This was an idea I could generalize. The positions of the arms and hands while walking form a social idiosyncrasy, they are not simply a product of purely

---

[281] See Cochoy, *Une sociologie du packaging.*

[282] As recent economic history shows, big decisions are less rational than small ones because they are much less equipped. No equipment, no rationality. There is a direct link in MacKenzie's work between his earlier study of theorems and his present study of markets. See Donald MacKenzie (2001), *Mechanizing Proof: Computing, Risk, and Trust* and MacKenzie, *An engine, not a camera.* The same trend is visible in Karin Knorr's moves from laboratory science, in Knorr-Cetina, *Epistemic Cultures,* to market 'rationality', in Knorr-Cetina and Bruegger, 'Global Microstructures'.

individual, almost completely psychical, arrangements and mechanisms. For example: I think I can also recognize a girl who has been raised in a convent. In general, she will walk with her fists closed. And I can still remember my third-form teacher shouting at me: 'Idiot! Why do you walk around the whole time with your hands flapping wide open?' Thus there exists an education in walking, too.

Another example: there are polite and impolite *positions for the hands* at rest. Thus you can be certain that if a child at the table keeps his elbows in when he is not eating, he is English. A young Frenchman has no idea how to sit up straight; his elbows stick out sideways; he puts them on the table, and so on.

Finally, in *running*, too, I have seen, you all have seen, the change in technique. Imagine, my gymnastics teacher, one of the top graduates of Joinville around 1860, taught me to run with my fists close to my chest: a movement completely contradictory to all running movements; I had to see the professional runners of 1890 before I realized the necessity of running in a different fashion.

Hence, I have had this notion of the social nature of the *habitus* for many years. Please note that I use the Latin word—it should be understood in France—*habitus*. The word translates infinitely better than *habitude* (habit or custom), the *exis*, the 'acquired ability' and 'faculty' of Aristotle (who was a psychologist). It does not designate those metaphysical *habitudes*, that mysterious 'memory', the subjects of volumes or short and famous theses. These 'habits' do not vary just with individuals and their imitations; they vary especially between societies, educations, proprieties and fashions, prestiges. In them we should see the techniques and work of collective and individual practical reason rather than, in the ordinary way, merely the soul and its repetitive faculties. (Mauss 1979: 100–1)

Cognitive abilities do not reside in 'you' but are distributed throughout the formatted setting, which is not only made of localizers but also of many competence-building propositions, of many small intellectual technologies.[283] Although they come from the outside, they are not descended from some mysterious context: each of them has a history that can be traced empirically with more or less difficulty. Each patch comes with its own vehicle whose shape, cost, and

[283] This propagation is key to the field of distributed cognition: 'Internalization has long connoted some thing moving across some boundary. Both elements of this definition are misleading. What moves is not a thing, and the boundary across which movement takes place is a line that, if drawn too firmly, obscures our understanding of the nature of human cognition. Within this larger unit of analysis, what used to look like internalization now appears as a *gradual propagation* of organized functional properties across a set of malleable media.' Hutchins, *Cognition in the wild*, p. 312 (my emphasis).

circulation can be mapped out—as historians of accounting, cognitive anthropologists, and psychologists have so forcefully shown. If there is one thing that is not 'in' the agent, it is those many layers of competence builders that we have to ceaselessly download in order to gain some sort of ability for a while. This should be the advantage of a flattened landscape: when I utter such an assertion, it no longer means that I have to fall back on the other symmetric solution and say that 'of course' they are held by some 'social context'. On the contrary, to say that they circulate through their own conduits means that they no longer come from either context or from the actor's subjectivity, or for that matter from any clever compromise between the two.

But what about me, the *ego*? Am I not in the depth of my heart, in the circumvolutions of my brain, in the inner sanctum of my soul, in the vivacity of my spirit, an 'individual'? Of course I am, but only as long as I have been individualized, spiritualized, interiorized. It is true that the circulation of these 'subjectifiers' is often more difficult to track. But if you search for them, you will find them all over the place: floods, rains, swarms of what could be called psycho-*morphs* because they literally lend you the shape of a psyche. Take for instance, love talks. If you doubt the efficacy of this kind of transportation, do the experiment. Try living without them for a bit and see how fast 'you'—yes, the primeval 'you'—will simply wither away.[284] Even love, love especially, can be construed as that which comes from the outside, as a somewhat miraculous gift to create an inside. And it is certainly the way it has been traced in poems, songs and paintings, not to mention the countless retinue of angels, cherubs, putties, and arrows whose objective existence, yes *objective*, should also be taken into account. Even love has to have its vehicle, its specific techniques, its conduits, its equipment just as much as a trading room, a headquarters, or a factory. Of course, the medium will be different and so will be *what* is transported, but the general abstract shape will be the same—and it is this purely theoretical shape that I wish to capture for now.

What I am trying to do here is simply show how the boundaries between sociology and psychology may be reshuffled for good. For this, there is only one solution: make every single entity populating the former inside come from the outside not as a negative constraint

---

[284] There is a small but telling set of literature from the classic Denis De Rougemont (1983), *Love in the Western World* to Ulrich Beck and Elisabeth Beck-Gernsheim (1995), *The Normal Chaos of Love* and Sabine Chalvon-Demersay (1999), *A Thousand Screenplays: The French Imagination in a Time of Crisis*. But no one peeled back all the successive layers of all the equipment necessary better than Michel Foucault (1990), *The History of Sexuality: An Introduction*.

'limiting subjectivity', but as a positive *offer* of subjectivation.[285] As soon as we do this, the former actor, member, agent, person, individual—whatever its name—takes the same star-shaped aspect we have observed earlier when flattening the global and re-dispatching the local. It is *made to be* an individual/subject or it is *made to be* a generic non-entity by a swarm of other agencies. Every competence, deep down in the silence of your interiority, has first to come from the outside, to be slowly sunk in and deposited into some well-constructed cellar whose doors have then to be carefully sealed.[286] None of this is a given. Interiorities are built in the same complicated way as Horus's chamber in the center of the pyramid of Cheops. The old empiricist motto was not that off the mark: *nihil est in intellectu, quod non sit prius in sensu*, although its meaning (nothing is inside which has not come from the outside) is a bit different. Nothing pertains to a subject that has not been given to it. In a way, is this not the strongest intuition of social sciences: 'Have we been made up?' Of course, the meaning of this tricky phrase depends entirely on what is meant by this innocent little word 'outside'.

From actors to attachments

Have I not drifted from Charybdis to Scylla? What does it mean to say that psycho-morphs come from the outside? Have I fought so fiercely against the global/local dichotomy that I have ended up reinstating it in its oldest guise, namely the interior/exterior opposition, the stock-in-trade dispute between psychology and sociology? What a huge step backward! Do I really want to revert to the time where actors were considered as so many puppets manipulated, in spite of themselves, by so many invisible threads?[287] What's the use of having done away with global structure and face-to-face interactions if it is to drown the

---

[285] Foucault's later work is a good example of the richness of this line of thought, although the construction of human interior psyches is somewhat obfuscated by the earlier theme of the 'death of the subject'. In spite of his own affirmation, the two are parallel, not contradictory.

[286] Durkheim showed how all logical and personal categories inside are in some ways the translation and interiorization of the outside. But this outside was mistaken for a society thus opening, in spite of Tarde's warnings, the empty debate between psycho- and socio-logy. Compare the sociology of logics in Gabriel Tarde (1893), *La logique sociale* with Emile Durkheim (1915), *The Elementary Forms of the Religious Life*.

[287] As this label indicates, post-structuralism is the survival of structuralism after the structure is gone, much like a chicken that goes on running after its head has been cut off. Although it has abandoned the search for coherence, post-structuralism has retained the same definition of causality: a few causes followed by long chains of passive place-holders or what I have called intermediaries.

person's most intimate subjectivity in fields of anonymous forces? Acting without actors! Subjectivity without subjects! Back to the glorious Sixties! But what is gained? Well, that's exactly where ANT's gain may reside. After this flattening of the landscape, the outside itself has changed a lot: it's no longer made of society—and nor is it made of nature. In doing away *both* with ungraspable subjectivity and with intractable structure, it might be possible to finally place at the forefront the flood of *other* more subtle conduits that allow us *to become* an individual and *to gain* some interiority.[288]

The difficulty in following these types of 'subject-carrying' or psycho-morph mediators is that since they come from the 'outside', they seem to transport the *same sort of constraints* as the one imagined by sociologists of the social for their definition of society.[289] And sure enough, given what they meant by 'outside', namely the constraining power of context or the causal determination of nature, there was not the slightest chance for plug-ins to deposit anything *positive* inside the actor. Structural forces had to do most of the work—give or take a few small marginal adjustments by the individuals. In their fanciful theory of action, this was the only way sociologists had imagined that the string of the puppeteer's hand could activate the puppet.[290] But we have no longer any reason to be intimidated by this odd way of conceiving the import of an outside force because we have detected two successive mistakes in the notion of the sociology of the social: one in the definition of the cause and the other in the vehicle that was supposed to transport the effect. The relationship between puppeteers and their puppets is much more interesting than that.[291] Besides, we have also learned how to redress two misconceptions: we know that mediators are not causes and that without transformations or translations no vehicles can transport any effect. Something happens along the strings that allow the marionettes to move.

The hopeless division of labor between psychology and sociology may begin to change once the definition of the 'outside' has been dissolved and replaced by the circulation of plug-ins. While none of the the plug-ins have the power to determine, they can simply *make*

[288] Peter Sloterdijk with his three-volume book on different types of spheres has offered a new and powerful metaphor to get out of the inside/outside dichotomy. Unfortunately, his work is not yet available in English. See Peter Sloterdijk (2004), *Sphären, 3 Bde.*

[289] See Anne-Nelly Perret-Clermont (1979), *La Construction de l'intelligence dans l'interaction sociale* and her early critique of Piaget's linkage between social theory and epistemology.

[290] And so does my version of the *Roget's Thesaurus*! It proposes the following entries: 'dupe', 'image', 'non-entity', 'slave'. No wonder the debate between psychology and sociology never goes anywhere.

[291] See p. 58 and Bruno Latour (1999a), 'Factures/fractures. From the Concept of Network to the Concept of Attachment'.

someone *do* something. We are now in a position to bring the two points together and refurbish for good the notion of an outside: it's not situated at the same place and the influence it exerts keeps acting through a totally different theory of action. The outside is not a context 'made of' social forces and it doesn't 'determine' the inside.

The gravest consequence of the notion of context was that it forced us to stick to double-entry accounting so that whatever came from the outside was *deducted* from the total sum of action allotted to the agents 'inside'. With that type of balance sheet, the more threads you added in order to *make you act* from the outside, the *less* you *yourself* acted: the conclusion of this accounting procedure was inescapable. And if you wished, for some moral or political reason, to save the actor's intention, initiative, and creativity, the only way left was to increase the total sum of action coming from the inside by *cutting some of the threads*, thus denying the role of what is now seen as so many 'bondages', 'external constraints', 'limits to freedom', etc. Either you were a free subject or you lived in abject subjection. And of course critical sociologists reinforced this tendency since they couldn't talk about the 'outside force' of the social, except by gloating over the 'narrow constraints' put by 'the anonymous weight of society' over 'personal freedom'. But this odd landscape does not depress us any longer. The outside never resembles some Gobi desert invented by sociologists of context, nor is it simply populated by matters of fact; the inside never resembles an inner sanctum surrounded by cold social forces like a desert island circled by hungry sharks.[292] Ins and outs, like ups and downs, are results not causes. The sociologist's job is not to fix their limits in advance.[293]

The difference between the two theories does not reside only in the number of bonds, but also in the theory of action that connects any one of those bonds. We saw earlier that what was wrong with the metaphor of marionettes was not their activation by the many strings firmly held in the hands of their puppeteers, but the implausible argument that domination was simply *transported* through them without translation. Of course marionettes are bound! But the consequence is certainly not that, to emancipate them, you have to cut all the strings. The only way to liberate the puppets is for the puppeteer to be a *good* puppeteer. Similarly for us, it is not the *number of connections* that we have to diminish in order to reach at last the sanctuary of the self. On the contrary, as William James so magnificently demonstrated, it is by multiplying the connections with the outside that

---

[292] This move is complementary to what I did with the 'outside' of nature in Chapter 5 of Latour, *Politics of Nature*.

[293] On Durkheim's misreading of Tarde's psychology, see Louise Salmon (2004), *La pensée politique de Gabriel Tarde*.

there is some chance to grasp how the 'inside' is being furnished.[294] You need to subscribe to a lot of subjectifiers to become a subject and you need to download a lot of individualizers to become an individual—just as you need to hook up a lot of localizers to have a local place and a lot of oligoptica for a context to 'dominate' over some other sites.

It is only once the alternative between actor and system is ignored— note that I do not say overcome, reconciled, or solved—that the most important topic of sociology can begin to shine through. This had been Tarde's major contribution against Spencer's organism and Durkheim's society. He clearly articulated the obligation for a social scientist to generate *intra*-psychology through the many mediations offered by *inter*-psychology, the former one being conceived as a sort of bridgehead for the later.[295] We might end up gaining some 'intra-psyche' only if we are entering into a relationship with a lot of 'extra-psyches', or what could be called mind-churning substances, namely psycho-*tropes* or—to use still another expression about soul generating entities—psycho-*genes*.[296] If you treat what comes from the outside as mediators offering an occasion to the next agent to behave as a mediator, the whole scene of the inside and outside might be modified for good. The puppeteer still holds many strings in her hands, but each of her fingers is itching to move in a way *the marionette* indicates. The more strings the marionettes are allowed to have, the more articulated they become.[297]

We are now at least free from a whole set of discussions considering the 'relative weight' of 'individual freedom' over 'structural determin-ation': every mediator along any chain of action is an individualized event because it is connected to many other individualized events. This might offer a good place to bid farewell to the notion of 'actor' that I have used all along as a provisional placeholder. What's wrong with the word is not that it is often limited to humans—this limit we have learned to encroach upon—but that it always designates a *source* of initiative or a starting point, the extremity of a vector oriented toward some other end. Of course, when the sociology of the social held sway, it was important to insist on actors, activity, initiative,

[294] The classic work on this 'exteriorisation' remains William James (1890), *The Principles of Psychology*.

[295] But unfortunately he did not have the allegory of information technologies to materialize his web of connections and instead had to rely on the loose metaphor of 'imitative rays'. On Tarde's limits see Bruno Karsenti (2002), 'L'imitation. Retour sur le débat entre Durkheim et Tarde'.

[296] See Gomart, 'Surprised by Methadone' and Gomart 'Methadone: Six Effects in Search of a Substance'.

[297] Witness the powerful effect on the audience of puppets held by visible manipula-tors in Japanese *bunraku* theater.

interpretation, improvisation, justification, interactions, and so on, because the only possible activity that context could bring was that of a cause in search of consequences, of a mediator looking for some passive intermediaries that would faithfully carry its forces. But this is no longer the case with ANT: the theory of action itself is different, since we are now interested in mediators *making* other mediators *do* things. 'Making do' is not the same thing as 'causing' or 'doing': there exists at the heart of it a duplication, a dislocation, a translation that modifies at once the whole argument. It was impossible before to connect an actor to what made it act, without being accused of 'dominating', 'limiting', or 'enslaving' it. This is no longer the case. The more *attachments* it has, the more it exists. And the more mediators there are the better.[298]

Now it's the actor, which so far in this book was kept as a point, an atom, or a source, that has to be flattened out and forced to take a star-like shape. What should we call this newly 'flattened' element? Is it something that is 'made to act'? Is it something that is 'triggered into being triggered into action'?[299] Why not use actor-network? I know this expression remains odd because it could mean just the opposite as well, namely a solution to the actor/system quandary we have just rejected. But we have the word already at hand, and it's not that badly designed in the end. So, an actor-network is what is made to act by a large star-shaped web of mediators flowing in and out of it. It is made to exist by its many ties: attachments are first, actors are second. To be sure, such an expression smacks of 'sociologism', but only as long as we put too much in 'being' and not enough in 'having'. As Tarde insisted long ago, the family of 'to have' is much richer than the family of 'to be' because, with the latter, you know neither the boundary nor the direction: to possess is also being possessed; to be attached is to hold and to be held.[300] Possession and all its synonyms are thus good words for a reworked meaning of what a 'social puppet' could be. The strings are still there, but they transport autonomy or enslavement depending on *how* they are held. From now on, when we speak of actor we should always add the large network of attachments making

[298] Attachment is another word for what I tried to capture under the makeshift expression 'factish'. See also Emilie Gomart and Antoine Hennion (1998), 'A sociology of attachment: music amateurs, drug users'.

[299] See François Jullien (1995), *The Propensity of Things: Toward a History of Efficacy in China*.

[300] 'So far, all of philosophy has been founded on the verb *To be*, whose definition seemed to have been the Rosetta's stone to be discovered. One may say that, if only philosophy had been founded on the verb *To have*, many sterile discussions...would have been avoided. From this principle "I am", it is impossible to deduce any other existence than mine, in spite of all the subtleties of the world. But affirm first this postulate: "I have" as the basic fact, and then the *had* as well as the *having* are given at the same time as inseparable.' Tarde, *Monadologie et sociologie*, p. 86.

it act. As to emancipation, it does not mean 'freed from bonds' but *well*-attached.

In spite of the criticism I made earlier about the notion of society— by opposition to what I proposed to call the collective—an even more radical solution would be to consider these bundles of actor-networks in the same way that Whitehead considers the word 'society'. For him societies are not assemblages of social ties—in the way Durkheim or Weber could have imagined them—but are all the bundles of composite entities that *endure* in time and space.[301] In his words, a society needs new associations in order to persist in its existence. And of course, such a labor requires the recruitment, mobilization, enrollment, and translation of many others—possibly of the whole universe. What is so striking in this generalized definition of societies is that the respective meanings of subjectivity and objectivity are entirely reshuffled. Is a subject whatever *is* present? Is an object whatever *was* present? So every assemblage that pays the price of its existence in the hard currency of recruiting and extending is, or rather, *has* subjectivity. This is true of a body, of an institution, even of some historical event which he also refers to as an organism. Subjectivity is not a property of human souls but of the gathering itself—provided it lasts of course. If we could retain this vastly expanded meaning of society, then we could again understand what Tarde meant when he said that 'everything is a society and that all things are society'.

---

[301] 'The point of a "society", as the term is used here, is that it is self-sustaining; in other words, that it is its own reason.' Alfred North Whitehead (1929/1978), *Process and Reality. An Essay in Cosmology*, p. 89. See Didier Debaise (2003), 'Un empirisme spéculatif: Construction, Processus et Relation chez Whitehead'.

Third Move: Connecting Sites

I s not the 'Tortoise and the Hare' fable rather like that of the 'Ant and the Hare' story? One character jumps, runs, leaps, slumbers, wakes up, and summersaults, so sure he is of winning the race and snatching the prize. But the other one never sleeps. He trudges along, masticating endlessly; he allows himself no break in digging around minuscule galleries, the walls of which are nothing but clay and saliva through which he travels back and forth. And yet is it not fair to say that the Ant, much to the hare's great surprise, is going to win? By sticking obstinately to the notion of a flatland and by inserting clamps every time there is a temptation to take three-dimensional shapes for granted, we have been highlighting types of connections that had no recognizable existence before—even though everyone felt they had to be there. By refusing to leap to context or to stick to the local or to take any position in between, are we not registering now in our account a view of the social rarely seen before?

In the first chapter of Part II, we reckoned that the abrupt alternation between micro and macro, actor and system, was not due to some essential trait of sociology, but rather to the shadow projected over society by the body politic. For this reason, we then imagined two solutions to break the urge that was leading the observer from the local interaction to context or from structure to situated practice. The first move transferred the global, the contextual, and the structural inside tiny loci; it allowing us to identify through which two-way circulations those loci could gain some relevance for others. The second move transformed every site into the provisional endpoint of some other sites distributed in time and space; each site becomes the result of the action at a distance of some other agency. As I warned the reader several times, it's only once the two corrective moves have been practiced assiduously that a third phenomenon appears, the only one worth the efforts of abstraction that we had to go through.

Now is the time for the Ant to fetch its prize. What happens when we practice the two gestures—localizing the global and distributing the local—*together*? Every time a connection has to be established, a new conduit has to be laid down and some new type of entity has to be transported through it. What circulates, so to speak, 'inside' the conduits are the very acts of giving something a dimension. Whenever a locus wishes to act on another locus, it has to go through some medium, transporting something all the way; to go on acting, it has to maintain some sort of more or less durable connection. Conversely, every locus is now the target of many such activities, the crossroads of many such tracks, the provisional repository of many such vehicles. Sites, now transformed into actor-networks for good, are moved to the background; connections, vehicles, and attachments are brought into the foreground. As soon as we do this, we end up with a superposition of various canals as entangled and varied as those that an anatomist would see if she could simultaneously color all the nerve, blood, lymph, and hormone pathways that keep organisms in existence. 'Admirable networks' (from *retia mirabilia*) is the expression histologists have used to register some of these wondrous shapes. How even more miraculous than the body does the social now appear! Could sociology, as Whitehead said of philosophy, not only begin but also *end* in wonder?

I hope it's clear that this flattening does not mean that the world of the actors themselves has been flattened out. Quite the contrary, they have been given enough space to deploy their own contradictory gerunds: scaling, zooming, embedding, 'panoraming', individualizing, and so on. The metaphor of a flatland was simply a way for the ANT observers to clearly distinguish their job from the labor of those they follow around. If the analyst takes upon herself to decide in advance and a priori the scale in which all the actors are embedded, then most of the work they have to do to *establish* connections will simply vanish from view. It is only by making flatness the default position of the observer that the activity necessary to generate some difference in size can be detected and registered. If the geographical metaphor is by now somewhat overused, the metaphor of accounting could do just as well—even though I may have used it too much already. The transaction costs for moving, connecting, and assembling the social is now payable to the last cent, allowing us to resist the temptation that scaling, embedding, and zooming can be had for nothing without the spending of energy, without recruitment of some other entities, without the establishment of expensive connections.

Whatever metaphors we want to cling to, they do nothing more than help us counterbalance the weight of social inertia. They are part of our infra-language. Once again, everything happens as if ANT did not locate social theory at the same level as sociologists of the social. What the latter means by theory is a positive, substantive, and synthetic view of the ingredients out of which the social is fashioned—and those accounts may often be very suggestive and powerful. With ANT, we push theory one step further into abstraction: it is a negative, empty, relativistic grid that allows us *not* to synthesize the ingredients of the social in the actor's place. Since it's never substantive, it never possesses the power of the other types of accounts. But that's just the point. Social explanations have of late become too cheap, too automatic; they have outlived their expiration dates—and critical explanations even more so. So many ingredients have been packed into society, individual, cognition, market, empire, structure, face-to-face interactions, that it has become as impossible to unpack them as it is to read the hundred thousand lines of code making up a proprietary operating system—not to mention trying to rewrite it. This is why we have to make sure that every entity has been reshuffled, redistributed, unraveled, and 'de-socialized' so that the task of gathering them again can be made in earnest. When we shift to ANT, we are like lazy car drivers newly converted to hiking; we have to relearn that if we want to reach the top of the mountain, we need to take it one step at a time, right foot after left foot, with no jumping or running allowed, all the way to the bitter end! I will show in the Conclusion why this point is so important not only for science but also for politics.

Three new questions may now be tackled in our discussion. The first is to detect the type of connectors that make possible the transportation of agencies over great distance and to understand why they are so efficient at formatting the social. The second is to ask what is the nature of the agencies thus transported and to give a more precise meaning to the notion of mediator that I have been using. Finally, if this argument about connections and connectors is right, it should be possible to come to grips with a logical consequence that readers must have already puzzled about: What lies *in between* these connections? What's the extent of our ignorance concerning the social? In other words, how vast is the *terra incognita* we will have to leave blank on our maps? After having complained too often in this book that the social of sociologists was so badly packaged—we could not inspect its composition any more than we could check its degree of freshness—the time has now come to take much more positively the work done by the social sciences to render the social traceable.

From standards to collecting statements

Before proceeding forward, let's do a little test to see whether we are able to tackle a topic where scale is obviously involved *without* ourselves making any assumption about the respective dimensions of all the agents along the chain. This will allow us to verify how nimble we have become in avoiding the local as well as the global.

Consider for instance this series of photos that show Alice voting in France for a general election. Go from the first to the last and try to decide which one is more local or more global than the other. The first, where Alice ponders the newspaper *Le Monde* to make up her mind about which party to vote for, cannot be said to be local simply because she is alone reading at her breakfast table. The same issue of this newspaper is read that day by millions. Alice is bombarded by a flood of clichés, arguments, columns, and opinions out of which she has to make up her own mind. But the last image that sums up the result of the election day cannot be said to be global either under the pretext that it's the 'whole of France' that is summarized in one pie chart on television (with the surprising result that the Left has been winning). On the television inside Alice's apartment, this pie chart is a few centimeters wide. So, once we realize that none of the successive images in this photomontage can be said to be smaller or bigger than any other, the key feature of their *connectedness* becomes fully visible— although it is not graspable on any single photograph![302] Something is circulating here from the first to the last. In the opaque voting booth, Alice's opinion is transformed into a piece of paper certified by her signature and then placed by scrutinizers into a ballot box, where it is then ticked off as one anonymous dot in a tally whose sum is wired to the Ministry of the Interior's central bureau to be merged inside other double checked additions. What's the relationship between the 'small' Alice and 'France as a whole'? *This path*, laid down by *this* instrument, makes it physically possible to collect, through the circulation of paper technologies, a link between Alice and France whose exacting traceability has been slowly elaborated through two centuries of violent political history and contested voting reforms.[303] The gap between 'interaction' and 'context' would hide the complex machinery establishing continuous connections between the sites, none of which is either big or small.

As soon as we concentrate on what circulates from site to site, the first type of entities to snap into focus are *forms*.[304] Few words are more ambiguous, and yet this is just the sort of topic that the shift in social

[302] This is the central argument about image flaws and image *flows* in Latour and Weibel, *Iconoclash*. More can be seen on this 1996 election example in Latour and Hermant, *Paris the Invisible City*.

[303] See Latour and Weibel, *Making Things Public*; Heurtin; *L'espac public*.

[304] Let us remember that any site will be taken as an actor network if it is the source of what acts at a distance on other sites—hence giving it a star-like shape—and is the end point of all the transactions leading to it—hence giving it the same star-like shape. So the word 'site' should not be taken as a synonym of the local that we have abandoned in the previous chapter.

theory allows us to see in a new light.[305] Usually, form is taken not in a material but in a formal sense. And it's true that if you forget that in a flat world no jumping is allowed, then formalism becomes an adequate description of itself: you will attempt to give a formal description of formalism—and God knows that there has been no lack of such endeavors. But as soon as you notice that each site has to pay the connection with another site through some displacement, then the notion of form takes a very concrete and practical sense: a form is simply something which allows something else to be transported from one site to another. Form then becomes one of the most important types of translations.

Such a displacement from ideal to material can be extended to *information*. To provide a piece of information is the action of putting something into a form.[306] But now the word takes a very mundane, practical meaning; it can be a paper slip, a document, a report, an account, a map, whatever succeeds in practicing the incredible feat of transporting a site into another one without deformation through massive transformations.[307] Watch in the case of Alice's vote how many metamorphoses her opinion has undergone even though it has been faithfully registered—provided there has been no fraud along the way. It is to register such contradictory requirements of formalism that I had proposed long ago the expression of 'immutable mobiles'.[308] Once again, scientific activity offers many privileged cases of transportation through transformations: from the humble and smelly tasks of the taxidermy of rare animal specimens[309] to the

[305] I introduced the expression of inscription devices in Bruno Latour and Steve Woolgar (1986), *Laboratory Life: The Construction of Scientific Facts*.

[306] French speakers have the great advantage of still hearing in their word *forme* the same etymology as in their beloved *fromages*, cheese being literally fermented milk that is put into a *forme* or a *fourme*. Gastronomy and epistemology are close enough for them!

[307] There is a rich literature on the 'matter of form', including Jacques Derrida (1998), *Of Grammatology*; François Dagognet (1974), *Ecriture et iconographie*; Elizabeth Eisenstein (1979), *The Printing Press as an Agent of Change*; and Goody, *The Domestication of the Savage Mind*. For recent work on formalism see Eric Livingston (1985), *The Ethnomethodological Foundations of Mathematical Practice*; MacKenzie, *Mechanizing Proof*; Hélène Mialet (2003), 'Reading Hawking's Presence: An Interview with a Self-Effacing Man'; Rosental, *La Trame de l'évidence*; Bryan Rotman (1993), *Ad Infinitum: The Ghost in Turing Machine. Taking God out of Mathematics and Putting the Body Back In*; and Andrew Warwick (2003), *Masters of Theory: Cambridge and the Rise of Mathematical Physics*. Derrida has never stopped meditating on the odd sort of materiality implied by archives—see Derrida (1995), *Archive Fever: A Freudian Impression*.

[308] An expression I introduced in Latour, *Science In Action* to describe not displacement *without* transformation but displacement *through* transformations. See also the seminal paper by Thévenot, 'Rules and implements: investment in forms' that links standardization, economization, and formatting together.

[309] Susan Leigh Star and Jim Griesemer (1989), 'Institutional Ecology, "Translations" and Boundary Objects: Amateurs and Professionals in Berkeley's Museum of Vertebrate Zoology, 1907–1939'.

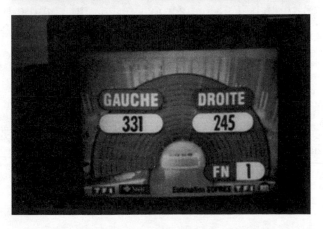

GAUCHE DROITE
331 245
FN 1

most elevated, but just as practical, writing of equations, through the building of a statistical apparatus or the even humbler task of paper clippings and file making of all hues and colors. Whatever the medium, a material description of formalism is now possible which takes very seriously the connecting ability of forms—conceived as physically as possible—while shedding the idea that formalisms could themselves be formally described.[310]

The first important consequence of becoming attentive to the material traceability of immutable mobiles is to help us locate what has been so important with the sociology of the social from its inception. This will also be the occasion to make amends for the apparently cavalier way in which I have treated my elders and betters. I can now confess that it's not without scruples that, throughout this book, I had to be so critical of the ways the social sciences approached the question of formatting. In truth, the sociology of the social has been amazingly successful. Its achievements are truly impressive and has made it possible for us all to 'have' a society to live in.[311] I knew from the beginning that, although those sociologies make for awkward social theory because they interrupt the task of assembling the social, this is just the reason why they are so good at *performing* it, that is, at *formatting* the relations between sites. Their weakness is just what makes them so strong, or rather their strength at fixing up the social is what makes them so unwieldy when reassembling it. Thus, all things considered, critiques of sociology of the social are misdirected if they forget to consider their extraordinary efficacy in generating one form of attachments: the social ones, or at least that part of the social that has been stabilized. There cannot be anything wrong in forming, formatting, or informing the social world.[312]

To reproach the social sciences for being formal would be like criticizing a dictionary for ranking words from A to Z or a pharmacist for having labels on all his vials and boxes. The task of stabilizing the five sources of uncertainty is just as important as that of keeping them open. Even though it's a dangerous mistake to confuse the two, it would be ridiculous not to tackle the second under the pretext that

[310] Harry Collins (1990), *Artificial Experts: Social Knowledge and Intelligent Machines* and MacKenzie, *Mechanizing Proof* provide many powerful examples of the richness of a redescription of formalism as does Galison, *Image and Logic*.
[311] See Alain Desrosières (2002), *The Politics of Large Numbers: A History of Statistical Reasoning*; Theodore M. Porter (1995), *Trust in Numbers: The Pursuit of Objectivity in Science and Public Life*; and Norton Wise (1995), *The Values of Precision and Exactitude*.
[312] This is why there is no reason to deplore the empire of what Garfinkel designates, somewhat derogatively, by FA, that is, 'Formal Analysis' of the 'worldwide social movement'. 'Thinking like a sociologist involves a commitment to the belief that there is no orderliness in the concreteness of everyday life.' Garfinkel, *Ethnomethodology's Program*, p.136.

the first has to be dealt with. On the contrary, once the task of deploying controversies about the social world is fully undertaken— as I did in Part I—then the crucial importance of the second task of enforcing boundaries, categories, and settlements has to be fully recognized as well.[313] If it is such a grave methodological mistake to limit in advance and in the actor's stead the range of entities that may populate the social world, it would be equally pathetic to ignore the constant work they do so as to restrict the repertoire of actants and to keep controversies at bay. Once again, even if it has become somewhat irritating, the only viable slogan is to 'follow the actors themselves'; yes, one must follow them when they *multiply* entities and again when they *rarefy* entities.

We now must learn to pay respect to the formalizers, pigeonholers, categorizers, and number crunchers just as we had to learn earlier to reject them for interrupting too early the task of association and composition. I recognize that this new corrective calisthenics might make us sore, but who said the practice of social science should be painless? If the actors are busy doing many things at once, should we not become as pliable, articulate, and skillful as they are? If the social sciences per-*form* the social, then those forms have to be followed with just as much care as the controversies. This is especially the case now that we no longer run the risk of confusing such a study of formalism with its formalist description. Forms have not 'lost' anything. They have not 'forgotten' any sort of human, concrete, lived-in dimension. They are neither 'cold' nor 'heartless', nor are they devoid of a 'human face'. Following the making, the fine-tuning, the dissemination, and upkeep of immutable mobiles will not for one second take us away from the narrow galleries of practice.[314] If there is one opposition that no longer holds us back, it's the one that was supposed to pit positivist against interpretative sociologies. Once carefully relocated, their intuitions reveal two successive aspects of social assemblages.[315]

In following the stabilization of controversies, we are greatly helped if we bring to the foreground the crucial notion of *standards*. We can say that the sociology of the social circulates in the same way as physical standards do or, better yet, that social sciences are part of *metrology*. Before science studies and especially ANT, standardization

---

[313] This is a restatement of the principle of irreduction as defined in Latour *Irreductions*.

[314] A telling example is provided in Bowker and Star, *Sorting Things Out*. It would be a case of 'misplaced concreteness' to criticize those formatting as being 'abstract'. This is the limit of Lave *Cognition in Practice*, which otherwise shows a welcomed attention to the practice.

[315] When we deal later with plasma, we will once again reconsider the great advantage of Garfinkel's position and understand why it has most likely been misdirected due to his attachment to phenomenology.

and metrology were sort of dusty, overlooked, specialized, narrow little fields. This is no wonder since their truly wonderful achievements were cut off by the gap between local and global that we have now recognized to be an artifact. As soon as local and global disappears, the central importance of standards and the immense advantages we draw from metrology—in the widest acceptance of the term—become obvious.

Take, for instance, the case of the platinum kilogram maintained by the International Bureau of Weights and Measures (*Bureau International des Poids et Mesures*) in a deep vault inside the Breteuil Pavillon at the Sèvres park outside of Paris. Is it a convention? Yes. Is it a material object? Yes. Is it an international institution? Once more, yes. Does it represent the head of a metrological chain, the ideal model to which all other inferior copies are compared in a solemn ceremony once every two years? Again, yes. There is no doubt that it is a hybrid. And yet it is exactly those confusing entities that allow all the metrological networks of the world to have some sort of 'common weight'. Is a metrological reference like the kilogram local or global? Local, since it always resides somewhere and circulates inside special boxes using specific signals, at certain specified times, following specific protocols.[316] Is it global? Sure, since without standards like the watt, the newton, the ohm, the ampere, that is, without the *Système International d'Unités*, there would be no global of any sort because no locus would have the 'same' time, the 'same' distance, the 'same' weight, the same intensity of electric current, the same chemical 'reagents', the 'same' biological reference materials, etc. There would be no baseline, no benchmark. All sites would be incommensurable for good.

Standards and metrology solve practically the question of relativity that seems to intimidate so many people: Can we obtain some sort of universal agreement?[317] Of course we can! *Provided* you find a way to hook up your local instrument to one of the many metrological chains

---

[316] There is now a rich literature on the practical extension of networks through standards. See Ken Alder (1995), 'A Revolution to Measure: The Political economy of the Metric System in France'; Rexmond Canning Cochrane (1976), *Measures for Progress: A History of National Bureau of Standards*; Alexandre Mallard (1996), 'Les instruments dans la coordination de l'action: pratique technique, métrologie, instrument scientifique'; Mélard 'L'autorité des instruments'; and Joseph O'Connell (1993), 'Metrology: the Creation of Universality by the Circulation of Particulars'. The most decisive work has been done in Simon Schaffer (1988), 'Astronomers Mark Time: Discipline And The Personal Equation' and (1991b), 'A Manufactory of OHMS, Victorian Metrology and its Instrumentation'.

[317] A stunning example of the use of metrology in the arm's race debate has been provided by Don MacKenzie (1990), *Inventing Accuracy: A Historical Sociology of Nuclear Missile Guidance*. See also Galison, *Einstein's Clocks*.

whose material network can be fully described, and whose cost can be fully determined. Provided there is also no interruption, no break, no gap, and no uncertainty along any point of the transmission. Indeed, traceability is precisely what the whole of metrology is about! No discontinuity allowed, which is just what ANT needs for tracing social topography. Ours is the social theory that has taken metrology as the paramount example of what it is to expand *locally everywhere*, all the while bypassing the local *as well* as the universal. The practical conditions for the expansion of universality have been opened to empirical inquiries. It's not by accident that so much work has been done by historians of science into the situated and material extension of universals. Given how much modernizers have invested into universality, this is no small feat.

As soon as you take the example of scientific metrology and standardization as your benchmark to follow the circulation of universals, you can do the same operation for other less traceable, less materialized circulations: most coordination among agents is achieved through the dissemination of *quasi*-standards. For many types of traces the metaphor is pretty easy to follow: What would be the state of any economical activity without accounting codes and summaries of best practices? If, for instance, you shift from the North American to the European Union accounting format, you offer investors different handrails to help them make calculations: profitable European companies will fall in the red, while others will jump into black.[318] Of course, those who believe the economy to be an infrastructure would not be moved by this 'little difference' in accounting; they will say that it is moot compared to the 'real impact' of economical forces down below. But those of us who have to understand what it means to calculate something, to externalize some elements and to internalize others to take them, literally, *into* the *account*, are going to follow nonetheless every little detail of this 'technical dispute' because explaining what is a profit, an exploitation, or a plus value depends entirely upon such niceties.[319] If *economies* are the outcome of *econom-*

[318] Consider the standards of the International Accounting Standards Board (IASB), a private firm based in London to which the European Union has delegated some of the work. Many powerful examples of the way 'micro' techniques of accounting hold the 'macro' consequences of profit and economical theories can be found in the journal *Accounting, Organizations and Society*. See also Tomo Susuki (2003), 'The epistemology of macroeconomic reality: The Keynesian Revolution from an accounting point of view'.

[319] See Alexandra Minvielle (forthcoming), 'De quoi une enterprise est-elle capable?'. On all those questions of 'spreading' in time and space by 'making' space and time, see the special issue of *Organizations* and especially G. Jones, C. McLean and Paolo Quattrone (2004), 'Spacing and Timing': Introduction to the Special Issue of *Organization* on 'Spacing and Timing'.

ics, as Michel Callon has argued, the humble paper tools allowing coordination are at once placed in the foreground.

Other circulations of standards seem more tenuous, even though their tractability is fairly good as long as the observer does not let the irruption of the 'social explanation' break this Ariadne thread. How would you know your 'social category' without the enormous work done by statistical institutions that work to calibrate, if not to standardize, income categories? How would one identify oneself as 'upper-middle class', 'yuppy', or 'preppy' without reading the newspapers? How would you know your 'psychological profile' without more statistical surveys, more professional meetings, more consensus conferences? How would a psychiatrist categorize a mental patient without the DSM?[320] It is no use saying that those categories are arbitrary, conventional, fuzzy, or, on the contrary, too sharply bounded or too unrealistic. They do solve practically the problem of extending some standard everywhere locally through the circulation of some traceable document—even though the metaphor of a document might dim somewhat. It is not the case that some powerful people unfairly 'pigeon-hole' other people whose 'ineffable interiority' is thus ignored and mutilated; rather, the circulation of quasi-standards allow anonymous and isolated agencies to slowly become, layer after layer, *comparable* and *commensurable*—which is surely a large part of what we mean by being human. This common measurement depends, of course, on the *quality* of what is transferred. The question is not to fight against categories but rather to ask: 'Is the category subjecting or *subjectifying* you?' As we saw at the end of the last chapter, freedom is getting out of a *bad* bondage, not an *absence* of bonds.

Viewed in this way, we can now understand the great services, albeit unwittingly, that the sociology of the social can render to our inquiry. It has rendered traceable that portion of the social that is going to be stocked and stabilized just as much as utility companies, information technology, bureaucracies and, more generally, the dissemination of formats and benchmarks have been rendering the cost of generating universality visible. This is why the social sciences are as much a part of the problem as they are a solution: they ceaselessly kept churning out the collective brew. Standards that define for everyone's benefit what *the social itself* is made of might be tenuous, but they are powerful all the same. Theories of what a society is or should become have played an enormous role in helping actors to define where they stand, who they are, whom they should take into account, how they should justify themselves, and to which sort of forces they are allowed to

---

[320]   Stuart A. Kirk and Herb Kutchins (1992), *The Selling of DSM: The Rhetoric of Science in Psychiatry*.

bend. If natural sciences, like physics or chemistry, have transformed the world, how much more have the social sciences transformed what it is for humans to be connected to one another? Actors can download those theories of the social as effectively as they do MP3 files. And of course the very idea that 'we are members of a society', that we are 'accountable', that we have 'legal responsibility', that 'gender is different from sex', that 'we have a responsibility toward the next generation', that we have 'lost social capital', etc., does circulate through conduits that intellectual historians can reconstruct almost as precisely as their colleagues do for the International clock, the ohm, the meter, double-entry bookkeeping, or the spread of ISO-9000 standards. Social theories are not behind all this but are very much in the foreground. Each one is trying to expand or is, as Tarde noted, 'dreaming like Alexander of conquering the world'. Even if one social theory had reached hegemony, it would never be more universal than the meter, and like it, it would not survive a minute longer than the metrological chains that sustain it.[321]

As soon as we become good at tracing it, we can use this topography to tackle other conduits that are not materialized continuously by some state apparatus but whose movements have nonetheless the same effect. *Collecting statements* play exactly the same role, on condition that we don't see them as simply 'representing' or 'distorting' existing social forces. For example, the medieval expression *Vox populi, vox Dei* does not simply 'express' some widely held popular belief residing in the eternal wisdom of the people. As Alain Boureau has done, you can document most of the occurrences of this speech act during the Middle Ages, draw the networky shape of its usage and show that every time it has been uttered, it has modified, albeit slightly, the distribution of roles and powers among *deus, populus, vox*, and *rex*.[322] We have learned from the first source of uncertainty that even a tiny change in the ways of talking about groups would change the performance of those groups. This is even truer when a statement carries a different social theory as is the case with this highly unstable expression which implies, like a delicate relief carved on the

---

[321] It does not require some heroic feat of reflexivity to apply this principle to Tarde's sociology and to ANT itself. No privileged position is required to make this point, nor any absolute frame of reference.

[322] In addition to Alain Boureau (1992), 'L'adage *Vox Populi, Vox Dei* et l'invention de la nation anglaise (VIIIe-XIIe siècle)', a modern day example is provided by the word 'environnement' in Florian Charvolin (2003), *L'invention de l'environnement en France. Chroniques anthropologiques d'une institutionnalisation*. For a general theory of macro-actors, see Cooren, *The Organizing Property of Communication*. In a different vein, Jean-Pierre Faye (1972), *Langages totalitaires* offers another way to take seriously the connecting power of specific statements. For the use of socio-linguistics tools, see Lorenza Mondada (2000), *Décrire la ville: La construction des savoirs urbains dans l'interaction et dans le texte*.

surface of a gem, a whole interpretation of the linkages between theology and politics.

These collecting statements are not rare and exotic cases. Think of what is achieved when an American proudly exclaims 'This is a free country!' or when a Frenchman retorts '*On est en République quand même!*' Consider how many positions are modified when the 'principle of precaution' is invoked by European bureaucrats against the more classical American definition of risk.[323] Fathom what is triggered in a Middle Eastern audience when you speak of an 'Axis of Evil' or plead for 'an Islamic Enlightenment'. Collecting statements not only traces new connections but also offers new highly elaborated theories of what it is to connect.[324] They perform the social in all practical ways. Such is the power of the 'justifications' analyzed by Boltanski and Thévenot: they have no size but they leave 'sizings', so to speak, in their wake since those expressions allow people to rank themselves as well as the objects in dispute. Every time an expression is used to justify one's action, they not only format the social but also provide a second order description of how the social worlds should be formatted.[325] It's precisely because scale is not a fixed feature of the social that those collecting statements play such an important role. As soon as they are allowed to simply represent, reify, or objectify something else, for instance the social context behind them, they efficacy stops being visible. But as soon as they are taken again as so many standards circulating along tiny metrological chains, they clearly become the source of what we mean by being in a society. Without collecting statements, how could the collective be collected?

Mediators at last

Now that we understand how to navigate our way through the flattened landscape and how to pay our respects to the formatting power of the sociology of the social, the next step is as difficult as it is logical. The very metrological power of the social sciences is just what makes it

---

[323] In his work on the expression 'precautionary principle' in European offices, see Jim Dratwa (2003), 'Taking Risks with the Precautionary Principle'.

[324] A beautiful example of the connecting ability of arguments is provided in Michael Baxandall (1985), *Patterns of Intention. On The Historical Explanation Of Pictures*. Timothy Mitchell (2002), *Rule of Experts: Egypt, Techno-Politics, Modernity* provides one of the best cases of the richness of studying in addition to the collecting statement 'development' the formatting power of intellectual technologies.

[325] Boltanski and Thévenot, *On Justification*. Boltanski's sociology is half Kantian philosophy and half a new attention toward collecting and circulating statements. There should be no difficulty in relocating the second and getting rid of the first.

difficult for them to encounter the social as associations. It's precisely because it is so good at calibrating and benchmarking *stabilized* definitions of the social that it finds so impractical the sizing up of newcomers that are constantly imported in the course of controversies. The better you are at defining the 'older' social, the worse you are at defining the 'new' one. The situation is exactly the same with the technical fields of metrology: they allow all the other laboratories to do science, but they are not themselves the sources of much discovery—even though they are quick to use any new fact to improve the accuracy of their instruments by a few more decimal places.[326] Metrology is no more the whole of science than the sociology of the social is the whole of sociology. The social that makes up society is only one part of the associations that make up the collective. If we want to reassemble the social, it's necessary, aside from the circulation and formatting of traditionally conceived social ties, to detect other circulating entities.

This detection is made easier once we know that we should not confuse the already assembled social with the work of reassembling it, and once we learn how not to substitute the entities we are looking for with something made out of social stuff. By localizing the circulation, production, formatting, and metrology of the social inside tiny, expansive, and expensive conduits, we have already opened a space in which other types of entities may begin to circulate.

But if we wish to profit from this small 'window of opportunity', we have to modify the default setting of our inquiries. We should not state that 'when faced with an object, ignore its content and look for the social aspects surrounding it'. Rather, one should say that 'when faced with an object, attend first to the associations out of which it's made and only later look at how it has renewed the repertoire of social ties'. In other words, what we have to understand is why sociologists are so shy to meet the non-social entities that make up the social world, even though this wondrous encounter is a most common experience. It's as if we could not stand meeting face-to-face the puzzling phenomena that keep proliferating whenever we feel that collective life is breaking down. Why is it that when faced with religion, we tend to limit our inquiry to its 'social dimensions' and take as a scientific virtue *not* to study religion itself? When faced with science, why is our first reaction to politely stick to its 'social biases' and *not* to account for objectivity itself? Why is it that when inquiring about art we restrict ourselves only to 'what is social' in the appreciation of a masterpiece and not to

[326] See Cochrane, *Measures for Progress*. Unfortunately, the amazing article by P. Hunter (1980), 'The National System of Scientific Measurement', to my knowledge, has not been updated.

the many other sources from which its worth could come from? When we study economics, why are we so hesitant at going to the heart of our attachments to goods and instead limit ourselves to 'the something sociological' that seems to 'embed' the purely rational calculations? And so on. It's as if our first reaction was to welcome associations only if they had first been covered in a coat made of social ties; as if we could never accept to talk with the original characters but only with the social forces that act as their proxies. In a period not known for its chastity, such prudishness is rather extraordinary: 'Hide, please hide, I can't bear to see those associations!' or 'Before entering the palace of social sciences please conceal yourself under the chador of social explanations.'

Although our most common encounter with society is to be overloaded by new elements that are not themselves part of the social repertoire, why do we keep insisting that we should stick to the short list of its accepted members? Such a limitation made sense during the time of modernization. To mark a clean break with the past, it was logical to limit in advance society to a small number of *personae gratae*. But this doesn't mean that sociology should accept forever to be an object-*less* discipline, that is, a science *without object*. Respecting the formatting power of the sociology of the social is one thing, but it's another to restrict oneself to metrology and abandon the discovery of new phenomena. How could we call empirical a discipline that excises out of the data only those that can be packaged into 'social explanations'? It does not take much courage or imagination to see that, once modernism is put aside, such an attitude no longer makes moral, scientific, or political sense.

Consider for instance what would happen if we were approaching the study of religion while keeping the older default settings. Pious souls have an uncanny obstinacy to speak as if they were attached to spirits, divinities, voices, ghosts, and so on. All of those entities would have, of course, no existence at all in the observer's agenda since they would not pertain to the limited repertoire of agencies fixed at the onset. So what should we do with what the actors designate ceaselessly as 'real beings'? We would have to put scare quotes around them, bracket their existence out, and locate them firmly in the believer's mind. We would literally have to *invent a believer*.[327] A first fanciful sphere would begin to develop. Now since those entities don't exist but are nonetheless 'taken as' being real, they have to come from the inside of one's spirit or brain.

---

[327] That belief is a modernist institution coming from critique is one of the important aspects of the study of iconoclasm and of the whole repertoire of critical gestures. See Latour and Weibel, *Iconoclash*.

But divinities, spirits, and voices live a rather cramped life inside the individual person's sphere. They are too precise, too technical, too innovative. They move too wildly and they obviously overflow the individual capacity of invention, imagination, and self-delusion. And besides, actors still insist they are made to do things by those real entities 'outside' of them! Ordinary persons don't want them to be just an object of belief and so those entities have to come from the outside after all. Does this mean that we have to accept their real existence? No, no, since they don't exist—that's supposedly the only 'sure fact' of the matter. What is the only reality which is outside the individual and which has the strength to sustain the existence of non-existing phenomena? The answer of course is society, the social made of social stuff. Here, a second even bigger sphere would begin to develop out of our own studies: the non-existing social stuff in charge of maintaining the existence of non-existing entities that populate the narrow mind of deluded members. And all of that would be in the name of good science and serious scholarship! All the while, ordinary folks would keep insisting that they are made to act by real entities *outside* of themselves.

But any science has to invent risky and artificial devices to make the observer sensitive to new types of connections. Is it not obvious that it makes no empirical sense to refuse to meet the agencies that make people do things? Why not take seriously what members are obstinately saying? Why not follow the direction indicated by their finger when they designate what 'makes them act'? A (surely fake) Chinese proverb says that 'When the wise man shows the moon, the moron looks at the finger'. I find it impossible to accept that social sciences could be so debased as to create entire disciplines to make scholars moronic. Why not say that in religion what counts are the beings that make people act, just as every believer has always insisted?[328] That would be more empirical, perhaps more scientific, more respectful, and much more economical than the invention of two impossible non-existing sites: the mind of the believer and the social reality are hidden behind illusions propped up by even more illusions. Besides, what is so scientific in the notion of 'belief'?

If such a default setting is accepted—look at the object first and only later at the standardized social—there is of course a catch. I am not deluded enough to believe that ANT could escape the fate of all theories: to think is not to solve arduous problems, only to displace them. For such an encounter with objects to take place, other circulating entities have to be granted back some rights of citizenry, so that they, too, can have a seat with the older members. But aren't sociologists of

[328] Claverie, *Les Guerres de la Vierge*.

the social proud of having dissolved all those exotic objects? Do we really have to bring back the gods when talking of religion, masterpieces when analyzing art, and objective facts when studying science? Is this not exactly the obstacle that social science is proud of having left behind? By invoking the existence of non-social circulating entities, is this not taking the most reactionary, backward, and archaic move possible? This is where the Ant wins or loses. Can we anticipate a social science *that takes seriously the beings that make people act?* Can sociology become *empirical* in the sense of respecting the strange nature of what is 'given into experience', as zoologists do with their zoos and botanists with their herbariums? Can we trace social connections shifting from one non-social being to the next, instead of replacing all entities populating the world by some ersatz made 'of' social stuff? Even simpler: can social science have a *real object* to study?

Before answering emphatically 'no', consider for a minute what it would do to the sensitivity of our instruments were we to change the default setting and consider objects first, rather than beat around the bush in search of social explanations. Then, compare it with the ways in which religion was mishandled in the example just mentioned. Take works of art, for instance.[329] Apart from religion, no other domain has been more bulldozed to death by critical sociology than the sociology of art. Every sculpture, painting, *haute cuisine* dish, techno rave, and novel has been explained to nothingness by the social factors 'hidden behind' them. Through some inversion of Plato's allegory of the Cave, all the objects people have learned to cherish have been replaced by puppets projecting social shadows which are supposed to be the only 'true reality' that is 'behind' the appreciation of the work of art. Nowhere has social explanation played more the role of a negative King Midas transforming gold, silver, and diamonds into dust. And yer, as one sees in religion, if you are listening to what people are saying, they will explain at length how and why they are deeply *attached, moved, affected* by the works of art which 'make them' feel things. Impossible! Forbidden! To be affected is supposed to be mere affectation.[330] So what should we do if we keep the old setting? Well, here again, as for religion, science, and politics, people are made to delude themselves by the 'scientific' grasp of social science: they are transmogrified, once more, into believers! And here again, as always, some people, infuriated by the barbarous irreverence of 'social explanations', come forth and defend the 'inner sanctity' of the work of art against barbarians. And sadly—the slope is steep, the outcome

---

[329] I have already shown in Part I what it did to the study of science.
[330] I am following here Antoine Hennion (1993), *La passion musicale: Une sociologie de la médiation.*

inevitable—we end up swinging gently between 'internalism' and 'externalism', esthetic and social explanations, all the way back to kindergarten.

Of course, this is not what is empirically given because the beings to which we are attached via the mediation on the works of art, if they never resemble the social of sociologists, *never look* like the insulated 'object' of esthetics with its 'inner core' of 'ineffable beauty'. While in the old paradigm you had to have a zero-sum game—everything lost by the work of art was gained by the social, everything lost by the social had to be gained by the 'inner quality' of the work of art—in the new paradigm you are allowed a win/win situation: the more attachments the better.[331] Is this not the most common experience? You watch a painting; a friend of yours points out a feature you had not noticed; you are thus *made to see* something. Who is seeing it? You, of course. And yet, wouldn't you freely acknowledge that you would have not seen it *without* your friend. So who has seen the delicate feature? Is it you or your friend? The question is absurd. Who would be silly enough to *deduct* from the total sum of action the influence of pointing something out? The more influence, the better. And if you are allowed progressively to influence the quality of the varnish, the procedures of the art market, the puzzles of the narrative programs, the successive tastes of collectors making up a long retinue of mediators, then the 'inner' quality of the work will not diminish but, on the contrary, be reinforced.[332] The more 'affluence', the better.[333] It is counterintuitive to try and distinguish 'what comes from viewers' and 'what comes from the object' when the obvious response is to 'go with the flow'. Object and subject might exist, but everything interesting happens upstream and downstream. Just follow the flow. Yes, follow the actors themselves or rather that which makes them act, namely the circulating entities.

In the pre-relativist definition of the social, what had been brought to the foreground was the human participant and then, through a sharp discontinuity, the social world of beyond. Nothing was allowed to encounter humans unless it was made of social ties. Such was the etiquette of this odd diplomacy. In the new definition it's just the opposite: human members and social context have been put

---

[331] See Antoine Hennion and Geneviève Teil (2003), 'Le goût du vin: Pour une sociologie de l'attention' and Joseph Leo Koerner (2004), *The Reformation of the Image*.

[332] The treatment of masterpieces by some art historians, see Svetlana Alpers (1988), *Rembrandt's Enterprise: The Studio and the Market*, is an excellent model for treating the rest of the social, even for those who like Francis Haskell (1982), *Patrons and Painters: A Study in the Relations Between Italian Art and Society in the Age of the Baroque* don't indulge in any explicit social theory whatsoever.

[333] Neologism in Yaneva, 'L'affluence des objets'.

into the background; what gets highlighted now are all the mediators whose proliferation generates, among many other entities, what could be called quasi-objects and quasi-subjects. To take up and reverse the rather unfortunate astronomical simile rendered even shakier by Kant's use of it, instead of objects turning around social aggregates as in the pre-Copernican sociology, various social aggregates are emanating out of the many attachments which now occupy the center of the social universe. No matter how hesitant the metaphor, it is such a shift in perspective that ANT is looking for. Things, quasi-objects, and attachments are the real center of the social world, not the agent, person, member, or participant—nor is it society or its avatars. Is this not a better way, to use another of Kant's expressions, of rendering sociology able at last to 'walk onto the sure path of science'?

The reader might remember that in the very first pages of this book, when I had to define as sharply as possible the difference between sociology of the social and sociology of associations, I had to say, following Tarde, that the first had simply confused the *explanans* with the *explanandum*: society is the consequence of associations and not their cause. At the time, this trenchant distinction could not be very convincing because it simply reversed the direction of causal efficacy. I might now be in a position to offer a more precise definition: there are many other ways to retrace the entire social world than the narrow definition provided by standardized social ties.

I could of course maintain the simplified argument and claim, for instance, that it's not science that is explained by social factors, but scientific *content* that explains the shape of its *context*; that it's not social power that explains law, but legal practice that defines what it is to be *bound*; that it's not technology that is 'socially shaped', but rather techniques that grant extension and durability to social *ties*; that it's not social relations that 'embed' economical calculations, but economists' calculations that provide actors with the competence to behave in an economic way, and so on. Although every one of these inversions would be right in terms of ANT, they would remain partial because I have kept the two positions of what explains and what should be explained intact, simply substituting one for the other. In this first formulation it's not the social that accounts for associations but rather associations that explain the social.

But now that we are getting used to traveling in the new flatland, the two positions themselves have vanished together with the very urge for a social explanation that would appeal to the stock of already stabilized social ties: social is not a place, a thing, a domain, or a kind of stuff but a provisional movement of new associations. This change of topography allows for the same ANT argument to be now presented in a more interesting light, offering, so to speak, landing strips for other entities to enter the collective, entities just as complete, ubiquitous, respectable, and empirical as the social of sociologists but not as thoroughly followed by them.

It's not only that law, for instance, is unexplainable by the influence social forces exert over it; and it's not even true to say that law has to explain in turn what society is, since there is no society to be explained. Law has much better things to do: one of them is to circulate throughout the landscape to associate entities *in a legal way*. Science cannot of course be explained by its social context, but nor does it really have to be used in order to explain the ingredients of social relations. It, too, has much better things to do: one of them is to circulate throughout, tying entities together *in a scientific way*. Although it would be pretty empty to explain religion as a fanciful embodiment of society, doing the reverse would be only slightly better because religion does not even aim at explaining the shape of society either. It, too, has much more potent things to do, namely gathering all the same entities as law and science did but tying them together *in a religious way*. Since explaining politics by power and domination is a moot point, there would be no sense either in simply reversing the argument, since politics has a much more important task to fulfill, namely to trace again and again the paradoxical shape of the body politic in *a political way*. And the same could be said of many other types of *connectors* which are now center stage because it is their displacements that trace social connections—an expression that, as we know, does not mean 'connections made of social', but new associations between non-social elements.

Now comes the tricky part as here comes the straw that breaks the camel's back: displacement yes, but *of what*? What does it mean to speak of legal, religious, scientific, technical, economical, and political 'ways' of associating? And how could this be comparable with the traces left by the calibrated definitions of social ties? This is where the simile of the Copernican revolution is but a meek understatement; this is where the real rupture is going to occur with any sort of 'social' science if we don't modify for good the meaning of this adjective—and this is where the few readers I have managed to keep until now may well abandon the theory for good.[334] To understand what I take to be the ultimate goal of ANT, we have to let out of their cages entities which had been strictly forbidden to enter the scene until now and

---

[334] This is also the place where I have to part company finally with Tarde, who never thought it necessary to differentiate the types of threads with which he was weaving his definition of the social world. In this sense, Tarde maintained a substantive and not a relativist definition of sociology.

allow them to roam in the world again.[335] What name could I give them? Entities, beings, objects, things, perhaps refer to them as invisibles.[336] To deploy the different ways in which they assemble the collective would require an entirely different book, but fortunately I don't need to make the point positively, only to indicate the direction and explain why we keep minimizing our chances of being 'objective' when we stick too long to the sociology of the social.

I might have used the relativity metaphor too often but the parallel is striking: abandoning social explanation is like abandoning the ether; nothing is lost except an artifact that made impossible the development of a science by forcing observers to invent entities with contradictory features, blinding them to the real ones. What I see as the major advantage of the odd move I propose is that it allows social scientists to get an empirical grasp on what all members actually do. Once social explanations are relocated into the making and dissemination of standards, the other beings that gather the collective in their own ways may be emphasized at last. No pious soul ever accepted to be merely a believer, so why act as if belief was the only way to 'explain' religion? No amateur ever alternated between 'subjectivity' and 'objectivity', so why force the whole sociology of art into this artificial quandary? No engineer ever distinguished the assembly of people and the assemblage of parts, so why explain things as if society and technology had to be kept separate? No laboratory scientist was ever confronted with an object 'out there' independently of the work to 'make it visible', so why act as if the alternative between 'realism' and 'constructivism' was interesting? No politician was ever confronted with mere domination, so why pretend that the distinction between formal procedures and real social forces was important? If the word 'empirical' means 'faithful to experience', then is this not a way to respect what is given in the most common encounters with the social?

Mediators have finally told us their real names: 'We are beings out there that gather and assemble the collective just as extensively as what you have called so far the social, limiting yourselves to only one standardized version of the assemblages; if you want to follow the actors themselves, you have to follow us as well.' When you begin addressing mediators that scrupulously, you realize that very few of them are content with the ontological repertoire granted by the two former collectors of society and nature. Law, science, religion, economies, psyches, moralities, politics, and organizations might all have

[335] It's possible that such a move is beyond the reach of social science and that it leads to philosophy. But I have learned from Mol that 'empirical philosophy' might be another way to do social science.

[336] If I was accused of positivism in rejecting every hidden force (see the second source of uncertainty, p. 43), I hope it's now clear that it was only a momentary impression.

their own modes of existence, their own circulations. The plurality of inhabited worlds might be a farfetched hypothesis but the plurality of regimes of existence in our own world, well that's a *datum*.[337] Is there any reason why sociology should keep ignoring it?[338]

The problem is that the social sciences have never dared to really be empirical because they believed that they simultaneously had to engage in the task of modernization. Every time some enquiry began in earnest, it was interrupted midway by the urge to gain some sort of relevance. This is why it's so important to keep separate what I earlier called the three different tasks of the social sciences: the deployment of controversies, the stabilization of those controversies, and the search for political leverage. But before we take up this last question of political epistemology, I have to point out another puzzling feature that is the reason for writing this introduction. Contrary to all the other 'clamps' I managed to put in place, this one will break the continuity of the networks, the *terra firma* of traces and documents. This one will lead us back to the sea, the sea of our common ignorance.

Plasma: the missing masses

What a great relief it is to discover that we are not 'in' society—no more than we are 'in' nature. The social is not like a vast impalpable horizon in which every one of our gestures is embedded; society is not omnipresent, omniscient, ubiquitous, watching every one of our moves, sounding every one of our most secret thoughts like the omnipotent God of older catechisms. When we accept to draw the flattened landscape for which I offered a list of props, tricks, grids, and clamps, the social—at least that part that is calibrated, stabilized, and standardized—is made to circulate inside tiny conduits that can expand only through more instruments, spending, and channels. The total, that is the systematic or structural, is not ignored but rather carefully situated inside one of the many Omnimax theaters offering complete panoramas of society—and we now know that the more thrilling the impression, the more enclosed the room has to be. Society is not the whole 'in which' everything is embedded, but what travels 'through' everything, calibrating connections and offering every

---

[337] This is what renders so interesting a philosophy such as that of Etienne Souriau (1943), *Les différents modes d'existence*. To define and explore them is my next project, which I call an inquiry into regimes of enunciation.

[338] Luhmann's masterly attempt at respecting the differences through the notion of autonomous spheres was unfortunately wasted because he insisted in describing all the spheres through the common meta-language borrowed from a simplified version of biology.

entity it reaches some possibility of commensurability. We should now learn to 'hook up' social channels like we do cable for our televisions. Society does not cover the whole any more than the World Wide Web is really world*wide*.

But then the next question is so simple, the step forward so inevitable, the consequence so logical to draw that I am sure every reader has already anticipated this last aspect. If it is true, as ANT claims, that the social landscape possesses such a flat 'networky' topography and that the ingredients making up society travel inside tiny conduits, *what is in between* the meshes of such a circuitry? This is why, no matter its many defects, the net metaphor remains so powerful. Contrary to substance, surface, domain, and spheres that fill every centimeter of what they bind and delineate, nets, networks, and 'worknets' leave everything they don't connect simply *unconnected*. Is not a net made up, first and foremost, of empty spaces? As soon as something as big and encompassing as the 'social context' is made to travel throughout the landscape much like a subway or gas pipes, the inescapable question is: What sort of stuff is it that does *not* get touched by or is *not* hooked up on those narrow sort of circulations? Once this question is raised, it's as if a vertiginous reversal of background and foreground had taken place. Once the whole social world is relocated inside its metrological chains, an immense new landscape jumps into view. If knowledge of the social is limited to the termite galleries in which we have been traveling, what do we know about what is *outside*? Not much.

In a way, this is the consequence of taking formalism materially. If formalism doesn't offer a complete description of itself, this means that in order to complete any act of formalism you need to *add something* that is coming from elsewhere and which, by definition, is not itself formal. This is Wittgenstein's greatest lesson: what it takes to follow rules is not itself describable by rules. As usual, it's Garfinkel who offers the starkest definition of the 'outside' to which we should appeal in order to complete any course of action: 'The domain of things that escape from FA [Formal analytic] accountability is astronomically massive in size and range.'[339] Even though he did not realize the true importance of standardization, Garfinkel's metaphor is not an exaggeration: the ratio of what we have formatted to what we ignore is indeed astronomical. The social as normally construed is but a few specks compared to the number of associations needed to carry out even the smallest gesture.

---

[339] Garfinkel, *Ethnomethodology's Program*, p. 104.

You find this same bewilderment in many different schools of social theory: *action doesn't add up*. For instance, it's the great virtue, not to say the charm, of Howie Becker's accounts of social practices. If his descriptions remain always incomplete, open-ended, hesitant, if they begin midway and stop for no special reason, this is not a weakness on his part but the result of his extreme attention to the vagaries of experience.[340] To learn a tune, to coordinate a band, you need to fathom a large number of unlearned, uncoordinated fragments of action. This is also the reason, to take a different school of thought, why Thévenot has to multiply the different regimes of action so as to simply begin to cover the simplest behavior. As soon as a non-formal description of formalism has to be given, every thinker becomes another Zeno, multiplying the intermediary steps *ad infinitum*. It's also why Law, when trying to define his ANT perspective, insists that 'the alternative metaphysics assumes out-thereness to be overwhelming, excessive, energetic, a set of undecided potentialities, and an ultimately undecidable flux'.[341]

But it is Tarde, not surprisingly, who offered the most radical insights about the background necessary for every activity to emerge.[342] This is the consequence of his interpretation of the links between the big and the small that I have already used in the previous chapters. The big (states, organizations, markets) is an amplification but also a *simplification* of the small. Only Tarde could reverse common sense that much in quietly stating that: 'So, too, there is generally more logic in a phrase than in a discourse, and more in a single discourse than in a succession or group of discourses; there is more in one special rite than in a whole religion, in one point of law than in a whole legal code, in one particular scientific theory than in the whole body of science; and there is more in a single piece of work executed by one workman than in the sum total of his performances.'[343] With this principle we should not consider that the macro encompasses the micro, but that the micro is made of a proliferation of incommensurable entities—what he calls 'monads'—which are simply lending one of their aspects, a 'façade of themselves', to make up a provisional whole. The small holds the big. Or rather the big could at any moment drown again in the small from which it emerged and to which it will return. Whatever the expression, it seems that no understanding of the social can be provided if you don't turn your attention to another range of

---

[340] See Howard Becker (1991), *Outsiders: studies in the sociology of deviance* and Becker, *Art Worlds*.
[341] Law, *After Method*, p. 144.
[342] Tarde, *Psychologie économique*, p. 220.
[343] Tarde, *Social Laws*, p. 76.

unformatted phenomena. It's as if at some point you had to leave the solid land and go to sea.[344]

I call this background *plasma*, namely that which is not yet formatted, not yet measured, not yet socialized, not yet engaged in metrological chains, and not yet covered, surveyed, mobilized, or subjectified.[345] How big is it? Take a map of London and imagine that the social world visited so far occupies no more room than the subway. The plasma would be the rest of London, all its buildings, inhabitants, climates, plants, cats, palaces, horse guards. Yes, Garfinkel is right, 'it's astronomically massive in size and range'.

Once we recognize the extent of this plasma, we may relocate to the right place the two opposite intuitions of positivist and interpretative sociologies: yes, we have to turn our attention to the outside to make sense of any course of action; and yes, there is an indefinite flexibility in the interpretations of those courses. But the outside is not made of social stuff—just the opposite—and interpretation is not a characteristic of individualized human agents—just the opposite.

To interpret some behavior we have to add something, but this does not mean that we have to look for a social framework. Of course, sociologists were right to look for some 'outside', except this one does not resemble at all what they expected since it is entirely devoid of any trace of calibrated social inhabitant. They were right to look for 'something hidden behind', but it's neither behind nor especially hidden. It's *in between* and not made of social stuff. It is not hidden, simply *unknown*. It resembles a vast hinterland providing the resources for every single course of action to be fulfilled, much like the countryside for an urban dweller, much like the missing masses for a cosmologist trying to balance out the weight of the universe.

To interpret some behavior we have indeed to be prepared for many different versions, but this doesn't mean that we have to turn to local interactions. At many points in this book I have criticized phenomenologists, and perhaps also humanists, for believing that face-to-face interactions, individual agents, and purposeful persons provided a more realist and lively locus than what they called the vain abstractions of society. Although they were right in insisting on uncertainties, they have misplaced their sources. It's not that purposeful humans, intentional persons, and individual souls are the only interpretative agents in a world of matters of fact devoid of any meaning by itself.

[344] Sloterdijk with his philosophy of explicitation of the envelopes in which we are all folded—although very different from the metaphorical circulation of network—offers a powerful new description of what is always missing from any account.

[345] See Emmanuel Didier (2001), 'De l'échantillon à la population: Sociologie de la généralisation par sondage aux Etats-Unis' for a remarkable example of plasma before it has been turned into numbers.

What is meant by interpretations, flexibility, and fluidity is simply a way to register the vast outside to which every course of action has to appeal in order to be carried out. This is not true for just human actions, but for every activity. Hermeneutics is not a privilege of humans but, so to speak, a property of the world itself. The world is not a solid continent of facts sprinkled by a few lakes of uncertainties, but a vast ocean of uncertainties speckled by a few islands of calibrated and stabilized forms.

Do we really know that little? We know even less. Paradoxically, this 'astronomical' ignorance explains a lot of things. Why do fierce armies disappear in a week? Why do whole empires like the Soviet one vanish in a few months? Why do companies who cover the world go bankrupt after their next quarterly report? Why do the same companies, in less than two semesters, jump from being deep in the red to showing a massive profit? Why is it that quiet citizens turn into revolutionary crowds or that grim mass rallies break down into a joyous crowd of free citizens? Why is it that some dull individual is suddenly moved into action by an obscure piece of news? Why is it that such a stale academic musician is suddenly seized by the most daring rhythms? Generals, editorialists, managers, observers, moralists often say that those sudden changes have a soft impalpable liquid quality about them. That's exactly the etymology of plasma.[346] This does not mean that the solid architecture of society is crumbling behind, that the Great Leviathan has feet of clay, but that society and the Leviathan circulate inside such narrow canals that in order to be activated they have to rely on an unaccounted number of ingredients coming from the plasma around them. So far I have insisted too much on continuity, which is achieved through traceable connections that have always to be considered against a much vaster backdrop of discontinuities. Or to put it another way, a sociology has to emerge whose contradictory intuitions have to be maintained: it is hard and soft at the same time. We have to be able to consider both the formidable inertia of social structures and the incredible fluidity that maintains their existence: the latter is the real milieu that allows the former to circulate.

To every action I have described so far, you have to add an immense repertoire of missing *masses*. They are needed to balance the accounts, but they are *missing*. The good news is that social paraphernalia do not occupy much space; the bad news is that we don't know much about this outside. And yet there exists a reserve, a reserve army, an immense territory—except it's neither a territory nor an army—for every formatted, localized, continuous, accountable action to be carried out in.

---

[346] See the index in Cassin, *L'effet sophistique*.

It might be understood now why I have been so obstinate in criticizing the social of sociologists because it was a package not easily opened for inspection. If I have insisted a lot on not confusing the social as society with the social as association, it was to be able in the end to mobilize this reserve. How could any political action be possible if it couldn't draw on the potentials lying in wait?

The laws of the social world may exist, but they occupy a very different position from what the tradition had first thought. They are not *behind* the scene, *above* our heads and *before* the action, but *after* the action, *below* the participants and smack in the *foreground*. They don't cover, nor encompass, nor gather, nor explain; they circulate, they format, they standardize, they coordinate, they have to be explained. There is no society, or rather, society is not the name of the whole terrain. Thus we may start all over again and begin exploring the vast landscape where the social sciences have so far only established a few tiny bridgeheads. For sociology the era of exploration may start again, provided we keep reminding ourselves of this motto: *don't fill in the blanks*. Why should we be impatient with this discipline? Sociology is a new science that was born last in a large family of many older brothers and sisters. It's comprehensible that it tried at first to emulate their successes by imitating their definition of science and of the social. It takes time to discover one's own way.

Conclusion: From Society to Collective—Can the Social Be Reassembled?

The alternative I have proposed in this book is so simple that it can be summarized in one short list: the question of the social emerges when the ties in which one is entangled begin to unravel; the social is further detected through the surprising movements from one association to the next; those movements can either be suspended or resumed; when they are prematurely suspended, the social as normally construed is bound together with already accepted participants called 'social actors' who are members of a 'society'; when the movement toward collection is resumed, it traces the social as associations through many non-social entities which might become participants later; if pursued systematically, this tracking may end up in a shared definition of a common world, what I have called a collective; but if there are no procedures to render it common, it may fail to be assembled; and, lastly, sociology is best defined as the discipline where participants explicitly engage in the reassembling of the collective.

In spite of my overall tone, the goal I set myself at the beginning of this work was restricted enough: Is a *science* of the *social* possible again provided we modify, because of what has been learned from the sociology of science, what is meant by 'social' and what is meant by 'science'? As I warned the reader at the onset, I did not try to be fair and balanced, only coherent in drawing as many consequences as possible of this odd starting point.

We have now reached the end of our trip. We can already conclude that the social, as usually defined, is but a moment in the long history of assemblages, suspended between the search for the body politic and the exploration of the collective. The broad project that had given its impetus to the sociology of the social, from its inception in the mid-19th century to the end of the last one, has now weakened. But that is not a reason for despair. On the contrary, it simply means that another project, one that is just as broad as the former one, should take the relay. Since the sociology of the social is only one way to get at the collective, the sociology of associations takes up the mission of collecting which the idea of the social has left suspended. To pay justice to the efforts of our predecessors and to remain faithful to their tradition, we have to take up their goal, understand why they thought it had been prematurely completed, and see how it can be pursued with slightly better chances of success.

If I might have seemed unfair or even nasty with the older definitions of the social, it's because they seem recently to have had greater difficulty in resuming the task of exploring the common world. Once new associations have been stocked in the package of social forces, there is no way to inspect their content, to check their expiration dates, to verify if they really possess the vehicles and the energy to be transported all the way to what they claim to explain. As we have just seen in the previous chapter, this is not to deny the formatting power of the social sciences. On the contrary, it's precisely because they are so good at calibrating the social world that they are ill-adjusted in following associations made of many non-social entities. The same repertoire that equips you so well to find your way through society paralyzes you in times of crisis. So the temptation is to stick to the repertoire of already accepted social members and to excise out of the data those that don't fit. In resuming the project of the social sciences and bringing it back to the source of bewilderment from which it first grew, it is important to become sensitive again to very odd types of assemblages. When we believed that we were modern, we could content ourselves with the assemblies of society and nature. But today we have to restudy what we are made of and extend the repertoire of ties and the number of associations way beyond the repertoire proposed by social explanations. At every corner, science, religion, politics, law, economics, organizations, etc. offer phenomena that we have to find *puzzling again* if we want to understand the types of entities collectives may be composed of in the future. Since it now appears that the collectors are not comprehensive enough, let's go back to the drawing board.

Although I can expect some embarrassment from the sociologists of the social at the idea that the task of tracing connections has to be resumed and redirected toward all those objects they had thought reasonable to leave aside, the continuity of ANT with their project should nonetheless be clear enough. There might be many methodological disagreements and some grumbling, but they should not find such a resumption of their own project unsettling.

The situation is different with critical sociology. I have given this label to what happens when you not only limit yourself to the calibrated social repertoire and leave aside the objects, as the other schools are often tempted to do, but when you claim in addition that those objects are *made of* social ties. This trend is rendered all the more worrying once the indignant reactions of the actors themselves are taken not as a sign of the danger of such a reduction, but as the best proof that this is the only scientific way to proceed. If the objects of study are made of social ties, namely what earlier social scientists have taken to be part of the official repertoire, and if you cut off the only source of falsification, that is, the objections of those that have been 'explained', then it's hard to see the compatibility with ANT. Whatever its claims to science and objectivity, critical sociology cannot be sociology—in the new sense that I propose—since it has no way to retool itself to follow through on the non-social elements. When faced with new situations and new objects, it risks simply repeating that they are woven out of the same tiny repertoire of already recognized forces: power, domination, exploitation, legitimization, fetishization, reification. Law may be socially constructed but so is religion, economics, politics, sport, morality, art, and everything else built with the same material; only the name of the 'field' changes. The problem of critical sociology is that it can never fail to be right.

And yet I must, in this conclusion, come to grips with this way of doing social critique because behind the apparent question of what is a good science there is the much trickier question of political relevance. If the first kindles passion, the second triggers rage—and rages, too, have to be respected.

As should now be clear from the very structure of this book, I have claimed that to be faithful to the experience of the social we have to take up three different duties *in succession*: deployment, stabilization, and composition. We first have to learn how to deploy controversies so as to gauge the number of new participants in any future assemblage (Part I); then we have to be able to follow how the actors themselves stabilize those uncertainties by building formats, standards, and metrologies (Part II); and finally, we want to see how the assemblages thus gathered can renew our sense of being in the same collective. Until now I have simply tried to delay the moment when this last duty has to be fulfilled. The time has now come to tackle the question of what I have called political epistemology.

What sort of political epistemology?

After having made amends for castigating much of the sociology of the social when I relocated its formidable formatting power, I now have to reexamine my assessment of critical sociology. The mistake was not to wish to have a critical edge, but to reach for it at the wrong moment and before the other tasks of sociology had been fulfilled. I reproach critical sociology for having confused society and collective. Its mistake wasn't that it appeared political or confused science with politics, but that it gave a definition of both science and politics that could only fail since it did not care to measure up the number of entities there was to assemble in the first place. Critical sociologists have underestimated the difficulty of doing politics by insisting that the social consists of just a few types of participants. It did not care to notice that there was not much chance for politics to succeed if the list of *bona fide* members making up the social world was drastically restricted in advance.

Several times in this book I showed why you can't multiply the number of entities, follow their intricate metaphysics, fathom the extent of their controversies, and try simultaneously to exclude most of them as fanciful, arbitrary, outdated, archaic, ideological, and misleading. Born at an inauspicious time, sociology tried to imitate the natural sciences at the height of scientism and to shortcut due political process in order to answer the urgent calls for a solution to the social question. But in fusing science and politics too readily, it never followed through to explain what sort of non-social stuff the social was made of, nor had it any freedom to elaborate its own conception of science. Sociologists were not wrong to do this; they simply thought they already had the solution close at hand by using 'the social', and especially society, to define the common world. They wanted to have a say regarding the political questions of their time, to do something about the swift path of modernization, or at the very least apply the laws of their sciences to social engineering.

But no matter how respectable these reasons may appear, they should not suspend the labor of deploying and collecting the associations. If what is to be assembled is not first opened up, de-fragmented, and inspected, it cannot be reassembled again. It does not require enormous skill or political acumen to realize that if you have to fight against a force that is invisible, untraceable, ubiquitous, and total, you will be powerless and roundly defeated. It's only if forces are made of smaller ties, whose resistance can be tested one by one, that you might have a chance to modify a given state of affairs. To put it bluntly: if there is a society, *then no politics is possible*.[347] So, contrary to the first impression, there is a strong conflict between gaining political relevance and offering social explanations. Or, at the very least, there is no

---

[347] I am generalizing Bauman's argument that society was invented to replace revolutionary politics. See Bauman, *Postmodernity and its Discontents* and Frédéric Audren's thesis on the history of the social sciences—Audren, 'Les juristes et les sociologues'.

guarantee that critical sociology will automatically give you some critical edge.

As I have already stated several times, the great danger of critical sociology is that it never fails to explain. This is why it always runs the danger of becoming empirically empty and politically moot. Leaving open the possibility for failure is important because it's the only way to maintain the quality of the scientific grasp and the chance of political relevance. The definition of a social science I have proposed here by building on the sociology of science should be able to reclaim an empirical grasp, since it travels wherever new associations go rather than stopping short at the limit of the former social. It should regain political significance since it tackles again the question of assembling with the new participants that which has been ferreted out. But that requires a simultaneous tuning of science and politics. Not 'seeing double' is what we have learned from studying science *and* society.[348] The idea is not to strive for a purely objective science of the social, nor is it, if the dream of a disinterested science is abandoned, to see the social sciences bogged down in the dirty tricks of politics forever. It simply means that another distribution of roles between science and politics should be attempted. The difficulty comes from deciding what it means to study something if it is not to alternate between the dream of disinterestedness and the opposite dream of engagement and relevance.

It's worth noting at this point that ANT has been accused of two symmetric and contradictory sins: the first is that it extends politics everywhere, including the inner sanctum of science and technology; the second is that it is so indifferent to inequalities and power struggles that it offers no critical leverage—being content only to connive with those in power.[349] Although the two accusations should cancel each other out—how can one extend politics so much and yet doing so little for it?—they are not necessarily contradictory. Since the Left has always leaned on some science to reinforce its project of emancipation, politicizing science amounts to depriving the exploited from the only chance they have of redressing the balance by appealing to objectivity and rationality.[350] Although the false sciences have to be

---

[348] This is the expression used by Shapin and Schaffer, *Leviathan and the Air Pump*. Political epistemology describes the repartition of powers between science and politics while epistemology is a theory of science cut away from politics.

[349] See Alan D. Sokal and Jean Bricmont (1999), *Fashionable Nonsense: Postmodern Intellectual's Abuse of Science*; Langdon Winner (1993), 'Upon Opening the Black Box and Finding It Empty: Social Constructivism and the Philosophy of Technology.'; and Mirowski and Nik-Khah, 'Markets Made Flesh'.

[350] During the somewhat silly episodes of the 'Science Wars', it was mainly in the name of the Left that the fight against science studies and especially ANT was waged. See Meera Nanda (2003), *Prophets Facing Backward: Postmodern Critiques of Science and Hindu*

exposed—they are nothing but barely disguised ideology—there resides in the purely scientific ones the only court of appeal capable of adjudicating all the disputes. Only the most reactionary people rejoice at a weakening of reason. If not, the underdogs are left with 'mere' power relations—and at that game the lambs will be eaten much faster than the wolves. Moreover, by delivering the keys of a politicized science to the hands of the powerful, ANT turns into nothing but a 'sociology of engineers', or worse, a group of consultants teaching those who have been freed from the disciplining power of reason to be even more Machiavellian, even more scheming, even more indifferent to the difference between science and ideology. In the name of the extension of networks, the naked emperor gets more of the latest 'wearables'.[351] ANT is nothing but an extended form of Machiavellianism.

I have always been puzzled by those critiques. It seems to me, on the contrary, that those who call themselves men and women of progress should not tie themselves to the social theory least able to accommodate their various programs of emancipation. If there is no way to inspect and decompose the contents of social forces, if they remain unexplained or overpowering, then there is not much that can be done. To insist that behind all the various issues there exists the overarching presence of the same system, the same empire, the same totality, has always struck me as an extreme case of masochism, a perverted way to look for a sure defeat while enjoying the bittersweet feeling of superior political correctness. Nietzsche had traced the immortal portrait of the 'man of resentment', by which he meant a Christian, but a critical sociologist would fit just as well.

Is it not obvious then that only a skein of weak ties, of constructed, artificial, assignable, accountable, and surprising connections is the only way to begin contemplating any kind of fight? With respect to the Total, there is nothing to do except to genuflect before it, or worse, to dream of occupying the place of complete power. I think it would be much safer to claim that action is possible only in a territory that has been opened up, flattened down, and cut down to size in a place where formats, structures, globalization, and totalities circulate inside tiny conduits, and where for each of their applications they need to rely on masses of hidden potentialities. If this is not possible, then there is no politics. No battle has ever been won without resorting to new combinations and surprising events. One's own actions 'make a difference'

Nationalism in India, who accuses science studies of providing Hindu fundamentalists with help in restricting reason.

[351] The proximity of the notion of networks with the 'fluid artist' capitalism described in Boltanski and Chiapelllo, *The New Spirit of Capitalism* makes the connection tempting enough.

only in a world made of differences. But is this not the topography of the social that emerges once we practice the three moves I proposed in Part II? When pointing out the 'plasma', don't we discover a reserve army whose size is, as Garfinkel said, 'astronomically bigger' than what it has to fight? At least the odds of winning are much better—and the occasions to nurture masochism much rarer. Critical proximity, not critical distance, is what we should aim for.

If it has been difficult to pinpoint exactly where ANT's political project resides—and thus where it errs and should be redressed—it's because the definition of what it is for a social science to have political relevance has also to be modified.[352] Politics is too serious a thing to be left in the hands of the few who seem allowed by birthright to decide what it should consist of.

A discipline among others

When I claim that critical sociology has confused science with politics, the last thing I want is to revert to the classical separation of politics and epistemology. The claim would anyway look very odd coming from a sociologist of science! I cannot pretend that it should not be the business of a respectable science to have a political project—even if the two heroes I have chosen, Tarde and Garfinkel, are not known for their political fervor. However, the opposition between a detached, disinterested, objective science and an engaged, militant, passionate action becomes meaningless as soon as one considers the formidable *collecting* power of any scientific discipline—and it makes no difference if it's 'natural' or 'social'. If anything, the social ones have simply to catch up with the assembling power of the natural ones. Political epistemology is not a way to avoid the 'pollution' of good science by 'dirty political considerations', nor is it the way to prevent positivists from 'hiding themselves behind the pretence of objectivity'. Since no one knows what ties them all together—the five uncertainties reviewed in Part I—we surely need a concerted, artificial, earnest, and inventive effort that uses a specific set of disciplines. But those disciplines have to be understood in the same way as chemistry,

---

[352] See Michel Callon (1999), 'Ni intellectuel engagé, ni intellectuel dégagé: la double stratégie de l'attachement et du détachement'. For an extreme case of non-participation, see Michel Callon and Vololona Rabeharisoa (2004), 'Gino's lesson on humanity: genetics, mutual entanglements and the sociologist's role'. Much of the argument against the traditional French figure of the 'intellectuel engagé' can be found in a moving interview with Michel Foucault (1994), *Dits et écrits: Tome 2*, p. 306.

physics, mechanics, etc., that is, as so many attempts at collecting in some systematic way new candidates to form the world.

The parallel with the natural sciences is inescapable at this point because both types of science have to escape from the idea that the collection is already completed. In another work, I showed that nature shares this characteristic with society.[353] Under the same 'external reality', the notion of nature conflates two different functions at once: on the one hand, the *multiplicity* of beings making up the world; on the other, the *unity* of those assembled in one single undisputable whole. Appealing to realism is never enough, since it means throwing together in one package multiple matters of concern as well as unified matters of fact. So, when people doubt the existence of 'nature' and 'outside reality', you never know if they are contesting the premature unification of matters of concern under the hegemony of matters of fact, or whether they deny the multiplicity of entities revealed by the sciences. The first is indispensable, the second is plain silly.

To break the package open and allow public scrutiny, I proposed distinguishing the question that deals with multiplying the entities with which we are led to live—*how many are we?*—from another thoroughly different question, namely that of deciding whether the assembled aggregates form a livable world or not—*can we live together?* Both endeavors must be tackled by the various skills of scientists, politicians, artists, moralists, economists, legislators, etc. Those various trades are not distinct by the *domains* they deal with, but only by the different *skills* they apply to the *same* domain, much like different professions—electricians, carpenters, masons, architects, and plumbers—work successively or in parallel on one single building. Whereas the tradition distinguished the common good (a moralist concern) and the common world (naturally given), I proposed replacing 'the politics of nature' by the *progressive composition of one common world*. This was, in my view, the way to redefine science and politics and to carry out the task of political epistemology forced upon us by the various ecological crises.

We may now see what the two collectors, nature and society, have in common: they are both premature attempts to collect in two opposite assemblies the one common world.[354] This is what I have called the *Modern Constitution*, using the legal metaphor to describe the joint achievements of political epistemology. So the redefinition of politics as the progressive composition of the common world has to be applied

[353] I summarize here the solution proposed in Latour, *Politics of Nature*.
[354] The politics of wildlife offers a marvelous example of the necessity of a symmetric approach. See Charis Thompson (2002), 'When Elephants Stand for Competing Philosophies of Nature: Amboseli National Park, Kenya'.

to the former assemblages of society as well as to the former assemblages of nature. The difficulty is that there is a slight breach of symmetry at this point, and this is the reason why it would be so deleterious to confuse this new definition of politics with critical sociology.

While recalcitrant objects from the former natural realm remain in full view no matter what natural scientists say about them, recalcitrant *subjects* from the former society might be easily subdued because they rarely complain when 'explained away', or at the very least, their complaints are rarely recorded with as much care.[355] Too often social sciences tend to offer a more vivid imitation of the bleak and blank scientistic realm (populated with matters of fact and a strict chain of causalities) than most natural sciences! And yet in both cases what is to be collected, namely the former members of the old assemblages of nature and society which I have called mediators, circulating objects and beings, resembles neither matters of fact nor social actors.

To grasp this point, we have to remember that being a matter of fact is not a 'natural' mode of existence but, strangely enough, an *anthropomorphism*.[356] Things, chairs, cats, mats, and black holes never behave like matters of fact; humans sometimes do, for political reasons, to *resist* enquiries. So it's absurd to resist 'treating humans like objects'. At worst, it would simply put humans *on par* with other matters of concern in physics, biology, computer science, etc. Complexity will simply be added to complexity. Far from being 'lowered down', 'objectified humans' will instead be *elevated* to the level of ants, chimps, chips, and particles! To be 'treated like things', as we understand it now, is not to be 'reduced' to mere matters of fact, but allowed to live a life as multifarious as that of matters of concern. Reductionism is not a sin one should abstain from or a virtue one should firmly stick to: it is a practical impossibility since the elements to which one 'higher level' is being reduced will be as complex as the 'lower level'. If only humans in the hands of critical sociologists could be treated *as well as* whales in zoology, genes in biochemistry, baboons in primatology, soils in pedology, tumors in cancerology, or gas in thermodynamics! Their complex metaphysics would at least be respected, their recalcitrance recognized, their objections deployed, their multiplicity accepted. Please, treat humans as things, offer them at least the degree

---

[355] On the comparative recalcitrance of human and non-human entities, see Despret, *Naissance d'une théorie éthologique* and Stengers, *The Invention of Modern Science*.

[356] 'Inanimism' is just as much a figuration as 'animism'. For the notion of figuration see p. 53. For a masterful inquiry into the distribution of those various functions in the world, see Descola, *La nature des cultures*—especially the chapter proving the anthropomorphic character of naturalism.

of realism you are ready to grant humble matters of concern, materialize them and, yes, *reify* them as much as possible!

Positivism—in its natural or social form, in its reactionary or progressive form—is not wrong because it forgets 'human consciousness' and decides to stick with 'cold data'. It is wrong politically. It has reduced matters of concern into matters of fact *too fast, without due process*. It has confused the two tasks of realism: multiplicity and unification. It has blurred the distinction between deploying the associations and collecting them into one collective. This is what the advocates of a hermeneutic sociology have rightly felt but without knowing how to get out of the trap, so bizarre were their ideas about natural sciences and the material world. Together with the reductionists they love to hate, they have misunderstood what it means for a science—social or natural—to have a political project; hence, the false alternative between being, on the one hand, a 'disinterested' scientist and, on the other, being 'socially relevant'. This is why it is puzzling to see that the sociology of associations has often been accused of being 'just descriptive' and 'without a political project' when it is, on the contrary, the sociology of the social which has alternated feverishly between a disinterested science it could never deliver and a political relevance it could never reach.

Instead, two other sets of procedures should be brought into the foreground: a first set that makes the deployment of actors visible; and a second that makes the unification of the collective into a common world acceptable to those who will be unified. It's because of the first set that ANT looks more like a disinterested science combating the urge of sociology to legislate in the actor's stead. It's because of the second set that ANT should most resemble a political engagement as it criticizes the production of a science of society supposed to be invisible to the eyes of the 'informants' and claims by some avant-garde to know better. We wish to be more disinterested than was possible with the social engineering project of traditional sociology since we pursue controversies much further. But we also wish to be much more engaged than what was possible with the scientistic dream of a disinterested gaze. And yet, something like disinterestedness is offered by the deployment of the four sources of uncertainty reviewed earlier, while engagement comes from the possibility offered by the fifth uncertainty of helping assemble in part the collective, that is, to give it an arena, a forum, a space, a representation through the very modest medium of some risky account that is most of the time a fragile intervention consisting only of text.

So, to study is always to do politics in the sense that it collects or composes what the common world is made of. The delicate question is to decide what sort of collection and what sort of composition is needed. This is where ANT might render its contrast with the sociology of the social more vivid. We claim that the controversies about what types of stuff make up the social world should not be solved by social scientists, but should be resumed by future participants and that at every moment the 'package' making up existing social links should be opened for public scrutiny. This means the two tasks of *taking into account* and *putting into order* have to be kept separate. The test is now to detect which social sciences are good at maintaining this distinction.

All the disciplines from geography to anthropology, from accounting to political science, from linguistics to economics, enter the scene as so many of the ways through which the ingredients of the collective are first juxtaposed and then turned into some coherent whole. To 'study' never means offering a disinterested gaze and then being led to action according to the principles discovered by the results of the research. Rather, each discipline is at once *extending* the range of entities at work in the world and actively participating in *transforming* some of them into faithful and stable intermediaries. Thus economists, for instance, are not simply describing some economic infrastructure which has always been there since the beginning of time. They are revealing calculative abilities in actors who did not know before they had them and making sure that some of these new competences are sunk into common sense through the many practical tools of bank accounts, property rights, cash register slips, and other plug-ins. Sociologists of the social, as we have seen, have done much more than 'discover' what a society is. They have always actively engaged in multiplying the connections among actors who did not know before they were related by 'social forces' and they have also offered the actors many ways to be grouped together. Psychologists are simultaneously populating the psyche with hundreds of new entities—neurotransmitters, the unconscious, cognitive modules, perversions, habits—and stabilizing some of them as routine parts of our common sense. Geographers are able to represent the idiosyncratic varieties of rivers, mountains, and cities and create a common inhabitable space by using maps, concepts, laws, territories, and networks. The same instrumental activities are seen in the language of linguists, the history of historians, the cultural diversity of anthropologists, etc. Without economics there are no economies; without sociology there is no society; without psychology there is no psyche; without geography there is no space. What would we know of the past without historians? How would the structure of language be accessible to us without grammarians? Just as a spider casts a web, *economization* is what is crafted by economists, *socialization* by sociology, *psychologization* by psychology, *spatialization* by geography.

This does not mean those disciplines are fictions, inventing their subject matter out of thin air. It means that they are, as the name nicely indicates, *disciplines*: each has chosen to deploy some sort of mediator and favored some type of stabilization, thus populating the world with different types of well-drilled and fully formatted inhabitants. Whatever a scholar does when she writes an account, she is already part of this activity. This is not a *defect* of the social sciences, as if they would be better off by freeing themselves out of this loop. It simply means that they are like all the other sciences, involved in the normal business of multiplying agencies and stabilizing or disciplining some of them. In this sense, the more disinterested the science, the more engaged and politically relevant it already is. The ceaseless activities of the social sciences in making the social exist, in churning the collective into a coherent whole, make up a large part of what it is to 'study' the social. Every account added to this mass also consists of a decision about what the social should be, that is, on what the multiple metaphysics and singular ontology of the common world should be. Rare are the group formations today that are not equipped and instrumented by economists, geographers, anthropologists, historians, and sociologists, who are hoping to learn how the groups are made, what are their boundaries and functions, and how best to maintain them. It would make no sense for a social science to wish to escape from this ceaseless work. But it makes a lot of sense to try to do this work *well*.

A different definition of politics

So in the end, what is ANT's political project? Since this tiny school is nothing more than a complicated way to go back to the surprise at seeing the social unravel—an experience which has been somewhat dulled by the recent history of the social sciences—the only way to register again what we mean by politics is to get even closer to the original experience.

During the 19th century it was easy to see how this feeling was constantly refreshed by the surprising emergence of masses, crowds, industries, cities, empires, hygiene, the media, and inventions of all sorts. Strangely enough, this insight should have been even stronger in the next century with its catastrophes and innovations, increasing numbers of threatened humans, and ecological crises. That this was not the case was due to the very definitions of society and of social ties that tried to mop up a few elements while excluding vast numbers of candidates. Where naturalism reigned, it was very difficult to scrutinize the composition of the social for any length of time with any seriousness.[357] What ANT has tried to do is make itself sensitive again to the sheer difficulty of assembling collectives made of so many new members once nature and society have been simultaneously put aside.

The feeling of crisis I perceive to be at the center of the social sciences could now be registered in the following way: once you extend the range of entities, the new associations do not form a livable assemblage. This is where politics again enters the scene if we care to define it as the intuition that associations are not enough, that they should also be *composed* in order to *design one* common world. For better or for worse, sociology, contrary to its sister anthropology, can never be content with a plurality of metaphysics; it also needs to tackle the ontological question of the unity of this common world. This time, however, it has to be done not inside the panoramas I have presented, but outside and for good. So it's perfectly true to say that no sociology can be content with 'just describing' associations, and nor can it simply enjoy the spectacle of the sheer multiplicity of new connections. Another task also has to be fulfilled to deserve the label of 'a science of living together', to use again Laurent Thévenot's paradoxical expression.[358] If sociology is a science, what does it have to do with 'living together'? If the question is one of cohabitation, why would we need a science? Answer: because of the number of new candidates in existence and because of the narrow limits of the collectors imagined to render the cohabitation possible.

The LSE student that was so puzzled by ANT in the Interlude was right to strive for political relevance; so are all the young fellows who enter into departments of political science, science studies, women studies, and cultural studies to gain a critical edge, to 'make a difference', and to render the world more livable. Their formulations may be naive, but it's hard to see how one could call oneself a sociologist and look down on them as if theirs was just some adolescent dream. Once this urge for political involvement is no longer confused with the two other duties, once the recruitment process of new candidates for collective life is not interrupted, the burning desire to have the new entities detected, welcomed, and given shelter is not only legitimate, it's probably the only scientific and political cause worth living for.

The words 'social' and 'nature' used to hide two entirely different projects that cut across both of those ill-assembled assemblies: one to trace connections among unexpected entities and another to make those connections hold in a somewhat livable whole. The mistake is not in trying to do two things at once—every science is also a political

---

[357] I have tried to capture this difficulty in Latour, *We Have Never Been Modern*. Modernism has never been able to catch up with its own time.
[358] Thévenot, 'Une science de la vie ensemble dans le monde'.

project—the mistake is to interrupt the former because of the urgency of the latter. ANT is simply a way of saying that the task of assembling a common world cannot be contemplated if the other task is not pursued well beyond the narrow limits fixed by the premature *closure* of the social sphere.

It is hard to believe that we still have to absorb the same types of actors, the same number of entities, the same profiles of beings, and the same modes of existence into the same types of collectives as Comte, Durkheim, Weber, or Parsons, especially after science and technology have massively multiplied the participants to be cooked in the melting pot. Yes, sociology is the science of immigrant masses, but what do you do when you have to deal with electrons and electors, GMOs and NGOs all at once? For the new wine of new associations, a dusty old flask just won't do. This is the reason why I defined the collective as an expansion of nature and society and sociology of associations as the resumption of the sociology of the social.

This is what I take to be the political project of ANT, what I mean by a search for political relevance. Once the task of exploring the multiplicity of agencies is completed, another question can be raised: What are the *assemblies* of those *assemblages*?

We should be careful here in not confusing this formulation with another one that has a strong resemblance to it, but which would lead us back to an entirely different project. To raise a political question often means to reveal behind a given state of affairs the presence of forces hitherto hidden. But then you risk falling into the same trap of providing social explanations I criticized earlier and end up doing exactly the opposite of what I mean here by politics. You use the same old repertoire of already gathered social ties to 'explain' the new associations. Although you seem to speak *about* politics, you don't speak *politically*. What you are doing is simply extending one step further the same small repertoire of already standardized forces. You might feel the pleasure of providing a 'powerful explanation', but that's just the problem: you partake in the expansion of power, but not in the re-composition of its content. Even though it resembles political talks, it has not even begun to address the political endeavor, since it has not tried to assemble the candidates into a new assembly adjusted to their specific requirements. 'Drunk with power' is not an expression fit only for generals, presidents, CEOs, mad scientists, and bosses. It can also be used for those sociologists who confuse the expansion of powerful explanations with the composition of the collective. This is why the ANT slogan has always been: 'Be sober with power', that is, abstain as much as possible from using the notion of power in case it backfires and hits your explanations instead of the target you are aiming for. There should be no powerful explanation without checks and balances.[359]

So in the end there is a conflict—no need to hide it—between doing critical sociology and being politically relevant, between society and the collective. Retracing the iron ties of necessity is not sufficient to explore what is possible. Provided we accept a detoxification of the powerful explanations of critical sociology, being politically motivated now starts to take a different and more specific meaning: we look for ways to register the novelty of associations and explore how to assemble them in a satisfactory form.

In the end, strangely enough, it's only the freshness of the results of social science that can guarantee its political relevance. No one has made the point as forcefully as John Dewey did with his own definition of the public. For a social science to become relevant, it has to have the capacity to renew itself—a quality impossible if a society is supposed to be 'behind' political action. It should also possess the ability to loop back from the few to the many and from the many to the few—a process often simplified under the terms of representation of the body politic.[360] So the test for political interest is now slightly easier to pass: one must practice sociology in such a way that the ingredients making up the collective are regularly refreshed. Clear the path for the composition so that it can go through the complete loop and take it up again, making sure that the number, modes of existence, and recalcitrance of those that are thus assembled are not thwarted too early. Every reader can now judge what sort of social theory is best able to fulfill these goals.

Our distinctive touch is simply to highlight the stabilizing mechanisms so that the premature transformation of matters of concern into matters of fact is counteracted. ANT argues that it should be possible to clarify this confusion, to distinguish the two tasks of deployment and unification, to spell out the procedures for due process, thus modifying what it means for a social science to be more politically relevant *and* more scientific.[361] In this sense we share the same keen interest in science and in politics as our predecessors, although ANT diverges from it because of the way the deployment is accepted and the way the collection is achieved. So far, the sociology of the social has not been especially interested in proposing explicit procedures *to distinguish* the two tasks of deployment and collection. We simply claim to be a bit better at those two opposed and complementary moves precisely because the conception of what science and society is has

---

[359] For a more complete elaboration of these points and especially the crucial notion of assembly, see Latour and Weibel, *Making Things Public*.
[360] Dewey, *The Public and Its Problems*.
[361] Callon, Lascoumes and Barthe, *Agir dans un monde incertain*.

been modified due to the emergence of a hard-headed sociology of science.

There exists a link, in my view at least, between the end of modernization and the definition of ANT. If we were still modern, we could simply ignore this soul-searching and hair-splitting. We could continue the earlier tasks of modernization and strive for a disinterested science and/or a scientifically-based politics. The reason is that the sociology of the social has always been very strongly linked to the superiority of the West—including, of course, its shame at being so overpowering and so hegemonic. So, if you really think that the future common world can be better composed by using nature and society as the ultimate meta-language, then ANT is useless. It might become interesting only if what was called in the recent past 'the West' decides to rethink how it should present itself to the rest of the world that is soon to become more powerful. After having registered the sudden new weakness of the former West and trying to imagine how it could survive a bit longer in the future to maintain its place in the sun, we have to establish connections with the others that cannot possibly be held in the nature/society collectors. Or, to use another ambiguous term, we just might have to engage in cosmopolitics.[362]

I am well aware that I have not said enough to substantiate any of these numerous points. This book is just an introduction to help the interested reader in drawing the social theory consequences of the sociology of science. It's not for me to say if anyone will end up using these tricks in any trade. At least now nobody can complain that the project of actor-network-theory has not been systematically presented. I have voluntarily made it such an easy target that a sharpshooter is not needed in order to hit it.

I have completed what I promised at the beginning, namely to be one-sided enough so as to draw all the consequences from a fairly implausible starting point. And yet, I can't totally shake the impression that the extreme positions I have taken might have some connections with common sense. In a time of so many crises in what it means to belong, the task of cohabitation should no longer be simplified too much. So many other entities are now knocking on the door of our collectives. Is it absurd to want to retool our disciplines to become sensitive again to the noise they make and to try to find a place for them?

---

[362] In the sense developed in Isabelle Stengers (1996), *Cosmopolitiques - Tome 1: la guerre des sciences* and not in the Stoic or Kantian one, which implies an already unified cosmos. For a review of the latter tradition see Daniele Archibugi (2003), *Debating Cosmopolitics*.

BIBLIOGRAPHY

Abbott, E. (1992). *Flatland: a romance of many dimensions (illustrated by the author; with an introduction by Banesh Hoffmann)*. New York: Dover.

Akrich, M. (1992). 'The De-Scription of Technical Objects', in *Shaping Technology-Building Society: Studies in Sociotechnical Change*. (eds. Bijker, W. and Law, J.) Cambridge, Mass.: MIT Press, 205–224.

Akrich, M. (1993). 'A Gazogene in Costa Rica: An Experiment in Techno-Sociology', in *Technological Choices: Transformation in Material Cultures since the Neolithic*. (ed. Lemonnier, P.) London: Routledge.

Akrich, M. and Bouiller, D. (1991). 'Le mode d'emploi: genèse et usage', in *Savoir faire et pouvoir transmettre* (ed. Chevallier, D.) Paris: Editions de l'EHESS, 112–131.

Akrich, M. and Latour, B. (1992). 'A Summary of a Convenient Vocabulary for the Semiotics of Human and Non-Human assemblies', in *Shaping Technology-Building Society: Studies in Sociotechnical Change*. (eds. Bijker, W. and Law, J.) Cambridge, Mass.: MIT Press, 259–264.

Alder, K. (1995). 'A Revolution to Measure: The Political economy of the Metric System in France', in *The Values of Precision*. (ed. Wise, N.) Princeton: Princeton University Press, 39–71.

Alpers, S. (1988). *Rembrandt's Enterprise: The Studio and the Market*. Chicago: University of Chicago Press.

Anderson, W. (1990). *Diderot's Dream*. Baltimore: John Hopkins University Press.

Aquino, P. d. (1998). 'La mort défaite: Rites funéraires du candomblé', *L'homme*, 147: 81–104.

Archibugi, D. (ed.) (2003). *Debating Cosmopolitics (New Left Review Debates)*. Verso Books.

Audren, F. (forthcoming). 'Les juristes et les sociologues', Ph.D. thesis, Paris: Paris Sorbonne.

Auroux, S. (1999). *La raison, le langage et les normes*. Paris: PUF.

Barnes, B. (1983). 'Social Life as Bootstrapped Induction', *Sociology*, 17/4: 524–545.

Barry, A. (2001). *Political Machines: Governing a Technological Society*. London: Athlone Press.

Bastide, F. (1990). 'The Iconography of Scientific Texts: Principle of Analysis', in *Representation in Scientific Practice*. (eds. Lynch, M. and Woolgar, S.) Cambridge, Mass.: MIT Press, 187–230.

Bastide, F. (2001). *Una notte con Saturno: Scritti semiotici sul discorso scientifico.* (trans. Roberto Pellerey). Rome: Meltemi.

Bastide, F., Callon, M. and Courtial, J. P. (1989). 'The Use Of Review Articles In The Analysis Of A Research Area', *Scientometrics,* 15/5–6: 535–562.

Bastide, F. and Myers, G. (1992). 'A Night With Saturne', *Science, Technology and Human Values,* 17/3: 259–281.

Bauman, Z. (1992). *Intimations of Postmodernity.* London: Routledge.

Bauman, Z. (1997). *Postmodernity and its Discontents.* London: Polity Press.

Bauman, Z. (2000). *Liquid Modernity.* Cambridge: Polity Press.

Baxandall, M. (1985). *Patterns of Intention: On The Historical Explanation Of Pictures.* New-Haven: Yale University Press.

Beck, U. (1992). *Risk Society: Towards a New Modernity.* London: Sage.

Beck, U. and Beck-Gernsheim, E. (1995). *The Normal Chaos of Love.* London: Polity Press.

Beck, U., Giddens, A. and Lash, S. (1994). *Reflexive Modernization: Politics, Tradition and Aesthetics in the Modern Social Order.* Stanford: Stanford University Press.

Becker, H. (1982). *Art Worlds.* Berkeley: University of California Press.

Becker, H. (1991). *Outsiders: studies in the sociology of deviance.* New York: Free Press.

Benjamin, W. (2002). *The Arcades Project.* Cambridge, Mass.: Harvard University Press.

Bensaude-Vincent, B. (1986). 'Mendeleev's periodic system of chemical elements', *British Journal for the History and Philosophy of Science,* 19: 3–17.

Bentham, J. and Foucault, M. (1977). *Le Panopticon précédé de l'oeil du pouvoir: entretien avec Michel Foucault.* Paris: Pierre Belfond.

Berg, M. and Mol, A.-M. (1998). *Differences in Medicine: Unraveling Practices, Techniques and Bodies.* Durham: Duke University Press.

Biagioli, M. (ed.) (1999). *The Science Studies Reader.* London: Routledge.

Bijker, W. (1995). *Of Bicyles, Bakelites, and Bulbs: Towards a Theory of Sociotechnical Change.* Cambridge, Mass.: MIT Press.

Bijker, W. and Law, J. (eds.) (1992). *Shaping Technology-Building Society: Studies in Sociotechnical Change.* Cambridge, Mass.: MIT Press.

Bijker, W. E., Hughes, T. P. and Pinch, T. (eds.) (1987). *The Social Construction of Technological Systems: New Directions in the Sociology and History of Technology.* Cambridge, Mass.: MIT Press.

Blix, H. (2004). *Disarming Iraq.* New York: Pantheon Books.

Bloor, D. (1976/1991). *Knowledge and Social Imagery (second edition with a new foreword).* Chicago: University of Chicago Press.

Bloor, D. (1999). 'Anti-Latour'. *Studies in History and Philosophy of Science,* 30/1: 81–112.

Boltanski, L. (1987). *The Making of a Class: Cadres in French Society* (trans. Arthur Goldhammer). Cambridge: Cambridge University Press.

Boltanski, L. (1990). *L'amour et la justice comme compétences.* Paris: A.-M. Métailié.

Boltanski, L. (1999). *Distant Suffering: Morality, Media and Politics* (trans. Graham D. Burchell). Cambridge: Cambridge University Press.

Boltanski, L. and Chiapelllo, E. (1999/2005). *The New Spirit of Capitalism* (trans. Gregory Elliott). W W Norton & Co Inc.

Boltanski, L. and Thévenot, L. (1999). 'The Sociology of Critical Capacity', *European Journal of Social Theory*, 2/3: 359–377.

Boltanski, L. and Thévenot, L. (forthcoming). *On Justification* (trans. Catherine Porter). Princeton: Princeton University Press (translation of Boltanski, L. and Thévenot, L. (1991). *De la justification. Les économies de la grandeur*. Paris: Gallimard).

Boudon, R. (1981) *The logic of social action: an introduction to sociological analysis* (trans. David Silverman). London: Routledge.

Bourdieu, P. (1972). *Outline of a Theory of Practice*. Cambridge: Cambridge U.P.

Bourdieu, P. (1975). 'Le Couturier et sa griffe: contribution à une théorie de la mode', *Actes de la Recherche en Sciences Sociales*, n°1: 7–36.

Bourdieu, P. (1991). 'Delegation and Political Fetishism', in *Language and symbolic power* (edited and introduced by John B. Thompson; trans. Gino Raymond and Matthew Adamson). Cambridge: Polity Press.

Bourdieu, P. (2001). *Science de la science et réflexivité*. Paris: Raisons d'agir.

Bourdieu, P., Chamboredon, J.-C. and Passeron, J.-C. (1968). *Le métier de sociologue. Préalables épistémologiques*. Paris: Mouton.

Bourdieu, P., Chamboredon, J.-C. and Passeron, J.-C. (1991). *Craft of Sociology: Epistemological Preliminaries*. Walter de Gruyter Inc.

Boureau, A. (1992). 'L'adage *Vox Populi, Vox Dei* et l'invention de la nation anglaise (VIIIe-XIIe siècle)', *Annales ESC*, 4–5: 1071–1089.

Bowker, G. (1994). *Science on the Run: Information Management and Industrial Geographics at Schlumberger, 1920–1940*. Cambridge, Mass.: The MIT Press.

Bowker, G. C. and Star, S. L. (1999). *Sorting Things Out: Classification and Its Consequences*. Cambridge, Mass.: MIT Press.

Boyer, R. (2004) 'The Rediscovery of Networks - Past and Present - An Economist's Perspective', in *50th Annual Meeting of the Business History Conference*, Le Creusot.

Bremmer, J. and Roodenburg, H. (1992). *A Cultural History of Gesture: From Antiquity to the Present Day*. Cambridge: Polity Press.

Brun-Cottan, F. et al. (1991). *The workplace project: Designing for diversity and change (Videotape)*. Palo Alto, CA.: Xerox Palo Alto Research Center.

Bucchi, M. (2004). *Science in Society: An Introduction to the Social Studies of Science*. London: Routledge.

Butler, S. (1872) *Erewhon*. Harmondsworth, Middlesex: Penguin Book.

Byrne, R. and Whiten, A. (eds.) (1988). *Machiavellian Intelligence: Social Expertise and the Evolution of Intellects in Monkeys, Apes and Humans*. Oxford: Clarendon Press.

Calbris, G. (1990). *The Semiotics of French Gesture*. Bloomington: Indiana University Press.

Callon, M. (1981). 'Struggles and Negotiations to Decide What is Problematic and What is Not. The Socio-logic Translation', in *Knorr K. R. Krohn & R. Whitley*, 197–220.

Callon, M. (1986). 'Some elements of a sociology of translation domestication of the scallops and the fishermen of St Brieux Bay', in *Power, Action and Belief. A New Sociology of Knowledge?* (ed. Law, J.), 196–229.

Callon, M. (ed.) (1989). *La science et ses réseaux: Genèse et circulation des faits scientifiques*. Paris: La Découverte.

Callon, M. (1998a). 'An Essay on Framing and Overflowing: Economic Externalities Revisited by Sociology', in *The Laws of the Market*. (ed. Callon, M.) Oxford: Blackwell, 245–269.

Callon, M. (ed.) (1998b). *The Laws of the Markets*. Oxford: Blackwell.

Callon, M. (1999). 'Ni intellectuel engagé, ni intellectuel dégagé: la double stratégie de l'attachement et du détachement', *Sociologie du travail,* 1: 1–13.

Callon, M. (2001). 'Les méthodes d'analyse des grands nombres', in *Sociologie du travail: quarante ans après*. (ed. Pouchet, A.) Paris: Elsevier, 335–354.

Callon, M., Lascoumes, P. and Barthe, Y. (2001). *Agir dans un monde incertain: Essai sur la démocratie technique*. Paris: Le Seuil.

Callon, M. and Latour, B. (1981). 'Unscrewing the Big Leviathans: How Do Actors Macrostructure Reality', in *Advances in Social Theory and Methodology: Toward an Integration of Micro and Macro Sociologies*. (eds. Knorr, K. and Cicourel, A.) London: Routledge, 277–303.

Callon, M. and Latour, B. (1992). 'Don't throw the Baby out with the Bath School! A reply to Collins and Yearley', in *Science as Practice and Culture*. (ed. Pickering, A.) Chicago: University of Chicago Press, 343–368.

Callon, M., Law, J. and Rip, A. (eds.) (1986). *Mapping the Dynamics of Science and Technology*. London: Macmillan.

Callon, M. and Rabeharisoa, V. (1999). *Le pouvoir des malades*. Paris: Presses de l'Ecole nationale des mines de Paris.

Callon, M. and Rabeharisoa, V. (2004). 'Gino's lesson on humanity: genetics, mutual entanglements and the sociologist's role', *Economy and Society,* 33/1: 1–27.

Cambrosio, A., Keating, P. and Mogoutov, A. (2004). 'Mapping Collaborative Work and Innovation in Biomedicine: a Computer Assisted Analysis of Antibody Reagent Workshops', *Social Studies of Science,* 34/3: 325–364.

Cambrosio, A., Limoges, C. and Pronovost, D. (1990). 'Representing biotechnology: an ethnography of Quebec Science Policy', *Social Studies of Science,* 20: 195–227.

Candolle, A. de (1873/1987). *Histoire des sciences et des savants depuis deux siècles d'après l'opinion des principales académies ou sociétés scientifiques*. Paris: Fayard, Corpus des Oeuvres de Philosophie.

Canguilhem, G. (1968/1988). *Ideology and Rationality in the History of the Life Sciences*. Cambridge, Mass.: The MIT Press.

Cassin, B. (1995). *L'effet sophistique*. Paris: Gallimard.

Castells, M. (2000). *The Rise of the Network Society*. Oxford: Blackwell.

Castoriadis, C. (1998). *The Imaginary Institution of Society* (trans. Kathleen Blamey). Cambridge, Mass.: MIT Press.

Chalvon-Demersay, S. (1999). *A Thousand Screenplays: The French Imagination in a Time of Crisis* (trans. Teresa Lavender Fagan). Chicago: University of Chicago Press.

Chandler, A. D. (1977). *The Visible Hand: The Managerial Revolution in American Business*. Cambridge, Mass.: Harvard University Press.

Charvolin, F. (2003). *L'invention de l'environnement en France. Chroniques anthropologiques d'une institutionnalisation*. Paris: La Découverte.

Claverie, E. (2003). *Les Guerres de la Vierge: Une anthropologie des apparitions*. Paris: Gallimard.

Cochoy, F. (2002). *Une sociologie du packaging ou l'âne de Buridan face au marché.* PUF: Paris.

Cochrane, R. C. (1976). *Measures for Progress: A History of the National Bureau of Standards.* New York: Arno Press.

Collins, H. (1985). *Changing Order: Replication and Induction In Scientific Practice.* London-Los-Angeles: Sage.

Collins, H. (1990). *Artificial Experts: Social Knowledge and Intelligent Machines.* Cambridge, Mass.: MIT Press.

Collins, H. (2004). *Gravity's Shadow: The Search for Gravitational Waves.* Chicago: University of Chicago Press.

Collins, H. and Kusch, M. (1998). *The Shape of Actions: What Human and Machines can do.* Cambridge, Mass.: MIT Press.

Collins, H. and Yearley, S. (1992). 'Epistemological Chicken' In *Science as Practice and Culture.* (ed, Pickering, A.) Chicago: University of Chicago Press, 301–326.

Collins, H. M. and Pinch, T. (1982). *Frames of Meaning: the Social Construction of Extraordinary Science.* London: Routledge and Kegan Paul.

Collins, R. (1998). *The sociology of philosophies: a global theory of intellectual change.* Cambridge, Mass.: Harvard University Press.

Comment, B. (2003). *The Panorama.* London: Reaktion Books.

Conein, B., Dodier, N. and Thévenot, L. (eds.) (1993). *Les objets dans l'action: De la maison au laboratoire.* Paris: Editions de l'EHESS.

Cooren, F. (2001). *The Organizing Property of Communication.* New York: John Benjamins Pub C°.

Cronon, W. (1991). *Nature's Metropolis: Chicago and the Great West.* New York: Norton.

Cussins, C. (1996). 'Ontological Choreography: Agency through Objectification in Infertility Clinics', *Social Studies of Science,* 26/26: 575–610.

Czarniawska, B. (1997). *A Narrative Approach To Organization Studies.* London: Sage.

Czarniawska, B. (2004). 'On Time, Space, and Action Nets', *Organization,* 16/6: 777–795.

Dagognet, F. (1974). *Ecriture et iconographie.* Paris: Vrin.

Daston, L. (1988). 'The Factual Sensibility: an Essay Review on Artifact and Experiment', *Isis,* 79: 452–470.

De Waal, F. (1982). *Chimpanzee Politics: Power and Sex Among Apes.* New York: Harper and Row.

Debaise, D. (2003). 'Un empirisme spéculatif: Construction, Processus et Relation chez Whitehead', Ph.D. thesis, Brussels: Université Libre de Bruxelles.

Deleuze, G. (1993). *The Fold: Leibnitz and the Baroque* (trans. Tom Conley). Athlone Press.

Denis De Rougemont (1983). *Love in the Western World* (trans. Montgomery Belgion). Princeton: Princeton University Press.

Denzin, N. K. (1990). 'Harold and Agnes: A Feminist Narrative Undoing', *Sociological Theory,* 8/2: 198–285.

Derrida, J. (1998). *Of Grammatology* (trans. Gayatri Chakravorty Spivak). Baltimore: John Hopkins University Press.

Derrida, J. (1995). *Archive Fever: A Freudian Impression* (trans. Eric Prenowitz). Chicago: University of Chicago Press.

Descola, P. (2005). *La nature des cultures*. Paris: Gallimard.

Descola, P. and Palsson, G. (eds.) (1996). *Nature and Society: Anthropological Perspectives*. London: Routledge.

Despret, V. (1996). *Naissance d'une théorie éthologique*. Paris: Les Empêcheurs de penser en rond.

Despret, V. (2002). *Quand le loup habitera avec l'agneau*. Paris: Les Empêcheurs.

Desrosières, A. (2002). *The Politics of Large Numbers: A History of Statistical Reasoning* (trans. Camille Naish). Cambridge, Mass.: Cambridge University Press.

Dewey, J. (1927/1954). *The Public and Its Problems*. Athens: Ohio University Press.

Dewey, J. (1930; repr. 1948; complete works 1982). *Reconstruction in Philosophy*. Carbondale: Southern Illinois University Press.

Diderot, D. (1964). 'D'Alembert's Dream' (trans. Ralph. H. Bowen), in *Rameau's Nephew and Other Works*. Indianapolis: Bobbs-Merrill.

Didier, E. (2001). 'De l'échantillon à la population: Sociologie de la généralisation par sondage aux Etats-Unis', Ph.D. thesis, Paris: Ecole des Mines.

Dodier, N. (2003). *Leçons politiques de l'épidémie de sida*. Paris: Presses de la Maison des Sciences de l'Homme.

Dratwa, J. (2003) 'Taking Risks with the Precautionary Principle', Ph.D. thesis, Paris: Ecole des Mines.

Duhem, P. (1904). *La Théorie Physique: Son objet sa structure*. Paris: Vrin.

Dumont, L. (1982). *Homo Hierarchicus: The Caste System and Its Implications* (trans. Mark Sainsbury and Basia Gulati). Chicago: University of Chicago Press.

Dupuy, J. P. (1992). *Introduction aux sciences sociales: Logique des phénomènes collectifs*. Paris: Editions Marketing.

Duranti, A. and Goodwin, C. (eds.) (1992). *Rethinking Context: Language as an Interactive Phenomenon (Studies in the Social & Cultural Foundations of Language)*. Cambridge: Cambridge University Press.

Durkheim, E. (1915/1947). *The Elementary Forms of the Religious Life* (trans. Joseph Ward Swain). New York: Free Press.

Durkheim, E. (1955). *Pragmatisme et sociologie; cours inédit prononcé à la Sorbonne en 1913–1914 et restitué par Armand Cuvillier d'après des notes d'étudiants*. Paris: Vrin.

Durkheim, E. (1966). *The Rules of Sociological Method* (trans. Sarah A. Solovay and John H. Mueller, edited by George E.G. Catlin). New York: Free Press.

Durkheim, E. (1983). *Pragmatism and sociology* (trans. J. C. Whitehouse; edited and introduced by John B. Allcock; with preface by Armand Cuvillier). Cambridge: Cambridge University Press.

Einstein, A. (1920). *Relativity, the Special and the General Theory*. London: Methuen And C°.

Eisenstein, E. (1979). *The Printing Press as an Agent of Change*. Cambridge: Cambridge University Press.

Epstein, S. (1996). *Impure Science: Aids, Activism and the Politics of Knowledge*. Berkeley: University of California Press.

Ewick, P. and Silbey, S. S. (1998). *The Common Place of Law*. Chicago: University of Chicago Press.

Farley, J. and Geison, G. L. (1974). 'Science, Politics and Spontaneous generation in 19th-century France: the Pasteur-Pouchet Debate', *Bulletin of the History of Medicine*, 48/2: 161–198.

Faye, J.-P. (1972) *Langages totalitaires*, Paris: Hermann.

Feuer, L. S. (1974). *Einstein and the Generations of Science*. New York: Basic Books.

Fleck, L. (1935/1981). *Genesis and Development of a Scientific Fact*. Chicago: University of Chicago Press.

Fleck, L., Cohen, R. S. and Schnelle, T. (1986). *Cognition and Fact Materials on Ludwik Fleck edited by Robert S. Cohen and Thomas Schnelle*. Dordrecht: Reidel.

Fontanille, J. (1998). *Sémiotique du discours*. Limoges: Presses de l'université de Limoges.

Foucault, M. (1973). *The Birth of the Clinic: An Archeology of Medical Perception*. New York: Random House.

Foucault, M. (1975). *Discipline and Punish: The Birth of Prison*. New York: Panthéon.

Foucault, M. (1990). *The History of Sexuality: An Introduction*. New York: Vintage Books.

Foucault. M. (1994) *Dits et écrits (1954–1970) Tome I*. Paris: Gallimard.

Foucault, M. (2003). *"Society Must Be Defended" : Lectures at the College de France, 1975–1976* (trans. David Mace). New York: Picador.

Fox-Keller, E. (2000). *The Century of the Gene*. Cambridge, Mass.: MIT Press.

Friedberg, E. (1993). *Le pouvoir et la règle: Dynamiques de l'action organisée*. Paris: Le Seuil.

Galison, P. (1997). *Image and Logic: A Material Culture of Microphysics*. Chicago: University of Chicago Press.

Galison, P. (2003). *Einstein's Clocks, Poincarés's Maps*. New York: Norton and Company.

Gane, N. (ed.) (2004). *The Future of Social Theory*. London: Continuum.

Garfinkel, H. (1967). *Studies in Ethnomethodology*. New Jersey: Prentice Hall.

Garfinkel, H. (2002). *Ethnomethodology's Program: Working Out Durkheim's Aphorism* (edited and introduced by Anne Warfield Rawls). Oxford: Rowman & Littlefield.

Garfinkel, H., Lynch, M. and Livingston, E. (1981). 'The Work of a Discovering Science Construed with Materials from the Optically Discovered Pulsar', *Philosophie of Social Sciences*, 11: 131–158.

Geison, G. G. (1995). *The Private Science of Louis Pasteur*. Princeton: Princeton University Press.

Gibson, J. G. (1986). *The Ecological Approach to Visual Perception*. London: Lawrence Erlbaum Associates.

Giddens, A. (1984). *The Constitution of Society*. Cambridge: Blackwell.

Ginzburg, C. (1980). *The Cheese and the Worms: The Cosmos of a 16th-Century Miller*. London: Routledge.

Ginzburg, C. (1999). *History, Rhetoric, and Proof: The Menachem Stern Lectures in History*. Hanover, NH : University Press of New England.

Goffman, E. (1959). *The Presentation of Self in Everyday Life*. New York: Double-day and Anchor Books.

Gomart, E. (1999). 'Surprised by Methadone', Ph.D. thesis, Paris: Ecole des Mines.

Gomart, E. (2002). 'Methadone: Six Effects in Search of a Substance', *Social Studies of Science*, 32/1: 93–135.

Gomart, E. and Hennion, A. (1998). 'A sociology of attachment: music amateurs, drug users', in *Actor Network Theory and after*. (eds. Hassard, J. and Law, J.) Oxford: Blackwell, 220–247.

Goodman, N. (1988). *Ways of Worldmaking*. New York: Hackett Publishing Company.

Goodwin, C. and Goodwin, M. (1996). 'Formulating planes: Seeing as a situated activity', in *Cognition and Communication at Work*. (eds. Engestrom, Y. and Middleton, D.) Cambridge: Cambridge University Press.

Goody, J. (1977). *The Domestication of the Savage Mind*. Cambridge: Cambridge University Press.

Gordon, D. (1999). *Ants At Work: How An Insect Society Is Organized*. New York: Free Press.

Gramaglia, C. (2005). 'La mise en cause environnementale comme principe d'association. Casuistique des affaires de pollution des eaux: l'exemple des actions en justice intentées par l'Association Nationale de Protection des Eaux et Rivières', Ph.D. thesis, Paris: Ecole des Mines.

Granovetter, M. (1985). 'Economic Action and Social Structure: The problem of Embeddedness', *AJS*, 91/3: 481–510.

Greimas, A. J. (1988). *Maupassant: The Semiotics of Text. Practical Exercises*. New York: John Benjamins Publishing Co.

Greimas, A. J. and Courtès, J. (eds.) (1982). *Semiotics and Language an Analytical Dictionary*. Bloomington: Indiana U.P.

Gross, P. R., Levitt, N. and Lewis, M. W. (eds.) (1997). *The Flight from Science and Reason*. New York: New York Academy of Science.

Hacking, I. (1992). 'The Self-Vindication of the Laboratory Sciences', in *Science as Practice and Culture*. (ed. Pickering, A.) Chicago: University of Chicago Press, 29–64.

Hacking, I. (1999). *The Social Construction of What?* Cambridge, Mass.: Harvard University Press.

Handley, S. (2000). *Nylon: The Story of a Fashion Revolution. A Celebration of Design from Art Silk to Nylon and Thinking Fibres*. Baltimore: John Hopkins University Press.

Haraway, D. (2000). *How like a Leaf: an Interview with Thyrza Goodeve*. London: Routledge.

Haraway, D. J. (1991). *Simians, Cyborgs, and Women: The Reinvention of Nature*. New York: Chapman and Hall.

Harman, G. (2002). *Tool-Being: Heidegger and the Metaphysics of Objects*. Open Court.

Harrison, S., Pile, S. and Thrift, N. (eds.) (2004). *Patterned Ground: Entanglements of Nature and Culture*. London: Reaktion Books.

Haskell, F. (1982). *Patrons and Painters: A Study in the Relations Between Italian Art and Society in the Age of the Baroque*. New Haven: Yale University Press.

Headrick, D. R. (1988). *The Tentacles of Progress: Technology Transfer in the Age of Imperialism, 1850–1940*. Oxford: Oxford University Press.

Heesen, A. t. (2004). 'Things that talk: News, Paper, Scissors. Clippings in the Sciences and Arts around 1920', in *Things that talk*. (ed. Daston, L.) New York: Zone Books, 297–327.

Heidegger, M. (1977). *The Question Concerning Technology and Other Essays*. New York: Harper Torch Books.

Hennion, A. (1993). *La passion musicale: Une sociologie de la médiation*. Paris: A.-M. Métailié.

Hennion, A. (2004). 'Pragmatics of Taste', in *The Blackwell Companion to the Sociology of Culture*. (eds. Jacobs, M. and M., H.) Oxford: Blackwell.

Hennion, A. and Teil, G. (2003). 'Le goût du vin: Pour une sociologie de l'attention'. *Terrain,*

Heurtin, J.-P. (1999). *L'espace public parlementaire: Essais sur les raisons du législateur*. Paris: PUF.

Hirschauer, S. (1991). 'The Manufacture of Bodies in Surgery', *Social Studies of Science*, 21/2: 279–320.

Hirschauer, S. (1998) 'Performing Sexes and Genders in Medical Practice', in *Differences in Medicine: Unraveling Practices, Techniques and Bodies*. (eds. Berg, M. and Mol, A.-M.) Durham: Duke University Press, pp. 13–27.

Hirschman, A. O. (1977). *The Passions and the Interests*. Princeton: Princeton University Press.

Houdart, S. (2000). 'Et le scientifique tint le monde: Ethnologie d'un laboratoire japonais de génétique du comportement', Ph.D. thesis, Nanterre: Université de Paris X, sous la direction de Laurence Caillet.

Houdé, O. (1997). *Rationalité, développement et inhibition: Un nouveau cadre d'analyse*. Paris: PUF.

Hughes, T. (2004). *Human-Built World: How to Think about Technology and Culture*. Chicago: University of Chicago Press.

Hughes, T. P. (1983). *Networks of Power: Electrification in Western Society, 1880–1930*. Baltimore: John Hopkins University Press.

Hughes, T. P. (1986). 'The Seamless Web: Technology, Science, Etcetera, Etcetera', *Social Studies of Science*, 16/2: 281–292.

Hunter, P. (1980). 'The National System of Scientific Measurement', *Science*, 210: 869–874.

Hutchins, E. (1995). *Cognition in the Wild*. Cambridge, Mass.: MIT Press.

Ihde, D. and Selinger, E. (eds.) (2003). *Chasing Technoscience: Matrix for Materiality*. Bloomingon: Indiana University Press.

Ingold, T. (2000). *Perception of the Environment: Essays in Livelihood, Dwelling and Skill*. London: Routledge.

Jacob, C. (1992). *L'empire des cartes: Approche théorique de la cartographie à travers l'histoire*. Paris: Albin Michel.

James, W. (1890). *The Principles of Psychology*. New York: Dover.

Jeanneret, Y. (1998). *L'affaire Sokal ou la querelle des impostures*. Paris: PUF.

Jensen, P. (2001). *Entrer en matière: Les atomes expliquent-ils le monde?* Paris: Le Seuil.

Jones, G., McLean, C. and Quattrone, P. (2004). 'Spacing and Timing': Intro-duction to the Special Issue of Organization on 'Spacing and Timing', *Organization,* 11/6: 723–741.

Jullien, F. (1995). *The Propensity of Things: Toward a History of Efficacy in China.* Cambridge, Mass.: Zone Books.

Jurdant, B. (ed.) (1998). *Impostures intellectuelles: Les malentendus de l'affaire Sokal.* Paris: La Découverte.

Kaiser, D. (2005). *Drawing Theories Apart: The Dispersion of Feynman Diagrams in Postwar Physics.* Chicago: University of Chicago Press.

Kantorowicz, E. (1997). *The King's Two Bodies.* Princeton: Princeton University Press.

Karsenti, B. (1997). *L'Homme total: Sociologie, anthropologie et philosophie chez Marcel Mauss.* Paris: PUF.

Karsenti, B. (2002). 'L'imitation: Retour sur le débat entre Durkheim et Tarde' In *La régularité.* (eds. Chauviré, C. and Ogien, A.) Paris: Editions de l'EHESS, 183–215.

Karsenti, B. (2003). 'Autorité, pouvoir et société: La science sociale selon Bonald', in *L'invention de la science sociale, XVIIIème et XIXème siècle.* (eds. Guillhaumou, J. and Kaufmann, L.) Paris: Editions de l'EHESS.

Keating, P. and Cambrosio, A. (2003). *Biomedical Platforms: Realigning the Nor-mal and the Pathological in Late-Twentieth-Century Medicine.* Cambridge, Mass.: MIT Press.

Keegan, J. (1987). *The Mask of Command.* New York: Viking.

Kidder, T. (1985). *House.* Boston: Houghton Mifflin Company.

Kirk, S. A. and Kutchins, H. (1992). *The Selling of DSM: The Rhetoric of Science in Psychiatry.* New York: Aldine de Gruyter.

Kitcher, P. (2003). *Science, Truth, and Democracy (Oxford Studies in the Philosophy of Science).* Oxford: Oxford University Press.

Knorr-Cetina, K. (1999). *Epistemic Cultures: How the Sciences Make Knowledge.* Cambridge, Mass.: Harvard University Press.

Knorr-Cetina, K. and Bruegger, U. (2002). 'Global Microstructures: The Virtual Societies of Financial Markets', *American Journal of Sociology,* 107/4: 905–950.

Koergte, N. (ed.) (1998). *A House Built on Sand: Exposing Postmodernist Myths about Science.* Oxford: Oxford University Press.

Koerner, J. L. (1993). *The Moment of Self-Portraiture in German Renaissance Art.* Chicago: University of Chicago Press.

Koerner, J. L. (2004). *The Reformation of the Image.* London: Reaktion Books.

Koolhaas, R. and Mau, B. (1995). *Small, Medium, Large, Extra-Large.* Rotterdam: Office for Metropolitan Architecture.

Kummer, H. (1995). *In Quest of the Sacred Baboon* (trans. M. Ann Biederman-Thorson). Princeton: Princeton University Press.

Kupiec, J.-J. and Sonigo, P. (2000). *Ni Dieu ni gène.* Paris: Le Seuil-Collection Science ouverte.

Lafaye, C. and Thévenot, L. (1993). 'Une justification écologique? Conflits dans l'aménagement de la nature', *Revue Française de Sociologie,* 34/4: 495–524.

Latour, B. (1984). *Les microbes, guerre et paix, suivi de Irréductions.* Paris: A.-M. Métailié La Découverte.

Latour, B. (1987). *Science In Action: How to Follow Scientists and Engineers through Society*. Cambridge, Mass.: Harvard University Press.

Latour, B. (1988a). *Irreductions part II of The Pasteurization of France*. Cambridge, Mass.: Harvard University Press.

Latour, B. (1988b). *The Pasteurization of France*. Cambridge, Mass.: Harvard University Press.

Latour, B. (1988c). 'A Relativist Account of Einstein's Relativity', *Social Studies of Science*, 18: 3–44.

Latour, B. (1993). *We Have Never Been Modern*. Cambridge, Mass.: Harvard University Press.

Latour, B. (1996). *Aramis or the Love of Technology*. Cambridge, Mass.: Harvard University Press.

Latour, B. (1999a). 'Factures/fractures: From the Concept of Network to the Concept of Attachment', *Res*, 36: 20–31.

Latour, B. (1999b). 'For Bloor and Beyond - a Response to David Bloor's "Anti-Latour"', *Studies in History and Philosophy of Science*, 30/1: 113–129.

Latour, B. (1999c). 'On Recalling ANT', in *Actor Network and After*. (eds. Law, J. and Hassard, J.) Oxford: Blackwell, 15–25.

Latour, B. (1999d). *Pandora's Hope: Essays on the reality of science studies*. Cambridge, Mass.: Harvard University Press.

Latour, B. (2002). 'Gabriel Tarde and the End of the Social', in *The Social in Question: New Bearings in the History and the Social Sciences*. (ed. Joyce, P.) London: Routledge, 117–132.

Latour, B. (2002) *La fabrique du droit. Une ethnographie du Conseil d'Etat*. Paris: La Découverte.

Latour, B. (2003a). 'The Promises of Constructivism', in *Chasing Technoscience: Matrix for Materiality*. (eds. Ihde, D. and Selinger, E.) Bloomington: Indiana University Press, 27–46.

Latour, B. (2003b). 'What if We Were Talking Politics a Little?', *Contemporary Political Theory*, 2/2: 143–164.

Latour, B. (2004a). 'How to Talk about the Body? The Normative Dimension of Science Studies' a symposium edited by Madeleine Akrich and Marc Berg, 'Bodies on Trial', *Body and Society*, 10/2/3: 205–229.

Latour, B. (2004b). *Politics of Nature: How to Bring the Sciences into Democracy* (trans. Catherine Porter). Cambridge, Mass.: Harvard University Press.

Latour, B. and Hermant, E. (1998). *Paris ville invisible*. Paris: La Découverte-Les Empêcheurs de penser en rond.

Latour, B. and Hermant, E. (2004) *Paris the Invisible City* (trans. by Liz Libbrecht) http://bruno.latour.name.

Latour, B. and Lemonnier, P. (eds.) (1994). *De la préhistoire aux missiles balistiques - l'intelligence sociale des techniques*. Paris: La Découverte.

Latour, B. and Weibel, P. (eds.) (2002). *Iconoclash: Beyond the Image Wars in Science, Religion and Art*. Cambridge, Mass.: MIT Press.

Latour, B. and Weibel, P. (eds.) (2005). *Making Things Public: Atmospheres of Democracy*. Cambridge, Mass.: MIT Press.

Latour, B. and Woolgar, S. (1979/1986). *Laboratory Life: The Construction of Scientific Facts* (second edition with a new postword). Princeton: Princeton University Press.

Lave, J. (1988). *Cognition in Practice: Mind, Mathematics and Culture in Everyday Life*. Cambridge: Cambridge University Press.

Law, J. (1986a). 'On Power and Its Tactics: A View From The Sociology Of Science', *The Sociological Review*, 34/1: 1–38.

Law, J. (1986b). 'On the Methods of Long-Distance Control: Vessels, Navigation and the Portuguese Route to India', in *Power, Action and Belief. A New Sociology of Knowledge?* (ed. Law, J.) Keele: Sociological Review Monograph, 234–263.

Law, J. (ed.) (1992). *A Sociology of Monsters: Essays on Power, Technology and Domination*. London: Routledge Sociological Review Monograph.

Law, J. (1993). *Organizing Modernities*. Cambridge: Blackwell.

Law, J. (2002). *Aircraft Stories: Decentering the Object in Technoscience*. Durham: Duke University Press.

Law, J. (2004). *After Method: Mess in Social Science Research*. London: Routledge.

Le Bourhis, J. P. (2004). 'La publicisation des eaux: Rationalité et politique dans la gestion de l'eau en France (1964–2003)', Ph.D. thesis, Paris: University Paris I Sorbonne.

Lemonnier, P. (ed.) (1993). *Technological Choices: Transformation in Material Cultures since the Neolithic*. London: Routledge.

Lépinay, V. (2003). 'Les formules du marché. Ethno-Economie d'une innovation financière: les produits à capital garanti', Ph.D. thesis Paris: Ecole des Mines.

Leroi-Gourhan, A. (1993). *Gesture and Speech*. Cambridge, Mass.: MIT Press.

Lewontin, R. (2000). *The Triple Helix: Gene, Organism and Environment*. Cambridge, Mass.: Harvard University Press.

Leyshon, A. and Thrift, N. (1996). *Money/Space: Geographies of Monetary Transformation (International Library of Sociology)*. London: Routledge.

Linhardt, D. (2004). 'La force de l'Etat en démocratie: La République fédérale d'Allemagne à l'épreuve de la guérilla urbaine 1967–1982', Ph.D. thesis, Paris: Ecole des Mines.

Lippmann, W. (1922). *Public Opinion*. New York: Simon & Schuster.

Lippmann, W. (1927/1993). *The Phantom Public*. New Brunswick: Transactions Publishers.

Livingston, E. (1985). *The Ethnomethodological Foundations of Mathematical Practice*. London: Routledge.

Livingstone, D. N. (2003). *Putting Science in Its Place: Geographies of Scientific Knowledge*. Chicago: University of Chicago Press.

Lowe, A. and Schaffer, S. (1999). *N01se, 1999*. An exhibition held simultaneously at Kettle's Yard, The Whipple Museum of the History of Science, Cambridge, the Museum of Archaeology and Anthropology, Cambridge and the Wellcome Institute, London. Cambridge: Kettle's Yard.

Luhmann, N. (1985). *A Sociological Theory of Law*. London: Routledge.

Lynch, M. (1985). *Art and Artifact in Laboratory Science: A Study of Shop Work and Shop Talk in a Research Laboratory*. London: Routledge.

Lynch, M. and Bogen, D. (1996). *The Spectacle of History: Speech, Text and Memory at the Iran Contra Hearings*. Durham: Duke University Press.

MacKenzie, D. (1990). *Inventing Accuracy: A Historical Sociology of Nuclear Missile Guidance*. Cambridge, Mass.: MIT Press.

MacKenzie, D. (2001). *Mechanizing Proof: Computing, Risk, and Trust (Inside Technology)*. Cambridge, Mass.: MIT Press.

MacKenzie, D. (forthcoming). *An engine, not a camera: finance theory and the making of markets*. Cambridge, Mass.: MIT Press.

MacKenzie, D. and Wajcman, J. (1999). *The Social Shaping of Technology. Second edition*. Milton Keynes: Open University Press.

Madsen, A. (1991). *Chanel: A Woman of Her Own*. New York: Owl Books.

Mallard, A. (1996). 'Les instruments dans la coordination de l'action: pratique technique, métrologie, instrument scientifique', Ph.D. thesis, Paris: Ecole des Mines.

Marin, L. (1989). *Opacité de la peinture: Essais sur la représentation*. Paris: Usher.

Marin, L. (1992). *Des pouvoirs de l'image: Gloses*. Paris: Le Seuil.

Marin, L. (2001). *On Representation* (trans. Catherine Porter). Stanford, CA.: Stanford University Press.

Marres, N. (2005). 'No Issue, No Politics', Ph.D. thesis, Philosophy Department, Amsterdam.

Maturana, H. R. and Varela, F. J. (1980). *Autopoiesis and Cognition: The Realization of the Living (Boston Studies in the Philosophy of Science)*. Dordrecht: Reidel.

Mauss, M. (1979). 'Body Techniques' in *Sociology and Psychology: Essays* (Trans. Ben Brewster). London: Routledge and Kegan Paul.

McNeill, W. (1976). *Plagues and peoples*. New York: Anchor Press.

Mélard, F. (2001). 'L'autorité des instruments dans la production du lien social: le cas de l'analyse polarimétrique dans l'industrie sucrière belge', Ph.D. thesis, Paris: Ecole des Mines.

Merton, R. K. (1973). *The Sociology of Science: Theoretical and Empirical Investigations*. Chicago: University of Chicago Press.

Mialet, H. (2003). 'Reading Hawking's Presence: An Interview with a Self-Effacing Man', *Critical Inquiry*, 29/4: 571–598.

Miall, R. C. and Tchalenko, J. (2001). 'A Painter's Eye Movements: A Study of Eye and Hand Movement during Portrait Drawing', *Leonardo*, 34/1: 35–40.

Miller, P. (1994). 'The Factory as Laboratory', *Science in Context*, 7/3: 469–496.

Minvielle, A. (forthcoming). 'De quoi une entreprise est-elle capable? Comptabilité sociale des entreprises', Ph.D. thesis, Paris: Ecole des Mines.

Mirowski, P. (2001). *Machine Dreams: Economics Becomes a Cyborg Science*. Cambridge: Cambridge University Press.

Mirowski, P. and Nik-Khah, E. (2004). 'Markets Made Flesh: Callon, Performativity, and a Crisis in Science Studies, augmented With Consideration of the FCC auctions'.

Mitchell, T. (2002). *Rule of Experts: Egypt, Techno-Politics, Modernity*. Berkeley: University of California Press.

Mol, A. and Law, J. (1994). 'Regions, Networks, and Fluids: Anaemia and Social Topology', *Social Studies of Science*, 24/4: 641–672.

Mol, A. (2003). *The Body Multiple: Ontology in Medical Practice (Science and Cultural Theory)*. Duke University Press.

Mondada, L. (2000). *Décrire la ville: La construction des savoirs urbains dans l'interaction et dans le texte (Collection Villes)*. Paris: Anthropos.

Monsaingeon, B. (1998) *Le chant possédé* (documentary by Bruno Monsaingeon), distribution Idéale Audience.

Morrison, P. and Morrison, P. (1982). *The Powers of Ten*. San Francisco: W. H. Freeman and Company.

Mumford, L. (1967). *The Myth of the Machine: Technics and Human Development*. New York: Harcourt, Brace & World, Inc.

Mundy, M. and Pottage, A. (2004). *Law, Anthropology and the Constitution of the Social: Making Persons and Things (Cambridge Studies in Law & Society)*. Cambridge: Cambridge University Press.

Muniesa, F. (2004). 'Des marchés comme algorithmes: sociologie de la cotation électronique à la Bourse de Paris', Ph.D. thesis under the direction of Michel Callon, Paris: Ecole des Mines.

Nanda, M. (2003). *Prophets Facing Backward: Postmodern Critiques of Science and Hindu Nationalism in India*. New Brunswick, N.J.: Rutgers University Press.

Napoli, P. (2003). *Naissance de la police moderne: Pouvoirs, normes, société*. Paris: La Découverte.

Nelson, V. (2002). *The Secret Life of Puppets*. Cambridge, Mass.: Harvard University Press.

Norman, D. A. (1988). *The Psychology of Everyday Things*. New York: Basic Books/Doubleday.

Norman, D. A. (1993). *Things that Make Us Smart*. New York: Addison Wesley Publishing Company.

O'Connell, J. (1993). 'Metrology: the Creation of Universality by the Circulation of Particulars', *Social Studies of Science*, 23/1: 129–173.

Oettermann, S. (1997). *The Panorama: History of a Mass Medium*. (trans. Deborah Lucas Schneider) New York: Zone Books.

Pasteels, J. and Deneubourg, J.-L. (eds.) (1987). *From Individual to Collective Behavior in Social Insects*. Bâle Boston: Birkhauser Verlag.

Pavel, T. (1986). *Fictional Worlds*. Cambridge, Mass.: Harvard University Press.

Pavel, T. (2003). *La pensée du roman*. Paris: Gallimard.

Perret-Clermont, A.-N. (1979). *La Construction de l'intelligence dans l'interaction sociale*. Berne: Peter Lang.

Pickering, A. (1995). *The Mangle of Practice: Time, Agency and Science*. Chicago: University of Chicago Press.

Piette, A. (1999). *La religion de près: L'activité religieuse en train de se faire*. Paris: Métailié.

Pietz, W. (1985). 'The Problem of the Fetish, I', *Res*, 9: 5–17.

Pietz, W. (1993). 'Fetishism and Materialism: the Limits of Theory in Marx', in *Fetishism as Cultural Discourse*. (eds. Apter, E. and Petz, W.) Ithaca: Cornell University Press, 119–151.

Polanyi, K. (1944). *The Great Transformation*. Boston: Beacon Press.

Ponge, F. (1972). *The Voice of Things*. Edited and translated by B. Archer. New York: McGraw-Hill Book C°.

Porter, T. M. (1995). *Trust in Numbers: The Pursuit of Objectivity in Science and Public Life*. Princeton: Princeton University Press.

Power, M. (ed.) (1995). *Accounting and Science: Natural Inquiry and Commercial Reason*. Cambridge: Cambridge University Press.

Powers, R. (1995). *Galatea 2.2*. New York: Farrar, Strauss and Giroux.

Powers, R. (1998). *Gain*. New York: Farrar, Straus & Giroux.

Quattrone, P. (2004). 'Accounting for God: Accounting and Accountability Practices in the Society of Jesus (Italy, 16th–17th centuries)', *Accounting, Organizations and Society*, 29/7: 647–683.

Riskin, J. (2002). *Science in the Age of Sensibility: The Sentimental Empiricists of The French Enlightenment*. Chicago: University of Chicago Press.

Robbins, E. (ed.) (1994). *Why Architects Draw*. Cambridge, Mass.: MIT Press.

Rogers, R. (2005). *Information Politic on the Web*. Cambridge, Mass.: MIT Press.

Rosental, C. (2003). *La Trame de l'évidence*. Paris: P.U.F.

Rotman, B. (1993). *Ad Infinitum: The Ghost in Turing Machine. Taking God out of Mathematics and Putting the Body Back In*. Stanford, CA.: Stanford University Press.

Ruellan, A. and Dosso, M. (1993). *Regards sur le sol*. Paris: Foucher.

Sahlins, M. (2000). *Culture in Practice*. New York: Zone Books.

Salmon, L. (2004). *La pensée politique de Gabriel Tarde*. Paris X: Economie, organisations, sociétés: Mémoire de DEA.

Sartre, J.-P. (1993). *Being And Nothingness* (trans. Hazel E. Barnes). Washington Square Press.

Schaffer, S. (1988). 'Astronomers Mark Time: Discipline And The Personal Equation', *Science In Context*, 2/1: 115–145.

Schaffer, S. (1991a). 'The Eighteenth Brumaire of Bruno Latour'. *Studies in History and Philosophy of Science*, 22: 174–192.

Schaffer, S. (1991b). 'A Manufactory of OHMS, Victorian Metrology and its Instrumentation', in *Invisible Connections*. (eds. Cozzens, S. and Bud, R.) Bellingham Washington State: Spie Optical Engineering Press, 25–54.

Schmitt, J. C. (1990). *La Raison des gestes dans l'Occident médiéval*. Paris: Gallimard.

Searle, J. (1995). *The Construction of Social Reality*. New York: Free Press.

Serres, M. (1974). *La Traduction (Hermès III)*. Paris: Minuit.

Serres, M. (1995). *Conversations on Science, Culture and Time with Bruno Latour*. Ann Arbor, MI.: The University of Michigan Press.

Shakespeare, W. (1988). *The Complete Works. Compact Edition edited by Stanley Wells and Gary Taylor*. Oxford: Clarendon Press.

Shapin, S. and Schaffer, S. (1985). *Leviathan and the Air-Pump: Hobbes, Boyle and the Experimental Life*. Princeton: Princeton University Press.

Sloterdijk, P. (1999) *Sphären. Bd.2 Globen*. Munich: Suhrkamp.

Sloterdijk, P. (2004). *Sphären, Bd. 3 Schaüme*. Munich: Suhrkamp.

Smith, B. C. (1997). *On the Origins of Objects*. Cambridge, Mass.: MIT Press.

Smith, B. C. (2003). 'The Devil in the Digital Details: Digital Abstraction and Concrete Reality', in *Digitality in Art* Special Symposium Calcografía Nacional (ed. Lowe, A.).

Smith, C. and Wise, N. (1989). *Energy and Empire: A Biographical Study of Lord Kelvin*. Cambridge: Cambridge University Press.

Sokal, A. D. and Bricmont, J. (1999). *Fashionable Nonsense: Postmodern Intellectuals' Abuse of Science*. New York: Picador.

Souriau, E. (1943). *Les différents modes d'existence*. Paris: PUF.

Sperber, D., Premack, D. and Premack, A. J. (1996). *Causal Cognition: A Multidisciplinary Debate (Symposium of the Fyssen Foundation)*. Oxford: Oxford University Press.

Star, S. L. and Griesemer, J. (1989). 'Institutional Ecology, "Translations" and Boundary Objects: Amateurs and Professionals in Berkeley's Museum of Vertebrate Zoology, 1907–1939', *Social Studies of Science,* 19: 387–420.

Stengers, I. (1991). *Drogues, le défi hollandais.* Paris: Les Empêcheurs.

Stengers, I. (1996). *Cosmopolitiques - Tome 1: la guerre des sciences.* Paris: La découverte & Les Empêcheurs de penser en rond.

Stengers, I. (1997). *Power and Invention. Situating Science* (trans. Paul Bains). Minneapolis: University of Minnesota Press.

Stengers, I. (2000). *The Invention of Modern Science* (trans. Daniel W. Smith). The University of Minnesota Press.

Stengers, I. (2002). *Penser avec Whitehead: Une libre et sauvage création de concepts.* Paris: Gallimard.

Stocking, G. W. (ed.) (1983). *Observers Observed: Essays on Ethnographic Fieldwork.* Madison: The University of Wisconsin Press.

Strathern, M. (1999). *Property, Substance and Effect: Anthropological Essays in Persons and Things.* London: Athlone Press.

Strum, S. (1982). 'Agonistic Dominance among Baboons an Alternative View', *International Journal of Primatology,* 3/2: 175–202.

Strum, S. (1987). *Almost Human: A Journey Into the World of Baboons.* New York: Random House.

Strum, S. and Fedigan, L. (eds.) (2000). *Primate Encounters.* Chicago: University of Chicago Press.

Strum, S. and Latour, B. (1987). 'The Meanings of Social: from Baboons to Humans', *Information sur les Sciences Sociales/Social Science Information,* 26: 783–802.

Suchman, L. (1987). *Plans and Situated Actions: The Problem of Human Machine Communication.* Cambridge: Cambridge University Press.

Susuki, T. (2003). 'The epistemology of macroeconomic reality: The Keynesian Revolution from an accounting point of view', *Accounting, Organizations and Society,* 28/5: 471–517.

Tang-Martinez, Z. (2000). 'Paradigms and Primates: Bateman's Principles, Passive Females, and Perspectives from Other Taxa', in *Primate Encounters.* (eds. Strum, S. and Fedigan, L.) Chicago: University of Chicago Press, 261–274.

Tarde, G. (1893/1999) *La logique sociale.* Paris: Les Empêcheurs de penser en rond.

Tarde, G. (1895/1999). *Monadologie et sociologie.* Paris: Les empêcheurs de penser en rond.

Tarde, G. (1899/2000). *Social Laws: An Outline of Sociology* (trans. Howard C. Warren). Kitchener, Ont.: Batoche Books.

Tarde, G. (1901/1989). *L'opinion et la foule.* Paris: PUF.

Tarde, G. (1902). *Psychologie économique.* Paris: Félix Alcan.

Tarde, G. (1969). *On Communication and Social Influence. Selected Papers. Edited by Terry N. Clark.* Chicago: University of Chicago Press.

Taylor, J. R. (1993). *Rethinking the Theory of Organizational Communication: How to Read an Organization.* Norwood, New Jersey: Ablex Publishing.

Teil, G. (1991). 'Candide™, un outil de sociologie assistée par ordinateur pour l'analyse quantitative de gros corpus de textes', Ph.D. thesis, Paris: Ecole des Mines.

Thévenot, L. (1984). 'Rules and implements: investment in forms', *Social Science Information*, 23/1: 1–45.

Thévenot, L. (2002). 'Which road to follow? The moral complexity of an "equipped" humanity', in: Social Studies of Knowledge Practices. *(eds. Law, J. and Mol, A.) Durham: Duke University Press, 53–87.*

Thévenot, L. (2004). 'Une science de la vie ensemble dans le monde', *La Revue semestrielle du MAUSS*, 24: 115–126.

Thompson, C. (2002). 'When Elephants Stand for Competing Philosophies of Nature: Amboseli National Park, Kenya', in *Complexities in Science, Technology, and Medicine*. (eds. Mol, A.-M. and Law, J.) Duke University Press.

Tiles, M. and Pippin, R. B. (eds.) (1984). *Bachelard: Science and Objectivity*. Cambridge: Cambridge University Press.

Tresch, J. (2001). 'Mechanical Romanticism: Engineers of the Artificial Paradise', Ph.D. thesis, Department of History and Philosophy of Science. Cambridge: University of Cambridge.

Vaughan, D. (1996). *The Challenger Launch Decision: Risky Technology, Culture and Deviance at NASA*. Chicago: University of Chicago Press.

Vinck, D. (1995). *La sociologie des sciences*. Paris: Armand Colin.

Vygotski, L. S. (1878) *Mind in Society: The Development of Higher Cognitive Processes (Texts edited by Michael Cole)*. Cambridge Mass: Harvard U.P.

Warwick, A. (2003). *Masters of Theory: Cambridge and the Rise of Mathematical Physics*. Chicago: University of Chicago Press.

Waters, L. (2004). *Enemies of Promise: Publishing, Perishing, and the Eclipse of Scholarship*. University of Chicago Press: Prickly Paradigm Press.

Weber, M. (1947). *The Theory of Social and Economic Organization*. New York: Free Press.

Whitehead, A. N. (1929/1978). *Process and Reality: An Essay in Cosmology*. New York: Free Press.

Wilson, E. O. (1975). *Sociobiology, the New Synthesis*. Cambridge, Mass.: Harvard University Press, The Belknap Press.

Winance, M. (2001). 'Thèse et prothèse. Le processus d'habilitation comme fabrication de la personne: l'association française contre les myopathies, face au handicap', Ph.D. thesis, Paris: Ecole des Mines.

Winchester, S. (2003). *The Meaning of Everything: The Story of the Oxford English Dictionary*. Oxford: Oxford University Press.

Winner, L. (1993). 'Upon Opening the Black Box and Finding It Empty: Social Constructivsm and the Philosophy of Technology', *Science, Technology and Human Values*, 18/3: 362–378.

Wise, N. (ed.) (1995). *The Values of Precision and Exactitude*. Princeton: Princeton University Press.

Woolgar, S. (1988). *Science The Very Idea*. London: Tavistock.

Woolgar, S. (1991). 'The Turn to Technology in Social Studies of Science', *Science, Technology and Human Values*, 16/1: 20–50.

Yaneva, A. (in press). 'Scaling Up and Down: Extraction Trials in Architectural Design', *Social Studies of Science*.

Yaneva, A. (2001). 'L'affluence des objets: Pragmatique comparée de l'art contemporain et de l'artisanat ∼ 2001', Ph.D. thesis, Paris: Ecole des Mines.

Yaneva, A. (2003). 'When a Bus Meet a Museum: To Follow Artists, Curators and Workers in Art Installation', *Museum and Society,* 1/3: 116–131.

Zourabichvili, F. (2003). *Le vocabulaire de Deleuze.* Paris: Ellipses.

INDEX

Abbott, E. 172n
  Flatland 204
accounts 80–81, 122–4, 127, 138
Accounting Standards Board
      (IASB) 229n
actant 54–5, 199
action 22, 44–7, 174
actor-network 133, 169, 179, 217–18
actor-network account, proportion of
      mediators to intermediaries is
      increased 133
actor-network-theory *see* ANT
actor/system quandary 169–70, 217
actors,
  able to propose their own *theories of
      action* 57
  can download theories of the social
      as effectively as MP3 files 231
  diffusion of word 'actor' 4n
  engage in criticizing other agencies
      accused of being fake and 56
  engaged in group formation and
      destruction and 47
  engaged in mapping 'social
      context' in which they are
      placed 32
  fully competent come in discreet
      pellets 207
  have to *do* things not be
      placeholders 154
  insist they are made to do things by
      entities 'outside' of them 235
  limited to humans but always
      designate *source* of
      initiative 216–17
  many philosophies and 52
  might be *associated* in way that
      they *make others do things* 107
  now fully artificial and fully
      traceable gathering 208

  treated as mediators render
      movement of social visible to
      reader 128
  unproblematic placeholders 46
  world-making activities and 24
actors and scholars, play role of group
      formation 34
adjective 'social', scientists and 1
agencies,
  'ceaselessly' debated 63, 87
  complexity, diversity and
      heterogeneity of action 44–5
  controversies about have way of
      ordering themselves 51–2
  more in the *pluriverse* than thought
      possible 116
  natural and/or social 109
  nature of and meaning of
      mediators 221
  presented as *doing* something 52–3
  scientific institutions and increase
      in range of 119
agents, coordination among
      achieved through *quasi*-
      standards 229
Akrich, M. 79n, 81n
Alice voting in France for general
      election 222–31
'alienation', how to denounce
      without Marx 28
amphitheatre 194–6
analysts 49, 85, 193
ANT 9–11, 15–16, 22, 24, 51, 176,
      217, 243–5
  negative argument 141, 200
  abstract *projection* principle for
      deploying *any* shape 178,
      221
  accused of two symmetric and
      contradictory sins 256